CAMBRIDGE

国际法与北极

International Law and the Arctic

[加] 迈克尔·拜尔斯 (Michael Byers) ◎著
陈子楠 ◎译

时事出版社
北京

目 录

英文版序言 ……………………………………………………（1）

中文版序言 …………………………………………………（10）

    一、中国和北极 ……………………………………………（10）

    二、北极资源 ………………………………………………（12）

    三、北极航运 ………………………………………………（13）

    四、近期发展 ………………………………………………（17）

第一章　领土 …………………………………………………（20）

    一、汉斯岛 …………………………………………………（20）

    二、斯瓦尔巴 ………………………………………………（26）

    三、格陵兰 …………………………………………………（31）

    四、斯弗德鲁普群岛 ………………………………………（34）

    五、小结 ……………………………………………………（36）

第二章　海上边界 ……………………………………………（37）

    一、1973 年《加拿大和丹麦边界条约》…………………（38）

    二、1990 年《白令海条约》………………………………（41）

    三、扬马延岛周边海上边界 ………………………………（45）

    四、2006 年《格陵兰和斯瓦尔巴边界条约》……………（46）

    五、2010 年《巴伦支海边界条约》………………………（47）

    六、林肯海边界 ……………………………………………（54）

    七、小结 ……………………………………………………（62）

第三章　波弗特海边界 (63)
- 一、背景 (64)
- 二、解决争端的努力 (67)
- 三、加拿大的法律立场 (69)
- 四、美国的法律立场 (72)
- 五、200海里内海上边界划定法律 (73)
- 六、200海里外海上边界划定法律 (76)
- 七、潜在谈判立场 (79)
- 八、美国和加拿大的合作选项 (88)
- 九、俄罗斯和加拿大波弗特海海上边界？ (94)
- 十、小结 (94)

第四章　外大陆架 (96)
- 一、大陆架制度 (97)
- 二、海底高地 (100)
- 三、北冰洋中部的地貌和地质特征 (108)
- 四、向大陆架界限委员会提交提案的选项 (112)
- 五、提案前先商定临时界线或永久边界 (117)
- 六、海上划界的选项 (119)
- 七、非北极国家和北极大陆架 (126)
- 八、小结 (128)

第五章　北极航道 (129)
- 一、西北航道 (132)
- 二、北方海航线 (143)
- 三、加拿大和俄罗斯法律立场评估 (149)
- 四、加拿大和俄罗斯合作 (151)
- 五、加拿大和美国合作 (154)
- 六、白令海峡 (157)
- 七、乌尼马克海峡 (159)

目 录

　　八、内尔斯海峡 ·· (161)

　　九、"海峡国"的多边机制 ······································ (163)

　　十、潜艇航行 ·· (167)

　　十一、小结 ·· (169)

第六章　环境保护 ·· (170)

　　一、物种保护 ·· (170)

　　二、渔业 ·· (176)

　　三、航运 ·· (183)

　　四、核事故 ·· (187)

　　五、深海采矿 ·· (188)

　　六、经空气传播的污染物 ·· (191)

　　七、石油泄漏 ·· (197)

　　八、基于生态系统的管理 ·· (210)

　　九、小结 ·· (212)

第七章　土著人民 ·· (213)

　　一、政治参与和自决 ·· (215)

　　二、土著人权利和主张 ·· (219)

　　三、土著跨国主义与国际立法 ···································· (222)

　　四、《极地因纽特人在北极主权的宣言》 ·························· (227)

　　五、主权是否"源于国内"？ ···································· (231)

　　六、海豹产品出口 ·· (233)

　　七、土著人民和人权 ·· (235)

　　八、土著人和捕鲸 ·· (237)

　　九、土著人与核武器 ·· (240)

　　十、小结 ·· (240)

第八章　安全 ·· (242)

　　一、缓和中的北极局势 ·· (245)

— 3 —

  二、中国 ·· （251）
  三、北极无核武器区 ·· （253）
  四、非国家行为体 ··· （258）
  五、搜索和救助 ·· （265）
  六、小结 ·· （275）

结　论 ·· （276）

参考文献 ··· （279）

中英译名索引 ·· （300）
  一、地理名称 ··· （300）
  二、主要法律文件名 ·· （305）

英文版序言

雷索卢特湾，加拿大康沃利斯岛上的一个因纽特人（Inuit）小村庄。2008年6月我来到这里，发现这是一个荒凉却引人注目的地方，尤其是在仲夏。午夜时分，漫步湾区，穿过冻结的砾石，像是行走在月球表面，一阵强风骤起，冰和着沙粒吹打着我的脸。雷索卢特湾位于北纬74度，此时太阳还在天空中高高地照耀着。我记得当时心想印度也是正午时分，那里的人们和我一样正享受着阳光。唯一的区别是，在雷索卢特湾光线是直射在北极点上空。

任何国家都不"拥有"北极。北极位于格陵兰岛以及加拿大、俄罗斯两国最北部岛屿以北约400海里，虽然靠近海岸的水域和海底属于沿岸国，但水面、水体和至少部分北冰洋中部海底区域属于全人类。与此同时，那里存在许多挑战，这些挑战首先也主要得依靠地理上接近的北极国家来解决，包括危及生命的事故、溢油和过度捕捞。随着气候变化、海冰融化和各种船舶进入，这些挑战将在未来数年和数十年内快速增加。

冷战期间，美国和苏联在北冰洋展开穿插对峙。核潜艇在冰面下潜行，远程轰炸机在高空巡逻。直到1990年，才有更为和平与合作的方式，当时两个超级大国通过协商划定了白令海、白令海峡和楚科奇海的海上边界。① 1996年，美国、俄罗斯、加拿大、丹麦、挪威、瑞典、芬兰和冰岛八个北极国家成立了北极理事会，作为讨论"军事安全"以外议题的政府间论坛。② 与此同时，俄罗斯在西方的帮助下，对苏联时

---

① Agreement between the United States of America and the Union of Soviet Socialist Republics on the Maritime Boundary (1990) 29 ILM 941, http://www.state.gov/documents/organization/125431.pdf.

② http://www.arctic-council.org/. On the origins of the Arctic Council, Evan T. Bloom, "Establishment of the Arctic Council" (1999) 93 American Journal of International Law 712.

代的核反应堆和核弹头进行退役和报废处理,①同意降低许多苏联时代战舰的性能,而美国和加拿大则选择不替换老化的破冰船。②

最近,气候变化正从根本上重塑北极地区。③除全球温室气体排放导致的温度上升外,这种变化还受到冰冻和液态水之间微妙平衡所产生的北极特有"反馈环"的推动。年均温度上升几分之一度就可以把反射性很强的海冰变为深色并且吸热的开阔大洋。随着温度升高,如岩石般坚硬、具有生物学上稳定性的永冻层将变成一堆腐败并且排放出甲烷气体的古代植物物质。在北极地区,年平均气温已经上升了 2 摄氏度以上。④

2012 年 9 月,北极海冰覆盖面积下降至 360 万平方千米,比 1979—2000 年间的平均值低了约 50%。⑤现在看来,不用到 2020 年就会出现夏末海冰完全融化的现象。⑥以往厚实坚硬的海冰消失,将打通北极大片区域,实现全年通航。北冰洋可能很快就会像波罗的海或圣劳伦斯湾那样,在强化抗冰船和破冰船护卫下,船队将能够在冬季航行。这将降低亚洲与欧洲、美国大西洋沿岸之间的航运成本,也有利于资源

---

① Brian D. Finlay, "Russian Roulette: Canada's Role in the Race to Secure Loose Nuclear, Biological, and Chemical Weapons." (2006) 61 International Journal 411.

② e. g., Polar Icebreakers in a Changing World: An Assessment of U. S. Needs (Report of the Committee on the Assessment of US Coast Guard Polar Icebreaker Roles and Future Needs, National Research Council) (Washington, DC: National Academies Press, 2007), http://www.nap.edu/catalog.php?record_id = 11753; Randy Boswell, "Shortsighted Politics, Forgotten Arctic Dreams: The Abandoned Polar 8 Icebreaker Ship Could Have Embodied Canada's Identity as a Circumpolar Power," Ottawa Citizen, August 10, 2007, A5.

③ For the most comprehensive (though already dated) examination, see Impacts of a Warming Arctic: Arctic Climate Impact Assessment (Cambridge University Press, 2004), http://www.acia.uaf.edu/.

④ "Sea Ice Loss Major Cause of Arctic Warming," Independent, April 30, 2010, http://www.independent.co.uk/environment/sea-ice-loss-major-cause-of-arctic-warming-1958815.html.

⑤ US National Snow and Ice Data Center, "Arctic Sea Ice News and Analysis," http://nsidc.org/arcticseaicenews/.

⑥ Margaret Munro, "Arctic Ice 'Rotten' to the North Pole, Scientist Says," Post Media News, October 1, 2012, http://www.vancouversun.com/technology/Arctic + Rotten + North + Pole + scientist + says/7279382/story.html. For a useful discussion of different scientificpredictions, Katherine Leitzell, "When Will the Arctic Lose its Sea Ice?" US National Snow and Ice Data Center, May 3, 2011, http://nsidc.org/icelights/2011/05/03/when-will-the-arctic-lose-its-sea-ice/.

勘探和开采。

随着易于获取的常规石油资源面临枯竭,各石油公司开始在不太宜居的地区搜寻石油,或者开发非传统资源,比如加拿大西部的油砂。因此,发现、生产和运输石油到市场的成本将会上升。2008年全球经济衰退之前,油价已经升至每桶140美元,此后也已回升至每桶100美元以上。① 有些专家认为,"石油峰值",即世界石油需求超过剩余储量的节点将很快达到或已经达到。② 正因如此,当美国地质调查局于2009年发布北极圈以北未探明石油和天然气资源预测时,人们才会异常兴奋:830亿桶石油,足以满足目前世界3年的需求量;44万亿立方米天然气,即大约14年的供应量。③

海冰融化加上高油价,人们有理由担心出现北极领土和资源潜在争夺。2007年,时任俄罗斯国家杜马副主席阿图尔·奇林加洛夫在北极海底插上一面钛制的国旗并宣称"北极是俄罗斯的",引发全球媒体哗然。④ 时任加拿大外交部长彼得·麦凯对此回应得同样有声有色:"嗨,这不是十五世纪。你不能到世界各地乱跑,插个旗帜说'我们要了这片领土。'而我们对北极的声索是有根有据的。"⑤

2008年,欧洲议会进一步推波助澜,呼吁以1959年《南极条约》为蓝本制定新的多边北极公约。⑥ 它这样一来,实际上是在含蓄地质疑

---

① International Energy Agency, "Oil Market Reports," http://omrpublic.iea.org/.

② John Collins Rudolf, "Is 'Peak Oil' Behind Us?" New York Times, November 14, 2010, http://green.blogs.nytimes.com/2010/11/14/is-peak-oil-behind-us/?partner=rssandemc=rss.

③ Donald L. Gautier, et al., "Assessment of Undiscovered Oil and Gas in the Arctic." (2009) 324 (5931) Science 1175.

④ Paul Reynolds, "Russia Ahead in Arctic 'Gold Rush'," BBC News, August 1, 2007, http://news.bbc.co.uk/2/hi/6925853.stm.

⑤ "Canada Rejects Flag-Planting as 'Just a Show'," Independent online, August 3, 2012, http://www.iol.co.za/news/world/canada-rejects-flag-planting-as-just-a-show-1.364759#.UHgzYo4_5UQ.

⑥ "European Parliament Resolution of 9 October 2008 on Arctic Governance," http://www.europarl.europa.eu/sides/getDoc.do?type=TA&reference=P6-TA-2008-0474&language=EN. For an excellent overview of similar proposals, Timo Koivurova, "Alternatives for an Arctic Treaty-Evaluation and a New Proposal." (2008) 17 Review of European Community and International Environmental Law 14.

北冰洋沿岸国家根据海洋法所声称的权利。① 同年,美国对外关系委员会的斯科特·柏格森将北极局势描述为可能导致严重后果的"混乱","新航线、市值数万亿美元的潜在石油和天然气资源,以及模棱两可的国家所有权,这几种情况相结合,酿造出某种有毒的大杂烩"。②

  幸运的是,头脑更冷静的人从此占了上风。一名参与北极插旗行动的俄罗斯科学家承认,这是缺乏法律相关性的宣传噱头。③ 丹麦外交大臣佩尔·斯蒂·默勒邀请其他四个北冰洋国家的同行前往格陵兰岛的伊卢利萨特,在此重申他们的承诺,愿在现有国际法框架内解决任何争端。④ 欧盟部长理事会发布一项北极政策承认,与南极不同,在一个以海洋为中心的区域内,海洋法是最重要的。⑤ 美国国务卿希拉里·克林顿谈到需要北极国家共同努力,她声称"因为事务繁多,时间紧迫,我们需要在座各位的帮助。"⑥

  即便是加拿大和俄罗斯的领导人,他们也明显采取了更为合作的立场,他们有时会出于国内政治目的而喜欢在北极问题上出风头。2010年1月,加拿大总理史蒂芬·哈珀对北约秘书长安诺斯·福格·拉斯穆森表示,"加拿大与俄罗斯在北极问题上存在良好合作关系",并且

---

① The law of the sea is made up of rules of customary international law which were codified, and supplemented with other rules and institutions, in the 1982 United Nations Convention on the Law of the Sea, 1833 UNTS 397, http://www.un.org/Depts/los/convention_agreements/texts/unclos/closindx.htm.

② Scott Borgerson, "Arctic Meltdown." (2008) 87 Foreign Affairs 63, http://www.foreignaffairs.com/articles/63222/scott-g-borgerson/arctic-meltdown.

③ Adrian Blomfield, "US Rises to Kremlin Bait," Daily Telegraph, August 4, 2007, http://www.telegraph.co.uk/news/worldnews/1559444/US-rises-to-Kremlin-bait.html.

④ "The Ilulissat Declaration," May 29, 2008, http://uk.nanoq.gl/Emner/News/News_from_Parliament/2008/05/~/media/66562304FA464945BB621411BFFB6E12.ashx.

⑤ Council of the European Union, "Council Conclusions on Arctic Issues," December 8, 2009, http://oceansnorth.org/resources/council-european-unionconclusions-arctic-issues. For an explanation of the shift in approach, Njord Wegge, "The EU and the Arctic: European Foreign Policy in the Making." (2012) 3 Arctic Review on Law and Politics 6.

⑥ "Hillary Clinton Criticises Canada over Arctic talks," BBC News, March 30, 2010, http://news.bbc.co.uk/2/hi/8594291.stm.

"北极国家不可能爆发战争"。① 8 个月后,哈珀政府发布一份《北极外交政策声明》,承诺加拿大将致力于解决该国遗留的北极边界争端。② 2010 年 9 月,时任俄罗斯总理(现任总统)弗拉基米尔·普京在北极专家国际会议上表示:"如果你孤军奋战,你无法在北极生存。自然条件促使人们和国家相互帮助。"③ 普京发表上述言论的一周前,俄罗斯和挪威签署巴伦支海边界条约,此前两国对这个面积为 5 万平方海里油气资源丰富的海底区域存在主权争议。④

简而言之,北极地区不存在为领土或资源进行的国家之间竞争,也没有爆发冲突的可能。相反,在地缘政治、环境和经济发生重大变化时期,北极正成为一个以合作和国际立法为标志的区域。

除了一个无关紧要的例外,该地区所有土地都无可置疑地属于这个或那个国家。这个例外就是汉斯岛,而它仅是一个位于格陵兰岛和加拿大之间的岩石小岛。北冰洋本身受到全球通行海洋法规则的管辖,包括美国在内的所有国家都将其视为国际习惯法。⑤ 这些规则是在几个世纪的国家实践和法律意见的基础上发展起来,并被编纂入 1982 年的《联

---

① US State Department cable # VZCZCXR03302, January 20, 2010, http://aptn.ca/pages/news/2011/05/11/while - harper - talked - tough - with - nato - on - arctic - u - s - believedpm - all - bark - no - bite/ (original cables are reproduced below the article).

② Statement on Canada's Arctic Foreign Policy, August 20, 2010, http://www.international.gc.ca/polar - polaire/assets/pdfs/CAFP_booklet - PECA_livret - eng.pdf.

③ Luke Harding, "Vladimir Putin Calls for Arctic Claims to Be Resolved under UN Law," Guardian, September 23, 2010, http://www.guardian.co.uk/world/2010/sep/23/putin - arctic - claims - international - law.

④ 2010 Treaty between the Kingdom of Norway and the Russian Federation Concerning Maritime Delimitation and Cooperation in the Barents Sea and the Arctic Ocean, English translation, http://www.regjeringen.no/upload/ud/vedlegg/folkerett/avtale_engelsk.pdf.

⑤ See, e.g., President Ronald Reagan, "Statement on United States Oceans Policy, March 10, 1983," http://www.oceanlaw.org/downloads/references/reagan/ReaganOceanPolicy - 1983.pdf; National Oceanic and Atmospheric Administration (NOAA), Office of General Counsel, "Law of the Sea Convention," http://www.gc.noaa.gov/gcil_los.html ("While it is not yet a party, the US nevertheless observes the Convention as reflective of customary international law and practice"). The International Court of Justice recently ruled that Art. 76 (1) of UNCLOS, on extended continental shelves, is part of customary international law. Territorial and Maritime Dispute (Nicaragua v. Colombia), November 19, 2012, p. 118, http://www.icj - cij.org/docket/files/124/17164.pdf.

合国海洋法公约》。①

  与世界其他地方一样，北极国家的领海扩展至海岸以外 12 海里。在此范围内，沿岸国对外国航运享有广泛的监管权力，并对渔业和海底资源享有绝对权利。在 12 海里和 200 海里之间的专属经济区内，沿岸国在航运方面权力较少，但仍对渔业和海底资源享有绝对权利。200 海里之外，沿岸国失去对渔业的权利，但只要这些国家能够通过科学方法证明海底是其陆地的"自然延伸"，就可能对那里的海底享有权利。正如第四章中将解释的那样，这意味着在北极海床插旗并不会比在月球插旗具有更多的法律意义。这还表明，大多数北极近海石油和天然气资源处于某个沿岸国无可争议的管辖范围之内，因为从有机物中提取的近海石油和天然气通常在大陆架的沉积层中被发现。

  数十年来，国际法在确定海岸相邻国家之间海上区域边界方面发挥了核心作用。如上所述，美国和苏联于 1990 年签署白令海、白令海峡和楚科奇海的边界条约。② 21 年后，俄罗斯和挪威在巴伦支海达成类似条约。③ 如第三章所释，北极目前仅剩一处尚未解决的海上边界，即美国和加拿大在波弗特海的边界。

  为解决上述争端，美国和加拿大在获得两国大陆架外部边界相关地质和地貌证据方面展开了合作。作为《联合国海洋法公约》的缔约国，加拿大将很快向大陆架界限委员会提交其数据，该委员会是由科学家组成，只有发布"建议"权，以使得到支持的大陆架划界提案合法化。同样的数据也将与更北部区域有关，在这里加拿大、俄罗斯和丹麦的外大陆架沿着数条海底海脊存在重叠。由于委员会没有解决此类重叠问题的授权，在北冰洋中部的边界最终可能必须通过谈判解决，当然，这将在现有国际法框架内进行。

  在第五章中将讲到，西北航道和北方海航线的法律地位也存在争议。两个争议都是双边的，都涉及到美国，而俄罗斯和加拿大各自声称这些北极海峡是"内水"，受其完全管辖和控制。俄罗斯已经成功阻止

---

① n. 15, above.
② n. 1, above.
③ n. 24, above.

了对其法律立场的任何挑战,而加拿大已经管控该争议超过四十年,包括在1988年谈判达成《北极合作协议》,协议中美国承诺在派遣海岸警卫队破冰船通过西北航道之前将寻求加方许可。① 当前,随着海冰消退和各种船只的到来,该协议亟待更新。

船舶安全、溢油预防和渔业管理等问题也值得关注。北极现实条件需要更高的船舶建造标准,包括冰区强化和双层船壳、完全封闭的救生艇和最先进的导航和通讯设备。国际海事组织花费数年时间就航运"极地规则"进行谈判,但是该文件在2002年通过之前被降级为一套指导方针。② 旨在升级该指导方针并将其转化为有约束力条约的谈判正在进行。

在北极,清理重大溢油事故是一项难以企及的任务。北极八国均已批准了1990年《国际油污防备、反应和合作公约》,该公约是在国际海事组织主持下谈判达成的。③ 除要求采取储备溢油处理设备等措施外,该公约推动了区域协议的发展。北极理事会已签署一份关于北极海上石油污染防备和响应的条约草案,预计于2013年通过。④ 但新条约的重点在于提升事故发生时的沟通和协调,不太可能超过《国际油污防备、反应和合作公约》的规定,解决诸如同季减压井和责任上限等更棘手的问题。正如第六章所述,北极真正需要的是一份关于溢油预防的条约。

在不久将来的某个时候,远洋捕鱼船队将探索北冰洋中部新出现的无冰水域。在世界各地公海,或在公海和沿岸国专属经济区之间游动的鱼类资源极易受到过度捕捞的影响。第六章中将提出,在商业捕鱼开始之前,北冰洋需要成立一个区域性渔业组织。

---

① Agreement between the Government of Canada and the Government of the United States of America on Arctic Cooperation, Canada Treaty Series 1988, No. 29; http://www.lexum.com/ca_us/en/cts.1988.29.en.html.

② The Guidelines were updated in 2009 but left unbinding. See Guidelines for Ships Operating in Polar Waters, December 2, 2009, http://www.imo.org/blast/blastDataHelper.asp?data_id=29985&filename=A1024(26).pdf.

③ 1990 International Convention on Oil Pollution Preparedness, Response and Co-operation, http://www.ifrc.org/docs/idrl/I245EN.pdf.

④ Task Force on Arctic Marine Oil Pollution Preparedness and Response, http://www.arctic-council.org/index.php/en/about-us/task-forces/280-oil-spill-task-force.

北极地区已存在数个区域性组织。1993 年，丹麦、芬兰、冰岛、挪威、瑞典、俄罗斯和欧盟签署《希尔克内斯宣言》，成立巴伦支海欧洲—北极理事会。① 与此同时，州省级政府、土著团体等也签署一项成立巴伦支区域理事会的议定书。这两个平行组织推动了就共同关心的问题开展合作，而由于该区域内的距离相近和历史因素，有可能实现特别高水平的信任和合作。

就在最近，北极理事会已成为北极地区最全面的国际机构。自1996 年以来，北极理事会取得了一系列成就，包括 2004 年《北极气候影响评估报告》② 和 2009 年《北极海运评估报告》③。2011 年，八个成员国成立了一个常设秘书处，可以说北极理事会正由政府间论坛向国际组织转变。④ 这些国家还谈判达成一项多边搜索和救援条约，这是在北极理事会主持下达成的首个具有法律约束力的文件。⑤

值得注意的是，自北极理事会成立以来，一直将土著居民作为"永久参与方"。他们与其他八个成员国一道，实时参与，这是一项基于共识、跌宕起伏的决策进程。⑥ 通过建立北极外交和立法核心论坛，北极理事会名声大振，它由政治家、外交官和其他专家组成，不断扩大，成为跨国共同体的"议政平台"。他们通过彼此间的反复磋商互动，逐步

---

① Declaration on Cooperation in the Barents Euro - Arctic Region, November 1, 1993, http://www.barentsinfo.fi/beac/docs/459_doc_KirkenesDeclaration.pdf.

② Arctic Climate Impact Assessment, n. 5, above.

③ 2009 Arctic Marine Shipping Assessment, http://www.pame.is/index.php/amsa-2009-report.

④ Nuuk Declaration, May 12, 2011, http://www.arctic-council.org/index.php/en/about/documents/category/5-declarations. Although the Arctic Council is based on a declaration rather than a founding treaty, such a treaty is not a necessary condition for an international organization. The Organization for Security and Cooperation in Europe (OSCE) is based on the "Helsinki Declaration" and has similarly evolved from an inter-governmental forum into an international organization. Final Act of the Conference on Security and Cooperation in Europe, August 1, 1975, 14 ILM 1292, http://www.umn.edu/humanrts/osce/basics/finact75.htm.

⑤ Agreement on Aeronautical and Maritime Search and Rescue in the Arctic, May 12, 2011, http://www.arctic-council.org/index.php/en/about/documents/category/20-main-documents-from-nuuk.

⑥ discussion, Chapter 7, below.

获得共同的期待、认同和利益。① 而这反过来又可以推动更多的合作和立法。

就像雷索卢特湾午夜的晨曦,本书试图管中窥豹,突出说明在快速变化的北极地区以法律为基础的合作具有日益重要的作用。要做到这一点,本书有时会讨论十分技术性的法律问题,并试图同时面向法律人士和非法律人士阐释这些问题。当代北极其他领域的问题,例如冷战后地缘政治、新生区域治理机制、油气资源与气候变化之间令人担忧的动态等,并非本书重点,他们仅作为现有规则或规则制定过程的相关背景资料稍带论及。北极地区国际立法的发展本身是一件非常重要的事情,鉴于北极当前存在盲目竞争和紧张冲突等报道甚嚣尘上,这种立法也是一种事实上的制约。

---

① For more on the "constructivist" dynamics of diplomacy and international law – making, Alexander Wendt, Social Theory of International Politics (Cambridge University Press, 1999); Michael Byers, Custom, Power and the Power of Rules (Cambridge University Press, 1999); Jutta Brunne'e and Stephen Toope, Legitimacy and Legality in International Law (Cambridge University Press, 2010).

中文版序言

2018年《中国的北极政策》白皮书提出，中国作为"近北极国家"，享有开展北极科研活动，共同应对全球变暖，助力北极社会和经济发展，以及"依据规则、通过机制"参与北极治理等一系列积极利益。①

本书研究的主要对象就是北极治理的规则和机制。

25年来，中方一直从言和行两方面表明，其接受北极国家领土主权、北极原住民权利、沿岸国和航运国根据1982年《联合国海洋法公约》（下称《公约》）所享之权利和义务，以及跨界污染、北极熊和渔业等领域国际环境法的不断扩展。

我诚恳希望本书有助于中国官员、学者和学生更好地了解北极治理相关规则和机制的全貌，进一步理解在北极开放性不断提升的背景下，这些规则是如何经受检验、调整并在一定情况下重新磋商的。作为大国，中国正在北极扮演越来越重要角色，可以为北极地区国际法的维护、发展和改变做出更多贡献。

一、中国和北极

中国于1995年派遣"雪龙"号科考破冰船开展首次北极航行，1996年加入国际北极科学委员会，2004年在斯瓦尔巴群岛建立科考站。② 2007

---

① State Council Information Office of the People's Republic of China, "China's Arctic Foreign Policy," 26 January 2018, http：//www.xinhuanet.com/english/2018 - 01/26/c_136926498.htm.

② Linda Jakobson, "China Prepares for an Ice - Free Arctic," SIPRI Insights on Peace and Security, 2 (2010), 3, http：//www.sipri.org/sites/default/files/files/insight/SIPRIInsight1002.pdf.

年，中国申请成为北极理事会观察员，并于 2013 年获得通过。[①] 2018 年，中国与北冰洋五国（加拿大、挪威、俄罗斯、丹麦和美国）以及冰岛、日本、韩国和欧盟共同签署禁止在北冰洋中部开展商业捕捞的条约，直至科学研究证明此类活动具备可持续性。[②]

目前，中国北极能力正迅速提升。2019 年，中国第 2 艘破冰船交付使用，现正筹划建造第 3 艘吨位更大的核动力破冰船。[③] 中国企业不断新建冰区加强型货船，并与俄罗斯合作开展北方海航线海上运输。[④] 中国海军也正着力发展可在冰面以下执行任务的核潜艇，提升北极军事能力。[⑤]

在与北极国家就区域问题开展紧密合作的同时，中国也与其中部分国家就某些国际问题存在分歧。例如，中国和美国就南海法律地位问题发生争执[⑥]、中国和加拿大的关系也受到中美贸易摩擦牵连。[⑦]

历史上看，国家间可以在某些区域或就具体议题保持良好合作关系，而在其他领域出现关系紧张。在冷战期间、冷战后和 2014 年克里米亚事件后，俄罗斯与其他北极国家仍在北极地区开展了广泛合作。[⑧] 2010 年以来，中国与挪威关系出现波动，但双方在北极地区的合作得

[①] Willis, Matthew, and Duncan Depledge. "How we learned to stop worrying about China's Arctic ambitions: Understanding China's admission to the Arctic Council, 2004 – 2013." *Handbook of the Politics of the Arctic*（2015）：388 – 407.

[②] 2017 *Agreement to Prevent Unregulated High Seas Fisheries in the Central Arctic Ocean*. http://eur-lex.europa.eu/legal-content/EN/ALL/? uri = COM：2018：454：FIN.

[③] Thomas Nilsen, "Details of China's nuclear-powered icebreaker revealed," *Barents Observer*, 21 March 2019, http://thebarentsobserver.com/en/arctic/2019/03/details-chinas-nuclear-powered-icebreaker-revealed.

[④] Malte Humpert, "Chinese Shipping Company COSCO To Send Record Number of Ships Through Arctic," *High North News*, 13 June 2019, http://www.highnorthnews.com/en/chinese-shipping-company-cosco-send-record-number-ships-through-arctic.

[⑤] Levon Sevunts, "Pentagon warns of risk of Chinese submarines in the Arctic," *CBC News*, 4 May 2019, http://www.cbc.ca/news/politics/china-arctic-military-submarines-pentagon-1.5123287.

[⑥] Bill Hayton, *The South China Sea*（New Haven：Yale University Press, 2014）.

[⑦] Jason Proctor, "Everything you need to know about Huawei, Meng Wanzhou and her possible extradition," *CBC News*, 12 December 2019, http://www.cbc.ca/news/canada/british-columbia/huawei-meng-extradition-questions-fraud-1.4943162.

[⑧] Michael Byers, "Crises and International Cooperation: An Arctic Case Study," *International Relations*, 31（4），375 – 402, http://journals.sagepub.com/doi/full/10.1177/0047117817735680.

以维持。事实上，各国在北极和外太空等"冷、暗、危"区域的持续合作，有助于防止国际危机扩散。①

二、北极资源

俄罗斯和加拿大是国土面积世界第一和第二大国，它们的大部分领土都位于北极地区。美国阿拉斯加州的面积大致等同于西欧。丹麦的格陵兰是世界上面积最大的非大陆类的岛屿。挪威的人均国内生产总值位居世界第三，其中很大部分收入来源于北极水域的油气资源开发。事实上，所有这些国家都拥有广阔的200海里专属经济区。如果地质和地貌数据表明存在"大陆架的自然延伸"，那么相关国家还可对专属经济区以外的海底资源享有主权权利。②

中国对北极资源的兴趣十分明显，这已经引发美国国务卿蓬佩奥所谓"侵略行为""军事化"和"竞争性领土主张"等一系列警告。③ 但这些警告都缺乏事实根据。从世界范围来看，中国一直坚持通过贸易和投资等方式和平地获取相关资源。正如俄罗斯亚马尔液化天然气④，中国、挪威和冰岛在冰岛水域油气开发⑤，格陵兰科瓦内湾铀稀土矿等项

---

① Michael Byers, "Cold, dark, and dangerous: international cooperation in the arctic and space." *Polar Record* (2019): 1 – 16, http://www.cambridge.org/core/journals/polar-record/article/cold-dark-and-dangerous-international-cooperation-in-the-arctic-and-space/EA8CD98F80BBFF8F14447F3613F6E06A.

② 1982 United Nations Convention on the Law of the Sea, 1833 U. N. T. S. 397, Articles 55 – 57 and 76, http://www.un.org/Depts/los/convention_agreements/texts/unclos/closindx.htm.

③ Michael R. Pompeo, "Looking North: Sharpening America's Arctic Focus," Remarks delivered in Rovaniemi, Finland, 6 May 2019, http://www.state.gov/looking-north-sharpening-americas-arctic-focus/.

④ Costas Paris, "China, Russia Carriers to Ship Gas on Arctic Route," *The Wall Street Journal*, 11 June 2019, http://www.wsj.com/articles/china-russia-carriers-to-ship-gas-on-arctic-route-11560284812.

⑤ Ragnhildur Sigurdardottir and Mikael Holter, "Iceland's Oil Dream Is in Peril," *Bloomberg*, 23 January 2018, http://www.bloomberg.com/news/articles/2018-01-23/iceland-s-oil-dream-in-peril-as-china-norway-give-up-last-block.

目所展现的，北极国家都愿意向中国敞开贸易大门。①

　　加拿大魁北克省迪塞普申湾附近的努纳维克铜镍矿属于中资项目。2014 年，加拿大冰区加强型货船装载该矿出产的第 1 船镍精矿经西北航道前往中国。② 规划中的魁北克北部 Lac Otelnuk 项目③和努纳武特西部 Izok Corridor 项目④同样有中国企业的身影。

　　中国于 1996 年批准《公约》，因此各方在北极大陆架资源开发合作问题上也不会出现任何不同。⑤ 但北极国家外大陆架以外的"深海海床"则另当别论，尽管该问题不会引发任何担忧。根据《公约》规定，该区域资源属于"人类的共同继承财产"，可以按照国际海底管理局的相关规定加以开采，其中部分收入需与"最不发达国家"分享。⑥ 中国已在世界其他地区深海海底开采活动中遵守了这些程序。⑦

三、北极航运

　　中国是全球第一大航运国。在"一带一路"倡议框架下，中国正致力于发展全球海上运输，其中之一便是穿过俄罗斯北方海航线的"冰

---

① Costas Paris, "China, Russia Carriers to Ship Gas on Arctic Route," *The Wall Street Journal*, 11 June 2019, http://www.wsj.com/articles/china-russia-carriers-to-ship-gas-on-arctic-route-11560284812.

② Peter Farquar, "A cargo ship just completed a historic trip through the Northwest Passage," *Business Insider*, 2 October 2014, http://www.businessinsider.com/a-cargo-ship-just-completed-a-historic-trip-through-the-northwest-passage-2014-10.

③ Nunatsiaq News, "Nunavik's Lac Otelnuk iron mine project on a fast-track to production," 30 October 2013, http://nunatsiaq.com/stories/article/65674nunaviks_lac_otelnuk_iron_mine_project_on_a_fast-track_to_production/.

④ Pav Jordan, "Nunavut mining rush attracts China-backed MMG," *The Globe and Mail*, 4 September 2012 (updated 8 May 2018), http://www.theglobeandmail.com/report-on-business/nunavut-mining-rush-attracts-china-backed-mmg/article4519069/.

⑤ Status of Treaties, https://treaties.un.org/pages/ParticipationStatus.aspx?clang=_en.

⑥ UNCLOS, Part XI, http://www.un.org/Depts/los/convention_agreements/texts/unclos/closindx.htm.

⑦ David Dodwell, "As China leads the hunt for deep-sea minerals, environmental and financial concerns come to the surface," *South China Morning Post*, 4 May 2018, http://www.scmp.com/comment/insight-opinion/article/2144647/china-leads-hunt-deep-sea-minerals-environmental-and.

上丝绸之路"。北方海航线将中国和欧洲西北部之间的距离缩短近6000千米。2012年，中国使用"雪龙"号测试该航线适航性，并从次年起派遣货船通过北方海航线。① 这些活动都得到了俄罗斯方面的协助。俄罗斯认为，北方海航线中最狭窄的部分属于俄方管辖和控制之下的"内水"。②

在加拿大一侧的北冰洋，西北航道同样为中国与加拿大东部北极地区、美国东北部之间的海上交通提供了更短的航线。在良好冰况下，船舶从魁北克北部启程途径西北航道前往中国，可比取道巴拿马运河缩短近40%的时间和燃料。2014年，即有1艘载有2.3万吨镍精矿的冰区加强型货船照此抵达中国。③

尽管何时北极冰况才能使货船通过西北航道更为可靠仍存在不确定性，但在既往12年中，北极海冰范围的最低值已经出现了12次。④ 然而，气候变化使得冰川进入大洋的速度提升，冰山数量不断增加，即使坚硬的"多年"海冰即将消失，西北航道对海上航运而言危险仍存。⑤ 北极开放水域增加同样会导致船舶"结冰"风险上升，即在强风和低温作用下，海浪冻结船只上层建筑，引发船只失衡等灾难性后果。⑥ 加拿大和美国之间就西北航道法律地位的争议也为该航线开发蒙上一层阴影。加拿大认为西北航道是处于加方完全管辖和控制之下的内水；美方

---

① Trude Pettersen, "China starts commercial use of Northern Sea Route," *Barents Observer*, 14 March 2013, http://barentsobserver.com/en/arctic/2013/03/china-starts-commercial-use-northern-sea-route-14-03.

② Government of the USSR, "*Aide mémoire* to the US embassy in Moscow," July 1964, reproduced in Office of Ocean Affairs, *Limits in the Seas No. 112: United States Responses to Excessive National Maritime Claims* (Washington, DC: US State Department, 1992) 71, http://www.state.gov/documents/organization/58381.pdf.

③ Peter Farquar, "A cargo ship just completed a historic trip through the Northwest Passage," *Business Insider*, 2 October 2014, http://www.businessinsider.com/a-cargo-ship-just-completed-a-historic-trip-through-the-northwest-passage-2014-10.

④ NOAA Arctic Program, "Arctic Report Card: Update for 2018", http://arctic.noaa.gov/Report-Card/Report-Card-2018/ArtMID/7878/ArticleID/771/2018-Headlines.

⑤ Julian A. Dowdeswell, "The Greenland ice sheet and global sea-level rise." *Science* 311.5763 (2006): 963-964.

⑥ J. E. Overland, et al. "Prediction of vessel icing." *Journal of climate and applied meteorology* 25.12 (1986): 1793-1806.

则主张其为"国际海峡",应不加限制的对所有国家船只开放。

西方媒体有时揣测中国会与美国采取相同立场,"中国准备挑战加拿大对西北航道的主权""中国是美加在西北航道分歧的最大变数"等标题时常见诸报端。① 事实上,中国或许会更倾向于支持或接受加拿大的内水主张。

中国已就本国船只通过西北航道与加拿大展开合作。2016 年,中国海事局发布船舶通过西北航道的航行指南。② 其中建议中国船只向加拿大政府申请许可并"遵守 2001 年《加拿大航运法》和 2010 年《加拿大北方船舶交通服务区规定》"。

2017 年,中国启动环北极航行项目,期间同样就"雪龙"号在西北航道开展海洋科研活动向加方提出申请。③ 因为他国无论在内水或国际海峡开展科学研究活动,均需要向沿岸国提出申请,所以该申请使得中国可以回避西北航道的法律地位问题。加拿大政府随后批准中方申请,并写道"在遵守治安、安全和环保法律的前提下,欢迎相关船舶在加拿大北极水域航行",同时建议中方雇佣一名加拿大冰区引航员。④ 中国不仅雇佣了引航员,而且提出加拿大科学家可以共同参与此次航行。

在实践和法律的战略层面,中国也有理由支持或至少接受加拿大的内水主张。西北航道位置偏僻、航行危险,根据所选路线不同,约有

---

① Nash Jenkins, "China Could be Preparing to Challenge Canada's Sovereignty over the Northwest Passage," *Time*, 20 April 2016, http://time.com/4302882/china-arctic-shipping-northwest-passage; Doug Tsuruoka, "China is Wild Card in US-Canada Split over Northwest Passage," *Asia Times*, 10 January 2017, http://www.atimes.com/article/china-wild-card-us-canada-split-northwest-passage.

② Adam Lajeunesse, "Chinese prepare to Use the Northwest Passage," *World Policy Blog*, 14 September 2016, http://www.worldpolicy.org/blog/2016/09/14/chinese-prepare-use-northwest-passage.

③ Robert Fife and Steven Chase, "Chinese ship sails Northwest Passage," *The Globe and Mail* 12 July 2017, http://www.theglobeandmail.com/news/politics/chinese-ship-making-first-voyage-through-canadas-northwest-passage/article36142513/.

④ Robert Fife and Steven Chase, "Chinese ship sails Northwest Passage," *The Globe and Mail* 12 July 2017, http://www.theglobeandmail.com/news/politics/chinese-ship-making-first-voyage-through-canadas-northwest-passage/article36142513/.

1500到2000千米长，航道两岸均为加方领土。故加拿大是唯一可为船舶航行提供海图、导航、气象和海冰预报、避难港、搜救，以及应对海盗、恐怖分子和走私威胁等支持的沿岸国。缺乏上述条件，商业航运将面临较大风险，导致事故率和保险费率攀升。

中美就中国大陆和海南岛之间琼州海峡的法律性质存在争议。这是中国支持或接受加拿大立场的法律层面原因。[1] 与加拿大在西北航道的情况类似，中国长期坚持琼州海峡构成历史性内水[2]；同加方一样，中国通过划设"直线基线"固化本国主张[3]；同加方一样，唯一反对中国主张的也是美国，其认为琼州海峡是国际海峡。[4]

这就导致一种情况，即中方在反对加拿大立场的同时也将损害本国法律主张。正如洪农（NONG HONG）所释：

中国和其他非北极国家所面临的一个基本问题是对西北航道和北方海航线法律地位的立场……若中国采纳美国立场……这将弱化中方对海南岛和大陆之间的琼州海峡属于中国内水的主张。[5]

中国有数个选项。一是不对西北航道争议持任何立场，并与加拿大就商业航运展开合作。甚至可以设想中国和加拿大之间达成北极合作协议，搁置西北航道法律地位，聚焦航线安全和效率。这与美加1988年《北极合作协议》的模式相类似。二是中国也可以发展北极航运合作并接受加方主张，以巩固自身在琼州海峡的法律立场。[6]

---

[1] Michael Byers & Emma Lodge, "China and the Northwest Passage," *Chinese Journal of International Law* 18.1 (2019): 57–90.

[2] Hungdah Chiu, "China and the Question of Territorial Sea," 1 *Maryland Journal of International Law* 29 (1975): 46, http://digitalcommons.law.umaryland.edu/mjil/vol1/iss1/6.

[3] Ibid.

[4] Michael Byers & Emma Lodge, "China and the Northwest Passage," *Chinese Journal of International Law* 18.1 (2019): 57–90.

[5] Nong Hong, "Emerging interests of non-Arctic countries in the Arctic: a Chinese perspective," *The Polar Journal*, 4 (2): 271–286, 277, citing Olga Alexeeva and Frederic Lasserre, "China and the Arctic," *Arctic Yearbook* (2012): 86.

[6] Michael Byers & Emma Lodge, "China and the Northwest Passage," *Chinese Journal of International Law* 18.1 (2019): 57–90.

四、近期发展

自本书英文版问世以来,国际法和北极均已出现一些重要进展。

2014年国际海事组织通过了《国际极地水域操作船舶规则》(《极地规则》)。《极地规则》规定了可在冰覆水域作业的三类船舶,并就保护船员、乘客和海洋环境提出建议。然而,《极地规则》原本应建立在《在北极冰覆盖水域内船舶航行指南》(《国际海事组织指南》)基础之上,但实际上其相关规定反而弱于后者。例如,《国际海事组织指南》第11.5.1条建议"所有救生艇……应为全封闭型,以充分掩蔽外部环境",而《极地规则》第8.3.3.3.1条却只要求"救生艇应是部分或全封闭型"。《极地规则》相对削弱也意味着加拿大和俄罗斯不太可能放弃在西北航道和北方海航线问题上的内水立场,以支持《极地规则》规范之下的国际海峡制度。因此,《极地规则》所取得的成效并不尽如人意。

在过去5年中,加拿大和丹麦向联合国大陆架界限委员会提交了北冰洋划界案,俄罗斯则提交了订正的划界案。如本书所释,任何国家都不会"拥有"地理学意义上的北极点。它位于格陵兰岛、埃尔斯米尔岛以及俄罗斯的法兰士约瑟夫地群岛等任何陆地的北部约400海里之外。沿岸国无法对12海里领海以外的水域享有完全主权,但对200海里专属经济区内海床和上覆水域的资源享有权利,有时还可对超出这一范围的的海底资源主张权利。

《联合国海洋法公约》第七十六条对沿岸国在200海里外的海底区域权利做出了规定,即如果海底形态、深度和沉积岩厚度等证明相关大陆架是沿岸国陆地领土的"自然延伸",则沿岸国可主张外大陆架权利。因此,如果俄罗斯、丹麦或加拿大能够从科学上证明北极海底是其大陆架的自然延伸,那么它们将获得对该区域的主权权利。但也仅此而已,其上覆水域和海冰仍属于公海。

第七十六条还要求沿岸国须向大陆架界限委员会提交自然延伸的科学证据,以供审议和提出建议。2001年,俄罗斯提交初步申请。在委员会要求提供更多北冰洋数据后,俄政府于 2015 年提交订正的申请。本书英文版出版后,加拿大计划于 2013 年 12 月提交全部划界案,但在最后关头决定只提交部分划界案。在进一步开展海底测绘后,加拿大于 2019 年提交了北冰洋海域大陆架划界案。丹麦也采取了类似方法,于 2014 年提交北冰洋海域大陆架划界案。三国主张的重叠区域沿着罗蒙诺索夫海岭。这个海底山脉位于北极点附近并将北冰洋一分为二。

俄罗斯、加拿大和丹麦均已表示,联合国大陆架界限委员会可以就重叠区域问题提出建议。委员会只有得到当事国同意后,才可审议争端区域内的划界案,但不会就海上划界问题做出决定。如果委员会认定两个及以上国家的外大陆架存在重叠,则当事国可选择自行协商解决方案、将之提交国际法庭或仲裁庭,亦或就存在争议达成一致并且不在争议区域颁发勘探许可。

2016 年,挪威、丹麦和加拿大在本国专属经济区内发现了俄罗斯的火箭舱段残骸。① 这使得此前被忽视的北极环境保护问题再度引发关注。这些火箭舱段原本用于极地轨道卫星发射活动,可能含有大量的偏二甲肼残留物。俄罗斯政府科学家此前也称,这种高毒性燃料与哈萨克斯坦和俄罗斯境内大范围健康和环境破坏存在关联。俄方此举显然是非法的,却也为海洋法和国际空间法发展提出了很多有意思的新问题。②

本书英文版中,我批评了 2011 年北极理事会成员国为吸纳观察员附加新条件的作法。根据该条件,申请成为观察员须以承认"北极国家

---

① Michael Byers and Cameron Byers, "Toxic splash: Russian rocket stages dropped in Arctic waters raise health, environmental and legal concerns." *Polar Record* 53.6 (2017): 580 – 591, http://www.cambridge.org/core/journals/polar-record/article/toxic-splash-russian-rocket-stages-dropped-in-arctic-waters-raise-health-environmental-and-legal-concerns/EAC6047606BDFFE6F8361F91EF02D14B.

② Michael Byers and Cameron Byers, "Toxic splash: Russian rocket stages dropped in Arctic waters raise health, environmental and legal concerns." *Polar Record* 53.6 (2017): 580 – 591, http://www.cambridge.org/core/journals/polar-record/article/toxic-splash-russian-rocket-stages-dropped-in-arctic-waters-raise-health-environmental-and-legal-concerns/EAC6047606BDFFE6F8361F91EF02D14B.

根据《联合国海洋法公约》管理北冰洋的权利"为前提。① 这意味着接受北极国家享有管理整个北冰洋的权利,而实际上中国和其他非北极国家有权在海岸线 12 海里外自由航行、在 200 海里外捕鱼、在沿岸国大陆架以外的海底区域开采资源。故我当时认为中方不会接受该条件。但据称中方虽感不快,② 但最终仍决定接受该条件,并在本书出版后不久的 2013 年 5 月成为北极理事会观察员。③ 中国自此可以参与北极理事会相关工作组等多方面事务,该决定亦为北极合作做出非常积极的贡献。

最后,中国和北极国家近期就北冰洋渔业科学管理等议题展开合作。2015 年,北冰洋沿岸五国通过一项中北冰洋宣言,意在预防五国船只在公海区域开展不管制商业捕鱼,同时希望非北极国家也做出相同承诺。④ 2017 年,中国与日本、韩国、冰岛和欧盟加入其中,通过条约形式承诺,在获得科学证据支持前不在北冰洋中部开展商业捕鱼。⑤

中国是全球主要国家,将在北极发挥重要作用。若此书中译本可为 2018 年《中国的北极政策》中有关"依据规则、通过机制"参与北极治理等核心内容有所助益,我将感到非常欣喜和荣幸。⑥

迈克尔·拜尔斯
加拿大不列颠哥伦比亚省盐泉岛
2019 年 7 月

---

① "Observers," http://www.arctic-council.org/index.php/en/about-us/partners-links.

② Linda Jakobson & Jingchao Peng, "China's Arctic Ambitions," SIPRI Policy Paper 34, November 2012, http://books.sipri.org/product_info?c_product_id=449.

③ Willis, Matthew, and Duncan Depledge. "How we learned to stop worrying about China's Arctic ambitions: Understanding China's admission to the Arctic Council, 2004 – 2013." Handbook of the Politics of the Arctic (2015): 388 – 407.

④ Canada, Denmark, Norway, Russia & US. (2015). Declaration Concerning the Prevention of Unregulated High Seas Fishing in the Central Arctic Ocean, http://www.regjeringen.no/globalassets/departementene/ud/vedlegg/folkerett/declaration-on-arctic-fisheries-16-july-2015.pdf.

⑤ 2017 Agreement to Prevent Unregulated High Seas Fisheries in the Central Arctic Ocean, http://eur-lex.europa.eu/legal-content/EN/ALL/?uri=COM:2018:454:FIN.

⑥ State Council Information Office of the People's Republic of China, "China's Arctic Foreign Policy," 26 January 2018, http://www.xinhuanet.com/english/2018-01/26/c_136926498.htm.

第一章 领土

2011年8月,我和我的大儿子搭乘"泽迪亚克"号穿越贝洛特海峡,这条水道狭窄蜿蜒,长达20海里,位于加拿大高北极地区。一条七节的潮汐裂口让旅行更为令人振奋。最令人兴奋的是在穿越海峡的途中,我们踏上了北美大陆的最北端。我们知道,自1880年英国将其北极领地转交加拿大以来,齐尼思角就一直属于加拿大,贝洛特海峡以北的群岛毫无疑问同样属于加拿大。[1] 当我们再次象征性地宣布这片土地属于我们国家时,地理发现的那股激情仿佛仍在我们的脊背上流淌。本章将聚焦领土问题,包括数个历史性的问题。本章将从该地区一处仍存领土所有权争议的地方讲起。

一、汉斯岛

在丹麦外交大臣的法律顾问托马斯·温克列尔大使办公室墙上,挂着一面已褪色并被风撕裂了的丹麦国旗。丹麦军队曾在汉斯岛升起这面旗帜,但之后加拿大军队将其撤下并寄回哥本哈根。

汉斯岛是个仅有一公里宽的贫瘠小岛,位于埃尔斯米尔岛和格陵兰岛西北部之间内尔斯海峡中的肯尼迪海峡。[2] 直至1973年,丹麦和加拿大外交官就格陵兰和加拿大之间这条1450海里长的大陆架边界展开谈

---

[1] An Order – in – Council dated July 31, 1880 transferred "all the British possessions on the North American continent, not hitherto annexed to any colony." Canada Gazette, October 9, 1880; Ivan Head, "Canadian Claims to Territorial Sovereignty in the Arctic Regions." (1963) 9 McGill Law Journal 200, 212.

[2] David H. Gray, "Canada's Unresolved Maritime Boundaries." (1997) 5 (3) IBRU Boundary and Security Bulletin 61 at 68 – 69, http://www.dur.ac.uk/resources/ibru/publications/full/bsb5 – 3_gray.pdf.

判之时①，他们才开始意识到两国对该岛所有权存在不同意见。但谈判人员没有因这个出乎预料却几乎无关大局的新情况而拖延会谈，仅是将该岛两端低潮点之间的部分排除于边界线之外。时至今日，虽然汉斯岛比某些从其附近漂过冰山还要小，但却是整个北极圈内唯一存在争议的领土。

2005年，另一位丹麦大使保罗·克里斯滕森在写给《渥太华公民报》编辑的信中，总结了该国对汉斯岛的主张：

普遍认为，1853年在经丹麦政府同意后开展的一次考察中，首次发现了汉斯岛，著名的格陵兰人"菲斯克奈瑟的汉斯·亨德里克"亦参与其中。此人在本次考察中所发挥的作用为其在探险史中赢得一席之地，该岛也正是以他的名字命名为"汉斯岛"。

自此之后，我们始终认为由于该岛属于格陵兰，所以是丹麦王国的一部分。地质和地貌等确定格陵兰区域的相关证据，明确地支持了这一观点。

1933年，国际常设法院对格陵兰岛法律地位的声明有利于丹麦，该法院特别引用英国政府代表加拿大发出的一份照会，其中英国在1920年向丹麦政府确认，该国承认丹麦对格陵兰岛主权。②

丹麦前格陵兰部长汤姆·贺耶姆提出了该国主张的另一个组成部分：

几个世纪以来，汉斯岛一直被格陵兰因纽特人作为观察海冰情况和对北极熊、海豹等进行狩猎观察的理想位置。事实上，汉斯岛是图勒因纽特人（Thule-Inuit）狩猎区的一部分。他们甚至给它起了当地的名字"塔图帕卢克"，即"肾脏"之意。③

然而，这些论据都经不起推敲。克里斯滕森大使没有提到汉斯·亨德里克参加的是美国考察队，但美国从未主张拥有汉斯岛。在涉及200海里以外的外大陆架问题时，地质和地貌证据才具有相关性，对于海岸

---

① For more on the Danish-Canadian maritime boundary, Chapter 2, below.
② Poul E. D. Kristensen, Ambassador of Denmark, Letter to the Editor ("Hans Island: Denmark Responds"), Ottawa Citizen, July 28, 2005.
③ Tom Høyem, "Mr. Graham, You Should Have Told Us You Were Coming," Globe and Mail, July 29, 2005.

线目视范围内的岛屿问题不具有相关性。① 由于 1931 年之前英国代表加拿大处理外交关系问题,所以 1920 年英国承认丹麦对格陵兰主权确实对加拿大有约束力,但是该承认只涉及格陵兰。格陵兰因纽特人对汉斯岛的使用是丹麦唯一有分量的论据,但是不具有决定性意义。同样的因纽特人也经常前往公认的加拿大领土埃尔斯米尔岛。

加拿大对汉斯岛主权主张是基于 1880 年英国将北美高北极岛屿(不包括格陵兰)转交给加拿大。该主张同样基于"使用和占领",因为根据国际法的规定,领土所有权必须通过经常性的活动加以巩固和维持。② 第二次世界大战期间,汉斯岛是加拿大科学基地所在地。1950 年,加拿大常设地名委员会正式采用"汉斯岛"的名称。3 年后,加拿大地形测量局的埃里克·弗赖伊对汉斯岛进行调查并树立了一块石碑,他在上面留下记录称该岛属于加拿大。1972 年,弗赖伊的测量点与格陵兰岛上的测量点一道通过角度和距离等测量后,连入加拿大控制的测量网络。这一工作由包括丹麦政府测量员在内的加拿大政府测量部门实施。③

1973 年,格陵兰和加拿大两国当时就海底边界展开谈判,这一争议由此到达"关键日期",也即各方明确在争端中的不同立场,随后采取的支持措施对法律分析均变得无关紧要。④ 自该时间点往后,一国外

---

① In the 1985 Libya-Malta Case, the ICJ made it clear that the evolution of distance-related foundations for maritime zones, most significantly in the form of the 200-nautical-mile EEZ, meant that geological and geomorphological features were to play no part in maritime delimitations where opposite coasts are less than 400 nautical miles apart. Indeed, it went so far as to specify that even evidence of a fundamental break in the continental shelf would not affect such delimitation. Case Concerning the Continental Shelf (1985) ICJ Reports 13 at 33 and 35, pp. 34、39, http://www.icj-cij.org/docket/files/68/6415.pdf. For more on extended continental shelves, Chapter 4, below.

② Island of Palmas Case (US v. Netherlands), Permanent Court of Arbitration, April 4, 1928, p. 35, http://www.pca-cpa.org/showfile.asp?fil_id=168.

③ Gray, n. 2, above, at 69.

④ Gerald Fitzmaurice defined the critical date as "the date after which the actions of the parties can no longer affect the issue." Fitzmaurice, The Law and Procedure of the International Court of Justice, Vol. 1 (Cambridge University Press, 1995), 260. Minquiers and Ecrehos Case (1953) ICJ Reports 59–60; L. F. E. Goldie, "The Critical Date." (1963) 12 International and Comparative Law Quarterly 1251; Robert Jennings and Arthur Watts, Oppenheim's International Law, 9th edn (London: Longman, 1992), 711–712; Marcelo Kohen, Possession conteste'e et souverainete' territorial (Paris: Presses universitaires de France, 1997), 169–183; Sovereignty over Pulau Ligitan and Pulau Sipadan (Indonesia/Malaysia), Judgment (2002) ICJ Reports 625 at 682, p. 135.

交抗议通常足以阻却另一国通过抗议行为获得主权权利。虽然存在这样的法律事实,围绕汉斯岛近乎无关紧要的争端还是引起不少荒谬和昂贵的故作姿态之举,包括从远距离外调集军机和军舰等情况。

20世纪80年代初,加拿大政府向加拿大多姆石油公司颁发一项土地使用许可,以建立科学营地研究被强水流冲击而下的海冰和冰山对汉斯岛北部海岸的影响。该研究旨在协助近海钻井平台建设中平台和人工岛礁的设计工作。1983年,联邦土地利用管理局局长乔·巴兰坦视察该营地时,丹麦军用喷气式飞机低空掠过该岛上空,发出的声响"把科学家们都吓坏了"。[1]

第二年,丹麦格陵兰部长汤姆·贺耶姆搭乘直升机飞往汉斯岛并插上丹麦国旗。加拿大政府提出外交抗议。1988年、1995年、2002年、2003年和2004年,相继出现丹麦插旗和加拿大抗议的活动。2000年,加拿大地理学会的一队地理学家访问该岛,标记地理位置,采集地质样本。尽管存在这么多的活动,但是双方对该争端都仍能保持幽默感。正如彼得·塔克苏·詹森在担任丹麦外交大臣法律顾问之时所说,"丹麦军队去那里时,他们会留下一瓶杜松子酒。而当(加拿大)军队到这时,他们会留下一瓶'加拿大俱乐部'牌威士忌并写上'欢迎来到加拿大'。"[2]

在加拿大,这一争端在2002年才开始引起公众注意,缘于《环球邮报》发表了一篇题为《维京人归来》的危言耸听的专栏文章。[3] 此前一年夏天,丹麦冰区加强护卫舰"瓦德伦"号运送士兵登陆汉斯岛。当时岛上没有其他访问者,加拿大政府以标准的外交抗议作为回应。但在报纸上,丹麦人被描述为"入侵的部落",在北约亲密盟友之间使用此类措辞显得十分奇怪。不幸的是,媒体对争议升级的报道直接影响了寻求获得选举优势的政客们。

距2001年11月丹麦大选仅数月之时,"瓦德伦"号驶往汉斯岛。

---

[1] Joe Ballantyne, Sovereignty and Development in the Arctic: Selected Exploration Programs in the 1980s (Whitehorse: self-published, 2009) 7 (on file with author).

[2] Christopher J. Chipello, "It's Time to Plant the Flag Again in the Frozen North," WallStreet Journal, May 6, 2004.

[3] Rob Huebert, "The Return of the Vikings," Globe and Mail, December 28, 2002.

2002年、2003年和2004年的插旗事件进一步强化了丹麦政府中的民族主义者在2005年2月大选中的领先地位。2005年7月插旗活动一周之后,国防部长比尔·格雷厄姆登上汉斯岛。这是加拿大最引人注目的回应动作,主要因为当时总理保罗·马丁领导的少数派自由党政府正深陷国内危机。

当认为争议对加拿大和格陵兰之间海上边界的位置或者其他权利没有影响之时,国内政治的作用就变得更为明显。1973年加拿大和丹麦划分加拿大和格陵兰之间的大陆架时,在汉斯岛南北两岸端点之间留下了875米的缺口。因此,任何解决争端的办法都不会对已按照条约划分的周边海底区域造成任何影响。[①] 其亦不会对周边水域产生影响,因为两国都使用同一条渔业分界线。

该争议几乎无关紧要的性质,使之更容易得到解决。这也许就是2005年9月加拿大和丹麦能够共同发表以下联合声明的原因:

> 我们承认,两国在汉斯岛主权问题上持有不同观点。自20世纪70年代双方达成加拿大和格陵兰海上边界协议以来,该领土争端一直存在。我们强调,该问题仅涉及汉斯岛,对上述协议没有影响。
>
> 我们坚定致力于和平解决争端,包括领土争端,我们在联合国和世界各地一贯支持该原则。为此,两国将继续努力,为解决汉斯岛争议达成长期解决方案。两国官员在不久的将来还将再次开会商讨解决该问题的办法,并将向部长们汇报进展情况。
>
> 在我们进行这些努力同时,我们已经决定,在不损害两国各自法律主张的情况下,我们将互相通报有关汉斯岛的活动。同样,任何一方与汉斯岛的联系均将以低调和克制的方式进行。[②]

---

① For more on the Danish-Canadian maritime boundary, Chapter 2, below.
② Canada-Denmark Joint Statement on Hans Island, September 19, 2005, New York, http://byers.typepad.com/arctic/canadadenmark-joint-statement-on-hans island.html.

解决该争议最简单的方法就是画一条直线：将海底分界线在汉斯岛的两个端点用直线连接起来。按此方法，各国均将获得该岛约50%的所有权，加拿大和丹麦将拥有一个很短且偏远的陆上边界。最近的报告表明，即将达成一项协议，其中一个可能结果是平分汉斯岛。①

另一种解决方案是宣布汉斯岛为共管区域，从某种意义上讲，加拿大和丹麦将分享该岛所有的主权。其他地区存在很多这种安排，包括法国和西班牙之间比达索亚河上的费伦特岛。② 两个国家共享该岛主权，由法国昂代伊和西班牙伊伦两市的市政当局每六个月交替承担行政责任。③

无论什么样的解决方案，加拿大和格陵兰的因纽特人都应参与其中，正如贺耶姆在2005年提出的建议："加拿大人和丹麦人应尊重并包容地方族群，不仅是在解决这一小争端中，而且是在未来北极战略发展过程之中。"④ 例如，格陵兰和努纳武特可能希望承担新边界或共管土地的管理责任。他们甚至可能希望仿照加拿大阿尔伯塔省和美国蒙大拿

---

① John Ibbitson, "Dispute over Hans Island Nears Resolution. Now for the Beaufort Sea," Globe and Mail, January 27, 2011, http：//www.theglobeandmail.com/news/politics/dispute – over – hans – island – nears – resolution – now – for – the – beaufort – sea/article563692/; Adrian Humphreys, "New Proposal Would See Hans Island Split Equally between Canada and Denmark," National Post, April 11, 2012, http：//news.nationalpost.com/2012/04/11/new – proposal – would – see – hans – island – split – equally – between – canada – and – denmark/.

② On condominiums generally, see Joel H. Samuels, "Condominium Arrangements in International Practice：Reviving an Abandoned Concept of Boundary Dispute Resolution." (2007 – 2008) 29 Michigan Journal of International Law 727. Most recently, the ICJ utilized the instrument of condominium in a maritime context in the Land, Island and Maritime Frontier Dispute (El Salvador/Honduras：Nicaragua intervening) (1992) ICJ Reports 350, pp. 601 – 604.

③ The Pheasant Island condominium was created by the 1659 Treaty of the Pyrenees. See Luis Careaga, "Un condominium franco – espagnol：L'iˆle des faisans ou de la confe´rence," thesis, Faculte´ de droit et des sciences politiques, University of Strasbourg, 1932; Peter Sahlins, Boundaries：The Making of France and Spain in the Pyrenees (Berkeley：University of California Press, 1989); Frank Jacobs, "The World's Most Exclusive Condominium," New York Times online, January 23, 2012, http：//opinionator.blogs.nytimes.com/2012/01/23/the – worlds – most – exclusive – condominium/.

④ Tom Høyem, "Mr. Graham, You Should Have Told Us You Were Coming," Globe and Mail, July 29, 2005.

州边界的"沃特顿——冰川国际和平公园",在此设立一个国际公园。①

在加拿大和丹麦通过协商达成任何解决方案之前,因纽特人甚至可以考虑提出他们自己对汉斯岛的主权。这一争论将揭示一个事实,即加拿大和丹麦均直到1973年才意识到两国对该岛存在争议,自那以后开始反对对方主张。因此,两国中的任何一国都可能无法使自身所有权主张完美无缺;换句话说,汉斯岛可能从未被殖民过。如果是这样,因纽特人可以说是保留了所有殖民前既有的权利。正如国际法院在"西撒哈拉案"咨询意见中所承认的那样,游牧民族存在享有领土之上某些权利的能力。② 虽然这些权利并不等同于国家地位,但确实阻却了该地成为无主之地,也即领土不属于任何人,因此所有国家均可通过占领的方式获得所有权。③

北极地区唯一的领土所有权争议为两国和原住民以创造性的方式考虑主权问题提供了机会。为了寻找灵感和另一种可能模式,他们只需参考仅800海里外的斯瓦尔巴群岛。

二、斯瓦尔巴

斯瓦尔巴群岛位于挪威大陆和北极之间的巴伦支海。④ 该群岛原名为斯匹茨卑尔根(荷兰语"参差不齐的山脉"之意),1920年《斯匹茨卑尔根条约》即是使用该名。斯瓦尔巴(挪威语"拥有寒冷海岸的陆地"之意)是现代名称,斯匹茨卑尔根之名目前只被用于指代该群岛中最大的岛屿,上述条约也越来越多地被称为《斯瓦尔巴条约》,下文中也将使用该名称。

斯瓦尔巴多峡湾和冰封山脉,群岛约有一半面积被冰川覆盖。斯瓦尔巴群岛陆地面积达62000平方千米,约为比利时两倍,但是人口较少,只有2500人在此生活,而且所有人都居住在斯匹茨卑尔根岛,没

---

① the UNESCO website, http://whc.unesco.org/en/list/354.
② Western Sahara, Advisory Opinion (1975) ICJ Reports 12 at 38 – 39, paras. 79 – 80.
③ Ibid.
④ For a map of Svalbard, http://ngm.nationalgeographic.com/2009/04/svalbard/svalbard-map.

有原住民。

一个多世纪以来，斯匹茨卑尔根岛上一直开采着煤矿，现在每年仍有大约 400 万吨煤炭运往欧洲。墨西哥湾暖流为此处提供了相对温和的温度和季节性的无冰水域，再加上良好的基础设施和与欧洲的航班联系，使得斯瓦尔巴群岛成为游客感受北极地区较为便捷和舒适之所。如今每年夏天，该群岛内均会有数十艘游轮运营，其中一些搭载超过 3000 名乘客。斯瓦尔巴也已成为北极的科研中心，包括中国和印度在内的许多国家在那里设立研究站。这里还是斯瓦尔巴全球种子库所在地，作为全球农作物多样性的终极安全政策，全世界成千上万的种子样品被保存在永久冰冻的山腰深处。①

领土主权通常属于国际习惯法问题，但就此地而言，1920 年《斯瓦尔巴条约》具有决定性意义。② 在 19 世纪，斯瓦尔巴被普遍认为是无主之地，因而对所有人开放。但是，随着一些国家的公司开始开采斯瓦尔巴丰富的煤矿资源，建立某种管理制度就成为现实需求。当时存在三个备选方案：第一，保留无主之地的地位，但赋予由挪威、瑞典和俄罗斯组成的三边委员会以治理权；第二，由国际联盟认定该群岛属于挪威所有；第三，承认挪威主权，但使其受制于其他国家经济活动准入的特殊条约权利。1919 年召开的巴黎和会选择了最后一个选项。1920 年 2 月，各国签署《斯瓦尔巴条约》并于五年之后生效。

包括英国、加拿大、中国、丹麦、法国、德国、印度、挪威、俄罗斯和美国在内的 40 个国家已批准《斯瓦尔巴条约》。③ 挪威认为，根据国际习惯法，该国对斯瓦尔巴的主权可对抗非缔约国，因为挪威有效占领该群岛并且其他国家没有提出反对。非缔约国不能根据该条约提出权利主张，但正如吉尔·乌尔夫斯坦指出的，这些国家仍然"可以自由批

---

① Svalbard Global Seed Vault, http：//www.croptrust.org/content/svalbard－global－seed－vault.

② Treaty concerning the Archipelago of Spitsbergen（"Svalbard Treaty"）（February 9, 1920）2 League of Nations Treaty Series 7, http：//www.lovdata.no/traktater/texte/tre － 19200209 － 001.html#map0.

③ "Traite' concernant le Spitsberg," http：//www.lovdata.no/cgi－bin/udoffles? doc = tra － 1920 － 02 － 09 － 001.txt&.

准《斯瓦尔巴条约》，从而受益于相关条款规定，这其中至关重要的就是不受歧视地参与该群岛经济性开发的权利。"①

俄罗斯是唯一一个有效利用其在该群岛陆上权利的缔约国，自1932年起，俄罗斯在斯匹茨卑尔根岛巴伦支堡的煤矿就一直处于运营状态。巴伦支堡500名居民几乎都是俄罗斯人或乌克兰人，而且其与仅相距50千米的挪威城镇朗伊尔城没有道路连接。

《斯瓦尔巴条约》禁止歧视的规定没能阻止挪威采取管理或禁止采矿、旅游和科研等活动的相关措施，只要这些规则同等适用于挪威人。正如乌尔夫斯坦解释道："挪威的主权包含对斯瓦尔巴颁布法律和法规并将之付诸实施的权利。挪威没有就斯瓦尔巴治理咨询其他国家的义务，这与其他国家管理本国领土一致。"② 这些权力被广泛运用于环境保护的目的，公园和自然保护区现已覆盖该群岛65%的面积。挪威权力的广泛使用将来可能会导致紧张局势，对此，查尔斯·埃默森警告说，"挪威实施强有力环境法规的权利，可能会与缔约国平等进入的权利产生冲突。"③

挪威也有权向外国公民征税，只要满足对挪威人也平等征收该税，以及"只能对上述领土进行专门征税，不能超过所虑及目标的必要限度"，也即仅限于对该群岛进行行政管理的目的。④ 正如乌尔夫斯坦指出的，后一个限制在今天来看是无关紧要的，因为行政成本远远超过了税收收入。⑤ 然而，如果斯瓦尔巴群岛或其周边出现大规模石油和天然气开发活动，则这一限制的重要性可能就会上升。⑥

目前对斯瓦尔巴的唯一争议是非歧视性的经济准入权利是否拓展至12海里领海之外。这个问题最早出现于1977年，当时挪威开始在该群

---

① Geir Ulfstein, "Spitsbergen/Svalbard," in Rudiger Wolfrum (ed.), Max Planck Encyclopedia of Public International Law (Oxford University Press, 2012), sec. 1, p. 24.

② Ibid., p. 23.

③ Charles Emmerson, The Future History of the Arctic (New York: Public Affairs, 2010), p. 93.

④ Treaty concerning the Archipelago of Spitsbergen, n. 24, above, Art. 8.

⑤ Ulfstein, n. 26, above, sec. 4, p. 31.

⑥ Ibid.

岛周边200海里范围实施渔业管制,认为关于平等经济准入的条款只适用于该群岛及其领水,而不包括专属经济区。自那以来,根据相关国家在该地开展传统渔业活动的实际情况,挪威已向多个国家发放专属经济区配额,但并不对冰岛等《斯瓦尔巴条约》其他缔约国适用。在数次事件中,挪威在斯瓦尔巴周边200海里内扣押了俄罗斯渔船,造成一些外交摩擦。[1] 这一争端近期已扩大至海底范围,包括200海里外大陆架区域,以及那里的石油和天然气开采潜力。[2]

《斯瓦尔巴条约》内若干条款明确规定,非歧视性经济准入权利延伸至领海。[3] 在条约缔约之时,挪威主张4海里领海。1970年,挪威政府围绕该群岛划设直线基线;2001年,其修改了这些基线;2003年,挪威采用12海里领海。然而,挪威也明确承认,《斯瓦尔巴条约》中非歧视性权利适用于上述扩大后的沿海区域,但不超过这一范围。

1920年,专属经济区和大陆架概念尚未进入国际法。现在挪威认为,《斯瓦尔巴条约》中对其主权权利的限制必须被严格解释,并且在缺乏书面依据的情况下,这种限制不应扩大至领海以外的新区域。挪威还认为,斯瓦尔巴群岛周边大陆架实际上是挪威本土海岸大陆架的延伸,出于这一新情况,这些区域不属于《斯瓦尔巴条约》中非歧视性权利的适用范围。[4]

反对挪威主张的立场有两种:第一,冰岛和俄罗斯直至最近都认为,根据《斯瓦尔巴条约》,挪威主权不仅受到内容上的限制,也受到地理范围制约,因此挪威在斯瓦尔巴群岛领海外不享有专属经济区或大

---

[1] e. g., Charles Digges, "Arrested Russian Fishing Trawler Flees for Home with Two Detained Norwegian Coast Guard Inspectors," October 18, 2005, Bellona Foundation (Norway), http://www. bellona. org/english_import_area/international/russia/nuke_industry/co - operation/40320.

[2] For more on extended continental shelves, Chapter 4, below.

[3] Art. 2 reads, in part: "Ships and nationals of all the High Contracting Parties shall enjoy equally the rights of fishing and hunting in the territories specified in Article 1 and in their territorial waters." Art. 3 reads, in part: "The nationals of all the High Contracting Parties... shall be admitted under the same conditions of equality to the exercise and practice of all maritime, industrial, mining or commercial enterprises both on land and in the territorial waters, and no monopoly shall be established on any account or for any enterprise whatever." Svalbard Treaty, n. 24, above.

[4] generally, Torbjørn Pedersen, "The Svalbard Continental Shelf Controversy: Legal Disputes and Political Rivalries." (2006) 37 Ocean Development and International Law 339.

陆架的权利。第二,英国所持立场更为微妙,它认为《斯瓦尔巴条约》必须依照1969年《维也纳条约法公约》所设立的一般解释规则进行解读。非歧视性权利是在承认挪威对斯瓦尔巴主权的同一句话中提出,由此可见,缔约国的意图是将非歧视性权利适用于该主权的所有地理范围。当挪威主权被扩展至这些新区域时,非歧视性权利也相应地扩大至覆盖专属经济区和大陆架。英国还认为,专属经济区和大陆架属于领海的功能延伸,其他任何结论都将造成一种奇怪的局面,即挪威在12海里外区域所享有的权利超出其在12海里范围内的权利。此外,在挪威与丹麦(格陵兰)就海上边界进行谈判并于2006年向联合国大陆架界限委员会提交有关外大陆架申请时,挪威自身并没有将斯瓦尔巴以北大陆架视为本土海岸大陆架的延伸。①

现在看来,俄罗斯和冰岛已经放弃了强硬立场。2009年,大陆架界限委员会对挪威提交的划界案做出积极回应。挪威在划界案中将斯瓦尔巴群岛作为对该群岛北部大片外大陆架区域主权权利主张的根据。②值得注意的是,俄罗斯、冰岛或其他任何国家都没有对大陆架界限委员会的建议表示反对,这意味着这些建议已是最终和有约束力的。2011年,挪威和俄罗斯缔结巴伦支海边界条约,暗含承认挪威在斯瓦尔巴群岛享有200海里专属经济区。③

然而,英国立场仍然有效,即如果《斯瓦尔巴条约》中规定的非歧视性权利适用于12海里之外,其也同样适用于外大陆架全部区域。当然,挪威对环境保护进行管理的权利也将适用于这一范围,包括对石油和天然气开发设置严格条件或直接加以禁止的权利。英国和挪威在这

---

① For a cogent expression of these arguments, David H. Anderson, "The Status under International Law of the Maritime Areas around Svalbard." (2009) 40 Ocean Development and International Law 373. For the executive summary of the Norwegian submission, http://www.un.org/depts/los/clcs_new/submissions_files/nor06/nor_exec_sum.pdf.

② "Summary of the Recommendations of the Commission on the Limits of the Continental Shelf in Regard to the Submission Made by Norway in Respect of Areas in the Arctic Ocean, the Barents Sea and the Norwegian Sea on 27 November 2006," March 27, 2009, http://www.un.org/Depts/los/clcs_new/submissions_files/nor06/nor_rec_summ.pdf.

③ Tore Henriksen and Geir Ulfstein, "Maritime Delimitation in the Arctic: The Barents Sea Treaty." (2011) 42 Ocean Development and International Law 1 at 9.

个问题上的关系可能会有些紧张。据报道,英国于 2006 年举办了俄罗斯、美国等一些《斯瓦尔巴条约》主要缔约国参加的会议。但直到会议结束后,挪威官员才知悉该会议。在得知这一情况后,"愤怒的"挪威外交大臣约纳斯·加尔·斯特勒立即致电英国外交大臣,要求其作出解释。①

《斯瓦尔巴条约》的最后一点是,通过禁止设立任何"海军基地"或"防御工事",声明该群岛"永远不得被用于战争目的",从而使该群岛有效地实现了非军事化。② 冷战期间,在挪威军舰和战机到访斯瓦尔巴和该群岛被置于北约指挥之下之时,苏联均提出此类行为违反条约中的限制条款。③ 如今,这些紧张局势已经消失。然而,作为首个规定在北极部分区域实施非军事化的文件,《斯瓦尔巴条约》构成倡导北极无核武区域的一个虽小却具有相关性的先例,或成为实现该目标的承上启下之举。④

如若斯瓦尔巴群岛是共享主权的一个例子,或者至少是藉由其他国家的条约权利对主权进行限制,那么格陵兰岛就是主权接近转移点的例子。作为世界范围内未被认定为大陆的最大岛屿,格陵兰岛正朝着成为首个因纽特人统治的国家前进。

三、格陵兰

格陵兰岛面积为 210 万平方千米,比法国、德国、意大利和西班牙加起来还要大。⑤ 根据冰岛的传奇故事,"红发埃里克"在 10 世纪发现该岛并将之命名为"绿地",以便吸引移民。因为整个岛的 80% 被巨大冰盖所覆盖,所以对其情况存在一定程度的误传。

---

① "Big Powers Discussed Spitsbergen Without Norway," April 18, 2007, http://www.spitsbergensvalbard.info/topical.html.
② Treaty concerning the Archipelago of Spitsbergen, n. 24, above, Art. 9.
③ Ulfstein, n. 26, above, sec. B, p. 15.
④ discussion, Chapter 8, below.
⑤ For a map of Greenland, showing its proximity to Canada, Iceland, and the Norwegian island of Jan Mayen, http://www.slaw.ca/wp-content/uploads/2009/06/canada-greenland.png.

1916 年，丹麦同意将维京群岛出售给美国后，其对格陵兰主权长期主张的重要性更为凸显。作为协议一部分，美国国务卿罗伯特·兰辛公开宣布："美国政府将不会反对丹麦政府将其政治和经济利益扩展至格陵兰全岛。"①

当挪威于 1931 年宣称对格陵兰东部享有主权时，丹麦将此问题提交国际常设法院。两年后，法院作出有利于丹麦的裁决，认为"如果其他国家不能提出具有更高效力的主张"，一国可以通过"很少实际行使主权权利"的方式设立和维持主权，"这种方式尤其适用于人口稀少或不稳定的国家对相关区域主张主权的情况。"②

1941 年，丹麦和美国签署《有关格陵兰岛防务的协议》，规定美国将接管该岛直至第二次世界大战结束。③ 1953 年，格陵兰成为丹麦王国不可分割的一部分。1979 年，该岛被授予自治权。六年后，格陵兰出于对欧洲经济共同体商业捕鱼法规和海豹皮制品禁令的担忧而退出该组织，并借此行使新权力。④ 因此，格陵兰当前不是欧盟成员国。

2008 年，关于更大范围自治的公投使得格陵兰将承担司法、治安和自然资源的责任。⑤ 目前，丹麦仍然控制格陵兰外交和国防政策，并在联合国和北极理事会等其他国际组织中代表格陵兰。

新的权力划分已经造成近海区域石油和天然气开发中的混乱。2010 年，一家苏格兰石油企业开始在巴芬湾的格陵兰一侧开展钻探活动，随即加拿大外交官对一份 1983 年与丹麦签订的海洋环境协议是否仍然适

---

① Convention between the United States and Denmark: Cession of the Danish West Indies, US Treaty Series No. 269, 39 Stat. 1706.

② Legal Status of Eastern Greenland Case (Denmark v. Norway) (1933) PCIJ Reports, Series A/B, No. 53, p. 46, http://www.icj-cij.org/pcij/serie_AB/AB_53/01_Groenland_Oriental_Arret.pdf.

③ 1941 Agreement Relating to the Defense of Greenland. (1941) 35 (3) American Journal of International Law Supplement 129.

④ "Greenland Out of EEC," New York Times, February 4, 1985, http://www.nytimes.com/1985/02/04/business/greenland-out-of-eec.html.

⑤ 2009 Act on Greenland Self-Government, http://uk.nanoq.gl/~/media/f74bab3359074b29aab8c1e12aa1ecfe.ashx.

用表示疑问。① 他们之后得出结论,格陵兰已经成功履行了丹麦在该协议下的义务。② 2012 年,权力划分也对林肯海边界条约谈判造成不利影响。加拿大和丹麦政府就该条约中划界问题进行磋商,之后加拿大又与格陵兰政府就跨界油气资源联合管理制度进行谈判。

自然资源可能将会导致格陵兰和丹麦之间关系发生进一步变化,正如一名格陵兰高级官员所称,该岛距离独立只有"发现一个大型油田"的距离。③ 事实上,自治协议中已经预料到这种情况,丹麦向格陵兰政府每年转移的 34 亿丹麦克朗(约 5.8 亿美元)经费将会随着当地自然资源收入的增加而减少。④ 自治协议也预见到,格陵兰最终将实现独立,尽管其强调这一结果将需要通过谈判实现,而不是单方面宣言。⑤ 由于 88% 的格陵兰人是因纽特人,这片土地正将成为世界上首个因纽特人统治的国家。这一发展不仅对格陵兰因纽特人而言具有重要意义,正如第七章所阐释的,对国际法中土著居民权利也同样具有很高重要性。

格陵兰实现独立的过程中也会出现一点具有讽刺意味的因素。如上所述,丹麦毫不犹豫地援引格陵兰因纽特人对汉斯岛的历史性"使用和占有"来支撑该国对汉斯岛的主权主张。下文中的例子将表明,丹麦并不是唯一如此行事的北极国家。

---

① Canadian Press, "Drilling Plans Near Greenland Spark Concern," April 30, 2010, http://www.ctv.ca/CTVNews/Canada/20100430/Greenland – drilling – warning – 100430/.

② the website of the Canadian Department of Foreign Affairs, "Denmark (Faroe Islands/Greenland)," http://www.international.gc.ca/arctic – arctigue/partners – international partenaires.aspx?lang = eng ("As a successor to the 1983 Danish-Canadian Agreement for Cooperation Relating to the Marine Environment, Greenland cooperates with Canada to develop effective oil and gas guidelines and prevent oil spills").

③ Environmental News Service, "Wikileaks Cables: 'Cold Peace' Among Resource – Hungry Arctic Nations," May 18, 2011, http://www.ens – newswire.com/ens/may2011/2011 – 05 – 18 – 01.html.

④ 2009 Act on Greenland Self – Government, n. 48, above, chap. 3, secs. 5 and 8.

⑤ Ibid., chap. 8, sec. 21.

四、斯弗德鲁普群岛

努纳武特北部的斯弗德鲁普群岛最初由著名的挪威探险家奥托·斯弗德鲁普发现、绘图并宣布为挪威领土，其于1989—1902年间，乘坐按他要求特别制造的"弗拉姆"号航行至此。① 尽管挪威政府没有兴趣对斯弗德鲁普提出权利主张，但是1930年，加拿大政府还是决定彻底打消这种可能性。因为涉及加拿大外交政策独立的《威斯敏斯特法令》一年之后才获得通过，所以在谈判之初需由英国政府充当中间人。加拿大提出购买斯弗德鲁普的地图和航行文件，表面上是为了帮助其退休，实际是为换取挪威正式承认加拿大主权。加拿大政府认为，若这个76岁的老探险家寿命异常漫长，按年支付费用的方式就会变得十分昂贵，遂同意一次性支付67000美元。② 巧合的是，斯弗德鲁普在谈判结果宣布两周后就去世了。但是加拿大政府通过"互换照会"的形式，即一系列表明国家间协议的信件，属于国际条约的一种，使该问题得到妥善解决。这些信件值得一读，因为他们展示了主张是多么容易被消灭，以及土著人权利最早何时出现在北极国际法中。

一封写于1930年8月8日的信中写道，挪威驻伦敦临时代办要求英国外交大臣"通知陛下在加拿大的政府，对斯弗德鲁普群岛没有主权主张的挪威政府，正式承认英王陛下对这些岛屿的主权。"③ 加拿大外

---

① The Fram Museum in Oslo, where the historic ship is housed, provides a useful summary of Sverdrup's expedition: http://www.frammuseum.no/Polar-Heroes/Main-Heroes/Main-Hero-3.aspx.

② It has been suggested that a side-deal also existed between Norway and the United Kingdom, with Norway recognizing Canadian sovereignty over the Sverdrup Islands in return for the United Kingdom recognizing Norwegian sovereignty over the island of Jan Mayen. See Thorleif Tobias Thorleifsson, "Norway 'must really drop their absurd claims such as that to the Otto Sverdrup Islands.' Bi-Polar International Diplomacy: The Sverdrup Islands Question, 1902-1930," MA thesis, Simon Fraser University, 2006, http://ir.lib.sfu.ca/retrieve/3720/etd2367.pdf. For a discussion of Jan Mayen, Chapter 2, below.

③ Exchange of Notes regarding the Recognition by the Norwegian Government of the Sovereignty of His Majesty over the Sverdrup Islands, Canada Treaty Series 1930, No.17, http://byers.typepad.com/arctic/1930.html.

交官很快实现了他们的目标,并且相对而言几乎没有成本,但挪威临时代办却遇到了严重的问题。他几乎立即写了第二封信:

> 关于我今年关于我国政府承认英王陛下对斯弗德鲁普群岛主权的照会,按我国政府指示,我很荣幸地通知您,上述照会所依据的前提是,挪威政府假设英王陛下在加拿大的政府愿意宣布,不会对挪威在上述承认的区域内捕鱼、狩猎或工业和贸易活动造成任何妨碍。①

然而,加拿大的主权已经得到承认,因此也没有什么留待谈判的事项了。加拿大人本可以直接忽略第二封信,但他们却提出了拒绝该请求的理由。1930年11月5日,英国驻奥斯陆临时代办写信给挪威外交部长:

> 如前述,根据1926年7月19日枢密院令及后续令,加拿大政府既定政策是,保护北极地区狩猎和捕获保护区只可供西北地区原住民使用,以避免其因白人猎人和商人对野生动物资源开发而陷入贫穷和饥饿的危险。除经西北地区专员许可外,除当地印第安人(Indians)或爱斯基摩人(Eskimos,也即因纽特人)外,任何人无论出于何种目的,都不允许在该大陆大片区域和整个北极岛屿区域内从事狩猎、诱捕、交易和贩运活动,巴芬岛南部区域除外。②

值得注意的是,非土著居民不仅被禁止在高北极地区狩猎和诱捕,而且还被禁止从事所有商业活动。

英国临时代办的信函以温和却无实际意义的提议结束:

---

① Exchange of Notes regarding the Recognition by the Norwegian Government of the Sovereignty of His Majesty over the Sverdrup Islands, Canada Treaty Series 1930, No. 17, http://byers.typepad.com/arctic/1930.html.

② Ibid.

但是，如果将来任何时候这些规定被改变，英王陛下在加拿大的政府将会以最友好的态度考虑挪威人就在上述被承认的区域内分享捕鱼、狩猎、工业或贸易活动所提出的申请。①

"以友好的态度加以考虑"这一措辞并未给挪威进入斯弗德鲁普群岛创设法律权利，当然，挪威公司可以根据管理外国投资的一般规定自由参与加拿大资源领域的活动。挪威国有企业，挪威国家石油公司已经活跃在加拿大西部油砂开发活动中，并可能向北部发展。得益于20世纪七八十年代开展的勘探工作，斯弗德鲁普群岛已探明的石油和天然气储量至少价值1万亿美元。②

五、小结

在北极政治中，领土所有权并不是主要问题，小小的汉斯岛是整个环北极地区唯一尚存争议的。只要将位于该岛两端的海上边界相连，即可轻松解决该争议。另一个解决方案是丹麦和加拿大设立一个共管区域，使得汉斯岛成为北极地区第二个共享或者有限主权的例子。自1920年以来，挪威对斯瓦尔巴群岛的所有权一直受制于其他国家从事经济活动的权利，例如俄罗斯在当地运营煤矿。另一方面，格陵兰逐步接近由丹麦主权领土转变为因纽特人治下完全独立国家的目标。然而，在围绕汉斯岛、斯瓦尔巴、格陵兰和北极其他区域的议题之中，海洋相关领域才是国际法所面临的最难和最紧迫问题。

---

① Exchange of Notes regarding the Recognition by the Norwegian Government of the Sovereignty of His Majesty over the Sverdrup Islands, Canada Treaty Series 1930, No. 17, http：//byers. typepad. com/arctic/1930. html.

② e. g., Zhuoheng Chen, et al., "Petroleum Potential in Western Sverdrup Basin, Canadian Arctic Archipelago." (December 2000) 48 (4) Bulletin of Canadian Petroleum Geology 323 – 338.

第二章 海上边界

詹姆斯·贝克的博士论文是关于国际关系学科中广泛存在的一种假设，即海上边界的历史和政治与陆地的情况相似。正如其所发现的，上述问题事实上存在着重要区别。最值得注意的是，历史上从来未有通过武力和征服的方式确定海上边界，而是通过发展和适用国际法规则来界定，基于近海权利是由陆权派生而来这一构想。

贝克的分析在北极地区显得尤为重要。与南极大陆被海洋环绕不同，北极是陆地包围着海洋。因此，北极治理很大程度上依赖海洋法，主要是不成文但具有约束力的国际习惯法规则，这些规则后于1982年被编纂为《联合国海洋法公约》。① 迄今为止，已有164个国家批准这个所谓"海洋宪法"，包括北冰洋五个沿岸国家中的四个：加拿大、丹麦（格陵兰）、挪威和俄罗斯。② 仅剩的北冰洋国家——美国，则承认《联合国海洋法公约》中的关键条款属于国际习惯法。③ 美国或许很快也会批准《联合国海洋法公约》，其对限制海洋航行自由对国家安全影响的担忧，已经被对恐怖主义和大规模杀伤性武器运输的担忧以及确保国际社会承认该国"外大陆架"主权权利的意愿所取代。

正如引言所述，每个沿海国均有权利主张12海里领海，也有权利主张12至200海里近海的专属经济区，顾名思义，其对该水域内水体和海床中的自然资源享有排他性权利。一项平行规则规定，每个沿海国享有在任何相邻大陆架进行资源开发的固有权利，大陆架是由大部分陆地延伸至相对较浅洋底的区域。20世纪70年代初，新技术和高油价最

---

① Introduction, n. 15, above.
② "Table Recapitulating the Status of the Convention and of the Related Agreements, as at 6 November 2012," http://www.un.org/Depts/los/reference_files/status2010.pdf.
③ Introduction, n. 25, above.

终将导致距离海岸超过 200 海里的石油和天然气开发的预期已经非常明确。因此,《联合国海洋法公约》第七十六条规定,如果海床的深度和形状以及海底沉积物的厚度表明该大陆架为沿海国陆地的"自然延伸",则该沿海国可在超过 200 海里外的外大陆架行使主权权利。①

相邻或相对沿海国之间不同海上区域(也即跨海湾、海峡或其他海洋部分)的边界问题在第三方争端解决机制中显得尤为突出,约占国际法院自 1947 年以来庭审案件的大约 1/5。② 然而,大多数海上边界都是通过谈判达成条约的方式得到解决,如下文所述,北极地区的情况尤为如此。包括北极地区在内,世界上仍有大量海上边界问题未得到解决。③

一、1973 年《加拿大和丹麦边界条约》

1969 年"曼哈顿"号超级油轮穿越西北航道之后,④ 加拿大将其领海由 3 海里拓展至 12 海里。⑤ 与此同时,加拿大忽略了新的界限已越过了埃尔斯米尔岛和格陵兰之间的"中间线"。⑥ 一旦实现这一结果,就需要同丹麦进行边界谈判。1973 年,两国同意使用中间线或"等距线"划分加拿大和格陵兰之间的洋底,也即沿着双方一致同意的 127 个"转

---

① The interpretation and application of Article 76 is discussed in Chapter 3, below.

② For a list of ICJ cases, http://www.icj-cij.org/docket/index.php? p1 = 3andp2 = 2.

③ For a visual depiction of the general situation, the Durham University International Boundary Research Unit map on "Maritime Jurisdiction and Boundaries in the Arctic Region" is an excellent place to start, http://www.dur.ac.uk/resources/ibru/arctic.pdf.

④ For more on the Northwest Passage dispute, Chapter 5, below.

⑤ Act to Amend the Territorial Sea and Fishing Zones Act, 1969 - 1970 Statutes of Canada, chap. 68, sec. 1243. The change, which was motivated at least partly by fisheries concerns elsewhere, took advantage of a developing rule of customary international law allowing states to claim twelve – mile territorial seas; by 1970, nearly sixty states had done just that. Pierre Trudeau, "Remarks to the Press Following the Introduction of Legislation on Arctic Pollution, Territorial Sea and Fishing Zones in the Canadian House of Commons on April 8, 1970." (1970) 9 ILM 600.

⑥ David H. Gray, "Canada's Unresolved Maritime Boundaries." (Autumn 1997) 5 (3) IBRU Boundary and Security Bulletin 61 at 68, http://www.dur.ac.uk/resources/ibru/publications/full/bsb5 - 3_gray.pdf.

折点"中 109 个距离双方相对海岸最近点距离相等点的一条线。① 自此,双方还利用由此产生的 1450 海里边界来确定两国渔业区,这意味着大陆架界限已经非正式地成为通用海上边界。②

该条约处理埃尔斯米尔岛和格陵兰岛之间汉斯岛争议问题的方式比较有趣,甚至没有提及该岛。③ 条约中使用两组大地测量线来确定内尔斯海峡的分界线,其中一条止于 122 号转折点处(位于 80°49.2′N,66°29.0′W),第二条则从 123 号转折点出发(位于仅半英里之外的 80°49.8′N,66°26.3′W)。④ 谈判代表们故意将 122 号转折点设置在汉斯岛南岸的低潮点,将 123 号转折点设置在该岛北岸低潮点。⑤ 但由于该条约涉及大陆架而非陆地划界,所以谈判代表显然认为没有必要提及这汉斯岛争议。

该条约中存在关于在边界线及其附近可能发现油气资源的条款。第三条则解决了新边界线精确性较低的特点。

鉴于某些区域现有的海道测量图存在不足,没有准确测定格陵兰岛和加拿大北极群岛东部海岸沿线所有区块的低潮线,在未获得另一方对有关区域附近分界线准确地理坐标点的事先同意之时,任何一方均不得签发在分界线附近区域开发矿产资源的许可证。⑥

与此相关的是,该条约解决了这种复杂性,但没有解决大地测量坐标系的罕见问题。大卫·格雷于 1997 年解释道:

---

① Agreement between the Government of Canada and the Government of the Kingdom of Denmark Relating to the Delimitation of the Continental Shelf between Greenland and Canada, December 17, 1973, http://www.un.org/depts/los/LEGISLATIONANDTREATIES/PDFFILES/TREATIES/DNK - CAN1973CS. PDF. The other points were either adjusted from the true equidistance line (110 - 113) or arbitrarily picked near the center of the channel (114 - 127).

② Gray, n. 9, above, at 68.

③ For more on Hans Island, Chapter 1, above.

④ Agreement between the Government of Canada and the Government of the Kingdom of Denmark, n. 10, above.

⑤ Although the two turning points later turned out to be just slightly off the low water marks, the common intent-to delimit the entire maritime boundary-was clear.

⑥ Agreement between the Government of Canada and the Government of the Kingdom of Denmark, n. 10, above, emphasis added.

从测量角度来看，加拿大的地图和图表是依据1927年北美基准点绘制，而丹麦的地图和图表则是根据使用不同地球椭球的努克基准点。技术专家们清楚大地坐标系之间存在差异，但无法测算其量级。所以，实际的解决办法是搁置该问题，留待以后考虑，并假设这两个坐标系是完全相同的。该协议中规定，当大地测量数据可用以联系两个大地基准，以及新的土地测量确定新的转折点并由其计算出等距线之时，该条约可重新开放修改。

1982年，两国同意就北纬75度以南的等距线进行重新计算，这项工作自此启动（并于2003年结束）。

因为现在有能力厘清努克基准点、1927年北美基准点、1983年北美基准点和世界大地坐标系统的内在关系，将来对坐标的修正案或以数个坐标系方式提出，并可能减少北纬75度以南现有113个边界转折点的数量。[1]

此程序在该条约中有明确规定，第四条第2款列出了相关后果：

若新的测量或由此产生的图表和地图表明分界线需要调整，双方同意将基于划定分界线时所使用的同样原则进行调整，此类调整应被作为该协议的议定书。[2]

第五条解决了在新边界及其更准确测定后，可能存在跨界油气资源或其他可开采海底资源的问题。但是与一些边界条约不同，[3] 它仅要求各方在这些情况下进行谈判，而不是提供解决问题的程序或机制：

---

[1] Gray, n. 9, above, at 68. In the end, only the southern 109 points were recomputed, and only on WGS–84, although NAD–83 is equivalent for all practical purposes. Personal communication from David Gray, November 2012.

[2] Agreement between the Government of Canada and the Government of the Kingdom of Denmark, n. 10, above.

[3] e. g., the Norway–Russia Barents Sea Treaty discussed later in this chapter.

若任何单一地质石油结构或矿田,或砂、砾石等任何其他矿床的单一地质结构或矿田延伸跨越分界线,位于分界线一侧的该结构或矿田具备可采性,无论是全部或部分来源于分界线另一侧,各方均应寻求就开采该结构或矿田达成协议。[1]

最后,谈判代表们选择不在82°13.0′N以北划定边界,在此位置上内尔斯海峡通向埃尔斯米尔岛和格陵兰附近的林肯海。该决定引发了另外两个问题:第一个问题将在本章下文中进行讨论,因就格陵兰岛西北部的博蒙特岛是否可被用于确定丹麦的直线基线存在不同意见,导致在距离海岸200海里内存在两个小透镜状的争议区域。第二个问题在第四章中讨论,它涉及加拿大与丹麦距离海岸200海里之外的相邻外大陆架的边界位置问题。然而,《加拿大和丹麦边界条约》本身就是相当标准的法律文书。基于等距原则和亲密盟友之间的持续合作关系,该条约提供了目前所需的一切东西。

二、1990年《白令海条约》

1990年,俄罗斯和美国就白令海、白令海峡和楚科奇海1600海里长通用海上边界协商达成一致,所以两国在北极不存边界争议。[2] 该条约由美国国务卿詹姆斯·贝克和苏联外交部长爱德华·谢瓦尔德纳泽签署,因此又被称为"贝克和谢瓦尔德纳泽线",这条边界基于1867年美国从俄罗斯购买阿拉斯加的条约中所描述的一条线:

> 领土和主权移交的西部边界经过,北纬65°30′的纬线与通过克鲁辛斯特恩岛与拉特曼诺夫岛之间中点的经线在白令海峡

---

[1] Agreement between the Government of Canada and the Government of the Kingdom of Denmark, n. 10, above.

[2] Agreement between the United States of America and the Union of Soviet Socialist Republics on the Maritime Boundary (1990) 29 ILM 941, http://www.state.gov/documents/organization/125431.pdf; generally, Robert W. Smith, "United States-Russia Maritime Boundary," in Gerald Henry Blake (ed.), Maritime Boundaries (London: Routledge, 1994), 91.

相交的一点，并由此继续向北延伸进入冰封大洋，没有尽头。该西部边界从上述点出发，向大约西南方向延伸穿过白令海峡和白令海，经过圣劳伦斯岛西北角和楚科奇角东南端之间中点，至西经172°度经线；从与该经线交点，向西南方向，通过北太平洋科曼多尔群岛中的雅图岛和铜岛之间中点，直到西经193°经线，以便包含该经线以东阿留申群岛全部领土。①

然而，1867年条约对描述边界时使用线、地图投影和水平基准点的种类都没有做出规定。由于两国采取不同的地图绘制方法，所以无法就该线的具体位置达成一致。正如弗拉德·卡钦斯基解释道：

> 制图者通常使用两种线划定海洋边界：恒向线和大地线（也被称为大圆弧）。两者分别被用于墨卡托投影和圆锥投影两种常见的地图投影。根据线和地图投影类型的不同，线将以直线或曲线的方式呈现。例如，恒向线是墨卡托投影中使用的直线，而大地线则是弯曲的。所有国家均将1867年《公约》中所描述的线解释为直线，但是苏联将白令海海上边界描述为墨卡托投影中的恒向线，而美国则在圆锥投影中使用大地线。尽管这两者在各自地图投影中均以直线显示，但其实各国欲借此差异最大化地主张本国控制的海洋区域和海底面积。②

结果就是造成约1.5万平方海里的争议区。③

1990年条约将有争议的区域大致一分为二，新的分界线明确划分

---

① Treaty concerning the Cession of the Russian Possessions in North America, June 20, 1867, Art. 1, http://avalon.law.yale.edu/19th_century/treatywi.asp.

② Vlad M. Kaczynski, "US-Russian Bering Sea Marine Border Dispute: Conflict over Strategic Assets, Fisheries and Energy Resources." (May 2007) 20 Russian Analytical Digest 2, http://www.laender-analysen.de/russland/rad/pdf/Russian_Analytical_Digest 20.pdf.

③ For a map showing the difference between the rhumb line on a Mercator projection and the geodetic line on a conical projection, see Figure 1 in Kaczynski, ibid., p. 3. The equidistance principle is applied -and sometimes modified-through a three-step approach. See discussion, Chapter 3, below.

渔业和海底资源的管辖范围。美国迅速批准该条约，参议院于1991年提出建议并同意批准该条约。但是，该条约在苏联和其后的俄罗斯国内引发相当大的反对，主要因为条约中规定的白令海分界线明显较等距线所在位置向西偏移，而等距线是国际法中默认采用的方法。① 该条约的反对者将这一结果归咎于谈判进行时苏联正在瓦解，致其谈判立场软弱，并且认为俄罗斯远东地区渔民的利益没有得到保护。②

1990年条约签署的同时，苏联和美国进行了一次互换照会，其中"在该协议生效前，两国政府同意遵守1990年6月15日协议的条款。"③ 两国互换照会符合1969年《维也纳条约法公约》第二十五条第1款，即"条约或条约之一部分于条约生效前在下列情形下暂时适用：条约本身如此规定；或谈判国以其他方式协议如此办理。"④ 此外，两国继续按照条约已生效的状态行事，卡钦斯基2007年报道称，两国已重新开始讨论"以试图解决该争议"。⑤

该条约目前一个相关方面涉及到这样一个事实：从白令海峡中一点（65°30′00″N, 168°58′037″W）向北，该边界沿着西经168°58′37″"在国际法允许的范围内"一直延伸至北冰洋。当然，国际法允许的情况会随着时间而改变。例如，《联合国海洋法公约》于1982年缔结，但直至1994年才生效。这意味着，《白令海峡条约》达成之时，《联合国海洋法公约》第76条尚未对双方产生约束力，其内容也没有成为国际习惯法的一部分。今天，沿岸国可对200海里外大陆架行使主权权利，第76条规定了在任何特定位置确定外大陆架界限的标准。⑥

---

① For a map showing the difference between the 1990 boundary and an equidistance line, see Figure 3 in Kaczynski, ibid., p. 5.

② Ibid., pp. 3 - 4.

③ The exchange of notes is reproduced in Alex G. Oude Elferink, "The 1990 USSR-USA Maritime Boundary Agreement." (1991) 6 International Journal of Estuarine and Coastal Law 41, Annexes 2 and 3.

④ 1969 Vienna Convention on the Law of Treaties, 1155 UNTS 331, 8 ILM 679, http://untreaty.un.org/ilc/texts/instruments/english/conventions/1_1_1969.pdf.

⑤ Kaczynski, n. 22, above, p. 5.

⑥ The International Court of Justice recently ruled that Article 76 (1) is part of customary international law: Territorial and Maritime Dispute (Nicaragua v. Colombia), Introduction, n. 25, above, p. 118. For more on the interpretation and application of Article 76, Chapters 3 and 4, below.

《白令海峡条约》谈判预见到了这些变化并提出了向北延伸的边界。

尽管如此，如第三章所释，美国和加拿大在波弗特海边界争议的解决可能会导致加拿大对外大陆架的主权权利最远延伸至西经168°58′37″经线。在此情形下，俄罗斯和美国的边界理论上只会向北延伸至美国管辖范围最远端（例如，俄罗斯和美国边界与加拿大和美国边界交汇点），导致俄罗斯和加拿大向北延伸的外大陆架存在未定边界。

《白令海条约》同样包含一些重要创新，例如"特别区域"的使用。在这些区域，因靠近缔约一方海岸线而产生的主权权利，被新划定的边界割离并移交给另一缔约方，以最大化国家管辖权的结合区域。

这一做法使得苏联和美国一致同意划设一条线，该线与苏联/俄罗斯海岸线上数个点之间距离小于200海里，同时与美国海岸线的距离超过200海里。[1] 按理说，该条线通常会有将苏联/俄罗斯的专属经济区外缘部分转变为公海的效力。但是谈判代表能够通过指定若干特殊区域的方式避免这一结果，在特殊区域中，由苏联/俄罗斯海岸线产生的专属经济区权利被分配给美国。[2] 在楚科奇海边界最北端设立了一个类似但面积相对较小的特别区域，这条线位于美国海岸线200海里内，但该区域距离苏联海岸超过200海里。在这里，专属经济区权利由美国海岸线产生，但被分配给苏联。这种做法产生这样一个问题，即对专属经济区权利的分配是否可对抗第三国。至少有一名俄罗斯国际法专家认为，适用特殊区域的尝试违反了国际习惯法和《联合国海洋法公约》。[3] 该问题的答案或许在于解决方式，因为第三国没有对这些特殊区域提出抗议。二十年后，美国和俄罗斯似乎可以公开提出，相关权利因默认而变为具有对抗效力，这一过程类似于通过时效获得领土或创设国际习惯法。[4]

---

[1] Agreement between the United States of America and the Union of Soviet Socialist Republics on the Maritime Boundary, n. 20, above.

[2] The map included in the treaty (ibid.) provides a useful visual image of the "special areas."

[3] Aleksandr Antonovich Kovalev, Contemporary Issues of the Law of the Sea: Modern Russian Approaches (trans. W. E. Butler) (Utrecht: Eleven International Publishing, 2004), pp. 67 – 68.

[4] For a similar view, see Kaczynski, n. 22, above, p. 5. On prescription, Jennings and Watts, Oppenheim's International Law, Chapter 1, n. 9, above, pp. 705 – 712. On customary international law, Byers, Custom, Power and the Power of Rules, Introduction, n. 39, above.

三、扬马延岛周边海上边界

扬马延岛是相对较小的岛屿，面积为373平方千米，位于格陵兰以东250海里，冰岛东北360海里，距离挪威600海里。在17世纪早期，它曾是荷兰捕鲸者的基地。1921年，挪威气象研究所在扬马延岛设立气象站，4年后，挪威吞并该岛。1930年，在确认英国将承认其主张后，挪威政府正式将该岛纳入挪威王国，这或许是由于挪威承认加拿大对斯维尔德鲁普群岛主权。① 现今，只有几十个人居住在扬马延岛，他们都是挪威武装力量或挪威气象研究所的雇员，然而扬马延岛周边的专属经济区却可支撑相当规模的渔业发展。

1993年，在丹麦提起的一个案件中，国际法院划定了格陵兰和扬马延之间的单一海上边界。② 法院以中间线为临时基础，然后考虑是否存在需要对该线进行调整的"特殊情况"，以达成"公平结果"。法院总结道，格陵兰海岸线要长得多，这一特殊情况要求划线需更靠近扬马延岛；该线也应稍微向东移动，使丹麦可公平地获得某些鱼类资源。

其他形式的争端解决方法也被运用于扬马延岛和位于其360海里之外冰岛之间的水域和海床划界。1981年，挪威和冰岛达成条约，同意冰岛专属经济区和大陆架从两岛之间区域的冰岛海岸向外延伸至200海里，使得该线更靠近挪威岛屿一侧。③ 然而，该条约同时给予挪威参与新边界以南冰岛大陆架部分区域中石油和天然气勘探25%的权益，给予冰岛参与新边界以北扬马延岛一部分大陆架石油和天然气勘探25%的权益。④ 该条约为跨界石油和天然气矿床开发创立了一体化协议。⑤

---

① Thorleifsson, Chapter 1, n. 55, above. For more on the Sverdrup Islands, see Chapter 1, above.

② Maritime Delimitation in the Area between Greenland and Jan Mayen (Denmark v. Norway) (1993) ICJ Reports 38, http://www.icj-cij.org/docket/files/78/6743.pdf.

③ Agreement on the Continental Shelf between Iceland and Jan Mayen, October 22, 1981, http://www.un.org/depts/los/LEGISLATIONANDTREATIES/PDFFILES/TREATIES/ISL-NOR1981CS.PDF.

④ Ibid., Arts. 5 and 6.

⑤ Ibid., Art. 8.

2008 年，两国通过后续条约，为跨界和两块 25% 参与区域的石油和天然气勘探①制定更为详细的框架。② 尽管最终设立的联合油气制度并非没有前例可循，但是这是首次在北极水域建立此类制度，可为美国和加拿大在波弗特海争议提供模板，对加拿大、丹麦和俄罗斯提交的有关北冰洋中部外大陆架权利重叠划界案亦有参考价值。③ 根据挪威外交部长约纳斯·加尔·斯特勒所称，这一安排为石油公司提供了所需的可预测性。④

四、2006 年《格陵兰和斯瓦尔巴边界条约》

2006 年丹麦和挪威就格陵兰和挪威北极斯瓦尔巴群岛之间通用海上边界进行谈判。⑤ 这条依据等距线划设的边界线长约 430 海里，因考虑到丹麦托拜厄斯岛距离格陵兰海岸约 38 海里的情况而稍加调整。⑥ 通过订立该条约，丹麦隐含承认挪威关于斯瓦尔巴存在专属经济区和大陆架的主张，这在第一章中有所讨论。该条约包括关于跨界矿产资源的规定，根据该规定，任何一方均就可能的合作解决方案启动谈判，但不

---

① Agreed Minutes concerning the Right of Participation pursuant to Articles 5 and 6 of the Agreement of 22 October 1981 between Iceland and Norway on the Continental Shelf in the Area between Iceland and Jan Mayen, November 3, 2008, http：//www. nea. is/media/olia/JM_agreed_minutes_Iceland_Norway_2008. pdf.

② Agreement between Iceland and Norway concerning Transboundary Hydrocarbon Deposits, November 3, 2008, http：//www. nea. is/media/olia/JM_unitisation_agreement_Iceland_Norway_2008. pdf.

③ Chapter 3 (Beaufort Sea) and Chapter 4, below (extended continental shelf).

④ Jonas Karlsbakk, "Norway and Iceland Sign Border Treaty," BarentsObserver. com, November 5, 2008, http：//barentsobserver. com/en/node/20950. According to the same report, the new treaty was signed just three days after the Norwegian Bank gave the Icelandic government a loan of approximately 1 million euros as part of Norway's assistance to Iceland during the global financial crisis.

⑤ Agreement between the Government of the Kingdom of Norway on the one hand, and the Government of the Kingdom of Denmark together with the Home Rule Government of Greenland on the other hand, concerning the delimitation of the continental shelf and the fisheries zones in the area between Greenland and Svalbard, Copenhagen, February 20, 2006, UNTS, vol. 2378, I-42887, p. 21, http：//treaties. un. org/doc/Publication/UNTS/Volume%202378/v2378. pdf.

⑥ generally, Alex G. Oude Elferink, "Maritime Delimitation between Denmark/Greenland and Norway." (2007) 38 Ocean Development and International Law 375.

要求双方承诺必须达成任何结果。

五、2010年《巴伦支海边界条约》

巴伦支海位于挪威芬马克地区和俄罗斯科拉半岛以北,在西北部挪威斯瓦尔巴群岛、东北部和东部法兰士·约瑟夫地和新地两个俄罗斯群岛之间。该区域约40万平方海里,周边水域平均深度只有230米。由于整个海床属于大陆架,使得巴伦支海成为鱼类、石油和天然气的最佳位置。挪威西北部的斯诺赫维特气田已经投产,储量估计为1930亿立方米。[①] 天然气通过洋底140千米管道输送至位于哈默菲斯特的液化工厂,之后经由超级冷冻油轮运送至日本、法国和西班牙。[②] 再往东,但仍在挪威管辖范围内,格里亚特油田可采储量估计为1.74亿桶。[③] 在巴伦支海的俄罗斯一侧,大规模的施托克曼天然气田估计有3.8万亿立方米天然气和3700万吨天然气凝析油。[④]

三十多年来,奥斯陆和莫斯科对大约5万平方海里,约占巴伦支海面积10%的区域存在争议。莫斯科争辩称,存在诸多与划界有关的"特殊情况",包括:俄罗斯海岸长度和形状;邻近地区各自人口规模;海冰情况;渔业、航运和其他经济利益;以及战略考量。其还认为,1920年《斯瓦尔巴条约》禁止该群岛上任何点对划界造成影响。[⑤] 在莫斯科看来,所有这些因素结合在一起构成了一条沿着32°04′35″E经线的区域分界线,该线只在斯瓦尔巴以东有所调整,以免侵犯《斯瓦尔

[①] "Offshore Field Development Projects: Snohvit," http://www.subseaiq.com/data/Project.aspx?project_id=223.

[②] "Snøhvit-Unlocking Resources in the Frozen North," http://www.statoil.com/en/OurOperations/ExplorationProd/ncs/Pages/SnohvitNewEnergyHistoryInTheNorth.aspx.

[③] "Offshore Field Development Projects: Goliat," http://www.subseaiq.com/data/Project.aspx?project_id=400.

[④] "Offshore Field Development Projects: Shtokman," http://www.subseaiq.com/data/Project.aspx?project_id=476.

[⑤] For more on the Svalbard Treaty, Chapter 1, above.

巴条约》中规定的区域。①

奥斯陆回应称,1926年苏联划设该区域分界线的唯一目的是确定几个近海岛屿的领土地位,没有划分海上区域的意图。它认为,应从挪威和俄罗斯位于芬马克和科拉半岛之间狭窄入口瓦朗尼治峡湾陆上边界的最上端引出一条中间线。这条线应是挪威和俄罗斯大陆海岸所有点的等距线;在更远处,其应是西边斯瓦尔巴和东边新地岛和法兰士·约瑟夫地岛之间的等距线。②

该争端始于20世纪60年代,当时挪威和苏联都依据1958年《日内瓦大陆架公约》主张近海权利。③ 1977年,当两国宣布200海里专属经济区包括渔业和海床资源时,其获得了更大的影响力。④ 此后,挪威和俄罗斯分别于1996和1997年批准《公约》,其中第七十六条承认,沿岸国可以在距海岸200海里外的外大陆架行使主权权利,只要证明该部分是其领土"自然延伸"。⑤ 然而,《公约》第八十三条也规定,海岸相向或相邻国家之间的大陆架划界"应在国际法的基础上以协议划定……以便得到公平解决"。第七十四条对专属经济区重叠区域划界做出同样的规定。

虽然该争端规模较大,重要性较高,两国在冷战中也处于对立立场,但是挪威和苏联及其后的俄罗斯都表现出值得称赞的克制。1975年,奥斯陆和莫斯科缔结《渔业事务合作协议》,强调养护和合理利用巴伦支海渔业资源的原则,并设立联合渔业委员会。⑥ 该委员会依据国

---

① Robin Churchill and Geir Ulfstein, Marine Management in Disputed Areas: The Case of the Barents Sea (London: Routledge, 1992), 63.

② Ibid.

③ 1958 Convention on the Continental Shelf, 499 UNTS 311, http://untreaty.un.org/ilc/texts/instruments/english/conventions/8_1_1958_continental_shelf.pdf. Tore Henriksen and Geir Ulfstein, "Maritime Delimitation in the Arctic: The Barents Sea Treaty." (2011) 42 Ocean Development and International Law 1 at 2.

④ Henriksen and Ulfstein, "Maritime Delimitation in the Arctic."

⑤ For more on the interpretation and application of Article 76, Chapters 3 and 4, below.

⑥ Agreement between the Government of the Kingdom of Norway and the Government of the Union of Soviet Socialist Republics on Co-operation in the Fishing Industry, April 11, 1975, 983 UNTS 8, http://treaties.un.org/doc/Publication/UNTS/Volume%20983/volume-983-I-14331-English.pdf.

际海洋考察理事会的科学建议，建议每年为不同种类渔业资源制定"总可捕量"，[1]并在挪威和俄罗斯之间平均分配。

1976年，一项后续协议明确承认，挪威和苏联在距海岸200海里内享有沿岸国渔业管理权。值得注意的是，该协议也授权一国进入他国专属经济区。[2] 1978年，两国开始在主张重叠区域实施渔业管理。所谓"灰色区域协议"一开始就规定，其不得损害任何一方法律立场。[3] 它承认，处于争议区域的挪威船由挪威实施专属管辖，俄罗斯船只则由俄方行使专属管辖权。其随后规定，第三方渔业船只获挪威或俄罗斯授权后，方可进入争议区域。在这种情况下，挪威对经其同意的船只行使管辖权，俄罗斯则对其所同意的船只拥有管辖权。"灰色区域协议"已良好运行逾三十年并且每年更新一次。

与此同时，两国渔业管辖范围扩大后，在巴伦支海中部留下了大约2.5万平方公里的公海。到20世纪90年代，冰岛船只在这一不受管制区域进行的过度捕捞已导致跨界鱼类资源枯竭，造成该国与挪威和俄罗斯之间关系紧张。1999年，挪威、俄罗斯和冰岛达成所谓"圈洞协议"，包括挪威与冰岛、俄罗斯与冰岛之间的双边协议。[4] 在新制度下，冰岛获得在挪威和俄罗斯专属经济区的捕鱼配额。作为回报，挪威渔民获得进入冰岛专属经济区权利，俄罗斯获得现金支付，三个国家都被要

---

[1] Norwegian Ministry of Fisheries and Coastal Affairs, "Fisheries Collaboration with Russia," http：//www. fisheries. no/resource_management/International_cooperation/Fisheries_collaboration_with_Russia/.

[2] Agreement between the Government of the Union of Soviet Socialist Republics and the Government of the Kingdom of Norway concerning Mutual Relations in the Field of Fisheries, October 15, 1976, 1157 UNTS 147, Art. 1, http：//treaties. un. org/doc/Publication/UNTS/Volume%201157/volume-1157-I-18273-English. pdf.

[3] Agreement on an Interim Practical Arrangement for Fishing in an Adjoining Area in the Barents Sea, January 11, 1978, original Norwegian text at (1978) Overenskomster med fremmede stater 436. See also Kristoffer Stabrun, "The Grey Zone Agreement of 1978: Fishery Concerns, Security Challenges and Territorial Interests." Fridtjof Nansen Institute Report 13/2009, http：//www. fni. no/doc&pdf/FNI-R1309. pdf.

[4] Agreement between the Government of Iceland, the Government of Norway and the Government of the Russian Federation concerning Certain Aspects of Co-operation in the Area of Fisheries, May 15, 1999, 2070 UNTS 204, http：//treaties. un. org/doc/Publication/UNTS/Volume%202070/v2070. pdf.

求阻止本国公民在巴伦支海使用方便旗或在没有配额情况下卸载鱼获。

挪威和苏联还同意推迟争议区域所有石油和天然气活动,并将重新致力于海上边界谈判。1957年,两国成功划定瓦朗尼治峡湾内领海边界。1970年两国进一步就海上边界展开非正式谈判,1974年开始正式谈判。① 但直到2007年,挪威和俄罗斯的谈判代表才最终成功地在领海之外划设首条20海里海上边界。②

2010年4月,剩余边界问题出现突破,挪威外交部长约纳斯·加尔·斯特勒和俄罗斯外交部长谢尔盖·拉夫罗夫在奥斯陆签署一项协议。协议承诺,两国将在"国际法基础上"划设通用边界"以实现公平解决方案",承认"相关因素……包括各国海岸长度主要差异的影响",同时将"整个有争议的区域划分为两个面积大致相等的部分"。③ 包含将8个指定点连接成大地测量线在内的最终条约于5个月后签署,挪威议会和俄罗斯杜马分别于2011年2月和3月批准了该条约。④

该条约为距海岸200海里内的专属经济区和大陆架、200海里外的外大陆架划设了单一海上边界。存在一个仅涉及有限权利的问题,即"协议达成的边界是应被称为修正的中间线(挪威主张),还是修正的区域线(如俄罗斯主张)",⑤ 因为该条约几乎将先前争议区域一分为

---

① Churchill and Ulfstein, n. 50, above, pp. 54 and 63.

② Agreement between the Russian Federation and the Kingdom of Norway on the Maritime Delimitation in the Varangerfjord Area, July 11, 2007, 67 UN Law of the Sea Bulletin 42, http://treaties.un.org/doc/Publication/UNTS/No%20Volume/45114/Part/I-45114-08000002801f5bf2.pdf.

③ "Joint Statement on Maritime Delimitation and Cooperation in the Barents Sea and the Arctic Ocean," Oslo, April 27, 2010, http://www.regjeringen.no/upload/UD/Vedlegg/Folkerett/030427_english_4.pdf.

④ 2010 Treaty between the Kingdom of Norway and the Russian Federation concerning Maritime Delimitation and Cooperation in the Barents Sea and the Arctic Ocean, English translation http://www.regjeringen.no/upload/ud/vedlegg/folkerett/avtale_engelsk.pdf. See also Henriksen and Ulfstein, n. 52, above; Thilo Neumann, "Norway and Russia Agree on Maritime Boundary in the Barents Sea and the Arctic Ocean." (November 9, 2010) 14 (34) ASIL Insight, http://www.asil.org/files/2010/insights/insights_101109.pdf. On the prompt ratifications, Walter Gibbs, "Norway Hails Barents Treaty OK by Russian Duma," Reuters, March 26, 2011, http://www.reuters.com/article/2011/03/26/barentstreaty-idUSLDE72P0HY20110326. For a map of the new boundary line, http://www.regjeringen.no/upload/UD/kart/kart_100914_ny.gif.

⑤ Henriksen and Ulfstein, n. 52, above, at 7.

二。如果存在区别的话，该线似乎是直接适用公平原则的结果，在涉及海上边界的有关司法或仲裁决定，该原则经常导致双方因对立的主张而发生分歧。①

该协议是其他领域双边合作的范例。正如 1990 年苏联和美国在《白令海峡条约》中所做的那样，②双方建立了"特别区域"，以最大限度提高两国主权权利结合程度。第三条第 1 款称：

> 海上分界线以西的区域（下文称"特别区域"），该分界线位于挪威测算其领海宽度的基线 200 海里之内，但位于俄罗斯测算其领海宽度的基线 200 海里之外的区域，俄罗斯联邦应自本条约生效之日起，有权行使挪威依据国际法享有的，自专属经济区管辖权派生出的主权权利和管辖权。

第三条第 2 款进一步承认：

> 如果俄罗斯联邦在本条规定的特别区域行使主权权利或管辖权，这种行使主权权利和管辖权行为源自于各方协议并且不构成对其专属经济区的扩展。为此，俄罗斯联邦应采取必要措施，确保其在特别区域内行使的主权权利或管辖权应在其相关法律、法规和图表中有所描述。与《白令海峡条约》一样，这一做法引发一个问题，即此类特别区域是否可以对抗第三国。③

考虑到一些油气资源可能会跨越该边界，挪威和俄罗斯同意共同管理此类矿床。第五条规定："若一方大陆架存在油气资源矿床已经确认，另一方认为该矿床延伸至己方大陆架，则后者可通知前者并提交其观点

---

① e.g., Prosper Weil, The Law of Maritime Delimitation-Reflections (Cambridge: GrotiusPublications, 1989), 9 – 14.

② discussion, above, pp. 35 – 36.

③ discussion, above, p. 36.

所依据的数据。"在这一点上,两国需要"就油气资源矿床的范围和将该矿床作为整体开发的可能性展开讨论",同时两国需"尽最大努力确保为这些讨论提供所有相关信息"。若证实该矿床延伸跨越了边界并且一方开发将影响另一方利益,任何一方可要求缔结"联合经营协议"。根据该协议,矿床应作为单一整体加以开发。据此,该条约对两国均施加了严格义务,以使私人公司可获得边界两边的开采权并签署"联合运营协议",并由"联合运营方"监督该矿床的勘探和开发。

两家公司之间协议在私法层面运行,但与联合经营协议存在不可分割的联系,后者作为国与国之间的协议是国际公法的一部分。例如,挪威和俄罗斯已通过该条约禁止一国在未与另一国协商的情况下,改变一方公司从矿床中勘探和开采油气资源的权利。此外,由于协商有时并不能解决所有分歧,该条约规定了争端解决程序,包括在未达成一致协议的情况下指定仲裁庭,在未能就某个油气资源矿床分配达成一致情况下指定独立专家。在两种情形下,该条约都认为争端解决结果"对各方均具有约束力"。

挪威和俄罗斯还同意在先前争议区域继续实施两国间长达数十年的共同渔业管理,在被专属经济区环绕包围的公海圈洞区域亦如此。该条约第四条规定:

1. 任何一方的捕鱼机会不因缔结本条约而受到不利影响。

2. 为此目的,各方应寻求在渔业领域开展密切合作,以期维持它们在总可捕量中的现有份额并确保各方对有关各类渔业资源的渔业活动相对稳定。

3. 各方应广泛实施预防措施,以养护、管理和开发共享的渔业资源,包括跨界渔业资源,以保护海洋生物资源和海洋环境。

4. 除本条款和附件一中规定外,本条约中任何内容均不影响各方对渔业合作协议的适用。

如托尔·亨里克森和吉尔·乌尔夫斯坦所释,"相对稳定"一词取自《欧盟共同渔业政策》,指的是基于可预测份额的渔业捕捞分配。[①]

[①] Henriksen and Ulfstein, n. 52, above, p. 8.

关于国际环境法的核心原则"预防性措施"的段落直接取自1995年《联合国跨界鱼类种群和高度洄游鱼类种群协议》。① 目前仍由联合渔业委员会负责执行这两种手段,如上文所述,该委员会已成功运作近40年。②

《巴伦支海条约》的重要性再怎么强调也不为过。需再一次提及,挪威和俄罗斯在冷战数十年中属于对峙的双方。挪威长期以来一直是北约成员国,拥有现代化的护卫舰和F-16战机;俄罗斯现有大部分核导弹潜艇都以巴伦支海沿岸为基地。解决北约国家和俄罗斯之间最后一个有争议的北极边界争议是对"重启"此前敌对双方之间关系的重大贡献,在美国总统巴拉克·奥巴马支持下,该目标也引领了之后俄罗斯和美国之间达成具有深远影响的核武器削减条约。③

《巴伦支海条约》对其他北极边界争端亦有影响,正如俄罗斯和挪威外交部长2010年9月联合在《环球邮报》撰写题为《加拿大,请记录:以下是解决海上争议的方法》的文章,以提醒加拿大政府。④ 当然,如果人口较少的挪威(500万人口)可以和强大的俄罗斯(1.4亿人口)谈判达成双赢的边界协议,那么其他任何北极边界争端都没有理由无法得到解决。如下面例子所示,加拿大正在遵循这一建议。

---

① 1995 UN Agreement for the Implementation of the Provisions of the United Nations Convention on the Law of the Sea of 10 December 1982 Relating to the Conservation and Management of Straddling Fish Stocks and Highly Migratory Fish Stocks, http://www.un.org/Depts/los/convention_agreements/convention_overview_fish_stocks.htm. For discussion of a proposed regional fisheries organization for the Arctic Ocean, Chapter 6, below.

② Annex I extends the application of the 1975 and 1976 Norwegian-Russian fisheries agreements by fifteen years while also providing for an additional six years of provisional application.

③ For more on the geopolitical context of the "reset," Chapter 8, below. New START Treaty ("Treaty between the United States of America and the Russia Federation on Measures for the Further Reduction and Limitation of Strategic Offensive Arms"), April 8, 2010, http://www.state.gov/documents/organization/140035.pdf; Peter Baker and Dan Bilefsky, "Russia and US Sign Nuclear Arms Reduction Pact." New York Times, April 8, 2010.

④ Sergei Lavrov and Jonas Gahr Støre, "Canada, Take Note: Here's How to Resolve Maritime Disputes." Globe and Mail, September 21, 2010, http://www.theglobeandmail.com/commentary/canada-take-note-heres-how-to-resolve-maritime-disputes/article4326372/.

六、林肯海边界

林肯海是北冰洋格陵兰岛和埃尔斯米尔岛以北的部分区域。受盛行风和洋流影响，海冰被推到两个岛屿之间的位置并在此停留数年，使得在这里可以发现北极最厚的海冰。如上所述，1973年划设加拿大和格陵兰之间海上边界的谈判人员最终停留在82°13′N，内尔斯海峡从这里通往林肯海，[①] 结果造成由此向北约200海里的大陆架（以及专属经济区）边界悬而未决。

1977年，加拿大主张沿其北冰洋海岸线划设200海里渔业区。该区域东边以等距线为界，将埃尔斯米尔岛、格陵兰岛以及数个边缘岛屿海岸的低潮线作为基点。[②] 三年后，丹麦在绘制直线基线后，采用了本国划设的等距线，其中两条以博蒙特岛作为基点。[③] 博蒙特岛面积10平方公里有余，距离格陵兰岛海岸超过12海里但不到24海里。第一条基线长42.6海里，从布赖恩特角（82°20.4′N，55°13.0′W）到博蒙特岛（82°45.2′N，50°46.0′W）西北角。第二条基线长40.9海里，从博蒙特岛同一点延伸至蒂斯坦特角（83°08.2′N，46°12.0′W）。受到使用直线基线和博蒙特岛将等距线稍向西移的影响，丹麦（格陵兰）的主张中增加了两块独立的透镜状区域，面积分别为31平方海里和34平方海里。

加拿大迅速对丹麦的直线基线提出抗议，尤其是针对使用博蒙特岛作为基点，理由有四个方面："博蒙特岛在其他岛屿西侧，因此不属于一系列岛屿的一部分；直线基线过长；未沿着海岸方向；没有跨过峡湾的入口，而是离海岸更远。"[④] 这些理由似乎来自于国际法院对直线基线影响深远的判决，即1951年"英挪渔业案"。[⑤]

[①] discussion, above, p. 32.
[②] Gray, n. 2, above, at 68.
[③] Executive Order No. 176 of 14 May 1980 on the fishing territory of Northern Greenland, http://faolex.fao.org/docs/pdf/den99033E.pdf.
[④] Gray, n. 9, above, at 68.
[⑤] Anglo – Norwegian Fisheries Case (1951) ICJ Reports 116.

2004 年，林肯海边界争端的范围减少，丹麦修改了该国的直线基线，适用更为准确的基点，使用一系列更短的基线替代博蒙特岛东部原先 40.9 海里长的基线，包括连接博蒙特岛和该岛链中下一个岛约翰·莫里岛的基线。① 同样在 2004 年，丹麦通过了一项新的"关于格陵兰专属经济区法生效的皇家法令"，重申了该国立场：

> 林肯海中专属经济区划界，在此格陵兰和加拿大相对海岸之间距离少于 400 海里，在不存在任何相关特别协议之情况下，应从第 127 点出发（1973 年商定边界的最北端），沿着在任何方向上与问题中海岸基线上最近点的距离相同的点所连成之线（中间线）。②

丹麦的改动成功缩小了最北端争议区的面积，几乎达到了消除该区域的程度，同时也强化了使用博蒙特岛作为基点的理由。③

在丹麦起初采用直线基线，加拿大提出抗议之后，《联合国海洋法公约》第七条将"英挪渔业案"中确定的规则立法化。具体而言，第七条第 1 款规定："在海岸线极为曲折的地方，或者如果紧接海岸有一系列岛屿，测算领海宽度的基线的划定可采用连接各适当点的直线基线

---

① °45.2′ "Royal Decree on Amendment of Royal Decree on Delimitation of the Territorial Waters of Greenland, 15 October 2004"（2005）56 Law of the Sea Bulletin 126 at 128, http://www.un.org/Depts/los/doalos_publications/LOSBulletins/bulletinpdf/bulletin56e.pdf. The new base points are as follow: Cape Bryant 82°20′.0.234N, 55°14′.0.984W; Northernmost point of Beaumont Island 82°45′.0.346N, 50°47′.0.051W; Northernmost point of John Murray Island 82°50′.0.190N, 49°03′.0.203W; Cape Bene′t 82°59′.0.816N, 47°16′.0.698W; Cape Payer 83°05′.0.275N, 46°15′.0.167W; Cape Ramsay 83°10′.0.915N, 44°53′.0.891W. Cape Distant is no longer used as a base point and now falls within the straight baseline connecting Cape Payer to Cape Ramsay. A useful map of the baselines is available in "Royal Decree," p. 132. Beaumont Island is almost bisected by the fiftieth meridian toward the top of the page.

② "Royal Decree," p. 135.

③ For a map showing the Danish equidistance line post-2004, see the map of the "Outer Limits of the Exclusive Economic Zone of Greenland," in "Executive Order on the Exclusive Economic Zone of Greenland, 20 October 2004"（2005）56 Law of the Sea Bulletin133 at 136, http://www.un.org/Depts/los/doalos_publications/LOSBulletins/bulletinpdf/bulletin56e.pdf.

法。"申言之,正如联合国针对直线基线的研究认为:"没有统一可证明的客观测试方法,可对紧挨海岸的一系列岛屿进行逐个认定。但各国应以第七条一般精神为指导。"①

国际法院之后在"黑海案"中明确表示,一国为设立外大陆架和专属经济区而划设基线,并不意味着这些相同的基线必然适用于相邻或相对国家大陆架和专属经济区的划界。正如法院写道:

> 在第二种情况下,涉及两个及以上国家海上区域划分时,法院不应仅依据争端各方中某一方选择的基点。法院在划定大陆架和专属经济区时必须参照相关海岸的地理位置选择基点。②

实际上,加拿大从未在林肯海边界问题上抱持特别强硬的立场。博蒙特岛确实位于格陵兰西北部其他一些岛屿的西面,但其确实属四个岛之一,这四个岛如链般延伸,几乎与海岸线平行,各岛之间存在深深的峡湾。关键是博蒙特岛距其东面下一个岛不到24海里,距大陆也不到24海里。在这一点上,联合国的研究报告认为:"这个描述性短语'紧邻海岸'是一个概念,其有明确的含义但没有绝对的检验标准……一般认为存在12海里领海,距离达24海里即满足该条件。"③

《联合国海洋法公约》或联合国研究报告都没有确定连接边缘岛屿直线基线的最大长度。然而,美国国务院一项研究建议:"任何直线基

---

① Office for Ocean Affairs and the Law of the Sea, The Law of the Sea-Baselines: An Examination of the Relevant Provisions of the United Nations Convention on the Law of the Sea (United Nations: New York, 1989), p. 21, p. 42, http://www.un.org/depts/los/doalos_publications/publicationstexts/The%20Law%20of%20the%20Sea_Baselines.pdf. The State practice on the interpretation of Article 7 is mixed, with Asian states being especially liberal with their straight baselines. Sam Bateman and Clive Schofield, "State Practice Regarding Straight Baselines in East Asia-Legal, Technical and Political Issues in a Changing Environment." Paper prepared for a conference at the International Hydrographic Bureau, Monaco, October 16–17, 2008, http://www.gmat.unsw.edu.au/ablos/ABLOS08Folder/Session7-Paper1-Bateman.pdf.

② Case Concerning Maritime Delimitation in the Black Sea (2009) ICJ Reports 44 at 108, p. 137, http://www.icj-cij.org/docket/files/132/14987.pdf.

③ Ibid., p. 22, p. 46.

线的长度都不应超过 48 海里。"① 因此，博蒙特岛最初的基线符合该建议的限制。

对于沿着海岸走向的基线，《联合国海洋法公约》第七条第 3 款规定："直线基线的划定不应在任何明显的程度上偏离海岸的一般方向，而且基线内的海域必须充分接近陆地领土，使其受内水制度的支配。"但是"明显的程度"究竟是什么意思？美国国务院研究建议：

> 最外缘岛屿走向（例如直线基线转折点所在的岛屿）不应与相对大陆海岸线偏离超过 20 度（包括任何横跨海湾、河口或港口的闭合线），或偏离相对大陆海岸线的一般方向，无论其是否更接近于平行于相关岛屿。②

在博蒙特岛及该岛链其他岛屿的情况中，其方向走势与格陵兰岛海岸一般方向的偏差不超过 10 度。

至于加拿大最为担忧的，直线基线"不会跨越峡湾口，而是更远离海岸。"第七条第 1 款指出，直线基线可被用于"在海岸线极为曲折的地方，或者如果紧接海岸有一系列岛屿。"在这两种地理情况并存的地点，沿岸国似乎可以享有选择权，丹麦选择对其最有利的方法是无可非议的。

就沿海区域的凹陷问题，相对保守的美国国务院研究报告建议，"占基线总长度 70% 的各基线分段，每段中海岸延伸与分段长度比例应至少达到 6∶10。"并且应满足"在任意给定区域至少应有三个明显的凹陷"。③ 就沿岸一系列岛屿的问题，该研究建议这些岛屿"应覆盖相对大陆海岸线的 50%"。④ 博蒙特岛的情况显然符合第一项建议的要求；第二项要求无法得到满足，但该岛覆盖的程度仍然很高，约为 25%至 30%。

---

① US State Department, Limits in the Sea (No. 106): Developing Standard Guidelines for Evaluating Straight Baselines (1987), 6, http://www.state.gov/documents/organization/59584.pdf.
② Ibid., p. 16.
③ Ibid., p. 6.
④ Ibid., p. 16.

这也不能成功地论证，为划定边界而使用直线基线不符合国际法。在回顾有关海上边界协议的国家实践后，路易斯·宋恩认为，"大约20个案件明确考虑了直线基线系统"以及"大约在50个案例中其被部分或全部忽略了。"① 在"厄立特里亚和也门仲裁案"中，仲裁庭依据埃塞俄比亚（厄立特里亚独立之前）采用的直线基线系统，并且根据《联合国海洋法公约》第七条第4款对直线基线设定的标准，拒绝将一个地物作为基点。② 在"卡塔尔诉巴林案"中，国际法院明显对两国领海边界划分中适用现有直线基线系统持开放态度，因为它拒绝巴林系统的实质理由是其主要岛屿海岸周边一群岛屿的数量太少，距离主要岛屿距离不足，不能被视为"沿海岸的一系列岛屿"。③

最后，大卫·格雷建议，"作为面积约4平方英里（10.3平方米），孤立和无人居住的岛屿，可以认为该岛（博蒙特岛）不能依据《联合国海洋法公约》第一百二十一条第3款的规定，由其自身产生专属经济区。"④ 要理解这一点，我们必须从《联合国海洋法公约》第一百二十一条第1款出发，该条将"岛屿"定位为"四面环水并在高潮时高于水面的自然形成的陆地区域"。根据第一百二十一条第2款，岛屿和其他陆地一样，可以产生领海、毗连区、专属经济区和大陆架权利。第一百二十一条第3款接着对岛屿种类的例外作出定义，即："不能维持人类居住或其本身的经济生活的岩礁，不应有专属经济区或大陆架。"⑤ 这些"岩礁"产生领海和毗连区，但是没有专属经济区或大陆架权利；

---

① Louis B. Sohn, "Baseline Considerations," in Jonathan I. Charney and Lewis M. Alexander (eds.), International Maritime Boundaries, Vol. 1 (Dordrecht: Martinus Nijhoff, 1993), 153 at 157.

② Award of the Arbitral Tribunal in the Second Stage of the Proceedings between Eritrea and Yemen (Maritime Delimitation) (1999), 22 Reports of International Arbitration Awards 335 at 366 – 367, http://untreaty.un.org/cod/riaa/cases/vol_XXII/335 – 410.pdf. Article7 (4) reads: "Straight baselines shall not be drawn to and from low – tide elevations, unless lighthouses or similar installations which are permanently above sea level have been built on them or in instances where the drawing of straight baselines to and from such elevations has received general international recognition."

③ Maritime Delimitation and Territorial Questions between Qatar and Bahrain (2001) ICJ Reports 40 at 67, p. 214, http://www.icj-cij.org/docket/files/87/7027.pdf.

④ Gray, n.9, above, p.68.

⑤ Introduction, n.15, above.

因此他们不能被用作划设直线基线。

目前,博蒙特岛缺乏人类居住和经济生活。然而,乔纳森·查尼考查了第一百二十一条的前期准备工作并总结道:"一个地物并不需要同时满足人类居住和维持自身经济生活两方面的内容。只要满足其中一项条件,就可将该地物从第一百二十一条第3款的限制中排除出去。"[1] 查尼还发现,"人类居住并不需要民众永久居住在该地物上,"而经济生活也不要求该地物"能够维持一个人全年的生活。"[2] 相反,"这句话似乎仅是要求证明,岩礁事实上具有一定供人类居住的能力或者对社会具有经济价值,"[3] 在北极地区存在巨大资源潜力的背景下,这一检验标准对丹麦而言并非难以实现。

该地物的大小或也具有相关性,正如查尼解释道:

> 对该条的初步工作进一步表明,"小岛"(islets)和"小岛"(small islands)等词语原本是用来定义最终纳入第一百二十一条第3款规定的那些地物。一些代表认为小于1平方公里的小岛,或"针头"般大小的,不应被授予任何海洋区域。另一些人则认为,小于10平方公里的岛屿不应被授予除12海里领海以外的海洋区域。然而,第一百二十一条第3款最终修订版本似乎适用于范围比这些更为狭窄的小型地物,也即只有不能维持人类居住或自身经济生活。[4]

博蒙特岛面积刚刚超过10平方公里。虽然查尼的观点不具有决定性意义,但就海洋法的目的而言,博蒙特岛更像是一个"岛",因此它

---

[1] Jonathan I. Charney, "Rocks that Cannot Sustain Human Habitation."(1999) 93 American Journal of International Law 863 at 868. See also Clive Schofield, "The Trouble with Islands: The Definition and Role of Islands and Rocks in Maritime Boundary Delimitation," in S. Y. Hong and Jon Van Dyke (eds.), Maritime Boundary Disputes, Settlement Processes, and the Law of the Sea (The Hague: Martinus Nijhoff, 2009), 19.

[2] Charney, ibid.

[3] Ibid.

[4] Ibid., p. 869.

成为直线基线的一个基点具有合理性。

尽管相较于丹麦的直线基线主张,加拿大的立场相对薄弱,但其仍可认为自己是幸运的。鉴于林肯海两边"相关海岸"的长度不同,在林肯海简单地适用等距线或显得有点慷慨。① 在加拿大一侧,埃尔斯米尔岛的海岸在哥伦比亚角(加拿大领土最北部)附近远离林肯海,距离罗伯逊海峡(内尔斯海峡最北部)西北约190千米。而在丹麦一侧,一直到格陵兰岛最北端的莫里斯·耶苏普角,海岸才开始远离林肯海,该地距离罗伯逊海峡东北部超过380公里。法院或仲裁庭可能会认为这些海岸的不同长度属于"相关情况"并最终将边界线向西移动。

在此前海上边界划定中,海岸线长度已被认为是相关情况,包括"扬马延案"②、"利比亚和马耳他案"③ 和"缅因湾案"④ 等案件。在"突尼斯和利比亚案"中,国际法院裁定:

> 双方各自海岸上都存在一个点,超过该点,所讨论的海岸就不再与另一方海岸的海床划界存在相关性。该点之外海岸的海床区域因此也不能成为双方外大陆架重叠区域,并因此与划界不存在相关性。⑤

同样,在"黑海案"中,国际法院没有考虑乌克兰的部分海岸,因为这些海岸对待划界区域没有影响。⑥

加拿大沿着埃尔斯米尔岛划设本国直线基线的方式,甚至可能削弱

---

① Alex G. Oude Elferink, "Arctic Maritime Delimitations: The Preponderance of Similarities with Other Regions," in Elferink and Donald Rothwell (eds.), The Law of the Sea and Polar Maritime Delimitation and Jurisdiction (Dordrecht: Kluwer Law International, 2001), 179 at 194.

② Maritime Delimitation in the Area between Greenland and Jan Mayen (Denmark v. Norway) (1993) ICJ Reports 38 at 69, p. 69, http://www.icj-cij.org/docket/files/78/6743.pdf.

③ Case Concerning the Continental Shelf (Libya/Malta) (1985) ICJ Reports 13 at 50, p. 68, http://www.icj-cij.org/docket/files/68/6415.pdf.

④ Gulf of Maine Case (Canada v. United States) (1984) ICJ Reports 246 at 334-335, p. 218, http://www.icj-cij.org/docket/files/67/6369.pdf.

⑤ Case Concerning the Continental Shelf (Libya v. Tunisia) (1982) ICJ Reports 62, p. 75, http://www.icj-cij.org/docket/files/63/6267.pdf.

⑥ Case Concerning Maritime Delimitation in the Black Sea, n. 82, above, p. 99-100.

了自身在林肯海的立场。1973 年,加拿大和格陵兰岛之间大陆架划界是采用沿着埃尔斯米尔岛东海岸划设基线的方法加以解决。① 1985 年,围绕加拿大公开宣布高北极岛屿基线和其他一些基线。② 那些基线中有一些被证明是有争议的,原因包括不寻常的长度和可能偏离海岸一般方向,这两个理由正是加拿大在 1980 年抗议丹麦直线基线时所使用的。

最后也最重要的是,由于两种原因之一或两者兼有,林肯海边界争议可能已经不复存在。第一,不清楚加拿大是否反对丹麦于 2004 年采用修改后的直线基线。③ 尽管可能已经发出一份外交照会,但是没有抗议的公开记录。这意味着双方或已经就基点及等距线存在隐含协议。第二,或许与此相关,加拿大外交部长约翰·贝尔德和丹麦外交大臣维利·瑟芬达尔于 2012 年 11 月宣布,双方谈判代表"已经就在林肯海设立海上边界达成初步协议。"④

显然,唯一有待磋商的重要问题是达成跨界油气资源矿床的联合管理制度。该问题不能由丹麦或加拿大谈判代表单独解决,因为尽管丹麦仍然负责格陵兰的外交政策,但是格陵兰政府自 2008 年开始行使对大陆架等自然资源的控制权。⑤ 尽管如此,双方可能会在 2013 年或 2014 年达成"林肯海边界条约"。联合管理制度已经成为海上边界条约的标

---

① "Report Number 1 - 1, Canada-Denmark (Greenland)," in Jonathan Charney and Lewis Alexander (eds.), International Maritime Boundaries: Volume I (Dordrecht: American Society of International Law/Martinus Nijhoff, 1993), 375 (Canada "established construction lines along its coast facing Greenland, up to the northeasternmost point of Ellesmere Island. It was not until September 1985, however, that Canada announced it considered the construction lines to be official straight baselines along its arctic archipelago").

② For a discussion of the relevance of the straight baselines to the Northwest Passage dispute, see Chapter 5.

③ discussion, above, pp. 47 - 48.

④ "Canada and Kingdom of Denmark Reach Tentative Agreement on Lincoln Sea Boundary," News Release, Canadian Department of Foreign Affairs, 28 November 2012 (with backgrounder), http://www.international.gc.ca/media/aff/newscommuniques/2012/11/28a.aspx? lang = eng. See also Kim Mackrael, "Canada, Denmark a step closer to settling border dispute," Globe and Mail, November 30, 2012, http://www.theglobeandmail.com/news/national/canada - denmark - a - step - closer - to - settling - border - dispute/article5831571/.

⑤ 2009 Act on Greenland Self - Government, http://uk.nanoq.gl/~/media/f74bab3359074b29aab8c1e12aa1ecfe.ashx.

准组成部分,包括在冰岛和扬马延岛之间以及在巴伦支海,这表明两国很容易就能找到最佳的实践样本。①

无论发生什么情况,林肯海边界争议都几乎没有什么实际意义。对于加拿大和丹麦相邻管辖范围在距海岸200海里外交汇的位置,从来没有任何意见分歧。这意味着,在距海岸200海里范围内发生的任何争端都与外大陆架划界没有法律相关性,这将是第四章的重点。

七、小结

大多数海上边界是通过谈判达成的,在北极地区更是如此。1973年,加拿大和丹麦划定加拿大与格陵兰之间1450海里长的边界;1990年,美国和苏联谈判达成白令海、白令海峡和楚科奇海1600海里边界;2006年,丹麦和挪威就格陵兰和挪威北极斯瓦尔巴群岛边界达成一致。这些努力为解决北极最大海上边界争议奠定了基础,即挪威和俄罗斯以北巴伦支海5000平方海里争议水域和海底区域。2010年,这两个国家签署条约确定了协商一致的边界,维持现有渔业管理合作措施,创设了跨界油气矿床的联合管理制度。《巴伦支海条约》的重要性怎么强调都不为过,其弥合了冷战时期的分歧,使俄罗斯在北极走上了国际合作的道路。最后,在格陵兰岛和埃尔斯米尔岛以北林肯海的一小段边界争议仍有待解决。2012年11月,加拿大和丹麦宣布一项临时协议,唯一有待谈判的问题是建立跨界油气资源联合管理制度。目前这一制度的最佳实践模式就在巴伦支海等地区。

---

① discussions above, pp. 37 - 38、44.

第三章　波弗特海边界

啊，这一次我要藉由西北航道，去探寻富兰克林伸向波弗特海的手。

斯坦·罗杰斯，"西北航道"①

2008至2011年的每个夏天，分属美国和加拿大的两艘强大的破冰船都会在阿拉斯加和加拿大育空地区以北的波弗特海相会。② 美国的"希利"号装备了可进行详细水深测量的先进多波束声呐系统，可以了解洋底地形信息。加拿大的"路易斯·圣劳伦特"号则携带一套精密的地震台阵，可以测量海底沉积物的特征和厚度。由于破冰时导致的振动会影响这些仪器的精度，这两艘船会轮流为对方开道，测量得到的声呐和地震数据由美国和加拿大共享。③ 这是一种与生俱来的伙伴关系，因为两国均未同时拥有可以胜任此项任务的两艘破冰船。此外，正如将在第四章中详细讨论的，两国需要对海床有完整的科学认知，以确定他们对距离海岸200海里之外的"外大陆架"主权权利的地理范围。

除此之外，200海里外的测绘合作也可以为解决整个北极圈内唯一的重要边界争端打开大门。近四十年来，美国和加拿大一直在争夺从阿

---

① "Stan Rogers," in The Canadian Encyclopedia, http://www.thecanadianencyclopedia.com/articles/stan-rogers.

② Randy Boswell, "'Astonishing' Data Boost Arctic Claim," Ottawa Citizen, November 12, 2008, at A3; Sian Griffiths, "US-Canada Arctic Border Dispute Key to Maritime Riches," BBC News, August 2, 2010, http://www.bbc.co.uk/news/world-United-States-Canada-10834006.

③ The quality of the data can also be affected by cavitation (i.e., air pockets) as well as chunks of ice passing along the bottom of the hull. Moreover, it is sometimes necessary for a ship to reverse when operating in ice, and this is difficult to do while towing a seismic array.

拉斯加和育空之间陆地边界终点向北延伸 200 海里的一块楔形海域，也即这两个沿岸国专属经济区的最远端。然而，最新的海底测绘将焦点集中到波弗特海中存在外大陆架的可能性，这些大陆架可以延伸到距离海岸 350 海里之处甚至更远。尽管美国和加拿大都没有明确提出两国在 200 海里之外的边界位置，但有趣和重要的是，如果两国仅是将各自在 200 海里之内边界争议的主张简单地适用于 200 海里之外的划界问题，那么由此产生的边界线都难以使己方获利。

一、背景

波弗特海属于北冰洋的浅水区，位于阿拉斯加和加拿大高北极岛屿之间，正好位于马更些河三角洲北部。早在 20 世纪 70 年代，地震调查和勘探钻井就发现此处海底沉积物中含有油气资源。① 2006 年，戴文加拿大公司在图克托亚图克以北发现一处潜在储量为 2.4 亿桶石油的油田，位于西北地区的一个小型因努维阿勒伊特人（Inuvialuit）社区。② 第二年，帝国石油公司和埃克森美孚加拿大公司承诺出资 5.85 亿美元购买附近海床区域开采权。③ 之后，英国石油公司于 2008 年同意斥资 12 亿美元勘探与"帝国和埃克森美孚许可证"相毗邻的一块区域。④ 2010 年，这三家公司成立了一家合资企业，共同在这两个近海地块勘

---

① For the 2011 "disposition map" of the Beaufort Sea and Mackenzie Delta produced by Aboriginal Affairs and Northern Development Canada, showing past discoveries and "shows," http://www.aadnc-aandc.gc.ca/DAM/DAM-INTER-HQ/STAGING/texte-text/nog_mp_bsmd_pg_1317059161670_eng.pdf.

② Gary Park, "Beaufort Find Is Oil, Not Gas," October 21, 2007, Petroleum News 12, http://www.petroleumnews.com/pntruncate/304958258.shtml.

③ Dina O'Meara, "Imperial Oil, Exxon-Mobil Canada Bet C $585M on Offshore Arctic Oil and Gas," July 19, 2007, Resource Investor, http://www.resourceinvestor.com/2007/07/19/imperial-oil-exxonmobil-canada-bet-c585m-on-offsho.

④ Scott Haggett, "BP Bids Big for Canadian Arctic Drilling Rights," Reuters, June 9, 2008, http://uk.reuters.com/article/2008/06/09/uk-energy-arcticidUKN0947438920080609.

探石油和天然气。① 在波弗特海美国一侧,壳牌石油公司花费数十亿美元准备勘探钻井活动,最初计划于 2010 年进行。但英国石油公司在墨西哥湾溢油事件引发监管担忧之后,该计划被推迟至 2012 年夏季,② 之后又推迟到 2013 年。③

1976 年以来,美国和加拿大就对波弗特海的边界位置存在分歧,当时美国对加拿大在签发石油和天然气开采权时所使用的边界线提出抗议。④ 第二年,两国各自划设了不同的 200 海里内专属渔业区,从而确认了争议的存在。⑤

该争议本身源于俄罗斯和英国(1867 年美国购买阿拉斯加后取得俄罗斯的条约权利;1880 年加拿大获得英国的权利)于 1825 年所签署的一项条约的措辞。⑥ 该条约规定阿拉斯加东部边界位于"西经 141 度的经线,一直延伸至冰冻的大洋"。⑦ 加拿大主张,该条约同时规定了陆地和海上边界,两者都必须沿着西经 141 度经线笔直向北延伸。与此相反,美国则认为该条约的划界只适用于陆地,海岸线以外区域适用海上边界划分的常规方法,在波弗特海案例中则应是一条等距线,即该线

---

① Shaun Polczer, "Firms Team Up in Arctic," Calgary Herald, July 31, 2010, http://www2.canada.com/calgaryherald/news/calgarybusiness/story.html?id=a3a43f92-a51d-4402-a76d-61362b8105b8.

② Kim Murphy, "Arctic Drilling: Beaufort Sea Oil Spill Response Plan Approved," Los Angeles Times, March 28, 2012, http://www.latimes.com/news/nation/nationnow/la-na-nn-arctic-drilling-20120328, 0, 2904392. story.

③ Kim Murphy, "Drill Rigs Wind up Operations in Arctic Alaska Seas," Los Angeles Times, October 31, 2012, http://www.latimes.com/news/nation/nationnow/la-na-nnarctic-drill-alaska-20121031, 0, 6809964. story.

④ Ted L. McDorman, Salt Water Neighbors: International Ocean Law Relations between the United States and Canada (New York: Oxford University Press, 2009), 184 (referring to Diplomatic Note, in Gulf of Maine Pleadings, 103 (May 20, 1976), vol. 5, Annex 8 to Reply of the United States, 529–530).

⑤ Gray, Chapter 2, n. 9, above, p. 62.

⑥ Great Britain/Russia: Limits of their Respective Possessions on the North-West Coast of America and the Navigation of the Pacific Ocean, February 16, 1825, 75 Consolidated Treaty Series 95.

⑦ Ibid., Art. 3. The 1825 treaty was written in French only, but the 1867 treaty both repeats the relevant passage in French and uses this English translation in an authentic text. Treaty concerning the Cession of the Russian Possessions in North America, Art. 1, Chapter 2, n. 21, above.

上每点至两侧两国海岸最近点的距离相等,这是在法律上和地理上更为合适的方法。① 从阿拉斯加巴罗角到马更些河,阿拉斯加、育空和西北地区的海岸线一直往东南方向倾斜,导致这条向加拿大一侧倾斜的等距线,在西经 141 度经线以东逐渐向东偏移,从陆地边界终点沿着大约东北偏北的方向直至 200 海里界限。由此,在距离海岸 200 海里范围内造成大约 6250 平方海里的扇形争议区域。②

如上文所述,各国也有权对 200 海里以外的海底资源主张主权权利,如果由该国大陆延伸出的大陆架超过该界限。1982 年《联合国海洋法公约》第七十六条规定了各国在确定对外大陆架管辖权的外部界限时所应采用的科学标准。③ 尽管美国尚未加入《联合国海洋法公约》,但却一再表示该公约主要条款反映了国际习惯法。④

《联合国海洋法公约》还设立了大陆架界限委员会,有权对各国向其提交科学数据的充分性提出建议,并据此宣布一国划设外大陆架外部界限的合法性。⑤ 所有希望对 200 海里外海底区域主张权利的国家,都需要在批准《联合国海洋法公约》后的 10 年内向大陆架界限委员会提交数据,尽管如下文所讨论的,各国可以选择提交部分或初步划界案,该划界案可在 10 年期限逾期后进行更新。⑥ 美国和加拿大在波弗特海 200 海里外开展测绘,是为两国对外大陆架部分区域主张管辖权做准备,就加拿大而言,是为在 2013 年,其 10 年期限截止之前,向大陆架

---

① e. g., US Department of State, Public Notice 2237, Exclusive Economic Zone and Maritime Boundaries (1995) 60 Fed. Reg. 43825 – 43829.

② McDorman, n. 11, above, pp. 181 – 190 for the definitive presentation of the dispute as previously understood.

③ Introduction, n. 15, above.

④ Introduction, n. 25, above.

⑤ Introduction, n. 15, above; Commission on the Limits of the Continental Shelf, http: // www. un. org/Depts/los/clcs_new/clcs_home. htm.

⑥ below, pp. 84 – 85. Coalter Lathrop, "Continental Shelf Delimitation Beyond 200 Nautical Miles: Approaches Taken by Coastal States Before the Commission on the Limits of the Continental Shelf," in David A. Colson and Robert W. Smith (eds.), International Maritime Boundaries (Leiden: American Society of International Law/Martinus Nijhoff, 2011), 4139.

界限委员会提交数据。[1]

如果将外大陆架引入这个关系，就会对波弗特海边界争议造成奇特的扭曲。因为假若将美国主张的等距线延伸至 200 海里之外，其很快就会改变方向，开始向西北方向移动。出现这种现象的原因是，马更些河三角洲东部的加拿大海岸方向发生了变化，甚至更多的是由于波弗特海东岸存在班克斯岛这个大型地物。班克斯岛的影响非常大，以至于等距线越过西经 141 度经线（该线一直向北自然延伸至北极点）后，将朝着美国和俄罗斯海上边界线的方向前进。[2] 这可能会导致西经 141 度经线东西两侧出现大片尚未明确的外大陆架区域，这与该争议区域以南的情况根本相反。从简单的空间角度而言，美国 200 海里外的划线似乎对加拿大有利，反之亦然。

截至目前，美国和加拿大都没有就专属经济区范围以外的权利公开表达立场。因此，我们不能假定任何一国或两国认为他们在 200 海里之内的论点决定了其在 200 海里以外区域的立场，这两个区域海上边界划分的法律原则之间可能存在不同。最重要的是，将争议扩大到 200 海里之外似乎将有助于通过谈判途径解决问题。

二、解决争端的努力

20 世纪 70 年代末，美国和加拿大试图将波弗特海争端和其他海上边界争端一并加以解决。[3] 当时，加拿大表示愿意以一揽子办法解决这些争端，并将以在波弗特海方面的损失换取其他地方的收益。[4] 双方还

---

[1] US Extended Continental Shelf Project, http://continentalshelf.gov/; Canadian Extended Continental Shelf Program, http://www.international.gc.ca/continental/index.aspx?lang=engandmenu_id=7andmenu=R.

[2] On the boundary between the United States and Russia, Chapter 2, above.

[3] McDorman, n. 11, above, pp. 188–189.

[4] Lorne Clark, Deputy Negotiator for Maritime Boundaries Canada/United States, Minutes of Proceedings and Evidence of the Standing Committee on Fisheries and Forestry, April 11, 1978, 30th Parliament, 3rd Session (1977–1978), No. 15 at 8, cited in McDorman, n. 11, above, p. 120.

调查了设立联合油气资源开发区的可能性,这一方案将在下文中详细讨论。① 双方最终都不愿对自身法律立场作出妥协,担心影响其他划界问题的处理。两国随即将重点放在最紧迫的缅因湾边界争端上,并同意将缅因湾争端提交国际法院的一个法庭处理。② 尽管如此,波弗特海争端仍得到妥善管控,两国在争议区域事实上暂停石油和天然气开发。③

如上所述,直至最近才形成了新的谈判环境,美国的传统法律立场有利于加拿大,而加拿大的传统法律立场则有利于美国。简言之,起初看起来是零和谈判的局面现在为创造性的权衡提供了机会。2010 年 2 月,加拿大外交部一名官员指出,两国对各自外大陆架权利下相关区域的看法可能存在重叠,这是重新努力解决波弗特海边界争端的主要原因。④ 之后,在 2010 年 3 月的《御前宣言》中,加拿大政府表达了"与其他北方国家合作解决边界分歧"的愿望。⑤ 在此之后,加拿大外交部长劳伦斯·坎农于 2010 年 5 月在华盛顿特区发表演讲时,公开邀请启动波弗特海边界问题谈判。⑥ 2010 年 8 月,坎农在发布加拿大《北极外交政策声明》之时,重申了解决边界争端的承诺,至少美国和加拿大外交官已经开始第一次会晤。⑦ 尽管这些讨论是在私下里进行的,但

---

① Christopher Kirkey, "Delineating Maritime Boundaries: The 1977 – 1978 Canada-US Beaufort Sea Continental Shelf Delimitation Boundary Negotiations." (1995) 25 Canadian Review of American Studies 49; McDorman, n. 11, above, p. 188; discussion, below, pp. 88 – 90.

② Gulf of Maine Case, Chapter 2, n. 100, above.

③ Gray, Chapter 2, n. 9, above, p. 63.

④ Randy Boswell, "Beaufort Sea Breakthrough," Vancouver Sun, February 17, 2010, http://byers.typepad.com/arctic/2010/02/beaufort – sea – breakthrough.html.

⑤ Speech from the Throne, March 3, 2010, http://www.speech.gc.ca/eng/media.asp?id =1388.

⑥ Randy Boswell, "Canada Ready to Settle Beaufort Sea Dispute with US: Cannon," Vancouver Sun, May 14, 2010, http://byers.typepad.com/arctic/2010/05/canada – ready – to – settle – beaufort – sea – dispute – with – us – cannon.html.

⑦ Department of Foreign Affairs, "Statement on Canada's Arctic Foreign Policy: Exercising Sovereignty and Promoting Canada's Northern Strategy Abroad." (2010), http://www.international.gc.ca/polar – polaire/assets/pdfs/CAFP_booklet PECA_livret – eng.pdf; Randy Boswell, "Work Underway to Resolve Beaufort Sea Boundary Dispute," Vancouver Sun, July 26, 2010, http://byers.typepad.com/arctic/2010/07/work – underway – to – resolve – beaufort – sea – boundary – dispute.html.

两国现有法律立场可能为其提供了出发点。

三、加拿大的法律立场

加拿大可以提出数个论据来支持其立场,也即除陆地边界外,1825年条约同时划分了阿拉斯加和育空以北的海上边界。第一,该条约的谈判是由俄罗斯沙皇亚历山大二世促成的,其1821年主张有权将外国人排除于北美西北海岸100海里之外。正如英国外交大臣乔治·坎宁当时所言:"我们本质上不是就边界线问题进行谈判。而是要求废除对无边大洋的一项无礼和不合理的排他性管辖权主张。我们就领土进行谈判,以囊括就原则问题提出的抗议。"① 结果,加拿大可能会据此辩称,1825年条约适用于波弗特海的海上边界符合条约的"目的和宗旨",这是国际习惯法和1969年《维也纳条约法公约》等规定的条约解释的指导原则之一。② 即便如此,查尔斯·伯恩和唐纳德·麦克雷考查1825年条约谈判的历史后,却并没有发现双方有意划定海上边界的证据。③ 此外,俄罗斯对海洋管辖权的主张不是在波弗特海,而是针对北太平洋。

第二,加拿大可以提出1825年条约的标准文本是法语的事实。1969年《维也纳条约法公约》第三十三条规定,条约的标准文本必须被用于解释的目的(以认证标准文字以外之他种文字作成之条约译本,仅于条约有此规定或当事国有此协议时,始得视为标准约文)。④ 不仅如此,该公约第三十一条规定解释必须符合"用语的通常意义"。⑤ 加拿大可以争辩称,在法语中,在"dans son prolongation jusqu'à la Mer

---

① Quoted in Charles B. Bourne and Donald M. McRae, "Maritime Jurisdiction in the Dixon Entrance: The Alaska Boundary Re-examined." (1976) 14 Canadian Yearbook of International Law 183.
② Vienna Convention on the Law of Treaties, Article 31 (1), Chapter 2, n. 27, above; Lord McNair, The Law of Treaties (Oxford University Press, 1961), 366–382.
③ Bourne and McRae, n. 32, above, pp. 175–223.
④ Vienna Convention on the Law of Treaties, Chapter 2, n. 27, above.
⑤ Ibid.

Glaciale"一句中，介词"jusqu'à"通常被解释为"包含与之相关的物体"。换句话说，在法语中"直至冰冻的大洋"是包含大洋本身的。①

第三，加拿大可以提出这样一个事实，即被用作俄罗斯和美国在白令海和楚科奇海海上边界基础的1867年《转让阿拉斯加条约》② 中明确提及1825年条约。③ 在第一条中，1867年条约提及1825年条约中所确定的领土东部边界，重申边界位置为"第141条经线，其延长线直至冰冻大洋"。④ 第一条还规定：

> 表明领土和统治权转移的西部界限，包含两条相交的线，一条是穿过白令海峡一点的北纬64°30′的纬线，另一条是穿过克鲁辛斯特恩岛的克鲁辛斯特恩岛与拉特曼诺夫岛或拉特曼诺夫岛之间的经线，一直向北延伸进入同一个冰冻大洋，没有尽头。

一个多世纪以来，双方都承认1867年条约划定了海上边界。⑤ 1990年，美国和苏联接受并更新该条约，使用西经168°58′37″经线并称其"在国际法允许范围内延伸进入北冰洋"。⑥

1993年，国际法院在挪威和丹麦的"扬马延案"中驳回了类似论

---

① Contrary views have been expressed by Donat Pharand, "Delimitation Problems of Canada (Second Part)," in Donat Pharand and Umberto Leanza (eds.), The Continental Shelf and the Exclusive Economic Zone: Delimitation and Legal Regime (Dordrecht: Martinus Nijhoff, 1993), 171 at 174 – 176; Karin L. Lawson, "Delimiting Continental Shelf Boundaries in the Arctic: The United States-Canada Beaufort Sea Boundary." (1981) 22 Virginia Journal of International Law 221 at 231 – 232.

② Treaty concerning the Cession of the Russian Possessions in North America, Chapter 2, n. 21, above.

③ Mark B. Feldman and David Colson, "The Maritime Boundaries of the United States." (1981) 75 American Journal of International Law 729 at 751 – 753.

④ Treaty concerning the Cession of the Russian Possessions in North America, Chapter 2, n. 21, above.

⑤ Feldman and Colson, n. 39, above, p. 752.

⑥ 1990 US-USSR Maritime Boundary Agreement, Chapter 2, n. 20, above. For more on the 1990 treaty, Chapter 2, above.

点，该岛与格陵兰边界必须与挪威和冰岛就边界达成的条款相类似。①然而，波弗特海的情况可以说是截然不同的，因为反对1825年条约适用于海上区域的一方已经事实上同意该条约确定了其他地方的海上边界。正如卡米尔·安提诺里在1987年评论称："美国事实上是讲，划设西部海上边界的条约没有划设东部海上边界。"②

第四，加拿大可以提出美国起初默许其使用西经141°经线作为海上边界。19世纪60年代末，加拿大在目前存在争议的区域发放石油和天然气勘探许可证，但没有引发美国抗议。③ 1970年，加拿大通过《北极水域污染防治法》确立了在目前争议区域的环境保护管辖权。④ 该法本身遭到美国抗议，但抗议并不是直接针对在波弗特海使用西经141°经线。⑤ 直到1976年，加拿大颁布更多石油和天然气特许权时，美国才首次就此提出抗议；在当年晚些时候加拿大使用西经141°经线划定200海里渔业区时，美国使用等距线主张本国的渔业区。⑥ 也就是说，从发放首个勘探许可到美国对此许可提出抗议之间存在10年的延迟，而且这些许可都没有导致在争议区域的钻探活动。至于《北极水域污染防治法》，当美国将该立法作为整体提出抗议时，是否仍有必要针对一个特定和相对较小的区域提出抗议仍存疑问。

最后，加拿大不能也没有依赖这一事实，即在20世纪早期，其将西经141°经线与"扇形理论"相结合，来定义该国直至北极点的管辖

---

① Maritime Delimitation in the Area between Greenland and Jan Mayen (1993) ICJ Reports 38 at 76 - 77, p. 86, http://www.icj - cij.org/docket/files/78/6743.pdf.

② Camille M. Antinori, "The Bering Sea: A Maritime Delimitation Dispute between the United States and the Soviet Union." (1987) 18 Ocean Development and International Law 1 at 34. Ted McDorman has suggested that, even if the parties cannot agree on whether the 1825 treaty applies as a treaty in the Beaufort Sea, the US maritime boundary with Russia in western Alaska at least indicates "what the United States might consider an equitable result" in eastern Alaska. McDorman, n. 11, above, p. 187.

③ Donat Pharand, Canada's Arctic Waters in International Law (Cambridge University Press, 1988), 58.

④ Arctic Waters Pollution Prevention Act, 1969 - 70 Statutes of Canada, chap. 47, sec. 2, http://laws - lois.justice.gc.ca/eng/acts/A - 12/FullText.html.

⑤ McDorman, n. 11, above, p. 184.

⑥ Ibid.

区域,① 早先对扇形理论的引用同时也是对加拿大就 1825 年条约解释的肯定。加拿大对扇形理论的态度很快转变为有意的模棱两可,② 直至 2006 年时任加拿大总理史蒂芬·哈珀完全放弃这一理论。③

四、美国的法律立场

美国还没有明确表明对加拿大法律论据的立场,但其可以使用几个理由来反驳加拿大的立场。首先,它可以主张按照 1825 年条约的字面结构进行理解,这与《维也纳条约法公约》中所规定的按照"用语通常意义"的方法一致。④ 将该方法应用于英文文本时,1825 年条约确定的边界在波弗特海海岸线终结,该水域在一年中的大部分时间处于冰冻状态。⑤ 但是,如上文所释,该条约的标准文本是法语,因此美国不得不主张将"通常意义"的方法适用于"dans son prolongation jusqu'à la Mer Glaciale"时也会产生相同结果。⑥ 其同样可以争辩说,1867 年条约英文文本中的这句话应被视为具有权威性,尽管该条约是与俄罗斯而不是英国签订的。

其次,美国可以指出,19 世纪初的国家管辖范围只延伸至近海的一小段距离,所以事实是 1825 年条约的谈判代表不可能对他们不知道

---

① Robert S. Reid, "The Canadian Claim to Sovereignty over the Waters of the Arctic." (1974) 12 Canadian Yearbook of International Law 115; Lester B. Pearson, "Canada Looks Down North." (1946) 24 Foreign Affairs 639.

② K. M. Shusterich, "International Jurisdictional Issues in the Arctic Ocean," in W. E. Westermeyer and K. M. Shusterich (eds.), United States Arctic Interests: The 1980s and 1990s (New York: Springer - Verlag, 1984), at 253, cited in McDorman, n. 11, above, p. 184.

③ Stephen Harper, "Securing Canadian Sovereignty in the Arctic," speech delivered at Iqaluit, Nunavut, August 12, 2006, http://byers.typepad.com/arctic/2009/03/securing-canadian-sovereignty-in-the-arctic.html.

④ Vienna Convention on the Law of Treaties, Chapter 2, n. 27, above.

⑤ Conceivably, the United States could argue the boundary terminates wherever the sea becomes covered in ice at any given point during the year, but this would produce an unprecedented and impractical result: a boundary that terminates at different places depending on the season and the on-going effects of climate change.

⑥ discussion, above, p. 64.

的区域划定边界。1985 年"几内亚和几内亚比绍仲裁案"为该论点提供了一些支持,该案中对历史性条约采取了谨慎的态度。①

最后,美国可以主张 1825 年条约和 1867 年条约在语言上存在差异,表明两者背后存在不同目的。1825 年条约规定了阿拉斯加和育空之间的分界线"直到冰冷的大海",而 1867 年条约却规定阿拉斯加和俄罗斯之间边界"延伸进同一个冰冻大洋"。后一种提法显然是为了划定海上边界,而前者则难以明确。②

若美国的论点令人信服,那么下一步就是考虑海上边界划分的国际法规则,首先是适用于距离 200 海里内的范围,其次是适用于该范围以外的外大陆架。

五、200 海里内海上边界划定法律

只有当美国关于 1825 年条约不适用于海上划界的立场胜出时,或者当该条约解释在谈判中成为一个要素时(这是可能的),海上边界划定的国际法才会和波弗特海争议存在联系。在该争端已存续的近四十个年头中,受到多边条约、判例法和具体争端谈判的影响,海上边界划定的规则已然经历了数个阶段的演变。

1958 年《日内瓦大陆架公约》赞成采用"等距线/特殊情况"方法划定边界。③ 这意味着,在没有商定边界的情况下,将使用等距线,若证明存在特殊情况,则通常会对该线进行调整。1982 年《联合国海洋

---

① Guinea-Guinea Bissau Dispute Concerning the Delimitation of the Maritime Boundary (1985) 25 ILM 251.

② Lawson, n. 37, above, p. 232. David Colson and Mark Feldman have further suggested that the terms of the 1867 treaty, which transferred "territory and dominion" rather than simply "possessions" as used in the 1825 treaty, can be understood to apply to continental shelf rights. Colson and Feldman, n. 39, above, pp. 750 – 751. Bourne and McRae, however, see no significance in the different wording and refer to the decision in the 1893 Bering Sea Seal Fishery Arbitration, which held that Russia had no exclusive fishing rights beyond the territorial sea. Bourne and McRae, n. 32, above, pp. 199 – 200.

③ 1958 Convention on the Continental Shelf, 499 UNTS 311, http://untreaty.un.org/ilc/texts/instruments/english/conventions/8_1_1958_continental_shelf.pdf.

法公约》采取了不同方法，该公约第八十三条第 1 款规定："海岸相向国或相邻国家间大陆架的界限，应在……国际法的基础上以协议划定，以便得到公平解决。"① 这种变化也可见诸判例法，国际法院一贯拒绝接受任何划界规则或原则约束，而是根据每一案件的是非曲直进行处理，以便取得公平结果。② 虽然人们批评判例法没有提供一套适用于所有案件的通用标准，③ 但近期判决已表现出更高的一致性，甚至为实现海上边界划定提供了某种程式。

在 2009 年"黑海案"中，国际法院将这一程序分为三步。④ 在大多数案件中，"法院所用方法的第一阶段是设立临时等距线"，⑤ 随后将"考虑是否存在需要调整或改变临时等距线的因素"。⑥ 第三步，也是最后一个阶段，法院将通过比较双方相关海岸线长度比率，检查海上区域划分是否存在显失公平的情况。⑦ 在 2012 年"尼加拉瓜和哥伦比亚案"中，法院即适用上述三步法划定边界。⑧

国际法院据以调整临时界限的因素或"相关情况"的性质全部属于地理性的。根据对陆地领土的主权产生海洋管辖权的原则，⑨ 法院已决定由"沿岸开放"的地理环境支配海上边界划分。⑩ 沿岸开放与海岸

---

① Introduction, n. 15, above, Art. 74 (relating to the EEZ) and Art. 83 (relating to the continental shelf).

② This practice began in the North Sea Continental Shelf Cases (Netherlands v. Germany; Denmark v. Germany) (1969) ICJ Reports 3, http://www.icj-cij.org/docket/files/51/5535.pdf. See, generally, Prosper Weil, The Law of Maritime Delimitation-Reflections (Cambridge: Grotius Publications, 1989), 9 – 14.

③ Gilbert Guillaume, "Speech to the Sixth Committee of the General Assembly of the United Nations," October 31, 2001, http://www.icj-cij.org/court/index.php?pr=81andpt=3andpl=1andp2=3andp3=1andPHPSESSID.

④ Case Concerning Maritime Delimitation in the Black Sea, Chapter 2, n. 82, above, pp. 118 – 122.

⑤ Ibid., p. 118.

⑥ Ibid., p. 120.

⑦ Ibid., p. 122.

⑧ Territorial and Maritime Dispute (Nicaragua v. Colombia), November 19, 2012, pp. 190 – 193, http://www.icj-cij.org/docket/files/124/17164.pdf.

⑨ North Sea Continental Shelf Cases, n. 59, above.

⑩ Case Concerning the Continental Shelf (Libya/Malta) (1985) ICJ Reports 13 at 39 – 40, p. 49, http://www.icj-cij.org/docket/files/68/6415.pdf.

线本身构造相关,并有别于一国陆地领土面积等其他地理因素。① 岛屿、不同海岸长度或海岸内凹属性等异常特征会对等距线造成不同程度的影响,在海上划界案中都被视为相关情况。②

这种对地理特征的关注是以牺牲各方有时认为具有相关性的其他因素为代价。在"缅因湾案"中,国际法院的一个法庭写道,临时界限不应因经济或安全原因加以调整,除非不这样做将造成灾难性后果:

> 与渔业(或航海、防卫、石油勘探和开发)有关活动的规模不能作为相关情况加以考虑,或作为决定划界时所适用的公平标准,如果偏爱适用这个词的话。被法庭视为一个合理顾虑的,不是在于整体结果,而是尽管通过适用公平标准并使用适当方法赋予这些标准具体效果,却意外出现根本性不公,也即可能对有关国家人民的生活和经济福利产生灾难性影响。③

地理特征在更早有关大陆架划分的判例法中同样起到主要作用,国家对其权利早于专属经济区的建立。1969 年"北海大陆架案"中,国际法院概述了各国对大陆架享有管辖权的理论基础:

---

① Case Concerning the Continental Shelf (Libya/Malta) (1985) ICJ Reports 13 at 39 – 40, p. 49, http: //www. icj – cij. org/docket/files/68/6415. pdf.

② On islands, Arbitration between the United Kingdom and France Concerning the Continental Shelf Boundary in the English Channel and South – Western Approaches (1979) 54 International Law Reports 6; Case Concerning Maritime Delimitation and Territorial Questions (Qatar v. Bahrain) (2001) ICJ Reports 68. On different coastal lengths, see Libya/Malta Continental Shelf Case, ibid. ; In the Matter of the Arbitration between Barbados and Trinidad and Tobago, Permanent Court of Arbitration, April 11, 2006, p. 334, http: //www. pca – cpa. org/showpage. asp? pag_id = 1152; and Gulf of Maine Case, Chapter 2, n. 100, above. On the concave nature of a given coastline, North Sea Continental Shelf Cases, n. 59, above. State practice increasingly reflects this approach, including in the Arctic. In 2010, Norway and Russia took "major disparities in the parties' coastal lengths" into account when negotiating the 2010 Barents Sea Treaty. Norwegian Ministry of Foreign Affairs, "The Background to the Treaty," http: //www. regjeringen. no/en/dep/ud/kampanjer/delelinje/forhistorie. html? id = 614274; discussion, Chapter 2, above.

③ e. g., Gulf of Maine Case, Chapter 2, n. 100, above, p. 100, p. 237.

国际法赋予沿海国对大陆架依法享有的所有权的依据在于,沿岸国已对相关领土拥有统治权,而有关海底区域可被视为该领土一部分的事实。也即从某种意义上讲,虽然被水覆盖,但它们仍属于该领土的延伸或延续,是其在海底的扩展。①

大陆架是一国陆地领土自然延伸的观点也被纳入《联合国海洋法公约》,其第七十六条第1款规定:"沿海国的大陆架包括其领海以外依其陆地领土的全部自然延伸,扩展到大陆边外缘的海底区域的海床和底土。"② 这句话导致数个国家根据海底的地质和地貌特征,对200海里内海洋管辖权提出进一步主张。③ 但1985年"利比亚和马耳他案"中,国际法院明确,专属经济区等以相关距离为基础的海洋区域发展表明,地质和地貌特征在相对海岸之间距离小于400海里的海上划界中不起作用。④ 其甚至明确指出,即使存在大陆架根本性断裂的证据也不会影响这种划界。⑤

六、200海里外海上边界划定法律

1985年"利比亚和马耳他案"中的决定引发了对地质和地貌因素与距海岸200海里外的海上边界划分存在多大程度相关性的问题。国际法院指出,距离因素在重叠专属经济区划界中的特殊地位,"并不是讲,自然延伸的理念现在已被距离概念所替代"。⑥ 然而,国际法院没有做出进一步决定来澄清地质和地貌特征是如何影响专属经济区之外的划界问题。

早先通过谈判划定外大陆架界限时,并没有考虑地质和地貌因素,

---

① North Sea Continental Shelf Cases, n. 59, above, p. 31, p. 43.
② Chapter 2, n. 100, above.
③ Gulf of Maine Case, Introduction, n. 15, above; Libya/Malta Continental Shelf Case, n. 67, above; see also Anthony Bergin, "The Australian – Indonesian Timor Gap Maritime Boundary Agreement." (1990) 5 International Journal of Estuarine and Coastal Law 383.
④ Libya/Malta Continental Shelf Case, n. 67, above, pp. 33 – 35, pp. 34 and 39.
⑤ Ibid.
⑥ Ibid.

因为双方对相关海底的特征缺乏足够资料。① 2003 年，在验证七项类似协议之后，戴维·科尔森总结认为它们存在数个共性，适用于 200 海里之内的划界方法在 200 海里之外并没有改变，第七十六条的标准是被用来确定边界的终点而非其走向。② 海底相关信息的不足也是"几内亚和几内亚比绍仲裁案"中仲裁庭在划设外大陆架边界时，没有考虑海底特征的部分原因。③

2004 年澳大利亚和新西兰之间的边界条约似乎考虑了某些 200 海里外的地貌和地质因素，因为新西兰比使用中间线获得了更多海底区域。④ 克莱夫·斯科菲尔德建议，谈判代表们将三王海岭作为新西兰陆地的延伸，尽管新西兰陆地与澳大利亚相关岛屿之间的距离也起到一定作用。⑤

最近，国际海洋法法庭处理了"孟加拉湾案"中孟加拉国和缅甸之间外大陆架划界问题。⑥ 孟加拉国认为，缅甸无权享有外大陆架，因

---

① Australia-France: Agreement on Maritime Delimitation, January 4, 1982, 1329 UNTS 107; Ireland-United Kingdom: Agreement Concerning the Delimitation of Areas of the Continental Shelf, November 7, 1988, 1564 UNTS 218; Trinidad and Tobago-Venezuela: Treaty on the Delimitation of Marine and Submarine Areas, April 18, 1990, 1654 UNTS 301; US-Russia Maritime Boundary Treaty, Chapter 2, n. 20, above. ; United States-Mexico: Treaty on the Delimitation of the Continental Shelf in the Western Gulf of Mexico Beyond 200 Nautical Miles, June 9, 2000, S. Treaty Doc. No. 106 – 39; Treaty between the Government of Australia and the Government of New ZealandEstablishing Certain Exclusive Economic Zone and Continental Shelf Boundaries, July 25, 2004, No. 4 Australia Treaty Series, 2006.

② David Colson, "The Delimitation of the Outer Continental Shelf between Neighboring States." (2003) 97 American Journal of International Law 96.

③ Guinea-Guinea Bissau Arbitration, n. 55, above, p. 300.

④ Australia-New Zealand Maritime Boundary Agreement, n. 77, above.

⑤ Clive Schofield, "Australia's Final Frontiers?: Developments in the Delimitation of Australia's International Maritime Boundaries." (2008) 158 Maritime Studies 2 at 6. It is noteworthy that Australia relies on a natural prolongation argument elsewhere, in its delimitation with Indonesia, where it continues to press for the boundary to follow the Timor Trough between it and Timor – Leste. Bergin, n. 73, above.

⑥ Dispute Concerning Delimitation of the Maritime Boundary between Bangladesh and Myanmar in the Bay of Bengal (Bangladesh/Myanmar), International Tribunal for the Law of the Sea, Case No. 16, March 14, 2012, p. 76, p. 240, http://www.itlos.org/fileadmin/itlos/documents/cases/case_no_16/C16_Judgment_14_03_2012_rev.pdf.

为存在地质上的中断,在距缅甸海岸 200 海里范围内,孟加拉湾的海床和缅甸陆地之间存在构造板块边界。① 孟加拉国的立场是,《联合国海洋法公约》第七十六条第 1 款提及"自然延伸"是为了提出一个地质解释,与缅甸不存在自然地理上的亲密关系的大陆架区域不可能属于该国管辖范围,例如处于板块边界之外。法庭否定了该论点,指出"第七十六条第 1 款中没有对自然延伸的概念做出详细说明",② 法庭不能接受自然延伸"构成某个沿海国为获得 200 海里外某个大陆架必须满足的一个区分和独立的标准"。③ 法庭认为,《联合国海洋法公约》第七十六条涉及的问题是,"某沿海国大陆架是延伸至大陆边的外缘还是延伸至 200 海里距离,这将取决于外缘的位置。"④ 由于《联合国海洋法公约》依据相关海床的地貌特征,给出了大陆架外部界限的定义,因此应根据这一定义来确定其影响。缅甸能够证明该国和孟加拉湾海床之间存在地貌连续性,因为沉积物已覆盖板块构造边界,所以有资格拥有 200 海里外的大陆架区域。此外,那些沉积物的来源对孟加拉国和缅甸主张外大陆架权利而言都不重要。

"孟加拉湾案"的法庭据此认为,其必须对各方存在重叠主张的大陆架进行划分。至关重要的是,法庭决定"该案中 200 海里之外大陆架划设的方法不应与 200 海里内的方法存在不同。因此,'等距线/相关情况'的方法继续适用于 200 海里外大陆架划界",因而拒绝了孟加拉国在地质上的进一步论点,即孟加拉湾构造成分和沉积物来源构成了一个特殊情况,因为它们更自然地与孟加拉国领土联系在一起。法庭决定,与 200 海里内依据海岸地理因素调整等距线相同的理由,也适用于该线

---

① Dispute Concerning Delimitation of the Maritime Boundary between Bangladesh and Myanmar in the Bay of Bengal (Bangladesh/Myanmar), International Tribunal for the Law of the Sea, Case No. 16, March 14, 2012, p. 76, p. 240, http://www.itlos.org/fileadmin/itlos/documents/cases/case_no_16/C16_Judgment_14_03_2012_rev.pdf, p. 112, p. 417.

② Ibid., p. 432.

③ Ibid., p. 435. This part of the decision was not unanimous. e.g., Judge Gao's separate decision, http://www.itlos.org/fileadmin/itlos/documents/cases/case_no_16/C16.sep_op.Gao.rev.Ewith_maps.pdf.

④ Ibid., p. 126, p. 429.

在 200 海里外部分的调整。①

总而言之，国际海洋法法庭已经帮助澄清了 200 海里内的地质因素在外大陆架权利和 200 海里外海上划界中的作用。海床的地貌而不是它与陆地的地质关系，决定了一个沿海国家的权利是否延伸至专属经济区以外。然而，在相邻或相对国家就共享大陆架进行划界的情况中，需要考虑的实质因素是海岸线的特征而非地貌。

但是，"孟加拉湾案"中没有涉及海岭或隆起的情况。正如第四章中详细解释的，在有关海岭的情况中，沿海国家权利限于距离海岸350 海里，而在隆起中的情况则不是。隆起与海岭不同，它是"大陆架的自然组成部分"，可以使用"2500 米等深线加 100 海里"的控制线。② 在波弗特海西部区域，被称为楚科奇海台的大型海底地物似乎延伸至距离海岸超过 350 海里之处。早在 1980 年，美国就表示，根据《联合国海洋法公约》，楚科奇海台属于隆起，因而不受 350 海里的限制。③

目前，外大陆架划界的判例法和国家实践仍过于有限和多变，无法明确表明从通常陆地边界一侧的大陆边扩展出的某个隆起，是否以及如何可被负责划定海上边界的国际法庭或仲裁庭视为具有相关性。然而，加拿大和美国已经合作测绘了该地区的外大陆架，这意味着缺乏信息不会成为在谈判或司法途径中使用地貌和地质特征的阻碍。

七、潜在谈判立场

（一）单方面承认他国立场

先前概述的一个奇特现象，即加拿大和美国各自在 200 海里之内的

---

① Ibid., p. 435. This part of the decision was not unanimous. e. g., Judge Gao's separate decision, http：//www.itlos.org/fileadmin/itlos/documents/cases/case_no_16/C16.sep_op.Gao.rev.Ewith_maps.pdf, p. 133, p. 461.

② Introduction, n. 15, above, Art. 76（6）.

③ Elliot Richardson, US Ambassador, "Statement," April 3, 1980（1981）13 Official Records of the Third United Nations Conference on the Law of the Sea 43.

法律立场若延伸至专属经济区之外的话，将事实上有利于对方国家，这可能有助于迅速解决波弗特海边界争端。任何国家都可以单方面承认对方立场，明确表明其既适用于 200 海里之内，也适用于 200 海里之外。这一举动将会率先阻止另一方对自身立场的任何改变，或许还可以劝阻其主张对两个区域应当分别适用不同的划界方法。然而，这将要求该国采取行动，接受用专属经济区内尚未确定的损失（或收益）换取外大陆架的收益（或损失）。这种不确定性来自于数个因素：更好的冰况、更浅的水域、与海岸设施距离更短，很可能会使 200 海里内争议三角区域比专属经济区以外新的和尚不明确的三角区域更为具有现实价值。此外，在进行地震调查和将测试井沉入这两个三角之前，油气资源的存在和位置仍然具有推测性。另一个不确定性因素存在于外三角，即大陆架实际上可以合法延伸多远的距离。在这些情况下，一方做出单方面承认的可能性不是很大，而美国和加拿大之间就海床测绘进行的合作将会具有新的重要性。

对 200 海里外海床进行更为详细的科学认知，再加上对外大陆架重要的新认识，可能会导致各国重新制定法律立场，以为严肃谈判作准备。另一选择是，各方可维持在专属经济区内的立场，并在不同法律论点之上提出对外大陆架的观点。然而，如上文所述，加拿大现有的立场并不适用于这种区别，因为它依据的是一项条约中的经线，该线在 200 海里限制概念提出之前 150 年既已存在。若加拿大是正确的，也即 1825 年条约旨在划定一条海洋边界，那么这条边界线除受到国家管辖范围的最终制约外，将不存在任何符合逻辑的终点。

（二）海岸长度

在坚持西经 141°经线上立场的同时，加拿大可能还会提出另一种观点，即接受等距线原则，但对海岸地理作出有利于加拿大的解释。该方法中的第一个要素涉及海岸长度。

在数个海上边界划定案中，海岸长度已被认为属于一种相关情况。在"扬马延案"中，国际法院认识到在划定边界线时，必须考虑海岸线长度的重大差异。① 法院在"利比亚和马耳他案"②和"缅因湾案"③中也得出了类似结论,"巴巴多斯和特立尼达和多巴哥仲裁案"④的仲裁庭也是如此。在"缅因湾案"中,即使是加拿大和美国在海岸长度上存在 1.38 比 1⑤的相对较小差异,也影响了部分边界线的位置选择,尽管该区域的一般特征进一步证实了这一结论。在所有其他案件中,都存在更大差异。⑥

在"黑海案"中,乌克兰海岸线长度是罗马尼亚的 2.8 倍,但是国际法院驳回了乌克兰的观点,即更长的海岸线有权在划界区域中享有更大份额。⑦ 重要的是,法庭明确认为海岸长度具有相关性,可是乌克兰的海岸线虽然更长,但其若干部分却投射到了相同海上区域,因而属于"强化了但没有在空间上扩大乌克兰的权利"。⑧ 在所有这些案件中,法院一直谨慎地强调,海岸长度不能以任何数学上机械的方式决定一个国家在近海的权利。

然而,数学计算是法院适用于划界第三步验证中比例性测试的核心内容。在此阶段,法院已经计算了各方海岸长度与争端部分长度之比,并将其与拟议的边界线授予两国的海上区域范围进行比较,以确定不存在显失公平。⑨

尽管在"巴巴多斯和特立尼达和多巴哥仲裁案"中海岸长度发挥

---

① Jan Mayen Case, Chapter 2, n. 35, above, p. 69.
② Libya/Malta Continental Shelf Case, n. 67, above, p. 68.
③ Gulf of Maine Case, Chapter 2, n. 100, above, p. 218.
④ In the Matter of the Arbitration between Barbados and Trinidad and Tobago, n. 69, above.
⑤ Gulf of Maine Case, Chapter 2, n. 100, above, p. 222. The ratio was 1.32 to 1 when Seal and Mud Islands were included.
⑥ Trinidad and Tobago had cited the difference between its coastal length and that of Barbados as being of a ratio of 8.2∶1. In the Matter of the Arbitration between Barbados and Trinidad and Tobago, n. 69, above, p. 326. In the Libya/Malta Continental Shelf Case, n. 67, above, p. 68, the International Court of Justice calculated the length of Malta's relevant coasts at twenty-four miles as opposed to 192 miles for those of Libya. In the 2012 Nicaragua-Columbia Case, n. 65, above, the ratio was 8.2 to 1 in favor of Nicaragua yet the adjudicated line is only three times further from Nicaragua than from the Colombian islands.
⑦ Black Sea Case, Chapter 2, n. 82, above, p. 215.
⑧ Ibid., p. 168.
⑨ For a discussion of the three-stage formula, see above, p. 69.

了作用，但海岸长度对外大陆架划界的相关性尚不清楚。① 然而，仲裁庭明确表示，特立尼达和多巴哥较长的海岸线具有相关性，仅因为其直接毗邻划界区域。② 明确哪段海岸线与划界区域相关是在确定海岸长度以及结果比例方面的关键一步。例如，加拿大或可争辩称，其高北极岛屿西北侧翼的长度和阿拉斯加北部海岸线长度之间的差异表明，需要对临时等距线进行有利于加拿大的调整。然而，美国可以反对称，加拿大群岛之间的中断部分不能作为海岸线以计算长度，只有加拿大海岸线上较短的一段与划界相关。

不同案例已经明确如何确定与划界有关的海岸线。在"突尼斯和利比亚案"中，国际法院写道：

> 双方各自海岸上都有一个点，超过该点的海岸就不再与对方海岸就海床划界存在相关性。超过该点的沿海海底区域因此构成双方外大陆架重叠区域，并因此与划界无关。③

法院接着定义了海岸的相关长度，端点位于突尼斯海岸的卡布迪亚角以及利比亚海岸的塔佐拉角，这两处都是海岸线与划界区域稍微偏离的地方。④ 在"黑海案"中，法院同样无视乌克兰海岸的某些部分，因为它们没有朝向划界区域。⑤ 因此，有观点会认为，加拿大海岸线与划界相关的部分仅是加拿大大陆、班克斯岛西岸，也许还有帕特里克王子岛西南角。类似的，可以提出美国海岸线的相关部分仅延伸至巴罗角，在这里海岸线开始远离波弗特海。在这些情形中，海岸长度的差异是最小的，并可以认为是无关紧要的。

(三) 岛屿的相关性

岛屿对边界线位置的影响是海上边界划分中长期存在的问题。如第

---

① In the Matter of the Arbitration between Barbados and Trinidad and Tobago, n. 69, above.
② Ibid., p. 331.
③ Case Concerning the Continental Shelf (Libya v. Tunisia) (1982) ICJ Reports 62, p. 75.
④ Ibid.
⑤ Black Sea Case, Chapter 2, n. 82, above, p. 99.

二章所述,"岛屿"(island)能够产生一整套从属于其自身的海洋区域,而不能维持人类居住或其本身经济生活的"岩礁"(rocks)只能拥有领海。① 面积为 7 万平方公里的班克斯岛,却明确享有其自身的大陆架和专属经济区。由此,该岛海岸线对任何等距线位置的影响都具有合理性。尽管国际法院和仲裁庭没有给予大陆国家远离海岸线的岛屿完全效力,只有在那些岛屿与海岸线之间符合一定距离限制或距离非常小的情况下,才能够产生相关影响。例如,"英国和法国仲裁案"中将海峡群岛作为飞地,因为该群岛远离法国海岸并且与英国存在一定距离,因而远远超出英吉利海峡中间线需要考虑的范围。② 与此相反,班克斯岛距离维多利亚岛不足 24 海里,而维多利亚岛本身距离加拿大大陆不超过 12 海里。此外,班克斯岛本身亦不是一个无足轻重的地物,它的存在将给等距线造成重要异常,否则等距线仍将由两国大陆海岸决定。

(四)海岸线的凹陷

海岸线的最后一个特征可能使得任何临时等距线都按照有利于加拿大的方式进行调整。大陆海岸在阿拉斯加和育空之间陆地边界终点以东马更些河的河口变得凹陷。再考虑到班克斯岛海岸线的情况时,海岸的凹陷程度将变得更为明显。海岸线凹陷已被国际法院认可为海上边界划分中的一个相关因素,特别是在德国和丹麦、德国和荷兰的"北海大陆架案"中,各国海岸线长度均差不多。③ 法庭表示:"在这种情况中不可接受的因素是,一国应享有的大陆架权利与其邻国存在相当大的不同。而这种不同仅是因为一方海岸线形状凸出,而另一方海岸线明显凹陷,尽管海岸线的长度类似。"④ 法庭的结论是,在修正了德国海岸线凹陷属性的公平解决方案中,可以通过在"相关海岸两个端点之间"划设一条直线基线,并在此基础上设立一条边界,而不是使用现实中的

---

① Introduction, n. 15, above, Art. 121. For a discussion of 'rocks' and 'islands' in the context of the Lincoln Sea, Chapter 2, above.
② Anglo – French Arbitration (1979) 18 ILM 397, p. 202.
③ For a similar, more recent result, Dispute Concerning Delimitation of the Maritime Boundary between Bangladesh and Myanmar in the Bay of Bengal, n. 82, above, pp. 290 – 297.
④ North Sea Continental Shelf Cases, n. 59, above, p. 50, p. 91.

德国海岸线。① 相较于使用等距线的情况，这种方法为德国提供了更为可观的海洋空间。

如果加拿大争辩称必须考虑该国海岸线的凹陷程度，并采取类似方法，那么接下来的问题就是这个"封闭线"的端点应置于何处，因为这些点决定了该线向海方向可达到的距离。一种可能是使用阿蒙森湾入口南侧的巴瑟斯特角作为东部端点，由此引出一条向西延伸至加拿大和美国陆地边界终点的线。如果该封闭线和从西经141°经线至巴罗港的阿拉斯加海岸随后被视为具有相关性的海岸，那么它们将具有大致相等的长度。这种方法将使加拿大在距离海岸200海里内受益，同时可能使得美国在这个距离以外的区域受益，因为班克斯岛将被从等距线的计算中移除。无论采取何种方式，海岸凹陷程度或许将在加拿大谈判立场中扮演重要角色，而波弗特海争端与"北海大陆架案"的不同之处在于加拿大在划界区域的两侧均没有处于不利位置。

（五）加拿大对专属经济区以外区域的立场

考虑到楚科奇海台的存在，西经141°经线美国一侧的大陆架自然延伸似乎比加拿大一侧更远。② 然而，加拿大可以提出大陆架制度应具有统一性，其结果就是地质和地貌因素与划界没有相关性，将相同的划界原则同时适用于200海里内外。如上所述，这正是海洋法法庭在"孟加拉湾案"中就地质、地貌和国际法适用问题所做出的总结。③ 只有存在两个明显不同的大陆边时，地质和地貌问题才可能会在大陆架划界中发挥作用，在涉及相对国家的情形下经常如此，但在涉及相邻国家的情形中则较少。由于这个原因，加拿大可能将至少对楚科奇海台拥有部分主权，这时等距线（特别是经修改的）将横跨该地物。

然而，这一结果也取决于《联合国海洋法公约》第七十六条第5款的适用，如第四章所释，该款对沿海国外大陆架的外部界限设置了一系列限制。因此，有可能加拿大的管辖权止于楚科奇海台以东某处，而

---

① North Sea Continental Shelf Cases, n. 59, above, p. 52, p. 98.
② discussion, above, p. 74.
③ discussion, above, pp. 72 – 74.

不考虑可能存在的共同大陆边。

（六）《因努维阿勒伊特最终协议》：一个复杂因素

加拿大在改变对波弗特海国际边界位置立场问题上确实面临重要的国内障碍。1984 年，在宪法承认的土地权利协议《因努维阿勒伊特最终协议》中，加拿大政府使用西经 141 度经线确定因努维阿勒伊特人安置区的西部边界。① 在安置区内，特别是被称为"育空北坡"的区域，包括国际陆地边界终点东北部的近海，加拿大承认因努维阿勒伊特人对渔业、博彩业的收益权并承诺保护该地区。②

根据国际法，加拿大可以与美国签订海上边界条约，该条约可以无视因努维阿勒伊特人的国内权利，并具有效力和约束力。③ 但是，根据加拿大法律，联邦政府有义务进行协商，以最大限度减少任何对原住民权利的侵犯，并通过议会法案明确此类限制措施和提供补偿。④ 因此，

---

① 1984 Inuvialuit Final Agreement (as amended), http：//www. daair. gov. nt. ca/_live/documents/documentManagerUpload/InuvialuitFinalAgreement1984. pdf. Under section 35 of the Constitution Act 1982, "rights that now exist by way of land claims agreements or may be so acquired" are "recognized and affirmed." http：//laws. justice. gc. ca/eng/Const/page – 12. html#sc：7_II.

② Inuvialuit Final Agreement, ibid., especially at sec. 12 (2): "The Yukon North Slope shall fall under a special conservation regime whose dominant purpose is the conservation of wildlife, habitat and traditional native use." Curiously, the Inuvialuit Settlement Area extends more than 600 nautical miles northward into the Beaufort Sea, well beyond Canada's exclusive jurisdiction over the living resources of the EEZ, though it is unclear whether Canada (in 1984 or at any time since) purports to exercise any exclusive jurisdiction beyond 200 nautical miles. For a map of the InuvialuitSettlement Area, http：//www. aadnc – aandc. gc. ca/eng/1100100031121/1100100031129#chp7.

③ Vienna Convention on the Law of Treaties, Chapter 2, n. 27, above, Art. 46 (1): "A State may not invoke the fact that its consent to be bound by a treaty has been expressed in violation of a provision of its internal law regarding competence to conclude treaties as invalidating its consent unless that violation was manifest and concerned a rule of its internal law of fundamental importance."

④ the Constitution Act 1982, n. 111, above, sec. 35; R. v. Sparrow, [1990] SCR 20 (Canada); Haida Nation v. British Columbia (Minister of Forests), [2004] SCR 73; and MikisewCree First Nation v. Canada (Minister of Canadian Heritage), [2005] SCR 69. In 2010, the Nunavut Supreme Court issued an injunction against seismic testing in Lancaster Sound on the grounds that the obligation to consult had not been fulfilled. See discussion, Chapter 7, below; Josh Wingrove, "Lancaster Sound: A Seismic Victory for the Inuit," Globe and Mail, August 14, 2010, http：//www. theglobeandmail. com/news/politics/lancaster – sound – a – seismic – victory – for – the – inuit/article1377067/.

加拿大政府最好同因努维阿勒伊特人就边界划定进行密切和持续的协商，并在与美国谈判中尽可能避免就边界线位置问题作出妥协。

例如，加拿大可以提出《因努维阿勒伊特最终协议》属于相关情况，需要据此调整任何向西的临时等距线。美国可能回应称，该协议于边界争端"关键日期"之后8年才达成，在"关键日期"之后支持一方或另一方立场的后续措施对法律分析而言都是无关紧要的。① 加拿大接着可以辩称，该协议只是承认了1976年之前加拿大公民中已经存在的土著人权利。

事实上，因努维阿勒伊特人长期以来一直在波弗特海中猎捕海豹、白鲸和露脊鲸，每年固定时间还会在冰上旅行和生活。② 国际法院在"西撒哈拉案"中承认了土著人民获得和转让主权权利的能力，尽管该案不涉及海上边界。③ 也许"巴巴多斯和特立尼达和多巴哥仲裁案"中的决定更值得关注，仲裁庭认为对一个区域的历史性使用不足以作为修改一条等距线的理由，除非一方绝大部分人口依赖那里的渔业资源。④ 不仅如此，仲裁庭还总结称，在边界线划设之后，各方可就跨界进入权利进行谈判，事实上这也是法律规定，作为《联合国海洋法公约》对各国施加的就保护和开发跨界渔业资源的措施达成一致义务的一部分。⑤

为此，波弗特海边界谈判的一个可能结果是，在加拿大因努维阿勒伊特人与美国政府之间就西经141度经线和该线以东两国协商达成边界之间的区域创设新的权利和义务。这样的协议将使加拿大政府可以在距

---

① On the critical date principle, references, Chapter 1, n. 9, above.

② That said, the Inupiat, the closely related indigenous people on the US side of the boundary, have also engaged in hunting and fishing activities in the disputed area.

③ Western Sahara, Advisory Opinion (1975) ICJ Reports 12, p. 79, recognizing that territories inhabited by indigenous peoples having a measure of social and political organization are not terra nullius, and thus conferring a limited but no less real international legal status on such groups.

④ In the Matter of the Arbitration between Barbados and Trinidad and Tobago, n. 69, above, p. 327.

⑤ Ibid. Also, in the Qatar-Bahrain Case, n. 69, above, p. 236, the Court found that pearling banks were not a relevant circumstance for adjusting a line, even though the Bahrainis argued they had predominantly engaged in diving there.

海岸200海里范围内做出让步,作为交换,美国可在200海里之外的海域做出让步。但为实现这一结果,需要将因努维阿勒伊特人纳入谈判。

(七)美国对专属经济区之外区域的立场

如上所述,1980年一名美国外交官表示,楚科奇海台是海底隆起,对其主权权利可以延伸至距海岸350海里之外。① 美国现在可以采取这样的立场,即一条等距线,无论是否经过调整,只适用于200海里内,而地质和地貌特征应决定更远的边界。该立场得到国际法院在"利比亚和马耳他案"② 中声明的支持,并与国际海洋法法庭在"孟加拉湾案"中的决定不矛盾。③

或者,美国可以提出波弗特海属于相对大陆架的情形。科尔森认为,在这种情况下,应依据陆坡脚的位置划定延伸范围,并在两者之间划设等距线。④ 尽管这种方法在两国属于完全相对位置时是可行的,但在波弗特海这种双方基本上处于一种"相邻和相对"混合关系的情况中,该方法就不那么容易移植了。班克斯岛和帕特里克王子岛或多或少位于阿拉斯加东北部海岸的相对一侧,但是这种相对位置是这两个岛在两国陆地边界附近与阿拉斯加海岸线处于一段相当长的相邻位置之后才出现。

最后,美国或加拿大中的一方可能提出界限是直至某点的相邻海岸关系的产物,同时也是该点之外海岸线相对关系的产物,并据此就200海里之内和之外的边界线位置提出异议。国际法院在"缅因湾案"⑤ 和"突尼斯和利比亚案"⑥ 中采纳了这种方法,尽管相对和相邻划界相关因素之间的区别近期已经变得模糊。⑦

---

① Richardson, n. 89, above. For more on submarine elevations, Chapter 4, below.
② Libya/Malta Continental Shelf Case, n. 67, above, p. 34.
③ Dispute Concerning Delimitation of the Maritime Boundary between Bangladesh and Myanmar in the Bay of Bengal, n. 82, above.
④ Colson, n. 78, above.
⑤ Gulf of Maine Case, Chapter 2, n. 100, above, p. 216.
⑥ Tunisia-Libya Case, n. 101, above, p. 126.
⑦ In the Matter of the Arbitration between Barbados and Trinidad and Tobago, n. 69, above, p. 315.

八、美国和加拿大的合作选项

上述可能的公开谈判立场中没有一个必然会缩小争议区域的面积。但是，大多数国家认为谈判是解决重叠海上主张的最佳途径。谈判可使当事方保持对划界进程的控制，并考虑法院或仲裁庭所允许的严格适用法律之外的更多因素。① 也就是说，以往海上边界谈判的结果表明，最终结果将或多或少地分割当事双方各自主张中存在差异的区域，无论这些主张是否基于本书所述的立场。在目前谈判变得愈发困难的情况下，当事方可以考虑几个更具创新性的选项，特别是在加拿大于 2013 年启动加入大陆架界限委员会进程之际。

（一）加拿大向大陆架界限委员会提交初步或部分划界案

大陆架界限委员会可以就向其提交的竞争性划界案中外大陆架区域的科学数据是否充分提出建议。但是，这种建议不影响现有海上划界事项，另一争端国总是可以向大陆架界限委员会提出，由于存在争议该程序不能继续进行。② 考虑到大陆架界限委员会被一个争端当事国阻碍的风险，沿海国可选择提交"表明外部界限的初步信息……以及准备情况概述和提交划界案的预期日期"。③ 此外，沿海国可选择部分提交划界案，不包括争议区域的数据，从而满足在 10 年内提交的要求，保证其在划界案审查队列中的位置，以及使得大陆架界限委员会可以继续审查

---

① Litigation or arbitration of the Beaufort Sea dispute seems particularly unlikely given US disappointment over the result in the 1984 Gulf of Maine Case. See A. L. Springer, "Do Fences Make Good Neighbours? The Gulf of Maine Revisited." (1994) 6 International Environmental Affairs 231; and McDorman, n. 11, above, pp. 148 – 149.

② Introduction, n. 15, above, Art. 76 (10).

③ Eighteenth Meeting of the States Parties, "Decision Regarding the Workload of the Commission and the Ability of States to Fulfil the Requirements of Article 4 of Annex II," Doc. SPLOS/183, June 20, 2008, paragraph 1, http: //www. un. org/Depts/los/meeting_states_parties/SPLOS_documents. htm. This document records the decision, by the parties to UNCLOS, that a preliminary submission is sufficient to meet the expectation of a submission within ten years of ratifying.

已经提交数据的那些区域。① 2013 年加拿大准备提交申请时将考虑这两个选项。尽管乍一看该方案似乎具有吸引力,但不幸的是,这种方法将外大陆架的外部界限问题遗留在一个单独区域中,而在此区域中,大陆架界限委员会有意避免的海上区域不确定性和潜在争议问题已然存在并将进一步恶化。②

(二)美国向大陆架界限委员会发出"无异议声明"

各国有时会同意不就大陆架界限委员会考虑争议区域的相关数据提出反对。尽管委员会迄今为止一直有意将沉默视为同意,但在理想情况下,此类同意会通过"无异议声明"的方式主动发送给大陆架界限委员会。挪威同意大陆架界限委员会审查俄罗斯2002年提交的首次划界案,2009年西非国家经济共同体一些成员国同意就外大陆架界限问题向大陆架界限委员会发出无异议声明。③ 提供此类声明往往符合一国利益,因为大陆架界限委员会的建议将明确沿岸国管辖权影响的最大区域,因而也是可供各方谈判的区域。如果美国和加拿大不能就更广泛的合作达成一致,他们最好采取这种方法,即前者向大陆架界限委员会发送对后者提交划界案的无异议声明。

---

① The Commission on the Limits of the Continental Shelf (CLCS) has indicated that submissions will be "queued in the order they are received." "Statement by the Chairman of the Commission on the Limits of the Continental Shelf on the Progress of Work in the Commission, 6 October 2006," at p. 38, http: // daccess - dds - ny. un. org/doc/UNDOC/GEN/N06/558/82/PDF/N0655882. pdf? Open Element. Alex G. Oude Elferink and Constance Johnson, "Outer Limits of the Continental Shelf and 'Disputed Areas': State Practice Concerning Article 76 (10) of the LOS Convention." (2004) 21 International Journal of Marine and Coastal Law 466. Cf. Bjørn Kunoy, "Disputed Areas and the 10 - Year Time Frame: A Legal Lacuna?" (2010) 41 Ocean Development and International Law 112.

② Lathrop, n. 20, above.

③ Permanent Mission of Norway to the Secretary - General of the United Nations, "Norway: Notification Regarding the Submission Made by the Russian Federation to the Commission on the Limits of the Continental Shelf," 2002, http: //www. un. org/Depts/los/clcs _ new/submissions _ files/rus01/CLCS_01_2001_LOS__NORtext. pdf; Lathrop, n. 20, above, p. 4155.

（三）加拿大和美国使用"特殊区域"的方式使联合专属经济区权利最大化

海上边界谈判中，在一国拥有管辖权而另一国没有管辖权的区域中，某些情况下可以将权利通过条约方式，由第一个国家授予给第二个国家，以便将保留这些管辖权利作为谈判一揽子方案的一部分。如第二章中所释，沿美国和苏联通过1990年条约在白令海边界确立的数个点确定边界线，该线距离苏联（现为俄罗斯）海岸线小于200海里，但是距离美国海岸线大于200海里。[1] 可以说，这样一条边界线具有把苏联专属经济区的外缘部分变为公海的效力。为避免这种可能的结果，谈判代表指定了数个"特别区域"，苏联将其专属经济区权利分配给美国，尽管那些权利是由苏联海岸线产生的。挪威和俄罗斯在2010年《巴伦支海条约》中采用了相同的方法，将距离挪威海岸线200海里内，但位于新边界线东部的海域明确分配给俄罗斯，即使该区域距俄罗斯海岸超过200海里。[2]

如果美国和加拿大就波弗特海等距线以西的边界进行谈判，那么在距离海岸200海里之内的区域也可以采取类似方法。由于这段海岸线凹陷的自然状态，这条线的改变将导致美国海岸线200海里范围内，目前美国主张的专属经济区内的一小片水域成为公海。[3] 这种权利的转移无需将该区域的海底权利划归加拿大管辖，因为它们可能将作为外大陆架而归属加拿大。然而，处理这种情况的最简单方式是，美国在边界条约中加入一个小的"特别区域"，将某些专属经济区权利让渡给加拿大。

（四）多功能划界

加拿大和美国可能会寻求通过谈判达成一项多功能划界条约，为不同区域划设不同边界线。澳大利亚和巴布亚新几内亚在《1978年托雷斯海峡条约》中就采取这样一种方式，为开放水体和海底资源权利划定

---

[1] US-Russia Maritime Boundary Treaty, Chapter 2, n. 20, above.
[2] Norway-Russia Barents Sea and Arctic Ocean Maritime Boundary Agreement, Chapter 2, n. 63, above, Art. 3.
[3] the map, above, p. 61.

了不同边界。① 此方法可能会满足《因努维阿勒伊特最终协议》中所承诺的一些权利。例如，如果加拿大保留开发直至西经 141 度经线和 200 海里外水体中资源的主权权利，即使美国对海底部分拥有管辖权，因努维阿勒伊特人食物收获权仍将称得上是完好无损。② 然而，同样有争议的是，这种妥协中加拿大所享有的管辖权将无法满足其对因努维阿勒伊特人的所有义务，例如保护他们狩猎和捕鱼权利不受石油和天然气勘探活动的不利影响。③ 与此类似的问题或许可以解释为什么《托雷斯海峡条约》是谈判达成单一海上边界一般实践的罕见例外。④

（五）经济准入权利条款

如上所述，如果加拿大和美国希望在因努维阿勒伊特安置区划定边界，妥协的一部分可能是美国同意加拿大因努维阿勒伊特人在直至西经 141 度经线继续行使传统权利，尽管事实上至少有一部分因努维阿勒伊特安置区将属于美国海上管辖区域。在世界的其他地方，各国有时会在划定海上边界之后，通常会同意邻国国民在有限期限之内继续在其水域内捕鱼，以使捕鱼业可以逐步适应新环境。⑤《托雷斯海峡条约》中就采取了这种办法，在该条约中，托雷斯海峡岛民和巴布亚新几内亚沿海民众有权在特定的保护区中继续他们的传统活动，不用考虑两国边界。⑥ 同样，经济准入权可能无法满足《因努维阿勒伊特最终协议》的

---

① Torres Strait Treaty (Australia-Papua New Guinea), No. 4, 1985 Australia Treaty Series.
② discussion, above, pp. 80 – 82.
③ e. g. , Inuvialuit Final Agreement, n. 111, above, Art. 13 (12): "The Government agrees that every proposed development of consequence to the Inuvialuit Settlement Region that is within its jurisdiction and that could have a significant negative impact on wildlife habitat or on present or future wildlife harvesting will be authorized only after due scrutiny of and attention to all environmental concerns and subject to reasonable mitigative and remedial provisions being imposed. "
④ In the Matter of the Arbitration between Barbados and Trinidad and Tobago, n. 69, above, p. 235.
⑤ For example, the China-Vietnam Fisheries Agreement, which accompanied the 2000 Gulf of Tonkin Boundary Treaty, provides for a transitional period of four years to enable Chinese fishermen to adjust to new fishing patterns. Zou Keyuan, "The Sino-Vietnamese Agreement on Maritime Boundary Delimitation in the Gulf of Tonkin. " (2005) 36 Ocean Development and International Law 16 – 21.
⑥ Torres Strait Treaty, n. 136, above, Art. 10.

全部要求，但它们可以有助于确保该协议成为一项新边界协议，这对于加拿大政府而言同样重要。

（六）联合开发安排

泰德·麦克道曼曾写道："波弗特海边界争端长期被视为建立某种石油和天然气资源联合开发制度的备选区域。"① 如上文所述，加拿大和美国在20世纪70年代海上边界谈判时，曾考虑在波弗特海设立一种联合开发区域。② 有关白鲸和北极熊的更大区域范围内的联合开发制度已经适用于一些争议区域，尽管这些协议是由边界两侧的土著人民以及阿拉斯加人达成，而不是在加拿大和美国政府之间实现。③

在世界其他地方，石油和天然气联合开发安排是解决海上边界争端的一种相对流行的做法。无论是否实现最终划界，均可以采取这些方法。黑兹尔·福克斯等人已就此提出三种通用类型：

模式一：国家或其国民之间的强制性联合经营制度；

模式二：具有许可和监管权力的联合机构代表各国管理联合开发区的开发活动。

模式三：由一国代表双方管理联合区域开发活动，另一国只参与收

---

① McDorman, n. 11, above, p. 188, citing as examples Dawn Russell, "International Ocean Boundary Issues and Management Arrangements," in David VanderZwaag (ed.), Canadian Ocean Law and Policy (Toronto: Butterworths, 1992), 496 – 498; Donald M. McRae, "Canada and the Delimitation of Maritime Boundaries," in Donald M. McRae and Gordon Munro (eds.), Canadian Oceans Policy: National Strategies and the New Law of the Sea (Vancouver, University of British Columbia Press, 1989), 159 – 160; and Donald R. Rothwell, Maritime Boundaries and Resource Development: Options for the Beaufort Sea (Calgary: Canadian Institute of Resources Law, 1988), 45 – 57.

② McDorman, n. 11, above, p. 189, explains: "The idea was that shared – access zones would be created adjacent to a negotiated maritime boundary. Although each State would have exclusive authority over the hydrocarbon activities within the zone on its side of the maritime boundary, each State would have a right of purchase to obtain one – half of the volume of the hydrocarbons produced within each shared – access zone."

③ Marie Adams, Kathryn J. Frostz, and Lois A. Harwood, "Alaska and Inuvialuit Beluga Whale Committee (AIBWC) -An Initiative in At Home Management." (1993) 46 Arctic 134; and Inuvialuit-Inupiat Polar Bear Management Agreement in the Southern Beaufort Sea, 2000, http：//pbsg. npolar. no/en/agreements/USA – Canada. html. See also, discussion, Chapter 6, below.

第三章 波弗特海边界

入分成和监督。[1]

实际上,这些模式只是单纯类型,他们之间可能存在大量重叠。每一种类型还包含派往联合机构的不同层级代表和将其适用于联合开发区时进行协调立法的问题。这些问题对于选择谈判达成某种形式联合开发制度的国家而言可能很重要,但是无论采取何种形式,就这些细节问题达成协议的困难有时与划定最终边界的困难同样显著。[2] 也就是讲,无论各方能否就最终边界位置达成一致,联合开发都有实现的可能性。

如第二章所释,1981年冰岛和挪威关于冰岛和扬马延边界的条约和2010年挪威和俄罗斯关于巴伦支海的条约,都为跨界石油和天然气矿床联合管理制度创设了诸多体系。[3] 即使双方通过谈判只能缩小有争议区域的范围,也可以考虑引入联合开发机制。[4] 最后,"模式三"(由一国代表双方管理开发活动)可能会成为加拿大维护其在《因努维阿勒伊特最终协议》中所做承诺的一种创造性方法。简而言之,加拿大可在与因努维阿勒伊特人协商后,管理争议区域南部的开发活动,并且只需向美国支付此处开采活动的一部分收入。

---

[1] Hazel Fox, et al., Joint Development of Offshore Oil and Gas: A Model Agreement for States for Joint Development with Explanatory Commentary (London: British Institute of International and Comparative Law, 1989).

[2] This situation is exemplified by the difficulties in setting up a "model 2" joint development zone between Thailand and Malaysia, which led to an eleven – year hiatus between the signing of the memorandum of understanding that expressed a desire for cooperation and its actual implementation in a considerably watered – down form. See David M. Ong, "The 1979 and 1990 Malaysia-Thailand Joint Development Agreements: A Model for International Legal Co – operation in Common Offshore Petroleum Deposits?" (1999) 14 International Journal of Marine and Coastal Law 207.

[3] Agreement on the Continental Shelf between Iceland and Jan Mayen, n. 36, above; Norway-Russia Barents Sea and Arctic Ocean Maritime Boundary Agreement, Chapter 2, n. 63, above, Annex II.

[4] This seems to have been the intent of the negotiators during the 1977 talks on the Beaufort Sea boundary who failed to reach agreement "as regards the number, size or configuration" of shared access zones. Lorne Clark, n. 24, above, p. 13, cited in McDorman n. 11, above, p. 189.

九、俄罗斯和加拿大波弗特海海上边界？

最后一个令人好奇的问题是美国和加拿大在波弗特海任何划界会产生的影响，也即加拿大和俄罗斯之间可能发生的边界争端。正如第二章所阐释的，美国已经与苏联（现在的俄罗斯）"在国际法允许的范围内"，达成一项沿着西经168°58′37″经线的边界协议。① 如果美国现在同意与加拿大依据等距线或修改后的等距线划定边界，美国与俄罗斯边界将自然会在和美国与加拿大边界线相交的那一点终止，只要加拿大能够证明其对外大陆架权利可以延伸到那么远。这可能需要加拿大和俄罗斯之间进行海上边界谈判，除非这两个国家继续使用西经168°58′37″经线。如第四章中所述，俄罗斯在2001年首次向大陆架界限委员会提交划界案时，尊重这条一直延伸到北极点的线。② 然而，如果美国和加拿大的新边界为美国管辖区域设置北部限制的话，俄罗斯有可能寻求将其管辖区域向西经168°58′37″以东扩展，例如，沿着阿尔法/门捷列夫海岭。③ 同样，如果地质和地貌条件允许，加拿大试图将管辖范围向该线以西扩展也不会存在任何障碍。

十、小结

由于海冰融化、近海石油和天然气开发潜力大幅提高、意识到争议海域存在延伸至200海里外的外大陆架等因素，波弗特海边界争端最近变得更为突出。加拿大和美国还没有公布他们就200海里以外边界的法律立场，这些立场的发展会因一些奇特的事实而变得复杂，也即一方在200海里范围内的立场将使得另一方在200海里之外的区域获利。虽然争端范围扩大为谈判达成协议提供了更大可能性，但在任何谈判中当事

---

① US-Russia Maritime Boundary Agreement, Chapter 20, n. 20, above, Art. 2（1）.

② "Submission by the Russian Federation: Summary," 2001, http://www.un.org/depts/los/clcs_new/submissions_files/submission_rus.htm.

③ For more on the Alpha/Mendeleev Ridge, Chapter 4, below.

双方将自然而然地谋求最大限度获益。因此，任何一方或双方都有可能部分或全部放弃现有法律立场并形成新立场。

例如，如果参考加拿大在划界区域东部海岸线的凹陷性质，对等距线进行修改，并且该线也被用于划设外大陆架的话，该国可以采取等距线立场。另一方面，美国可能会维持其在专属经济区内使用等距线的立场，同时主张应由地质和地貌特征决定之后更远边界的走向。例如，美国可以提出楚科奇海台是"海底隆起"，在此其可能拥有超过350海里的主权权利，而且这应被视为与任何划界都具有相关性。此类立场不太可能减少争议地区的面积，但是它们确实为谈判达成解决方案创造了空间，与诉讼或仲裁不同，谈判能够使得双方保留对划界进程的控制。双方也可以使用不涉及单一海上边界的创造性解决方案，虽然有些方案协商起来会十分困难。因努维阿勒伊特人安置区扩大至争议区域只会使问题复杂化，只有当因努维阿勒伊特人得到密切咨询并理想地参与到加拿大和美国之间的任何谈判之时，才能确保他们现有收益权在任何划界结果中都得到保障。

第四章　外大陆架

"北极是俄罗斯的。"① 2007年8月，阿图尔·奇林加洛夫带领探险队在北极点洋底插上钛制的国旗，并用几个简单的词语引发了全球媒体关注。俄罗斯政治观察家们知道奇林·加洛夫当时是处于竞选活动之中的俄罗斯杜马议员，正如一名参与此事的俄罗斯科学家后来承认，在北极点插旗是一个缺乏法律相关性的宣传噱头。② 然而，加拿大外交部长彼得·麦凯"上钩了"。"瞧，现在不是15世纪，"他呼喊道，"你不能走遍世界各地并且插上国旗，然后说，'我们占领这块领土'。我们对北极的主张是非常明确的。"③ 麦凯的声明掩盖了加拿大从未主张对北极拥有主权的事实。这同时也具有一些讽刺意味，因为加拿大士兵早在两年前就飞到汉斯岛并插上了一面加拿大国旗。④

俄罗斯、加拿大和丹麦政客们已经认识到，坚持主张北极主权权利是很好的竞选素材。然而，北极主权绝不仅仅是一个国内问题；其集中涉及与其他国家的关系，有时是相当强大的国家。主权牌打不好的话可能会对看似无关的具有全球重要性的问题产生负面影响，例如俄罗斯和美国之间的核裁军谈判。当记者们更多关注对抗的可能性而非合作的现实情况之时，负面影响就会被放大。奇林·加洛夫和麦凯的评论引发了对即将到来的北极资源争夺的激烈报道，一些新闻标题更是描绘了一个

---

① Paul Reynolds, "Russia Ahead in Arctic 'Gold Rush'," BBC News, August 1, 2007, http://news.bbc.co.uk/2/hi/6925853.stm.

② Adrian Blomfield, "US Rises to Kremlin Bait," Daily Telegraph, August 4, 2007, http://www.telegraph.co.uk/news/worldnews/1559444/US-rises-to-Kremlin-bait.html.

③ "Canada Rejects Flag-Planting as 'Just a Show'," Independent online, August 3, 2012, http://www.iol.co.za/news/world/canada-rejects-flag-planting-as-just-a-show-1.364759#.UHgzYo4_5UQ.

④ For more on Hans Island, Chapter 1, above.

处于战争边缘的北方地区。

有意对所有错误报道作出回应,2008年5月,丹麦政府邀请其他四个北冰洋沿岸国家外交部长前往格陵兰的伊卢利萨特。

此次峰会最大成果是达成《伊卢利萨特宣言》,五国政府重申承诺在现有国际法框架内共同努力。① "我们已从政治上承诺通过谈判解决所有分歧,"丹麦外交大臣派尔·史蒂格·莫勒解释称,"因此,我们满怀希望并一劳永逸地清除了所有'竞相前往北极'的谣言。"规则已经就位,五国政府现已宣布将遵守这些规定。"②

莫勒是正确的:规则已经就位并且已经存在一段时间了。

一、大陆架制度

北极位于加拿大、丹麦、挪威和俄罗斯最北部群岛逾400海里之外。根据国际法,沿岸国对水体的权利被限制在200海里内;超过这一距离,海洋的水面和水体就是"公海",任何国家都可以开发。如果主权权利扩展至200海里外,在大陆架制度下,这些权利就只能涉及海床和底土。

国家对大陆架资源的权利起源于20世纪上半叶。尽管对珍珠等海底资源的开发已经持续了几个世纪,但沿岸国对于大陆架权利的扩张始于1945年《杜鲁门大陆架宣言》的发表。③ 在《杜鲁门大陆架宣言》中,美国主张所有沿岸国对其领土之外的近海大陆架资源享有排他性权利。该主张本身的互惠性质导致许多其他国家在短短几年内扩张了本国

---

① "The Ilulissat Declaration," Arctic Ocean Conference, Ilulissat, Greenland, May 27 – 29, 2008, http://byers.typepad.com/arctic/ilulissat-declaration-may-28-2008.html.

② Andrew C. Revkin, "Countries Agree to Talk Over the Arctic," New York Times, May 29, 2008, http://www.nytimes.com/2008/05/29/science/earth/29arctic.html.

③ "Policy of the United States with Respect to the Natural Resources of the Subsoil and Sea Bed of the Continental Shelf," reproduced in (1946) 40 American Journal of International Law 45, http://www.ibiblio.org/pha/policy/1945/450928a.html.

的管辖范围。① 到 1958 年,《日内瓦大陆架公约》设法确定该管辖权的空间范围, 以及沿海国权利的内容和适用。② 《日内瓦大陆架公约》规定, 沿海国对水深 200 米或允许开发的深度以内的大陆架资源享有主权权利。正如第三章中所述, 国际法院在 1969 年"北海大陆架案"中为此提供了合理性依据, 也即"海底区域可被认为事实上是沿岸国现有领土的一部分, 从这个意义上讲, 尽管被水体覆盖, 该区域是领土的自然延伸或延续, 是其在海底的扩展。"③ 然而, 在大陆架和深海海底之间建立明确界限的努力的真正催化剂出现在 1967 年, 当时马耳他外交官阿维德·帕多将深海海底及其资源称为"全人类共同遗产"。④

目前大陆架法律制度是在第三次联合国海洋法会议期间谈判形成的, 并规定于 1982 年《联合国海洋法公约》的第六章。⑤ 作为专属经济区制度的一部分, 每个沿岸国均有权开发距离其领海基线 200 海里之内的海床和底土。那些大陆边的外缘超过 200 海里的国家可以进一步延伸其开发权利。第七十六条第 1 款规定:"沿海国的大陆架包括其领海以外依其陆地领土的全部自然延伸, 扩展到大陆边外缘的海底区域的海床和底土。"⑥ 因此, 大陆架仍被认为是一个连续的地貌特征。尽管对大陆架的科学和法律定义存在分歧,⑦ 当代法律制度同时使用海床的地

---

① James Crawford and Thomas Viles, "International Law on a Given Day," in Konrad Ginther, et al. (eds.), Vo lkerrecht zwischen normativem Anspruch und politischer Realita. Festschrift fur Karl Zemanek zum 65. Geburtstag (Berlin: Duncker and Humblot, 1994), 65; reprinted in James Crawford, International Law as an Open System: Selected Essays (London: Cameron and May, 2002), 69. Byers, Custom, Power and the Power of Rules, Introduction, n. 39, above, pp. 90 – 92.

② 1958 Geneva Convention on the Continental Shelf, 499 UNTS 311, http://untreaty.un.org/ilc/texts/instruments/english/conventions/8_1_1958_continental_shelf.pdf.

③ North Sea Continental Shelf Cases, Chapter 3, n. 59, above, p. 31, p. 43.

④ 1st Committee, 22nd Session, UN GAOR meeting., UN Doc. A/C. 1/PV. 1515 (November 1, 1967), http://www.un.org/Depts/los/convention_agreements/texts/pardo_ga1967.pdf.

⑤ UN Doc. A/CONF. 62/122 (1982), reproduced in (1982) 21 ILM 1261, http://www.un.org/Depts/los/convention_agreements/texts/unclos/closindx.htm.

⑥ Ibid.

⑦ Philip A. Symonds and Harald Brekke, "The Ridge Provisions of Article 76 of the UN Convention on the Law of the Sea," in Myron H. Nordquist, John Norton Moore, and Tomas H. Heidar (eds.), Legal and Scientific Aspects of Continental Shelf Limits (Dordrecht: Martinus Nijhoff, 2004), 170.

质和地貌特征来定义法律上大陆架的理论和界限。大陆边的定义是"沿海国陆块没入水中的延伸部分,由陆架、陆坡和陆基的海床和底土构成。"①

《公约》任何缔约国希望在200海里外设立相关权利,需要在《公约》批准后十年内向大陆架界限委员会提交有关其拟设立外大陆架界限的科学数据。② 一旦大陆架界限委员会以建议的形式做出回应,根据这些建议所设立的界限就对其他《公约》缔约国具有终局性和约束性的效力。③ 但是同样,如果一国大陆边扩展至200海里之外,其只需要提交数据;否则,该国可依据专属经济区制度(第五十五至七十七条)或第七十六条第2款之规定,主张200海里。④

第七十六条为提交申请规定了一套公式。各国可据此确定其法律意义上大陆架的向海界限:(1)沉积岩厚度或(2)至大陆坡脚距离,在没有相反证明的情形下,大陆坡脚应定为大陆坡底坡度变动最大之点。该界限应由长度不超过六十海里的若干直线标出,连接各确定的点,具体要求是(1)沉积岩厚度至少为从该点至大陆坡脚最短距离的百分之一,或(2)离大陆坡脚的距离不超过60海里。一国可在任何给定点上使用任一方法,并且通常会选择对其最有利的方法。更为复杂的事情是,一个沿岸国的外大陆架不能超过两条约束性界限:(1)2500米"等深线"(例如,水下深度等高线)100海里;或(2)领海基线350海里。对例如大西洋中的那些典型的大陆边而言,这些公式的适用较为容易。其他大陆架则更为复杂,也因此更具挑战性,这种情况在北冰洋

---

① UNCLOS, n. 12, above, Art. 76 (3).

② Ibid., Annex II, Art. 4. The CLCS is a body of scientists elected by the UNCLOS parties to issue recommendations on submissions concerning the outer limits of coastal states' rights over extended continental shelves.

③ Ted McDorman argues that the limits only become final and binding on the coastal state, with other states only becoming bound to respect such limits if they do not protest them and the limits become generally accepted. Ted L. McDorman, "The Role of the Commission on the Limits of the Continental Shelf: A Technical Body in a Political World." (2002) 17 International Journal of Marine and Coastal Law 301 at 315.

④ The second clause reads: "or to a distance of 200 nautical miles from the baselines from which the breadth of the territorial sea is measured where the outer edge of the continental margin does not extend up to that distance." UNCLOS, n. 12, above.

较为多见。

二、海底高地

　　增加复杂性的一种方式是通过海岭和其他海底"高地"的存在，罗恩·麦克纳布将其在第七十六条程序中的所起的作用比为"百搭牌"。[1] 这些高地在地球海底中所占比例要大大高于大陆边本身，覆盖面积约比后者多出1.7倍。[2] 它们具有不同的特征和起源，与大陆边存在不同的地质和地貌关系。菲利普·西蒙兹等人提供了"非聚敛型环境"（non-convergent settings）下的高地列表，例如某种情况下地球表面的构造板块不会被挤压在一起。

　　广泛分布的海岭是海底扩张在扩展地壳板块边界层面的产物，有可能是活动的，也有可能已经消失。

　　破裂带的海岭可能会沿着平移板块边界出现。当大陆分离时，可能会形成微大陆块。海洋高地反映了地幔热点的影响。热点海岭则反映了地幔热点的轨迹。[3]

　　在"聚敛型环境"中，可能会出现与潜没相关的"岛弧系统"和与碰撞相关的"造山带"（也即聚敛型海岭），或因先前存在的海岭与大陆边相结合而产生的增生海岭。这些地物的地理名称可能会有所不同，它们的地质和地貌特征也不会从名称中显示出来。

　　第七十六条包含对三种海底地物的不同规定，主要依据国家对其行使管辖权的程度不同。[4] 正如第三章中所提到的，海岭可以为确立大陆架外部边界提供有效依据，因此是国家管辖权对象，但不得超过距离海

---

[1] Ron Macnab, "Submarine Elevations and Ridges: Wild Card in the Poker Game of UNCLOS Article 76" (2008) 39 Ocean Development and International Law 223.

[2] Harald Brekke and Philip A. Symonds, "A Scientific Overview of Ridges," in Nordquist, et al., n. 14, above, p. 152.

[3] Philip A. Symonds, et al., "Ridge Issues," in Peter J. Cook and Chris Carleton, Continental Shelf Limits: The Scientific and Legal Interface (New York: Oxford University Press, 2000), 285 at 288.

[4] UNCLOS, n. 12, above, Art. 76 (3).

岸 350 海里，从而排除了"2500 米等深线加 100 海里"的选项。[①] 海底隆起是大陆边的自然组成部分，例如高地（plateaux）、隆起（rises）、盖岩（caps）、浅滩（banks）、山坡（spurs），也可为设立大陆架外部界限提供有效依据。但它们与海岭的不同之处在于，在计算管辖权范围时，任何一条约束线均可被采用。[②]《联合国海洋法公约》没有对这些地物作出进一步规定，也没有定义如"大陆边的自然组成部分"等关键术语。

（一）大洋海岭

大洋海岭与深海相关，被国际水道测量组织定义为"深海海底的较长隆起，地势不规则或平滑，边缘陡峭。"[③] 他们通常由大洋壳构成，并且完全位于大陆架地形之外。有时岛屿坐落于此类海岭顶部，就像冰岛和亚速尔群岛。一些作者认为，这些海岭的地质条件具有决定性意义，这些岛屿在 200 海里外不能产生法律意义上的大陆架。[④] 另一些人则认为，这些岛屿与之所处的海岭是经由同样过程形成的，可以使用关于海岭的条款将其大陆架权利延伸至 350 海里。[⑤] 问题是，由大洋壳构成的海岭有时与聚敛环境下的大陆边存在地貌上的联系，是否或何时将这些海岭降至国家管辖范围之内的问题尚未得到解决。[⑥]

1999 年，大陆架界限委员会发布了关于如何解释第七十六条的

[①] Ibid., Art. 76（6）. However, Kunoy, et al. argue that CLCS practice is inconsistent on this point. Bjørn Kunoy, Martin V. Heinesen, and Finn Mørk, "Appraisal of Applicable Depth Constraint for the Purpose of Establishing the Outer Limits of the Continental Shelf."（2010）41 Ocean Development and International Law 357.

[②] Ibid.

[③] International Hydrographic Organization, A Manual on Technical Aspects of the United Nations Convention on the Law of the Sea – 1982, 4th edn., Special Publication No. 51（2006）, Appendix I – 21, http：//www.gmat.unsw.edu.au/ablos/TALOS_ed4.pdf.

[④] Symonds, et al., "Ridge Issues," n. 21, above, p. 300.

[⑤] Ibid.

[⑥] Ibid.

《科学和技术准则》,包括有关海岭和隆起的条款,① 关于海底高地的一般种类,大陆架界限委员会写道:

> 第七十六条没有对不同类型的地壳做出系统性规定。相反,只是提到两个术语:"陆地领土……的自然延伸"和沿海国"陆块没入水中的延伸部分",作为深洋洋底及其洋脊的对立面。地质学意义上,"陆块"和"陆地领土"两词都属于描述地壳类型的中性术语,因此,委员会认为地质学上地壳种类不能成为将海底海岭和隆起分类对应第七十六条第6款中法律种类的唯一限定因素,即便是在岛屿国家的情况中。②

2010年,大陆架界限委员会对英国关于阿森松岛周边外大陆架的提案做出建议,证实大陆架界限委员会不会仅依据地壳种类阻止或限制对海岭的权利主张。③ 相反,它将建立一种基于以下考虑的观点:"一个海岭是否属于陆地领土和陆块的自然延伸,第七十六条第4款所规定的海岭形态及其和大陆边的关系,以及海岭的延续性。"④ 大陆架界限委员会强调,将根据个案具体情况,确定一个海岭是否属于大洋或海底的类别。

(二)海岭和隆起

海岭与隆起之间的区别一直存在争议。一个通常被引用的对"海岭"一词的定义是:"构成陆地领土自然延伸的海底纵长隆起,地形不规则或相对平缓,两侧陡峭。"⑤ 陆地领土的自然延伸是区分海岭和洋

---

① "Scientific and Technical Guidelines of the Commission on the Limits of the Continental Shelf," CLCS/11, May 13, 1999, http://www.un.org/depts/los/clcs_new/commission_documents.htm#Guidelines.

② Ibid., p. 54.

③ "Summary of Recommendations of the Commission on the Limits of the Continental Shelf in Regard to the Submission Made by the United Kingdom of Great Britain and Northern Ireland in Respect of Ascension Island on 9 May 2008," April 15, 2010, p. 22 and 23, http://www.un.org/Depts/los/clcs_new/submissions_files/gbr08/gbr_asc_isl_rec_summ.pdf.

④ Ibid.

⑤ International Hydrographic Organization, n. 25, above.

脊的关键之一。因此，相对确定的是，海岭必须位于地形上的大陆边，即第七十六条第 4 款所规定的"陆坡脚"范围内，以成为主权权利的对象。① 任何其他海岭都不能影响到大陆架的外部界限，无论地壳类型如何。② 此外，在将大陆架上下两部分分开的"鞍状"区域的情况下，就必须在地形上展现出足够的连续性，已确定该鞍状区域不是深海海底的组成部分。③

《联合国海洋法公约》可被解读为禁止在所有海脊状地物中使用"2500 米等深线加 100 海里"的限制线，基于此类地物一定属于海脊或洋脊中的一种。然而，另一种解释是无法区分海脊与"山坡"的定义，因此《联合国海洋法公约》承认某些海脊状结构是"大陆边自然组成部分的海底隆起"。④ 值得注意的是，大陆架界限委员会在对新西兰提案的建议中采用了后一种方法，将几处较长海脊状地物认定为海底隆起。⑤ 正如西蒙兹等人解释那样："在全球海洋中存在各种类似海脊的海底隆起。有些表现出明显大陆性的密切关系，有些表现出海洋性密切

---

① Harald Brekke and Philip A. Symonds, "Submarine Ridges and Elevations of Article 76 in Light of Published Summaries of Recommendations of the Commission on the Limits of the Continental Shelf." (2011) 42 Ocean Development and International Law 292.

② Symonds and Brekke, "The Ridge Provisions of Article 76 of the UN Convention on the Law of the Sea," n. 14, above, p. 185.

③ Brekke and Symonds note that Norway attempted to use foot of the slope points on the Mohns – Knipovich Ridge system, claiming that it was a submarine ridge because it was geomorphologically connected to Norway's continental margin by the Bjørnøya Fan. However, the CLCS decided that the seafloor in the area was too flat, and concluded that "the Mohns – Knipovich Ridge system, including its central valley, is considered to be part of the deep ocean floor and/or rise provinces on morphological and geological grounds." Similarly, the CLCS concluded that the United Kingdom could not use foot of the slope points on the mid – Atlantic Ridge because "Ascension Island is distinct from the surrounding ocean floor, morphologically, geologically, geophysically and geochemically." "Summary of Recommendations of the Commission on the Limits of the Continental Shelf in Regard to the Submission Made by the United Kingdom of Great Britain and Northern Ireland in Respect of Ascension Island on 9 May 2008," n. 31, above, p. 47; Brekke and Symonds, n. 14, above, p. 292.

④ Tomasz Gorski, "A Note on Submarine Ridges and Elevations with Special Reference to the Russian Federation and the Arctic Ridges." (2009) 40 Ocean Development and International Law 56.

⑤ "Recommendations of the Commission on the Limits of the Continental Shelf in Regard to the Submission Made by New Zealand on 19 April 2006," August 22, 2008, http://www.mfat.govt.nz/downloads/global – issues/cont – shelf – recommendations. pdf.

关系，有的则两者兼有"。① 这就提出了地壳类型与海底高地分类相关性的问题，在地形上毗邻大陆边的情况下，究竟是海岭亦或海底隆起。

1999年《科学和技术准则》，大陆架界限委员会表示：

第6款提及的"海底高地"一词包含多种高地。"海台、海隆、海峰、暗滩和坡尖等"，使用"等"一字意味着这并非详尽无遗。所有这些高地的共同点是它们都是大陆边的自然构成部分。因此宜考虑大陆边形成的过程和大陆形成的方式……因此，委员会将主要根据以下因素确定它对"海底高地"的看法：

就活动大陆边而言，来自海洋、岛弧或大陆的沉积物和地壳物质增生在大陆边是大陆生长的一个自然过程。因此，任何增生在大陆边上的地壳碎块或沉积楔均应被视为该大陆边的自然构成部分。

就被动大陆边而言，海底扩张使大陆分离之前大陆碎裂的自然过程涉及大陆地壳的减薄、拉张和断裂以及岩浆大量侵入该地壳和穿过该地壳大量喷发。这一过程促进了大陆生长。因此，由这一碎裂过程造成的任何海底高地均应被视为大陆边的自然构成部分，这些高地构成陆块延伸的组成部分。②

因此，这些地物的起源和地质特征，以及它们与大陆边的地貌关系，都关系到它们的法律地位。然而，大陆架界限委员会未能明确指出，由上述过程产生并带有海岭特征的地物是否仍可以或者可到某种程度被视为海底隆起。③

一部分问题是，第七十六条是两个相互竞争目标之间的妥协：（1）防止沿海国对构成全人类共同遗产的深海海底资源提出主权权利主张;④（2）向宽阔边缘的沿海国提供扩展大陆架的权利。这种紧张关系在有

---

① Symonds, et al., n. 21, above, p. 286.

② "Scientific and Technical Guidelines," n. 29, above.

③ Macnab, n. 19, above, p. 224.

④ Part XI of UNCLOS specifies that the "Area" beyond the continental shelf is the "Common Heritage of Mankind" and that "No State shall claim or exercise sovereignty or sovereign rights over any part of the Area or its resources, nor shall any State or natural or juridical person appropriate any part thereof.... All rights in the resources of the Area are vested in mankind as a whole, on whose behalf the Authority shall act," n. 12, above, Arts. 136 and 137.

关海脊的谈判中表现得很明显——苏联建议,"在包含淹没水中的洋脊的区域,大陆架界限不得超过 350 英里距离。"① 然而,代表们讨论的是由大洋壳形成的狭长高地,正如日本提议中反映的,构成洋脊一部分的海岭不能被纳入法律上的大陆架。② 这一结论得到托马斯·戈尔斯基的支持,他报告称,对海脊的单一 350 海里的约束是为了限制由位于洋中脊顶部的岛屿产生之主权权利。③ 国际法学会外大陆架委员会同样把"海脊"一词解读为"适用于(主要)起源于大洋并且是沿海国陆地领土自然延伸的海岭。"④ 然而,哈拉尔德·布雷克和西蒙兹的结论是,没有包含有关地壳种类的内容表明,组成洋脊的海岭或被作为自然组成部分纳入大陆边,若其与该大陆边具有形态和地质上的关系。⑤

在《联合国海洋法公约》谈判过程中,拥有宽阔边缘的沿海国曾主张将某些高地纳入法律意义上的大陆架。正如第三种中所提到的,美国坚持认为楚科奇海台是其大陆边的自然组成部分。⑥ 澳大利亚建议,"海台、海隆、海峰、暗滩和坡尖"是构成大陆边的海底隆起之例子。⑦ 丹麦后来解释称,其认为"本质上属于与陆地领土同样地质结构"的高地应是大陆边的自然组成部分。⑧

这种海底隆起从海脊中的分化使得布雷克和西蒙兹总结道,后者"不是大陆边自然组成部分的海岭,但仍是大陆边一部分,因为它们属于大陆坡脚的通常范围之内。"⑨ 这些海岭与大陆边向陆范围内存在地质学上的联系,与深海海底较远的向海部分也存在联系,同时在地貌上构成大陆边不可分割的一部分。布雷克和西蒙兹因此建议,那些在地貌

---

① Symonds, et al., n. 21, above, p. 287.
② Ibid.
③ Gorski, n. 37, above, pp. 51–60.
④ International Law Association, "Legal Issues of the Outer Continental Shelf," 2nd Report, Toronto Conference, 2006, p. 4, http://www.ila-hq.org/download.cfm/docid/435A6BA1-4F85-47B3-9ED23A6F64924414.
⑤ Brekke and Symonds, n. 14, above, p. 192.
⑥ Richardson, Chapter 3, n. 89, above.
⑦ Symonds, et al., n. 21, above, p. 287.
⑧ Ibid.
⑨ Brekke and Symonds, n. 14, above, p. 186.

上符合但是在其整个范围内在地质上与大陆边不存在连续性的海岭,应被认定为海脊,那些在地质和地貌上均存在连续性的应被认定为海底隆起。① 他们还建议地质连续性应从一般地质特征和成因两方面进行解释。②

简而言之,考虑到坡尖的定义与海岭的定义在本质上是无法区分的,而且《联合国海洋法公约》中海底隆起的最终列表并非穷尽列举,将海岭类地物视为大陆边自然组成部分似乎不存在障碍。③ 因此,这就表明可以使用任何一条从大路坡脚点引出的约束线,而该点由一个海岭状地物的计算得出,只要问题中的地物在其全部范围内在地貌和地质上与大陆边存在密切关系,在此情况下其可被称为海底隆起。④

这就是大陆架界限委员会在许多案件中采用的方法,正如比约恩·昆解释道:

委员会无论不批准或批准将海底高地划分为属于关系到相关沿海国的向海界限范围的大陆边自然组成部分的海底隆起,都缺乏地质学上的理由。在其向澳大利亚提出的建议中,委员会驳回了其在威廉姆斯海岭适用深度限制的申请,"因为第七十六条第6款中所规定的海底高地性质并未得到证明。"换句话说,因为缺乏地质过程,就不能接受将威廉姆斯海岭划分为大陆边自然组成部分的海底隆起。此外澳大利亚还提出,乔伊海岭是海底高地,"仅在形态学上"属于大陆边的自然组成部分。尽管认识到乔伊海岭是澳大利亚陆块淹没于水中的自然延伸,委员会基于提交的有关乔伊海岭起源的数据,并未接受该海岭属于大陆边自然组成部分的海底隆起的观点,认为其因"太稀疏而不能确定。"相比之下,在考虑地质因素的基础上,凯尔盖朗海台中部、凯尔盖朗海台南部和埃兰暗滩被"认为是赫德和麦克唐纳群岛大陆边的自然组成部

---

① Brekke and Symonds, n. 14, above. at p. 192.

② Ibid.

③ Weiguo Wang, "Geological Structures of Ridges with Relation to the Definition of Three Types of Seafloor Highs Stipulated in Article 76" (2011) 30 Acta Oceanologica Sinica 125 at 137.

④ Ibid. , p. 136.

分",并因此"可适用深度标准限制"。①

根据西蒙兹和布瑞克的说法,"大陆架界限委员会评估了此类隆起到达何种程度才会与沿海国陆块存在地理上的关联或延续,到达何种程度才能与周边深海海底相区别。"② 与此同时,他们指出一些国家不同意这种方法。③ 澳大利亚特别希望防止大陆架界限委员会发展一种先例,希望该委员会继续根据个案具体情况确定海脊的地位。④ 然而,正如梅尔·韦伯正确地总结道,最终大陆架界限委员会的实践将与国家实践相结合,以决定这场辩论的结果。⑤

总结这个高度技术性的章节,《联合国海洋法公约》关于海底高地的规定十分复杂,但对其含义的一些共识正在形成。洋脊通常但并非总是由大洋壳组成,其位于地貌上的大陆边之外,因此与深海海底相关。它们无助于设立大陆架的外部界限。海脊在地貌上与大陆边存在关联,同时在地质上与其具有连续性,国家管辖权范围限于距离海岸350海里之处。在地壳类型和地质起源方面,海底隆起与沿海国陆块具有地貌上的相关性和地质上的连续性。因此,它们是大陆边的自然组成部分。国家管辖权范围限制于350海里或2500米等深线外100海里,看两者哪个(在任意给定点)距离海岸更远。然而,尽管产生了这种共识,但必须永远记住,大陆架界限委员会对海底高地的特性描述视个案具体情况而定,这使得该程序中保留了持续的不确定性。

---

① Bjørn Kunoy, "The Terms of Reference of the Commission on the Limits of the Continental Shelf: A Creeping Legal Mandate." (2012) 25 Leiden Journal of International Law 109 at 120 – 121. See also Brekke and Symonds, n. 14, above, p. 299.

② Brekke and Symonds, n. 56, above, ibid.

③ Ibid. Australia argued that the geological test is relevant only in the case of ridges, with all other features being considered natural components of the continental margin on the basis of geomorphology alone. This approach seems problematic, given the non – exhaustive nature of the list and the definition of a spur.

④ Ibid.

⑤ Mel Weber, "Defining the Outer Limits of the Continental Shelf across the Arctic Basin: The Russian Submission, States' Rights, Boundary Delimitation and Arctic Regional Cooperation." (2009) 24 International Journal Marine and Coastal Law 653 at 669.

三、北冰洋中部的地貌和地质特征

北冰洋中部海底包括四个脊状结构——加克利海岭、罗蒙诺索夫海岭、阿尔法海岭和门捷列夫海岭。加克利海岭位于北冰洋欧亚海盆的欧洲一侧。罗蒙诺索夫海岭将欧亚海盆和美亚海盆分隔开,其从靠近格陵兰和加拿大埃尔斯米尔岛大陆架的区域向北延伸,经过但未跨越北极,并由此向南到达靠近俄罗斯新西伯利亚群岛大陆架的区域。阿尔法和门捷列夫海岭是同样的地貌,本书称之为阿尔法/门捷列夫海岭,位于罗蒙诺索夫海岭另一侧的美亚海盆。[1]

(一) 罗蒙诺索夫海岭

罗蒙诺索夫海岭长约900海里,宽约24—108海里,海面至海底高约为400—4000米。[2] 埃尔斯米尔岛和格陵兰边缘有一个"海槽"或"鞍状物"将大陆地壳分开,2006年加拿大和丹麦对该区域开展了联合调查,该调查以1979年确定罗蒙诺索夫海岭总体特征的调查为基础。加拿大外交和国际贸易部表示,2006年调查的目的是"利用地震仪记录沉积岩和地壳层声速,以表明该海岭与附近大陆区域存在密切联系"。[3]

2010年,加拿大科学家在《国际地球物理学报》杂志上发表了一篇文章。[4] 该文称,鞍状区域地质与周边深海海底不同,有连续的大陆

---

[1] The International Bathymetric Chart of the Arctic Ocean provides the most up-to-date and comprehensive picture, with the latest version dating to June 2012. International Bathymetric Chart of the Arctic Ocean, Version 3.0, June 8, 2012, http://www.ngdc.noaa.gov/mgg/bathymetry/arctic/arctic.html.

[2] H. Ruth Jackson, Trine Dahl-Jensen, and the LORITA working group, "Sedimentary and Crustal Structure from the Ellesmere Island and Greenland Continental Shelves onto the Lomonosov Ridge, Arctic Ocean." (2010) 182 Geophysical Journal International 11.

[3] Department of Foreign Affairs, "Extended Continental Shelf: International Cooperation," http://www.international.gc.ca/continental/collaboration.aspx?view=d. Presumably, the participating scientists would have conducted their research without any such pre-ordained conclusion.

[4] H. Ruth Jackson, et al., n. 62, above, p. 11.

地壳跨越鞍状区域,罗蒙诺索夫海岭被一段连续的陆坡脚包围并入北美大陆边。① 该文章还报道说,虽然海冰导致无法对该海岭大部分区域进行地质取样,收集到的含有锆石矿的样品支持了其属于"两面大陆边"的假设,在地貌上从属于加拿大/丹麦大陆边和俄罗斯大陆边。② 鞍状区域比深海底高出约 1000 米,大陆架界限委员会已接受了不同但具有相似比例的澳大利亚外大陆架申请。③ 罗蒙诺索夫海岭俄罗斯端存在相似地貌区域,它与西伯利亚大陆边相接,俄罗斯科学家报告称,该海岭同样也在此处陆坡脚包围之内。④

(二) 阿尔法/门捷列夫海岭

2011 年,美国和加拿大破冰船"希利"号和"路易斯·圣·劳伦特"号前往阿尔法海岭进行联合海底绘图,该海岭是从加拿大埃尔斯米尔岛西北侧延伸至俄罗斯弗兰格尔岛共 1100 海里长的海底山脉。阿尔法海岭位于罗蒙诺索夫海岭在地理上北极的对面一侧。一个关键问题是,阿尔法海岭是在北冰洋中部某个位置结束,还是与另一组称为门捷列夫海脊的由西伯利亚向北延伸的海底山脉相连。俄罗斯人也在问相同的问题,并已派遣"俄罗斯"号核动力破冰船和"费多罗夫院士"号调查船前往该地区绘制地图。"俄罗斯"号装备了地震阵列,"费多罗夫院士"号装备了多波束声呐系统,他们可以和"希利"号和"路易

---

① H. Ruth Jackson, et al., n. 62, above, p. 11.

② Ibid., p. 13. Ruth Jackson, et al., "The Structure of the Lomonosov Ridge, Arctic Ocean," American Geophysical Union, Fall Meeting 2010, abstract # T31A - 2122, http://adsabs.harvard.edu/abs/2010AGUFM.T31A2122J.

③ In the Australian submission, the CLCS was presented with a number of seafloor highs separated from other parts of the continental margin by a saddle. The Commission was satisfied with a depth difference of 2,000 m. and 700 m. above the deep ocean floor for the two saddle areas that connect the Macquarie Ridge Complex and the Australian continent (p. 71) and a difference of 1,000 m. for the saddle area that joins the South Tasman Saddle to the Australian continent (p. 94). "Summary of the Recommendations of the Commission on the Limits of the Continental Shelf (CLCS) in Regard to the Submission Made by Australia on 15 November 2004: Recommendations Adopted by CLCS on 9 April 2008," http://www.un.org/Depts/los/clcs_new/submissions_files/aus04/aus_summary_of_recommendations.pdf.

④ Macnab, n. 19, above, p. 226.

斯·圣·劳伦特"号一样进行协同工作。① 早期报告显示,俄罗斯仍有意愿限制其对西经168°58′37″经线(苏联和美国于1990年达成的协议构成两国"在国际法允许范围内"的大陆架权利边界)以西那些区域的主权权利主张,② 正如2001年向大陆架界限委员会提交的申请所表明的那样③。然而,如果加拿大也主张对阿尔法/门捷列夫海岭拥有主权,自我限制就不能继续,如果加拿大主张西经168°58′37″以西主权,其也肯定不能继续。因此,下文列出俄罗斯、丹麦和加拿大之间沿罗蒙诺索夫海岭进行协调及合作的可能选项,可以参照适用于俄罗斯和加拿大在阿尔法/门捷列夫海岭的活动。

(三)申请、回应和外交

俄罗斯在批准《公约》后仅仅4年就于2001年向大陆架界限委员会提交了相关数据。按照程序规则,申请是保密的并且只公布一份摘要和随附地图。④ 根据该地图,俄罗斯主张北冰洋海底很大一部分区域为其领土的自然延伸,总计约102000平方海里,并将权利拓展至北极点。⑤

2002年3月,在俄罗斯向大陆架界限委员会提交申请的陈述中,俄罗斯自然资源部副部长表示:

> 对穿越罗蒙诺索夫海岭的SLO-92地学断面进行深地震测深和高分辨率反射地震综合解释,提供了速度特征、地壳分层

---

① On the joint US-Canada mapping in the Beaufort Sea, Chapter 3, above.
② Alexandra Zakharova and Vitaly Radnayev, "Russia Proves Mendeleev Ridge Is Eurasian Continent Extension," Voice of Russia, November 1, 2012, http://english.ruvr.ru/2012_11_01/Russia-proves-Mendeleev-Ridge-is-Eurasian-continent-extension/. On the Russia-US boundary, Chapter 2, above.
③ discussion, next section.
④ "Submission by the Russian Federation: Summary," http://www.un.org/depts/los/clcs_new/submissions_files/submission_rus.htm.
⑤ "Area of the Continental Shelf of the Russian Federation in the Arctic Ocean beyond 200-Nautical-Mile Zone," http://www.un.org/depts/los/clcs_new/submissions_files/rus01/RUS_CLCS_01_2001_LOS_2.jpg.

和厚度等数据,这些都具有大陆型地壳特征。该结论符合普遍接受的概念。[1]

提案中的观点是,罗蒙诺索夫海岭和阿尔法/门捷列夫海岭两者都是俄罗斯大陆边的自然组成部分,但是终止于北极点表明,俄罗斯有意愿限制其主权权利主张。[2] 如上所述,俄罗斯提案使用与美国1990年海上边界条约中确定的横跨美亚海盆、阿尔法/门捷列夫海岭和罗蒙诺索夫海岭的西经168°58′37″经线作为其东部边界,同时使用"2500米等深线加上100海里"作为西部罗蒙诺索夫海岭和西伯利亚大陆架的限制线。[3]

尽管提案涉及的内容可能更为广泛,但并非所有俄罗斯海上邻国都愿意允许大陆架委员会程序在没有反对的情况下推进。大陆架界限委员会认为俄罗斯提案中包括挪威同样准备主张权利的区域,挪威对此表示赞成,[4] 而丹麦则表示,其不能就该提案是否会与其之后主张权利的区域发生重叠形成意见。[5] 丹麦和加拿大均表示,大陆架界限委员会对俄罗斯数据的审查并不意味着两国对该提案的同意,不会损害两国与俄罗斯之间海上边界划定。[6] 最重要的是,美国对罗蒙诺索夫海岭是海底山脉或高地的定位提出异议。尽管不是《公约》缔约国,美国提交了一份抗议书,声称罗蒙诺索夫海岭"是北冰洋海盆深海中的单独地貌,不是俄

---

[1] "Statement Made by the Deputy Minister for Natural Resources of the Russian Federation during Presentation of the Submission Made by the Russian Federation to the Commission on 28 March 2002," Doc. CLCS/31, 5 April 2002, p. 5, http://daccess-dds-ny.un.org/doc/UNDOC/GEN/N02/318/60/PDF/N0231860.pdf?OpenElement.

[2] Ted L. McDorman, "The Continental Shelf Beyond 200 nm: Law and Politics in the Arctic Ocean." (2009) 18 Journal of Transnational Law and Policy 155 at 176 – 177.

[3] Weber, n. 60, above, p. 660.

[4] Permanent Mission of Norway to the Secretary-General of the United Nations, Chapter 3, n. 132, above.

[5] Permanent Mission of Denmark to the United Nations, "Denmark: Notification Regarding the Submission Made by the Russian Federation to the Commission on the Limits of the Continental Shelf," 2002, http://www.un.org/Depts/los/clcs_new/submissions_files/submission_rus.htm.

[6] Ibid., Permanent Mission of Canada to the United Nations, "Canada: Notification Regarding the Submission Made by the Russian Federation to the Commission on the Limits of the Continental Shelf," 2002, http://www.un.org/Depts/los/clcs_new/submissions_files/submission_rus.htm.

罗斯或任何其他国家大陆边的自然组成部分。"① 大陆架界限委员会随后要求俄罗斯提供更多数据，表示无法依据当前提供的信息做出最终决定。②

丹麦也对从格陵兰延伸至北极点的罗蒙诺索夫海岭部分区域表现出兴趣，并计划将北极点纳入其向大陆架界限委员会提交的提案中。③ 然而，丹麦并没有参与格陵兰和俄罗斯海岸之间中线之外的海床地图绘制，该条中线位于北极点俄罗斯侧。这意味着其提案将不会包括整个罗蒙诺索夫海岭。但是丹麦可以在外部界限得以确定或就海上边界达成一致之前的某个时间点提出进一步提案。

加拿大也在准备提案，包含罗蒙诺索夫海岭的大部分区域，但与丹麦一样，其信息收集范围也没有越过与俄罗斯的中间线。所有这些可能会造成二到三个至少存在部分重叠区域的提案，重叠区域位于西经168°58′37″经线和中间线（格陵兰/埃尔斯米尔岛和俄罗斯海岸之间）之间，根据梅尔·韦伯的说法，共计仅为22000平方海里。④ 出于这些原因，随着俄罗斯、丹麦和加拿大加入大陆架划界委员程序，这些国家将有意愿考虑自身选项，其中一些可能有助于避免、管理或解决争议，客观上讲这些争议涉及的海底区域相对较小且非常边远，但却具有潜在难度。

四、向大陆架界限委员会提交提案的选项

尽管《公约》第九十六条第10款规定，大陆架界限委员会建议不

---

① "Letter from the Permanent Representative of the United States of America to the United Nations," UN Doc. CLCS. 01. 2001. LOS/USA, 28 February 2002, p. 3, http://www.un.org/depts/los/clcs_new/submissions_files/rus01/CLCS_01_2001_LOS_USAtext.pdf. The US view has apparently evolved more recently in light of new scientific data, and it might now be willing to consider the Lomonosov Ridge as susceptible to national jurisdiction. Betsy Baker, "Law, Science, and the Continental Shelf: The Russian Federation and the Promise of Arctic Cooperation." (2010) 25 American University International Law Review 251 at 269 – 270.

② "Oceans and the Law of the Sea: Report of the Secretary General, Addendum," UN Doc. A/57/57/Add. 1, 8 October 2002, p. 41, http://www.un.org/Depts/los/general_assembly/general_assembly_reports.htm.

③ Danish Continental Shelf Project. http://a76.dk/lng_uk/main.html.

④ Weber, n. 60, above, p. 672.

妨害划界问题，① 大陆架界限委员本身的程序规则排除了将存在陆地或海上争议的区域提交审议的可能性，除非获得所有争端方事先同意。② 相关程序可以将任何问题通知大陆架界限委员会和有可能受到潜在影响的国家。提交声明有义务告知大陆架界限委员会任何当前活跃的争议，保证提案不会对该问题造成损害。③ 此外，需要公开提案的执行摘要，以使得其他国家确定该提案是否侵犯了这些国家同样主张的权利。④ 然而，公开执行摘要也使得大陆架界限委员会在处理第二国提出的无效异议、非提案国以同意获得相关争议区域数据并提出建议的方式参与争议等事务时，获得比其自身规则所提供的更大灵活性。

与此同时，针对存在争议的区域或有潜在争议可能性，并且当事方不愿在提案之前解决相关争议的，可通过多种可能方式提交提案。值得注意的是，可以对某一区域采取多种方法的组合。

（一）不与他国协调的完全提案

任何国家均可在不与其他国家协调的情况下，向大陆架界限委员会提交完整的提案。然而，如上文所述，一国在其提案中包含争议或潜在争议区的数据，就会存在某个或多个其他国家就该提案向大陆架界限委员会提出反对。委员会届时将无法审议该数据，⑤ 因为审议相关数据可

---

① UNCLOS, n. 12, above.

② Rules of Procedure, Annex 1, Art. 5 (a), http://www.un.org/Depts/los/clcs_new/commission_rules.htm.

③ Ibid., sec. 2.

④ Lathrop, Chapter 3, n. 20, above.

⑤ The CLCS would likely be quite prompt in declaring itself unable to consider the data, as it did with regard to the UK submissions regarding the Hatton Rockall and Falkland Islands areas. On Rockall, "Statement by the Chairman of the Commission on the Limits of the Continental Shelf on the Progress of Work in the Commission," October 1, 2009, pp. 41 – 46, http://daccess-dds-ny.un.org/doc/UNDOC/GEN/N09/536/21/PDF/N0953621.pdf. On the Falkland Islands, "Statement by the Chairman of the Commission on the Limits of the Continental Shelf on the Progress of Work in the Commission," April 30, 2010, pp. 55 – 60, http://daccess-dds-ny.un.org/doc/UNDOC/GEN/N10/337/97/PDF/N1033797.pdf.

能会推迟对该问题的解决,并致使其成为持续紧张的可能来源。① 由于这些原因,俄罗斯、丹麦或加拿大在没有互相协调的情况下提交在北冰洋中部造成重叠的意见书是不明智的。

(二) 提案中排除所有争议或潜在争议区

第二种选项是俄罗斯、丹麦和加拿大只向大陆架界限委员会提交部分提案,因而排除任何可能存在争议的区域。② 这将使得各国有机会继续就其余大陆架界限问题提交提案,从而满足他们十年的期限,同时推迟审议可能重叠区域的界限。该方法在解决权利主张重叠的情况下最为有效,在此情形下,任何一方均不希望对方就争议区域采取任何行动。除共享现有或潜在主张的信息外,此种方式仅需要很少的合作和沟通。这种方式也增加了这些国家之后就争议或潜在争议区域提出联合提案的可能性,下面将讨论该问题。

然而,在一些国家将争议或潜在争议区域排除于大陆架界限委员会提案之外或导致国内政治风险,政府可能被描述为权利主张小于最大区域,即使该国政府保留其后进一步提交提案的权利。③ 延迟和不确定可能带来的风险,导致该选项将错过最后就确定边界方面取得一定进展的机会。最后,该选项似乎与俄罗斯、丹麦和加拿大声明中利用大陆架界限委员会程序明确向海方向主权权利的范围,根据国际法解决任何争议的意图背道而驰。④

---

① The CLCS is already experiencing a substantial backlog. "Delegates Offer Differing Views Regarding Workload of Commission on Limits of Continental Shelf as States Parties Continue Twenty – First Meeting," SEA/1954, June 14, 2011, http: // www. un. org/News/Press/docs//2011/sea 1954. doc. htm.

② discussion, above, pp. 84 – 85.

③ Lathrop, Chapter 3, n. 20, above, pp. 4151 – 4152.

④ "The Ilulissat Declaration," Arctic Ocean Conference, Ilulissat, Greenland, May 27 – 29, 2008, http: //byers. typepad. com/arctic/ilulissat – declaration – may – 28 – 2008. html; "Russia, Canada Back Science to Resolve Dispute over Arctic Claims," RIA Novosti, September 16, 2010, http: //en. rian. ru/world/20100916/160615112. html.

(三) 同意不反对大陆架界限委员会审议数据

正如第三章中解释的,各国有时同意不就大陆架界限委员会审查争议区域数据提出反对。理想状态下,这种协议将通过"无异议声明"的形式主动传递给大陆架界限委员会。这种协议仍会导致单独提案,但不会带来程序被中断或延迟的风险。虽然委员会的建议不会妨害任何划界,但同时他们可以提供有关国家管辖外部界限的信息,当各方决定通过谈判获得解决方案时,这些资料有利于各方。因此,俄罗斯、丹麦和加拿大可以同意,各方各自提交或重新提交划界案,也即在理想状态下是不发表反对声明。

(四) 协同提案

在单独提交的前提下,还有一种选择是通过分享地貌和地质数据并推动对相关数据共同解释的方式,更加紧密地协同提出提案。这种协同可能使得俄罗斯、丹麦和加拿大就北冰洋海底地质历史形成共同意见,以及基于对第七十六条对海底高地表述的共同理解,就罗蒙诺索夫海岭和阿尔法/门捷列夫海岭特征形成共同意见。这类协同或许可以提高大陆架界限委员会提案成功几率,同时有助于形成更为持久的合作动力,有利于未来划界工作。

(五) 联合提案

加拿大、丹麦和俄罗斯(或三国中任两国)可以向大陆架界限委员会提交联合提案,且据报道已就该选项进行了一些初步讨论。[1] 正如科尔特·莱思罗普解释称,联合提案可使未解决争议成为提案国之间的内部问题,确保大陆架界限委员会可以审查那些原本或许被排除在外的数据。[2] 这种方法可提供很多其他潜在的好处:成本分担和劳动分工,

---

[1] Randy Boswell, "Thaw May Be Underway in Ottawa-Moscow Arctic Issues," Vancouver Sun, May 12, 2009, http://byers.typepad.com/arctic/2009/05/thaw-may-be-underway-in-ottawa-moscow-arctic-issues.html.

[2] Lathrop, Chapter 3, n. 20, above, p. 4147.

更为完整和严格的数据集,透明度增强,以及促进未来就边界达成协议的合作动力。联合提案还将有助于防止争端恶化或媒体和公众对其的负面看法,与此同时这三个国家在等待十多年之后,大陆架界限委员会将很有可能审查该问题并提出建议。

从不利的方面来看,若各国已单独就相关问题收集大量数据的情况下,联合提案或许不能带来成本分担的优势,特别是在北极地区的情形下。若各方处于不同的数据收集阶段,对该地区地质历史存在不同理解,或者确定陆坡脚点或沉积岩厚度的方法不同,共同数据收集工作或许也将难以实现。此外,整合科学项目的工作已耗时数年,但直至目前仍在分别进行。考虑到加拿大和丹麦预计将分别于2013年和2014年提交提案,可能没有足够时间用来准备联合提案,除非他们只提交部分提案,将所有潜在重叠区域留待之后解决。

同样存在俄罗斯在大陆架界限委员会队列中位置的问题。俄罗斯目前有权要求大陆架界限委员会首先审查其再次提交的提案,然后再考虑其他国家在俄罗斯首次提案之后提交的相关提案。然而,若将相同数据作为联合提案的一部分提交,俄罗斯将失去该权利。联合提案的历史也并非是完全积极的。当比斯开湾周边沿岸国决定提交合并的数据,大陆架界限委员会要求这些国家根据各自主张分别提供数据,以证明他们具有对大陆架区域的单独权利。[1] 委员会最终拒绝了提案中的一部分内容,认为沿岸国作为一个整体所管辖的区域不能比各国单独提案中主张权利的区域更大。[2] 总之,第七十六条使用"沿岸国"时用的是单数,表明对大陆架的任何特定权利只能由单独一个国家产生。

---

[1] "Statement by the Chairman of the Commission on the Limits of the Continental Shelf on the Progress of Work in the Commission," October 4, 2007, pp. 26 – 29, http://daccess-dds-ny.un.org/doc/UNDOC/GEN/N07/529/89/PDF/N0752989.pdf.

[2] Commission on the Limits of the Continental Shelf, "Summary of the Recommendations of the Commission on the Limits of the Continental Shelf in Regard to the Joint Submission Made by France, Ireland, Spain, and the United Kingdom of Great Britain and Northern Ireland in Respect of the Area of the Celtic Sea and the Bay of Biscay on 19 May 2006," March 24, 2009, pp. 26、27, http://www.un.org/depts/los/clcs_new/submissions_files/frgbires06/fisu_clcs_recommendations_summary2009.pdf.

五、提案前先商定临时界线或永久边界

就大陆架界限委员会提案进行自我限制或合作的多种选择之外，俄罗斯、丹麦和加拿大将有意在提案完成之前，先谈判达成临时界线或永久边界。

（一）大陆架界限委员会提案前商定临时界线

俄罗斯、丹麦和加拿大可以谈判达成临时"约束线"，以完成各自向大陆架界限委员会的提案。的确，《公约》强烈鼓励在大陆架划界达成最终协议之前，使用"实际性的临时安排"，并规定这种安排"不妨害最后界限的划定"。① 任何一组界线均可以被合理运用于临时划界，一个明显的可能性是将北冰洋中部基于扇形进行划分，原因显而易见，因为俄罗斯在其2001年提案中选择了这一方法。丹麦已表示对北极点俄罗斯一侧区域感兴趣，因此可能会抵制这种方法。② 此外，在北冰洋中部适用扇形方式或人为地将美国卷入关于罗蒙诺索夫海岭和阿尔法/门捷列夫海岭的管辖权问题。因为，尽管阿拉斯加外大陆架不可能延伸至那么远，基于扇形方法的临时界线会将这两个海岭的一部分分配给一个国家，该国没有完善这种分配方式的现实可能。

更好的方法可能是将俄罗斯扇形作为该国临时约束线，并将阿尔法/门捷列夫海岭附近剩余海床临时分配给加拿大，罗蒙诺索夫海岭附近剩余海床分配给加拿大和丹麦。加拿大和丹麦之间的临时界线可沿着罗蒙诺索夫海岭的顶点，即双方"坡脚"之间的等距线，或者基于格陵兰北部海岸和加拿大高北极岛屿的等距线，这也是最为简单和更好的方法。加拿大和丹麦沿罗蒙洛索夫海岭的边界问题将在下文中更详细地讨论。③

关于临时界线的一个更为普遍的问题涉及到莱思罗普的观察，"在

---

① UNCLOS, n. 12, above, Art. 83 (3).
② the Danish Continental Shelf Project, http://www.a76.dk/.
③ discussion, below, pp. 120 – 122.

某些情况下，一国只有在对提案进行充分考虑的前提下，才会知道是否需要与领国就边界达成一致，或者在何种程度上的一致。"① 大陆架界限委员会可能最终建议，某个或更多国家不要使用罗蒙诺索夫海岭或阿尔法/门捷列夫海岭拓展其管辖权，由于临时界线的原因，其他各方不可提交提案将本国管辖权延伸至其他各方国家管辖权终结的位置。这将使得该国或数国处于不利境地，要么在未到实际自然延伸终点前结束管辖权，要么向大陆架界限委员会提交新的数据，随之而来的结果就是延迟。在大西洋东北部所谓的"南香蕉洞"的范围内，丹麦、冰岛和挪威通过提交超出已达成临时界线的区域相关数据的方式处理该问题。② 若大陆架界限委员会认定一方在一个特定区域内没有权利，为其他各方利益，该方应直接退出，边界也会相应作出调整。

在其他几个方法中，各国可就大陆架界限委员会的不同建议将如何影响临时界线事先达成协议。可以商定如果建议与之相符，临时界线将自动成为永久海上边界。同样，另外还可以商定临时界线将根据大陆架界限委员会建议结果进行调整，以符合具体规则。例如，可以商定，若一个区域内确定存在两个及以上国家的权利重叠，可通过调整临时界线，将重叠部分按比例分配给这几个国家。

（二）大陆架界限委员会提案前商定永久边界

最后一个选项是俄罗斯和加拿大就阿尔法/门捷列夫海岭达成永久边界，俄罗斯、加拿大和丹麦就罗蒙诺索夫海岭达成永久边界，再加上向大陆架界限委员会提交所有数据，并表明各国希望充分利用各国联合的管辖权以支持商定的边界。大陆架界限委员会建议一个或更多海岭仅是一国大陆边延伸的情况下，该国的权利将被转移给边界另一侧其他缔约国，就像距离海岸 200 海里内海床和水体的权利有时通过海上边界条约中所谓"特殊区域"的方式转移，正如第二章中解释的那样。

诚然，在外大陆架上使用这一方法将与大陆架作为某个沿岸国自然

---

① Lathrop, Chapter 3, n. 20, above, p. 4146.
② Ibid.

延伸的理念不符。在通常情况下不会获得相关权利的国家而言，这种做法也过于慷慨。但其确实有几方面优势：第一，提案之前确定的永久边界将提供高度确定性和稳定性，而且速度相当快。第二，该方法可为大陆架界限委员会认为某个沿岸国对阿尔法／门捷列夫海岭或罗蒙诺索夫海岭没有权利的风险提供一定保护。从这个意义上讲，在大陆架界限委员会建议之前商定永久边界，可以设立一个"无知之幕"，使得谈判中更容易实现公平分配。① 这就是说，在"无知之幕"被升起之后，将海洋空间分配给原本无权利的国家可能会导致政治紧张。

此外值得注意的是，必须将提案提交大陆架界限委员会，不仅是为支持该商定的永久边界，而且也决定了主权权利沿两个海岭侧翼延伸至北冰洋中部的范围，在必要的情况下，相关国家随后需调整划界以符合大陆架界限委员会的建议。最后，根据大陆架界限委员会建议，阿尔法／门捷列夫海岭或罗蒙诺索夫海岭是洋脊或海脊（与海底高地相对），将使得相关商定边界失效，因为相关该海岭的全部或部分将位于国家管辖范围之外。尽管如此，这种风险以及商定边界时耗费的时间和努力也会是合理的，因为其维持了这段期间的稳定，而大陆架界限委员会可将精力投入其他相当繁重的工作之中。

六、海上划界的选项

临时边界、调整临时边界的规则和永久边界均需要经过大量谈判。正如第二章和第三章所解释的，关于海上边界的谈判需要在法律规则的背景下进行。但是，人们可能希望边界划定的通常规则可以适用于北冰洋中部外大陆架，但一些学术研究却认为该区域所有海床都将以下两种方式中的一种来分配：（1）扇形原则，沿经线划设直达北极点的陆地或海上边界。（2）等距原则，外大陆架边界一点到相邻或相向海岸线最近点的距离相等。②

这两种方案都没有得到北极国家当前实践的支持。几十年来，俄

---

① e.g., John Rawls, A Theory of Justice (New York: Basic Books, 1974).
② e.g., Weber, n. 60, above.

罗斯一直主张扇形理论，但在 2010 年与挪威达成的《巴伦支海条约》中甚至都没有提及该理论。[1] 加拿大数十年来一直对扇形理论持模棱两可态度，直至 2006 年彻底放弃。[2] 挪威已经收到大陆架界限委员会建议，将其大陆架外部界限扩展至北极点以南。[3] 丹麦已经完成数据收集，准备向大陆架界限委员会提交提案。而美国似乎已将第七十六条视为国际习惯法，尽管美国不受条约义务的约束。[4] 此外，正如第三章中所解释的，国际海洋法法庭在"孟加拉湾案"中的决定可能对北冰洋中部问题缺乏指导意义，因为该案未涉及海底的海岭或隆起等情况。出于所有这些原因，有必要考虑，是否有国际法规则涉及该区域划界问题。

（一）海底高地划界

加拿大、丹麦和俄罗斯都认为罗蒙诺索夫海岭为其各自大陆边自然组成部分，重要的是考虑若该海岭（如上文所建议）在地貌学上与加拿大或丹麦大陆边或者与俄罗斯大陆边均存在联系情况下的影响。从逻辑上讲，如果加拿大和俄罗斯可以在那里发现相似科学证据，那么阿尔法/门捷列夫海岭也能得出类似结论。

近期科学家确实指出了罗蒙诺索夫海岭在地貌学方向上的问题。俄罗斯政府科学家主张罗蒙诺索夫海岭是名为"Arctida"的古代大陆的一

---

[1] Tore Henriksen and Geir Ulfstein, "Maritime Delimitation in the Arctic: The Barents Sea Treaty." (2011) 42 Ocean Development and International Law 1 at 6.

[2] Stephen Harper, "Securing Canadian Sovereignty in the Arctic, Speech Given at Iqaluit, Nunavut, 12 August 2006," http://www.byers.typepad.com/arctic/2009/03/securing-canadian-sovereignty-in-the-arctic.html.

[3] "Summary of the Recommendations of the Commission on the Limits of the Continental Shelf in Regard to the Submission Made by Norway in Respect of Areas in the Arctic Ocean, the Barents Sea and the Norwegian Sea on 27 November 2006," March 27, 2009, http://www.un.org/Depts/los/clcs_new/submissions_files/nor06/nor_rec_summ.pdf.

[4] The International Court of Justice has ruled that Article 76 (1) of UNCLOS is part of customary international law. See Territorial and Maritime Dispute (Nicaragua v. Colombia), November 19, 2012, Chapter 3, n. 65, above, p. 118.

部分,该大陆是欧亚和北美之间地壳构造上的桥梁,[①] 加拿大和丹麦政府的科学家认为其为北美和欧亚大陆仍然相连之时形成的"双面大陆边"。[②] 这就提出了一个问题:海岭在法律上是否可被视为一个以上大陆边的组成部分,从而受到两国或以上相向沿岸国的管辖?

《联合国海洋法公约》或《联合国大陆架界限委员会科学和技术准则》(以下简称《科学和技术准则》)似乎均未排除该可能性。《科学和技术准则》仅仅表明,海底扩张过程之前分裂过程中形成于被动大陆边的海岭很可能被认为是大陆边的自然组成部分,而没有考虑到此海岭与两个大陆边相连的可能性。[③] 因此,从属于一个以上大陆边的海岭可以被认定为其在地貌上所依附的所有大陆边的自然组成部分。

正如上文所述,俄罗斯2001年给大陆架界限委员会的提案止于北极点表明,至少莫斯科对主张整个海岭的权利不感兴趣。加拿大和丹麦缺乏跨过中间线的地图也表明,他们不会对整个地物提出主张。因此,存在一种可能,即部分或全部北冰洋国家可能更愿意使用某种等距或扇形规则将罗蒙诺索夫海岭划分为欧亚和北美两部分。

(二)使用扇形或等距规则划分海岭

无论使用扇形还是距离方法对罗蒙诺索夫海岭进行横向划界都可以减少产生科学分歧的可能性,该分歧可能导致问题复杂化或阻碍双方达成一致解决方案。2001年俄罗斯提案止于北极点可以被视为一个提议,或许加拿大和丹麦也将认为将北极点作为人为边界是合理的,无论是以完全意义上的扇形理论为基础,还是承认该地点的象征性意义。在后一

---

① e.g., E. V. Verzhbitskii, et al., "Age of the Alpha-Mendeleev and Lomonosov Ridges (Amerasian Basin)" (2011) 441 Doklady Earth Sciences 1587; N. P. Lavero, et al., "Basic Model of Tectonic Development of the Arctic as a Basis for Preparation of the Updated Submission of Russia to the UN Commission concerning the Establishment of the Outer Limits of the Continental Shelf." (2012) 2 (6) The Arctic: Ecology and Economy 4 (in Russian).

② e.g., Ruth Jackson, et al., "The Structure of the Lomonosov Ridge, Arctic Ocean," n. 66, above.

③ discussion, above, pp. 100 – 101.

种情况下,划设一条横跨该海岭靠近北极点部分的横向边界或许是合理的。① 相比之下,基于距离的方法将根据俄罗斯与格陵兰/埃尔斯米尔岛的相向海岸线划设横跨该海岭的中间线(例如等距线)。

那么第一个问题是,加拿大和丹麦两国是否能够接受将北极点作为某种横向边界的基础。很明显,如果整个罗蒙诺索夫海岭仅是其本国大陆边延伸,那么两国接受的可能性较小;如果该海岭是两国及俄罗斯大陆边的自然组成部分,则其接受的可能性更大。但是,即使在后一情况下,罗蒙诺索夫海岭最接近北极点的相关区域与格陵兰和埃尔斯米尔岛之间的距离比距俄罗斯海岸要小得多,这将被视为具有相关性。此外,韦伯指出,扇形划分与中间线法之间的差距约有2.2万平方海里。② 在其他条件都平等的情况下,使用北极点作为某种人为边界将对俄罗斯更为有利。为支持这一点,俄罗斯可以指出,其相较加拿大或丹麦而言,拥有更长的北冰洋海岸线,符合专属经济区内海上边界法律通常所采用的"等距线加相关情况"方法。③ 另一方面,亚历克斯·欧德·艾尔弗林克提议,丹麦或加拿大可提出由于俄罗斯更小岛屿与该国其他区域海岸之间的距离可能对其权益造成减损,要求对等距线做出调整。④

总而言之,如果加拿大、丹麦和俄罗斯希望在北冰洋中部划定永久海上边界,他们或者可以依据大陆架界限委员会的建议,或者寻求不通过该组织的方法。若各方继续相信,无论是否有大陆架界限委员会的建议,罗蒙诺索夫海岭都是各国大陆边的自然组成部分,他们可以使用北极点等界限(扇形或其他方法)或使用中间线(之后可能需要调整)划分该海岭及其周边海床。除横向划界之外,该海岭在北美一端还需要在加拿大和丹麦之间进行某种纵向划界,我们现在将要讨论这个问题。

---

① Conceivably, such a lateral line could follow the 1685803700W meridian, consistent with the 1990 Russia-US boundary treaty and Russia's 2001 submission to the CLCS, or be based on a modified equidistance line that tracked the contours of the Russian and Canadian/Greenland coasts.

② Weber, n. 60, above, p. 672.

③ On the law of maritime boundary delimitation within 200 nautical miles from shore, Chapter 3, above.

④ The islands in question are Henrietta and Jeannette Islands, which are only 3.4 and 11.9 square kilometers in size. Alex G. Oude Elferink, "Arctic Maritime Delimitations," Chapter 2, n. 97, above.

(三) 加拿大和丹麦沿罗蒙诺索夫海岭边界

正如在第二章中所解释的，1973 年加拿大和丹麦划定了格陵兰和加拿大东北部海岸之间长达 1450 海里的边界。该边界终止于内尔斯海峡通往林肯海的那一点，该区域北部近 200 海里大陆架（以及其后专属经济区）成了未解决的问题。2012 年 11 月，加拿大和丹麦两国外交部长宣布，谈判代表已经"就林肯海海上边界位置达成初步协议。"[1] 尽管即将就该条 200 海里范围内边界线达成最终条约或为进一步谈判创造动力，但是这与外大陆架划界几乎不存在法律相关性，因为加拿大和丹麦对相邻的 200 海里管辖权的位置没有争议。

加拿大和丹麦只需就 200 海里外边界进行谈判，如果两国将各自管辖范围扩大至该距离。正如上文所阐释，两国均认为情况确实如此，而且两国可以在向大陆架界限委员会提交提案之前或之后启动海上边界谈判，但应在大陆架界限委员会发布其意见之前。此外，加拿大和丹麦之间谈判没有理由必须等待两国与俄罗斯之间谈判的结果。罗蒙诺索夫海岭法律地位待定可能导致该边界只能是临时性质的，因此可以考虑将其谨慎地暂时终止于距离海岸 350 海里之处。或许更好的办法是简单规定，该边界将按照"在国际法允许的范围内"限制条款的相同方法延伸，如同 1990 年苏联和美国《白令海边界条约》所做的那样。[2]

加拿大和丹麦可以使用的第一种划界方法是基于经线（例如"扇形"），尽管两国已经在埃尔斯米尔岛和格陵兰 200 海里范围内使用等距法，这可能会造成一些麻烦或至少是不一致。[3] 第二种方法，在 200 海里外同样可以使用等距线，尽管越远离海岸确定基点会面临更多技术

---

[1] "Canada and Kingdom of Denmark Reach Tentative Agreement on Lincoln Sea Boundary," News Release, Canadian Department of Foreign Affairs, November 28, 2012 (with backgrounder), http://www.international.gc.ca/media/aff/news-communiques/2012/11/28a.aspx?lang=engan-dview=d. Kim Mackrael, "Canada, Denmark a Step Closer to Settling Border Dispute," Globe and Mail, November 30, 2012, http://www.theglobeandmail.com/news/national/canada-denmark-a-step-closer-to-settling-border-dispute/article5831571/.

[2] Chapter 2, n. 20, above, Art. 2 (1).

[3] On the maritime boundary in the Lincoln Sea, Chapter 2, above.

困难。此外，经线法和等距法均忽略了包括海岭或隆起等地质与地貌特征在外大陆架划界中的潜在关联。因此，沿着坡峰亦或沿着海岭每一个侧面的陆坡脚划设等距线，是划分该海岭比较可行的方法。

然而，沿着一些平坦延伸确定该海岭的坡峰可能存在困难，而由于不断出现具有挑战性的海冰条件，导致缺乏这些区域的科学数据，基于该海岭不同侧面陆坡脚各点划设等距线也将变得困难。幸好无需克服这些挑战，因为政治性和自然性地理因素的纯粹巧合，利用海岸线基点划设等距线将差不多就是沿着罗蒙洛索夫海岭中部区域延伸。因此，基于海岸线基点的等距线可被建议为在此情况下划设边界线的最佳和最易行方式。

无论采用哪种方法，加拿大和丹麦均希望对跨界油气资源和矿床的联合管理做出规定，正如第二章和第三章中讨论的。正如本章前面所讨论的，两国还应该考虑在任何边界协议中包含一项"特别区域"的规定，以此防止大陆架界限委员会建议两国中一国对罗蒙诺索夫海岭没有主权权利的风险。[1] 由于俄罗斯、美国和挪威已经在北极适用特别区域，尽管上述案例都是在距离海岸 200 海里内，但是加拿大和丹麦在适用该制度时可能默许其超出该距离。

（四）第三方争端解决

如果俄罗斯、丹麦和加拿大未能就其边界问题展开谈判，它们可以在几种有约束力的第三方争端解决方案中做出选择。备选方案包括国际法院、国际海洋法法庭、常设仲裁庭，或者为处理该问题而特别设立的法庭。[2] 裁判或仲裁可避免因谈判让步而造成的国内政治成本，但会导致丧失控制权并阻止考虑非法律因素，这些因素有可能是有利的，也可能是不利的。

裁决或仲裁可能是澄清罗蒙诺索夫海岭法律地位的一种方式。俄罗斯、丹麦和加拿大可以通过"特别协议"的方式向法庭或仲裁庭提出

---

[1] On special areas generally, Chapter 2, above.

[2] generally, Natalie Klein, Dispute Settlement in the UN Convention on the Law of the Sea (Cambridge University Press, 2004).

具体问题，而无需要求法庭或仲裁庭划定边界。裁决之后，各方可以在更为坚实的法律基础上就边界问题进行谈判，亦或者三国可要求法庭或仲裁庭确定海岭的地位并划定各自边界。

加拿大或丹麦也有可能根据国际法院的强制管辖权对彼此提出诉讼，因为两国都根据"任择性条款"做出了必要声明。[1] 然而，俄罗斯尚未发表类似声明，可能根据1953年"货币黄金案"中确定的原则，对未经其同意确定罗蒙诺索夫海岭地位提出反对。[2] 或许更为重要的是，三国均对排除《联合国海洋法公约》第十五部分强制性争端解决对海上边界争议的适用做出广泛声明，这可以排除任何一方在未获得他方同意的情况下，在任何法庭或仲裁庭提起与北冰洋中部有关的诉讼。[3] 但是如果没有在合理时间范围内谈判达成协议，他们可以根据《联合国海洋法公约》附件五第二节所规定的程序，保留要求另一方接受调解的选择。[4]

另一个重要的问题是关于任何诉诸裁判或仲裁：在大陆架界限委员会做出建议之前，任何国际法庭或仲裁庭是否有资格就相关问题提出建议或裁决？在"孟加拉湾案"中，国际海洋法法院总结称，其能够并且应当先行对外大陆架进行划界。其解释道：

《联合国海洋法公约》《委员会议事规则》或其实践中均没有任何内容表明，对大陆架进行划界会对委员会履职构成障碍。《联合国海洋法公约》第七十六条第10款规定，"本条的规定不妨害海岸相向或相邻国家间大陆架界限划定的问题"……正如委员会的职能不会影响海岸相向或相邻国家之间大陆架划界问题，所以，国际法庭或仲裁庭就划设大陆架等海上边界而践行司法管辖，不会损害委员会履行自身有关划定

---

[1] For Canada's declaration, http：//www. icj – cij. org/jurisdiction/index. php？p1 = 5andp2 = 1andp3 = 3andcode = CA. For Denmark's, http：//www. icj – cij. org/jurisdiction/index. php？p1 = 5andp2 = 1andp3 = 3andcode = DK.

[2] Monetary Gold Removed from Rome in 1943 (Italy v. France, UK and USA) (1954) ICJ Reports 19.

[3] Declarations of States Parties Relating to Settlement of Disputes in Accordance with Article 298 (optional exceptions to the applicability of Part XV, Section 2, of the Convention). http：//www. itlos. org/fileadmin/itlos/documents/basic_texts/298_declarations_June_2011_english. pdf.

[4] UNCLOS, n. 12, above, Art. 298 (1) (a) (i).

大陆架外部界限的职能。①

简而言之，划设大陆架外部界限和划设海上边界之间存在重要区别，前者是大陆架界限委员会的领域，后者是相关沿岸国的责任。这些国家可在任何地点划定边界，包括将相关问题提交裁判或仲裁。也就是说，如果法庭"得出结论认为该争议地区是否存在大陆边缘具有很大的不确定性，那么该法庭将会对划定超过 200 海里的边界犹豫不决"②。2001 年俄罗斯首次提交之后，大陆架界限委员会要求其提供更多数据，类似内容的建议至少对涉及北冰洋中部的问题有一定的借鉴意义。

任何关于向大陆架界限委员会联合提交的协议，也可能包含对裁决或仲裁的承诺。例如，加拿大、丹麦和俄罗斯可以同意将其所有数据提交给大陆架界限委员会，前提是明确了解其建议一旦收到，将立即传送给国际法院、国际海洋法法庭、常设仲裁法院，或者其他就划界问题而设的法庭。将整个北冰洋中部海床管辖权问题完全交由第三方机构处理，这样做的好处是可以避免其政治化，并且不会僭越大陆架界限委员会的角色。

七、非北极国家和北极大陆架

一些非北极国家对中北冰洋发出有兴趣的信号，中国则表示对这个国家管辖范围之外区域的完整性有特别关注。③ 2009 年，中国外交部部长助理胡正跃表示：

> 在确定外大陆架界限时，北极国家不仅需要妥善处理好彼此之间的关系，而且必须考虑外大陆架和作为全人类共同遗产

---

① Dispute Concerning Delimitation of the Maritime Boundary between Bangladesh and Myanmar in the Bay of Bengal (Bangladesh/Myanmar), Chapter 3, n. 82, above, pp. 111 – 112, pp. 377 – 379.

② Ibid. at p. 129, p. 443.

③ "China's Perspective on Arctic Matters." (2009) 55 (15) Shijie Zhishi, translated in Linda Jakobson, "China Prepares for an Ice – Free Arctic." SIPRI Insights on Peace and Security, No. 2010/2, March 2010, http://books.sipri.org/files/insight/SIPRIInsight1002.pdf.

的国际海底区域之间的关系,以确保沿岸国利益与国际社会共同利益之间的平衡。①

因此,一个或更多非北极国家将会反对加拿大、丹麦向大陆架界限委员会提交申请以及俄罗斯再次申请更新。非北极国家的抗议不能依据划界争端,因为这些国家在该地区没有主权权利,因此它们也无法影响大陆架界限委员会做出建议的法律权利。然而,麦克道曼认为,大陆架界限委员会不代表任何国家或国家集团,因此所有国家都有权利反对其建议或沿岸国在划设其大陆架时所采取的行动。② 他总结道,大陆架界限具有普遍约束力的唯一途径是使其在一段合理的时间内得到国际社会接受。③ 即使麦克道曼是不正确的,来自非北极国家的反对也可能会对大陆架界限委员会产生政治影响,抑制其任何批准的意愿,特别是雄心勃勃的申请。这也可能会为北极国家在提交其申请时保持克制,并在大陆架界限委员会程序内外仔细考虑其选项提供机会。

与此同时,《联合国海洋法公约》适用于全球,许多非北极国家将有机会就其本国海岸线以外的外大陆架提交申请。举例来讲,中国使用关于外大陆架的第七十六条规定支持其在东海的广泛主张。④ 中国还打算从《联合国海洋法公约》第十一部分所规定的规则中获益,该规定

---

① Ibid. The next year, Assistant Foreign Minister Liu Zhenmin said: "In accordance with the United Nations Convention on the Law of the Sea and other relevant international laws, Arctic states have sovereign rights and jurisdiction in their respective areas in the Arctic region, while non-Arctic states also enjoy rights of scientific research and navigation. To develop a partnership of cooperation, Arctic and non-Arctic states should, first and foremost, recognize and respect each other's rights under the international law." Liu Z., "China's View on Arctic Cooperation," July 30, 2010, http://www.fmprc.gov.cn/eng/wjb/zzjg/tyfls/tfsxw/t812046.htm.

② Ted L. McDorman, "The Role of the Commission on the Limits of the Continental Shelf: A Technical Body in a Political World." (2002) 17 International Journal of Marine and Coastal Law 301 at 313.

③ Ibid., p.317.

④ Alexander M. Peterson, "Sino-Japanese Cooperation in the East China Sea: A Lasting Arrangement?" (2009) 42 Cornell International Law Journal 441. China's disputes in the South China Sea revolve around quite different issues of title to land territory, in the form of islands and shoals, and the entitlements of such features to maritime zones.

给予所有国家在外大陆架之外进行深海海底采矿的权利。① 非北极的欧洲国家也是如此。英国依据第七十六条坚持主张对南乔治亚和南设得兰群岛外大陆架的主权权利。② 法国利用第七十六条主张在本国大西洋海岸和印度洋留尼汪岛周边权利,③ 等等。这些规则的互惠性可确保非北极国家将接受其在北极地区的关联性。

八、小结

北冰洋中部海床上有许多海底高地,其中最为突出的是罗蒙诺索夫海岭。《联合国海洋法公约》为沿岸国确定其对不同海底高地的管辖权提供了范式。加拿大、丹麦和俄罗斯可能享有主张罗蒙诺索夫海岭部分或全部区域为其大陆边缘(或被称为"海底隆起")自然组成部分的法律权利,同时加拿大和俄罗斯或享有主张阿尔法/门捷列夫海岭部分或全部的法律权利。这可能会让这些国家,连同美国一起,将他们的海床管辖范围扩展至除两个较小区域之外的整个北冰洋。然而,除非不同国家间相互合作,否则实现这一结果的过程将是漫长和困难的。加拿大、丹麦和俄罗斯可有效协调其提交大陆架界限委员会的申请,甚至可以联合提交,以确保大陆架界限委员会为他们提供永久解决这两个海岭法律地位的必要信息。加拿大、丹麦可以和俄罗斯一起划定临时或永久海上边界,以在等待大陆架界限委员会建议之时,建构更大程度的确定性和稳定性。三国中两国以上也可以求助于司法或仲裁途径,帮助解决目前普遍存在的法律不确定性。无论采取上述哪个步骤,都将会有助于维持北冰洋政治中特有的合作之健康动力。

---

① On deep seabed mining, Chapter 6, below.

② Submission by the United Kingdom of Great Britain and Northern Ireland in Respect of South Georgia and the South Sandwich Islands, 2009, http://www.un.org/Depts/los/clcs_new/submissions_files/gbr45_09/gbr2009fgs_executive%20summary.pdf.

③ Submission by the French Republic in Respect of La Re'union Island and Saint - Paul andAmsterdam Islands, 2009, http://www.un.org/Depts/los/clcs_new/submissions_files/submission_fra_40_2009.htm.

第五章 北极航道

"我需要寻找海冰，这是有生以来第一次。"2011年8月，亚历克斯·麦金泰尔站在"约飞院士"号的舰桥上发出这样的感慨。当时这艘悬挂俄罗斯国旗的冰区强化船刚穿过拉森海峡。麦金泰尔是一位有着40年北极航行经验的冰区引航员，他仍记得这条航线被十米多厚的海冰堵塞时的场景。现在，船上的80名生态游客热切地想要亲眼目睹海冰和聚集在海冰周围的海洋生物，但是出人意料的是，拉森海峡居然完全无冰。此前一天，我们穿过了贝洛特海峡，这是一条历史上曾被冰雪覆盖的西北航道咽喉要道，位于北极圈以北600千米。这条海峡很狭窄并伴有强大的潮汐流，但是由于没有海冰，在期间航行的难度也并不比土耳其西部的博斯普鲁斯海峡和达达尼尔海峡或者丹麦和瑞典之间的厄勒海峡高多少。

数十年来，由于厚实坚硬的"多年"海冰常年存在，只有重型破冰船才可以通过西北航道。沿俄罗斯北部海岸的北方海航线亦是如此，该航线有时被称为"东北航道"。但气候变化正导致冰层变薄和消退，这种现象在北极地区比在全球其他任何地区发展得都为迅速。2007年9月，北极出现史无前例的海冰融化现象，当季海冰覆盖率最低时仅有417万平方千米，比2005年的最低记录还少150万平方千米。① 这是西北航道和北方海航线首次出现暂时无冰并可向非破冰船开放的情况。2012年9月该记录再被打破，北极海冰覆盖区域降至341万平方千米，较1979至2000年间的平均水平下降49%。② 2007至2012年也不例外，北极海冰六次最低记录均发生在这六年间。③

---

① US National Snow and Ice Data Center, "Arctic Sea Ice News and Analysis," http://nsidc.org/arcticseaicenews/.

② Ibid.

③ Ibid.

现在看来，2020 年北极或在较晚季节出现完全无冰的现象，多年生海冰也将永久消失。① 欧洲航天局新型"冷卫星"2011 年拍摄的图像显示，多年生海冰已经从北冰洋大部分地区消失，现存区域的海冰也正迅速变薄。② 沿加拿大和俄罗斯北部海岸线的航道很快就会和波罗的海或者圣劳伦斯湾一样，冰区加强船只和破冰船护航船队将可在此实现全年运行。我们已经可以看到北极航运数急剧上升。1906 至 2005 年，西北航道通航的第一个百年中只有 69 次通过；而 2006 至 2010 年，只用了五年时间就再次出现 69 次通过，③ 其中 2009 和 2010 年均出现了 18 次通过。这种增长趋势仍在持续，2011 年出现 22 次通过，2012 年则有 30 次。④

伴随着航运增加而来的是环境和安全风险，在如此广袤和边远的区域，这些问题只能依靠距离最近的沿岸国妥善解决。相关风险包括致命事故、溢油、走私、非法移民、海盗和恐怖主义。⑤ 然而，沿岸国对西北航道和北方海航线的管辖存在冲突。美国认为，上述两条航线中最窄的部分均属于"国际海峡"，所有国家船只都可自由通行。

1949 年国际法院在"科孚海峡案"中为国际海峡设立的标准是"地理上连接公海的两个部分，并且存在用于国际航行的事实"。⑥ 当外国船舶必须在一个或多个沿岸国的 12 海里范围内航行通过国际海峡时，

---

① Peter Wadhams, "Arctic Ice Cover, Ice Thickness and Tipping Points." (2012) 41 AMBIO: A Journal of the Human Environment 1 at 31.

② "Cryosat Mission Delivers First Sea – Ice Map," BBC News, June 21, 2011, http://www.bbc.co.uk/news/science – environment – 13829785.

③ Donat Pharand, "The Arctic Waters and the Northwest Passage: A Final Revisit." (2007) 38 Ocean Development and International Law 3 at 38.

④ Emails from John North, Marine Communications and Traffic Services, Canadian Coast Guard, December 15, 2011 and November 29, 2012 (on file with author). The post – 2005 numbers do not include vessels under 300 tons which are not required to register with Transport Canada before entering Arctic waters. Already, dozens of smaller vessels, mostly private yachts, sail the Northwest Passage each summer.

⑤ the discussion of the 2009 Arctic Marine Shipping Assessment in Chapter 6, below.

⑥ Corfu Channel Case (UK v. Albania) (1949) ICJ Reports 4 at 28. The Court held that the test was not one of volume, while noting that 2,884 ships had passed through the Corfu Channel in a twenty – one – month period. Nor did the test concern the waterway's "greater or lesser importance for international navigation," providing that it is a "useful route for international maritime traffic."

与通常的领海"无害通过"权利不同,这些船舶享有经强化后的"过境通行"权利。① 该权利使得船舶通过上述海峡时既无需经过沿岸国批准,也不必受到其他限制。② 例如,外国潜艇可以潜航状态通过国际海峡,但这在通常的领海中是不可以的。③

加拿大和俄罗斯都坚持认为,沿两国北方海岸线的相关海峡(straits)和水道(channels)构成"内水"。内水不同于领海,未经沿岸国许可外国船舶无权进入该水域。当外国船舶经许可后进入内水时,其存在就不会损害一国的内水主张,例如船只每次均获得许可后进入他国港口。

内水存在于海湾或破碎海岸线,经由他国长期默示承认,或依据国际习惯法和国际法院1951年"英挪渔业案"判决,通过在岬和边缘岛屿划设"直线基线"获得。④

在只有重型破冰船才能通行西北航道和北方海航线时,对两者法律地位的争议并不引人重视。但由于海冰迅速融化和船运量不断增长,两条航道重要性较以往更为凸显,未来或将导致局势紧张。本章解释了这些航道在地缘政治语境下的法律问题,之后就沿岸国和航运国如何通过合作将北极航道转变为安全、可靠、高效和无争议的航运线路提出一系列建议。理论上讲,通过此类合作将有助于最终达成相关条约,承认这些海峡为俄罗斯和加拿大内水,以此换取沿岸国对外国船舶的进入保证以及在服务和基础设施方面的大规模投资。

---

① Art. 38, UNCLOS, Chapter 4, n. 12, above.

② The precise extent of freedom of navigation in international straits remains contested, with some authors questioning whether the relevant provisions of UNCLOS accurately reflect customary international law. e. g. , Tullio Scovazzi, The Evolution of the International Law of the Sea: New Issues, New Challenges (The Hague: Martinus Nijhoff, 2001), 174; Nihan U?nlu?, The Legal Regime of the Turkish Straits (The Hague: Martinus Nijhoff, 2002), 75.

③ Article 39 (1) (c) of UNCLOS states that ships exercising the right of transit passage "shall refrain from any activities other than those incident to their normal modes of continuous and expeditious transit unless rendered necessary by force majeure or by distress." Submarines, by definition, normally sail submerged. In contrast, Article 20 of UNCLOS states: "In the territorial sea, submarines and other underwater vehicles are required to navigate on the surface and to show their flag." UNCLOS, Chapter 4, n. 12, above.

④ Fisheries Case (UK v. Norway) (1951) ICJ Reports 116 at 128 – 129.

一、西北航道

西北航道由数条穿过加拿大高北极岛屿的潜在航道组成。自1880年英国向加拿大移交所有权以来，这里的数千个岛屿即归加拿大所有。当时此处海冰几乎无法被穿透，相关水域的所有权和控制权也就从未被讨论过，直到美国获得强大的破冰船和最近以来海冰大规模融化。

若西北航道属于加拿大内水，那么加拿大国内法将完全适用于该航道。如上文所述，内水不同于领水，未经沿岸国许可任何船舶均无权进入。内水产生于他国长期默认，或根据国际习惯法和"英挪渔业案"判决划设的直线基线。[①]

1985年，加拿大围绕高北极岛屿划设直线基线。加拿大还提出，作为海上原住民的因纽特人对这片海冰进行了数千年的使用和占有，基于这种历史性使用，相关水域属于内水。正如加拿大外交部长乔·克拉克在众议院所述：

> 加拿大对北极土地、海洋和海冰的主权不可分割。其不间断地延伸至北极岛屿向海的海岸线。这些岛屿通过彼此之间的水域连为一体，而不是孤立的。它们在一年中的大部分时间都通过海冰相连。自古以来，加拿大因纽特人即使用和占有这些海冰，正如同他们使用和占有土地。[②]

1993年《努纳武特领土声明协议》谈判之前，[③] 加拿大北极地区

[①] Ibid. Parties to the 1982 UNCLOS (Chapter 4, n. 12, above) wishing to draw straight baselines are subject to Articles 7 and 8. But Canada did not ratify UNCLOS until 2003.

[②] Joe Clark, Secretary of State for External Affairs, Statement on Sovereignty, September 10, 1985, reprinted in Franklyn Griffiths (ed.), Politics of the Northwest Passage (Kingston and Montreal: McGill-Queen's University Press, 1987), 269 at 270.

[③] 1993 Nunavut Land Claims Agreement, http://nlca.tunngavik.com/. In Canada, land claims agreements are "recognized and affirmed" by Section 35 of the Constitution Act 1982. http://laws.justice.gc.ca/eng/Const/page-12.html#sc:7_II.

因纽特人接受了有关传统狩猎和旅行模式的采访。由此得出的地图确认，埃尔斯米尔岛和斯弗德鲁普群岛南部冰封水域实际上是因纽特人和雪橇狗的高速公路，这片水域涵盖西北航道东部和中部区域。[1] 近期，因纽特遗产基金会采访了数位长者，收集西北航道沿线区域的因纽特语地名。[2] 这数千个地名证实了该水道在因纽特人语言、文化、历史和身份认同中的中心地位。

除历史使用和加拿大内水主张外，还可以提出因纽特人在欧洲人抵达之前即获得对西北航道的所有权，之后他们将这项权利转移给加拿大。[3] 在 1975 年《西撒哈拉问题的咨询意见》中，国际法院确认，拥有社会和政治组织的原住民所居住的领土不是无主地。因此，此类人群享有有限但明确的国际法地位。[4]

为推进这一论证，加拿大必须说服其他国家、国际法庭或仲裁庭：（1）海冰可像陆地一样被占有和占用；（2）根据国际法，原住民可获得并向政府转移主权权利；（3）因纽特人将该权利转移给了加拿大政府。

第一点最难以论证，尽管海冰几乎全年存在及其在因纽特人传统生活方式的中心地位，已经使得这种情况具有特殊性并因此令人信服。[5] 第二点需要对"西撒哈拉案"进行扩张性解释；如《联合国土著人民

---

[1] The map is reproduced in Donat Pharand, Canada's Arctic Waters in International Law (Cambridge University Press, 1988), 165.

[2] Inuit Heritage Trust, Place Names Project, http://www.ihti.ca/eng/iht-proj-plac.html.

[3] For an argument to this effect, Jose' Woehrling, "Les Revendications du Canada sur les eaux de l'archipel de l'Arctique et l'utilisation imme'moriale des glaces par les Inuit." (1987) 30 German Yearbook of International Law 120 at 139.

[4] Western Sahara, Advisory Opinion (1975) ICJ Reports 12, pp. 79 – 80.

[5] Susan B. Boyd, "The Legal Status of the Arctic Sea Ice: A Comparative Study and a Proposal." (1984) 22 Canadian Yearbook of International Law 98 at 105. The argument for the Inuit having rights over sea – ice is comparable to (and probably stronger than) similar arguments in favor of indigenous rights in the open water of Torres Strait between Australia and Papua New Guinea. See Monica Mulrennan and Colin Scott, "Indigenous Rights in Saltwater Environments." (2000) 31 Development and Change 681; Colin Scott and Monica Mulrennan, "Reconfiguring Mare Nullius: Torres Strait Islanders, Indigenous Sea Rights and the Divergence of Domestic and International Norms," in Mario Blaser, et al. (eds.), Indigenous Peoples and Autonomy: Insights for a Global Age (Vancouver: UBC Press, 2010), 148.

权利宣言》等近期相关发展降低了这一点的论证难度。① 最后一点最易证明,因为《努纳武特领土声明协议》确认,因纽特人有意向加拿大政府转移其根据国际法对西北航道所可能拥有的任何权利。②

1986年,美国抗议加拿大在北极采用直线基线,美国国务院汇编的美国海洋主张重申了摘编自国务院发送给一位美国参议员信函中的一段话,作为其立场的证据:

> 1985年9月10日,加拿大政府主张其北极岛屿间所有水域为内水,并在其北极群岛周边划设直线基线以确立主权主张。美国的立场是,加拿大的主张没有国际法依据。美国不能接受加拿大的主张,因为这样做将构成接受加拿大完全控制西北航道,并将终止美国依据国际法在西北航道所享有的航行权利。③

无论美国立场的价值为何,此封信中关于接受加拿大的直线基线将必然终止所有过境通行权利的观点是不正确的,因为直线基线并不享有封闭现有国际海峡之效力。④ 因此,加拿大和美国争端的一个关键点

---

① discussion, Chapter 7, below. The 2007 UN Declaration on the Rights of Indigenous Peoples is availableat: //www.un.org/esa/socdev/unpfii/documents/DRIPS_en.pdf. The UN Declaration may now be contributing to the development of customary international law. e.g., Mauro Barelli, "The Role of Soft Law in the International Legal System: The Case of the United Nations Declaration on the Rights of Indigenous Peoples." (2009) 58 International and Comparative Law Quarterly 957. However, the only reference to "waters and coastal seas" in the UN Declaration is in the context of "spiritual relationships." Ibid., Art. 25.

② 1993 Nunavut Land Claims Agreement, n.16, above, sec.15.1.1 (c) ("Canada's sovereignty over the waters of the arctic archipelago is supported by Inuit use and occupancy") and sec.2.7.1 (a) ("In consideration of the rights and benefits provided to Inuit by the Agreement, Inuit hereby: cede, release and surrender to Her Majesty The Queen in Right of Canada, all their aboriginal claims, rights, title and interests, if any, in and to lands and waters anywhere within Canada and adjacent offshore areas within the sovereignty or jurisdiction of Canada").

③ "Letter from James W. Dyer, Acting Assistant Secretary of State for Legislative and Intergovernmental Affairs, to Senator Charles Mathias, Jr. (R. Maryland), February 26, 1986," reproduced in Office of Ocean Affairs, Limits in the Seas No.112: United States Responses to Excessive National Maritime Claims (Washington, DC: US State Department, 1992), 30, http://www.state.gov/documents/organization/58381.pdf.

④ Arts. 8 (2) and 35 (1), UNCLOS, Chapter 4, n.12, above.

是，西北航道在1985年划设直线基线前是否属于"用于国际航行"。

甚至有可能1969年将成为西北航道相关问题的"关键日期"，意即在此时间点双方争议变得明确，随后任何意图支持各自立场的实践在法律上都是无关紧要的。①

（一）美国破冰油轮"曼哈顿"号的航行

1969年，埃克森公司派遣破冰油轮"曼哈顿"号（强化了破冰能力的超级油轮），测试将西北航道作为阿拉斯加通往美国大西洋沿岸航道的可行性。② 美国政府派遣海岸警卫队破冰船"北风"号提供协助。埃克森公司和美国政府行前均未寻求加拿大政府的许可。考虑到此举可能具有创设先例的效果，加拿大政府认为最好的应对措施是"友好的进攻"。加拿大政府先是强调双方已就此展开一些磋商的事实，然后以提供空中侦察和加拿大破冰船协助的形式，表明加拿大政府已批准此次航行。③

美国政府未事先申请许可或许是出于"曼哈顿"号和"北风"号将不会进入加拿大管辖区域的考虑。当时，加拿大仅主张拥有3英里领海，这就为通过西北航道留下了一条"公海"走廊。④ 因此，美国官员打算让这两艘船在整个航程中都保持位于公海之上，从东边的兰开斯特海峡进入西北航道，再经由西边麦克卢尔海峡驶出。⑤ 此次航行之前，

---

① references, Chapter 1, n.9, above.

② Bern Keating, The Northwest Passage: From the Mathew to the Manhattan, 1497 – 1969 (Chicago: Rand McNally and Company, 1970), p. 140.

③ As Prime Minister Pierre Trudeau told the House of Commons: "The legal status of the waters of Canada's Arctic archipelago is not at issue in the proposed transit of the Northwest Passage by the ships involved in the Manhattan project ... The oil companies concerned and the United States Coast Guard have consulted with appropriate Canadian authorities in the planning of the operation. The government will support the trials with the Canadian Coast Guard ice – breaker John A. Macdonald ... and will also provide aerial ice reconnaissance and assume responsibility for the coordination of such reconnaissance. The government has also selected and appointed an official Canadian government representative on board the S. S. Manhattan who will act as technical advisor and as co – ordinator of Canadian support for the operation." Parliament of Canada, House of Commons, Debates, 1st Session, 28th Parliament, 15 May 1969, pp. 8720 – 8721.

④ Robert S. Reid, "The Canadian Claim to Sovereignty Over the Waters of the Arctic." (1974) 12 Canadian Yearbook of International Law 111 at 120.

⑤ Ibid.

美国国务院通知加拿大政府，此次航行只是进行可行性研究，无意展示主张。① 然而，1969年9月10日，在首次尝试自东向西穿越麦克卢尔海峡之时，"曼哈顿"号被困在了冰层中。② "该船将其43000马力涡轮机中为生活区供热的蒸汽转用于提供额外的7000马力动力后，才得以脱困。即使这样，它也是在同行的加拿大破冰船'约翰·A.麦克唐纳'号帮助下才得以摆脱险境。"③ 在之后的航程中，"约翰·A.麦克唐纳"号至少又在另外11个情境下帮助"曼哈顿"号脱困。④

海冰情况迫使这艘超级油轮撤出麦克卢尔海峡，转而通过狭窄的威尔士王子海峡。正如多内特·法兰德解释道，"因为大公主岛的存在，该船不得不通过加拿大领水"。⑤ 无可争辩的是，进入加拿大领水、加拿大政府默示许可，以及加拿大海岸警卫队大量协助等意料之外的属性，导致"曼哈顿"号此次航行未能对该航道发展为一条国际海峡提供任何助益。

（二）美国海岸警卫队"极地海"号的航行

1985年夏天见证了关于西北航道的一系列外交照会。

5月，美国通知加拿大，美国海岸警卫队破冰船"极地海"号将通过西北航道，"因为是行使航行权利和自由，故无需事先通知"。⑥ 6月，美国重申其立场，"通过和相关准备活动均不会损害任何一方对西

---

① Jay Walz, "Oil Stirs Concern Over Northwest Passage Jurisdiction," New York Times, March 15, 1969.

② Larry Gedney and Merritt Helfferich, "Voyage of the Manhattan," December 19, 1983, Alaska Science Forum Article No. 639, http://www.gi.alaska.edu/ScienceForum/ASF6/639.html.

③ Ibid.

④ W. D. Smith, "Tanker Manhattan Is Escorted Into Halifax Harbor," New York Times, November 9, 1969.

⑤ Pharand, "The Arctic Waters and the Northwest Passage," n. 6, above, 38.

⑥ 1985 State Telegram 151842, May 17, 1985, quoted in Office of Ocean Affairs, Limits in the Seas No. 112, n. 24, above, at 73. The Polar Sea was returning to its homeport of Seattle after re-supplying the US airbase at Thule, Greenland.

北航道的法律立场"。① 7月，加拿大回复称，尽管该航道属于加拿大内水，但是加拿大政府"致力于为该航道航行提供便利"并"准备朝着该目标努力"。② 加拿大政府明确同意美国声明中关于此次航行不会损害两国法律立场的内容，但其随后的作法有些不必要并带有些许挑衅，它明确提供了华盛顿拒绝获得的许可。③ 9月，加拿大外交部长乔·克拉克表示，此次航行"未对加拿大北极主权造成任何影响"。④ 然而，正是"极地海"号此次航行促使加拿大政府明确阐明其内水立场，并通过划定直线基线的方式确定这些水域的外部界限。

一份详细的评估结果显示，加拿大的法律立场事实上并未受到明确挑战，因此此类"国际航行"也不会创设一个国际海峡。然而，一些加拿大专家认为，有必要论证即使存在这两次单方面通过行为，也不足以满足"科孚海峡案"中"用于国际航行"的标准。⑤ 大多数非加拿大学者都同意，至少有必要存在适当的航运量，正如理查德·巴克斯特在1964年写道："国际航道必须是很大程度上用于商业航行或非该海域周边沿岸国军舰航行的河流、运河和海峡"。⑥ 至于"科孚海峡案"中所使用的标准，巴克斯特总结称"较之于地理上的必要性，法院的考察方式更侧重于航运实践"。⑦

丹尼尔·奥康奈尔同样强调"实际使用"标准的重要性：

---

① State Department Note No. 222 of 24 June 1985, as quoted in Diplomatic Note No. 433, 31 July 1985, reprinted (in part) in Office of Ocean Affairs, Limits in the Seas No. 112, n. 24, above, p. 74.

② Diplomatic Note No. 433, 31 July 1985, reproduced fully only in the paper version of J. Ashley Roach and Robert W. Smith, Excessive Maritime Claims, 3rd edn. (Leiden: Martinus Nijhoff, 2012), p. 321.

③ Ibid.

④ Joe Clark, Secretary of State for External Affairs, Statement on Sovereignty, n. 15, above, p. 270.

⑤ For instance, Donat Pharand argues that "proof must be adduced that it has a history as a useful route for international maritime traffic." Pharand, "The Arctic Waters and the Northwest Passage," p. 35.

⑥ Richard R. Baxter, The Law of International Waterways (Cambridge, Mass.: Harvard University Press, 1964), p. 3.

⑦ Ibid., p. 9.

当论及法律上的海峡是指领海内连接公海两个部分的航道之时,不能从字面上进行解释,而应解释为意味着该航道通常承担大量国际航运,并且这些航运的目的地并非相关海岸线上的港口。与考察何为海湾不同,验证什么是海峡更多的是强调其功能因素,而不是地理因素。①

美国军方则认为,只要符合潜在使用条件即足够,② 甚至认为地理因素是唯一的考察标准。③ 然而,这些观点显然与国际法院在"科孚海峡案"中的判决和多数专家的意见相左。

(三)欧盟和中国

美国在西北航道问题上的立场得到欧共体(现为欧盟)的支持。1986年,欧共体同美国国务院一道抗议加拿大在高北极岛屿划设直线基线的做法。

其他国家基线的有效性取决于该案中对国际法相关原则的适用,包括划设基线不应明显偏离该国海岸一般方向的原则。成员国承认,纯粹地理因素以外的因素在特定情况下也可能与划设基线的目的具有相关性,但对现有基线仅在总体上进行合法性证明表示不满。此外,根据该指令,成员国不得承认将历史性所有权作为划设直线基线正当理由的有效性。④

---

① Daniel P. O'Connell, The International Law of the Sea, vol. 1, ed. Ivan Shearer (Oxford: Clarendon Press, 1982), 497. Daniel P. O'Connell, The International Law of the Sea, vol. 1, ed. Ivan Shearer (Oxford: Clarendon Press, 1982), p. 497.

② Richard J. Grunawalt, "United States Policy on International Straits." (1987) 18 Ocean Development and International Law 445 at 456.

③ James C. Kraska, "The Law of the Sea Convention and the Northwest Passage." (2007) 22 International Journal of Marine and Coastal Law 257 at 275.

④ British High Commission Note No. 90/86 of 9 July 1986, reprinted in Office of Ocean Affairs, Limits in the Seas No. 112, n. 24, above, 29 – 30. The United Kingdom was acting on behalf of all the members of the European Community, which in 1986 included Belgium, Denmark, France, Germany, Greece, Ireland, Italy, Luxemburg, the Netherlands, Portugal, Spain, and the United Kingdom.

"海岸一般方向"要求源于"英挪渔业案"。① 将其运用于加拿大高北极岛屿十分复杂,然而通过广泛使用"墨卡托"或"圆锥"投影法,可以扭曲两极附近地貌的大小和形状,从而使得沿岸群岛看起来像是北美大陆附属物,而不是其组成部分。地球仪可以更为准确地描述地理位置,同时也为加拿大法律立场增加更多可信度。法兰德已经确定,加拿大直线基线系统甚至符合美国制定的测试标准,即"大部分边远岛屿没有偏离海岸线或其一般趋势超过20度"。② 他还指出,美国的考察方式可能比国际法所要求的更为苛刻。③

欧共体抗议并且质疑"根据该命令,将历史性所有权作为划定边界正当理由的有效性"。然而,这并不是反对加拿大使用直线基线本身,而是指责数条基线不同寻常的长度。④ 但无论如何,欧洲似乎再未重复提出抗议。2009年,欧洲部长理事会发表有关北极的声明,其中提到了"过境通行"权利,意即表明该地区至少存在一条国际海峡。⑤ 但其更有可能针对的是美国阿拉斯加和俄罗斯远东地区之间的白令海峡,该海峡为国际海峡,其地位已被美国和俄罗斯承认。⑥

最后,尽管记者们有时会推测中国反对加拿大法律立场,但中国政府目前尚未对西北航道或北方海航线地位采取正式立场。介入北极沿岸国家争端不符合中国利益,因为加拿大和俄罗斯是唯一在实践中可以提供适当航海图、导航服务、避难港口、天气和海冰预报、搜寻和救助,威慑和处理海盗、恐怖主义、走私等警察力量的国家,而这些都是中国航运公司所需要的。⑦

---

① Anglo-Norwegian Fisheries Case (1951) ICJ Reports 116 at 133.
② Pharand, "The Arctic Waters and the Northwest Passage," n. 6, above, 19, quoting Office of Ocean Affairs, Limits in the Seas No. 106: Developing Standard Guidelines for Evaluating Straight Baselines (Washington, DC: US State Department), p. 16.
③ Ibid.
④ For a map of "Canadian Arctic Islands and Mainland Baselines," https://www.acls-aatc.ca/files/english/books/6.10.jpg.
⑤ Council of the European Union, "Council Conclusions on Arctic Issues," December 8, 2009, http://www.consilium.europa.eu/uedocs/cms_Data/docs/pressdata/EN/foraff/111814.pdf.
⑥ For more on Bering Strait, see below, pp. 157-159.
⑦ Michael Byers, "The Dragon Looks North," Al Jazeera, December 28, 2011, http://www.aljazeera.com/indepth/opinion/2011/12/20111226145144638282.html.

(四) 1988 年《北极合作协议》

自 1987 年美国总统罗纳德·里根访问渥太华以来,无论对加拿大或是美国,西北航道争议都没有造成任何难题。加拿大总理布赖恩·马尔罗尼在其办公室的一个地球仪上指出了西北航道的位置,他或许知道地球仪比平面地图更符合加拿大法律立场。[1] 里根的回应是,将要求其官员商讨解决方案,而结果就是 1988 年的《北极合作协议》。[2] 该协议解决了当时美国海岸警卫队破冰船在西北航道航行的棘手问题,方法是将该航道从法律争端中删除。美国承诺,"美国破冰船在加拿大主张的内水范围内所有航行均将经过加拿大政府同意。"同时,加拿大承诺为这些船只"航行提供方便"。两国还同意,"本协议中任何内容……或据此产生的实践,均不影响美国政府和加拿大政府在海洋法或其他海洋领域中的各自立场"。易言之,该条约从本质上讲,是同意各自保留不同意见。[3]

《北极合作协议》的目的是无限期地管控西北航道争议,因为当时厚且硬的海冰长期存在,航运仅限于破冰船。但问题同样是,如今海冰正变薄和减少,航运数量也在不断增加。现在通行该航道的多是外国油船和私人游艇,这可能引起走私和非法移民使用该线路进入北美地区的

---

[1] Interview with Brian Mulroney, "Leveraging Canada-US Relations 'to Get Big Things Done,'" Policy Options, March 2011, pp. 12 – 18, http://www.irpp.org/po/archive/mar11/mulroney.pdf. According to Christopher Kirkey, the US president "said something to the effect that 'that looks a little different than the maps they showed me on the plane coming to Ottawa.'" Kirkey, "Smoothing Troubled Waters: The 1988 Canada-United States Arctic Co-operation Agreement." (1994 – 1995) 50 International Journal 401 at 409.

[2] "Agreement between the Government of Canada and the Government of the United States of America on Arctic Cooperation," Canada Treaty Series 1988, No. 29, http://www.lexum.com/ca_us/en/cts.1988.29.en.html.

[3] In 2006, US Ambassador David Wilkins wrote that the agreement to seek Canadian permission was restricted to activities that are "not an exercise of the right of transit passage, such as marine scientific research," and that US icebreakers, "in the absence of marine scientific research, would not be required to seek Canadian consent before transiting the Northwest Passage." Letter from David Wilkins, Ambassador of the United States of America, to Peter Boehm, Assistant Deputy Minister, North America, Department of Foreign Affairs and International Trade, October 27, 2006, http://www.state.gov/documents/organization/98836.pdf.

风险。这给美国带来难题,自 2001 年"9·11"事件后,美国开始担忧恐怖分子可能利用西北航道潜入北美地区,或者"流氓国家"借由北美最长和几乎不设防的海岸线运输大规模杀伤性武器。一些美国人已经意识到,应对这些挑战的最佳方式是通过沿岸国国内刑事、海关和移民等方面法律,而不是依靠国际法中对国际海峡更为薄弱的管制权力。由于加拿大与美国军事和经济联系紧密,得出该结论就更为容易。

2004 年 10 月,时任美国大使保罗·塞卢奇表示,"我们看待任何事情都会透过恐怖主义的棱镜。我们首要任务是阻止恐怖分子。因此,当西北航道问题再次摆上台面时,我们可能会有不同看法。"① 5 个月之后,塞卢奇透露,他已经请求美国国务院依据恐怖主义威胁,重新检视美国立场。② 出于某种原因,加拿大政府未能跟进这一含蓄却明确的谈判邀请。直到 2007 年 8 月,加拿大总理斯蒂芬·哈珀向美国总统小布什提及塞卢奇观点时,此事才取得进一步进展。③ 但没有进行任何外交准备,该新闻就被置若罔闻。④

(五)对先例的担忧

美国海军尤为担忧,承认加拿大在西北航道法律地位可能为世界其他地区被美国主张为国际海峡的航道开设先例。2009 年 1 月,美国总统小布什在离任前签署指令,其中包含重申美国对西北航道属于国际海

---

① Greg Younger – Lewis, "US Might Be Safer if it Left Northwest Passage to Canada: US Ambassador," Canadian Press Newswire (Toronto), October 7, 2004.

② "North of Sixty: US Virtual Presence Posts in Canada," online dialogue with Ambassador Cellucci (March 9, 2005), http://web.archive.org/web/20080905100147/ http://www.canadanorth.usvpp.gov/yukon/chat.asp.

③ Tonda MacCharles and Bruce Campion – Smith, "Troops Out by '09, Bush Told," Toronto Star, August 21, 2007. At the same time, the by – then former ambassador made his personal views clear: "I think, in the age of terrorism, it's in our security interests that the Northwest Passage be considered part of Canada. That would enable the Canadian navy to intercept and board vessels in the Northwest Passage to make sure they're not trying to bring weapons of mass destruction into North America." Jim Brown, Canadian Press, "Ex – US envoy backs Canada's Arctic claim," Toronto Star, August 20, 2007, http://www.thestar.com/News/Canada/article/247881.

④ Several months later, in February 2008, Cellucci took part in a "model negotiation" between two teams of non – governmental experts. See discussion, below, p. 155.

峡长期立场的内容:"海洋自由是美国的最优先事项……维护北极地区航行和飞越相关权利和义务,支撑着美国在全球范围内行使通过战略海峡等相关权利的能力。"①

然而苏珊娜·拉隆德和弗雷德里克·拉塞尔分析了7个案例,"案例中,美国对其认为属于将国际海峡非法纳入某个沿岸国内水的行为提出抗议,从而捍卫航行自由原则"。② 第一个案例,日本为避免对美国利益造成任何威胁,以限制该国在宗谷、大隅和津轻海峡领海宽度的方式,确保国际航行,但日本同时宣布马关、丰予海峡和丰后水道等数个次要航道为内水。在其他三个案例中,印度和斯里兰卡之间的保克海峡,黑海和亚述海之间的刻赤海峡,意大利本土和厄尔巴岛之间的皮奥比诺海峡,因水深较浅、意义不大或存在更有利航线等因素,这些航道对美国实际价值较小。

拉隆德和拉塞尔得出的结论是:只有俄罗斯北方海航线、中国琼州海峡、黑德港水道(一个既窄又短,通过加拿大水域靠近美国缅因州的水道),和西北航道一样"引发同样法律担忧"并"对美存在不可否认和非常现实的战略利益"。③ 他们还推测,海冰融化可提升俄罗斯近海岛屿以北水域的通过能力,或事实上削弱北方海航线重要性,同时"可能对中国事实上对琼州海峡行使专属主权存在默示承认,并且这种情况或不会改变"。④ 至于黑德港水道,"其重要性更多体现在本身性质方面,因此或不会在全球战略评估中提及"。⑤

拉隆德和拉塞尔还注意到:"某些特定国家内水中包含的其他海峡

---

① National Security Presidential Directive 66 and Homeland Security Presidential Directive 25, January 9, 2009, http://www.fas.org/irp/offdocs/nspd/nspd-66.htm.

② Suzanne Lalonde and Fré′dé′ric Lasserre, "The Position of the United States on the Northwest Passage: Is the Fear of Creating a Precedent Warranted?" (2012) 43 Ocean Development and International Law 28.

③ Ibid. On the latter dispute, Jon M. Van Dyke, "Canada's Authority to Prohibit LNG Vessels from Passing through Head Harbor Passage to US Ports." (2008-2009) 14 Ocean and Coastal Law Journal 45.

④ Ibid. On the latter dispute, see Jon M. Van Dyke, "Canada's Authority to Prohibit LNG Vessels from Passing through Head Harbor Passage to US Ports." (2008-2009) 14 Ocean and Coastal Law Journal 45.

⑤ Ibid.

并未成为美国抗议的对象,因为它们受到特定国际条约或协议的管辖"。① 这个重要问题将在下文讨论美国和加拿大在海冰消融等环境根本性改变的情况下,寻求解决西北航道争议的选项时提及。②

最后,拉隆德和拉塞尔指出:大多数战略海峡(直布罗陀、霍尔木兹、马六甲、新加坡、托雷斯海峡等),在许多学术著作中被称受到西北航道先例的潜在影响,但实际上这根本不具有相关性。这些海峡不在与之毗邻的一国内水之中,因此不受这些国家的排他性控制。更为重要的是,这些主要海上通道目前毫无疑问被视为国际海峡,应适用过境通行制度。他们被认定为国际海峡,无论西北航道案最终结果如何,这些国际海峡的法律权利均不会受到合理的质疑。③

简而言之,由于各种因素结合,可以合法地将西北航道与其他现有或潜在国际海峡区别开来,如航道狭窄(例如小于 24 海里宽的咽喉要道)、没有特定条约制度、缺乏未经同意的外国穿越、存在原住民、几乎全年处于冰封状态等。这也与俄罗斯北方海航道中的部分北极海峡情况不同。

二、北方海航线

沿着俄罗斯北部地区,从大西洋一直延伸到太平洋的北方航海航线,已逐步实现季节性无冰。④ 2012 年夏季和秋季,有超过 46 艘船通过该航道,其中大部分船只将自然资源从俄罗斯港口运往亚洲市场。⑤

---

① Ibid. On the latter dispute, see Jon M. Van Dyke, "Canada's Authority to Prohibit LNG Vessels from Passing through Head Harbor Passage to US Ports." (2008 – 2009) 14 Ocean and Coastal Law Journal 45.
② discussion, below, pp. 154 – 157.
③ Ibid.
④ For a map of the Northern Sea Route, http://www.fni.no/insrop/nsrmap.jpg.
⑤ "46 Vessels through Northern Sea Route," BarentsObserver.com, November 23, 2012, http://barentsobserver.com/en/arctic/2012/11/46 – vessels – through – northern – sea – route – 23 – 11. In 2011, thirty – four ships traversed the route, up from just four in 2010. Ibid.

韩国造船厂正在建造冰区加强货轮和油轮,可以进一步延长通航季节,① 同时俄罗斯政府正建造新型破冰船,为商船队提供护航。②

俄罗斯政府有意将北方海航线转变为苏伊士运河和马六甲海峡的商业替代选项。普京于2011年9月11日表示:

> 欧洲最大市场和亚太地区之间的最短航线穿北极而过。该航线较传统航线缩短近三分之一。我想强调的是,北方海航线作为国际运输干线的重要性,其将在服务费用、安全和质量方面与传统贸易航线展开竞争。选择北极贸易航线的各国政府和私人企业无疑将获得经济优势。③

然而,这里存在一个外交问题:美国反对俄罗斯主张北方海航线中的维利基茨基海峡、绍卡利斯基海峡、德米特里·拉普捷夫海峡、桑尼科夫海峡属于俄罗斯内水。值得注意的是,其他国家都没有在该争议中选边站。1963年美国海岸警卫队破冰船"北风"号考察拉普捷夫海;次年夏天,"伯顿岛"号破冰船在东西伯利亚海进行相同活动。这些航行活动促使苏联政府于1964年7月向美国驻莫斯科大使馆发送辅助备忘录,清楚阐明这些海峡属于内水的立场:

> 北方海航线位于苏联北极沿岸附近。该航线距离国际航线较远,且仅有苏联船舶使用,或以北方海航道名义的包船。同样需要注意的是,北方海航道在某些地点需要穿过苏联领水和内水。具言之,这涉及卡尔斯基海所有东西向的海峡。由于他

---

① Steven Borowiec, "South Korea Angles for Influence on Arctic Policy," World Politics Review, September 25, 2012, http://www.worldpoliticsreview.com/articles/12366/south-korea-angles-for-influence-on-arctic-policy.

② Atle Staalesen, "Baltic Yard Wins Nuclear Icebreaker Contract," Barents Observer, August 6, 2012, http://barentsobserver.com/en/arctic/baltic-yard-wins-nuclear-icebreaker-contract-06-08.

③ Gleb Bryanski, "Russia's Putin Says Arctic Trade Route to Rival Suez," Reuters, September 22, 2011, http://ca.reuters.com/article/topNews/idCATRE78L5TC20110922.

们被苏联领水以及连接拉普捷夫海和东西伯利亚海的德米特里·拉普捷夫海峡和桑尼科夫海峡分为两节,并在历史上属于苏联。就目前所知,上述海峡中没有一个被用于国际航行。苏联国家边界保护法规在这些海峡的水域中完全适用,因此外国军事船舶需获得苏联政府事先同意后,才可通过苏联领海和进入苏联内水。①

1965年6月,美国政府以外交照会的方式加以回应,其中在总结苏联内水主张时仅使用"历史性水域"一词,并以明显的同义反复方式表明美国的立场,即俄罗斯北极海峡是国际海峡。

就德米特里·拉普捷夫和桑尼科夫海峡而言,即使国际法中的历史性水域原则可以适用于国际海峡,美国也不会认同可以基于历史性原因对这些水域提出主张。同时,美国赞赏苏联就开发北方海航线所做的努力,认识到这些水域对于苏联利益的重要性,但不认为这些因素具有改变该航道相关水域在国际法中地位的效力。关于所称与苏联领水重叠的卡尔斯基海中各海峡,必须指出的是,所有船舶在通过位于公海两部分之间用于国际航行的海峡之时,均享有无害通过权利,并且该权利不能被中止。在海峡内包含公海和领水的情况下,公海区域当然地享有不受限制的航行权利。出于上述原因,美国必须重申对自身权利的保留,美国国民在上述相关水域的地位将依据国际法原则而非沿岸国法律确定。②

通过坚称因为该航道是国际海峡,所以它是国际海峡的方式,美国试图回避一个尴尬的事实,即该航道并非用于国际航运,这也正是国际法院在"科孚海峡案"中设立的标准之一。③

(一)维利基茨基事件

美苏争议因所谓的"维利基茨基事件"迅速变得极为引人注目。

---

① Reproduced in: Office of Ocean Affairs, Limits in the Seas No. 112, n. 24, above, p. 71 (emphasis added).

② Ibid., p. 21, pp. 71 – 72 (emphasis added).

③ discussion, above, pp. 130 and 137.

维利基茨基海峡位于北地群岛南端布尔什维克岛和俄罗斯大陆最北端泰梅尔半岛之间。它们位于北纬78度，距离北极约800海里，使之成为北方海航线最为重要的咽喉要道。

1965年夏天，美国海岸警卫队"北风"号从西部接近维利基茨基海峡。苏联对此施加强大外交压力，根据美国国务院发言人称，若美方舰艇进入该海峡，苏联威胁将"奉陪到底"。① 美国政府的回应是要求"北风"号掉头航行。② 1967年夏天，美国海岸警卫队破冰船"艾迪斯托"号和"东风"号启程进行环北冰洋航行。向苏联政府通知的计划称，两艘舰艇将在新地群岛和北地群岛北部"完全的国际水域"航行。③ 恶劣的海冰情况迫使两艘舰艇改变航向，前往维利基茨基海峡。一份措辞谨慎的外交照会被送往莫斯科，以避免构成对俄请求许可："该编队将……和平和无害通过维利基茨基海峡，尽可能紧贴中心线航行，不会出现偏航或延迟。"④ 苏联当天以辅助备忘录回应，四天之后又发表口头声明，重申相关海峡属于苏联水域，外国船舶需提前30天提交进入申请。⑤ 美国政府中止其环北极航行计划，同时声称"强烈抗议""苏联毫无根据的立场，即所提'艾迪斯托'号和'东风'号的通过行为将违反苏联法规，并提升了苏联政府采取扣留船只或干扰航行等措施的可能性。"⑥

从法律角度来看，"维利基茨基事件"十分重要，因为国际法院对国际海峡设置的标准是某个海峡必须连接公海两部分并且被"用于国际

---

① Richard Petrow, Across the Top of Russia: The Cruise of the USCGC Northwind into the Polar Seas North of Siberia (London: Hodder and Stoughton, 1968), p. 352, cited in Erik Franckx, Maritime Claims in the Arctic: Canadian and Russian Perspectives (Dordrecht: Martinus Nijhoff, 1993), 148.

② Franckx, Maritime Claims in the Arctic, at 148. Curiously, the State Department account of the incident is limited to a single sentence suggesting, incorrectly, that the vessel stayed the course: "The Northwind conducted its transit from July to September of 1965." Office of Ocean Affairs, Limits in the Seas No. 112, n. 24, above, p. 72.

③ Office of Ocean Affairs, Limits in the Seas No. 112, n. 24, above, p. 72.

④ Robert D. Wells, "The Icy Nyet." (1968) 94 (782) US Naval Institute Proceedings 73 at 77.

⑤ Office of Ocean Affairs, Limits in the Seas No. 112, n. 24, above, p. 72.

⑥ Office of Ocean Affairs, Limits in the Seas No. 112, n. 24, above, p. 72.

航行"。① 俄罗斯北部地区的海峡明显不符合第二项功能标准。此外,唐纳德·罗思韦尔解释称,因为 20 世纪 60 年代的相关事件,"美国或其他国家再没有进一步积极尝试维护本国船只通过俄罗斯北极海峡的航行自由权利"。②

(二) 开放北方海航线

1985 年,苏联采用直线基线连接新地群岛、北地群岛和新西伯利亚群岛内一系列岛屿。③ 此举或受到《联合国海洋法公约》谈判催动,因为相较于先前国际习惯法,该公约关于直线基线规定对沿岸国较为不利,而当时苏联已签署《联合国海洋法公约》但尚未批准。④ 1987 年苏联总书记米哈伊尔·戈尔巴乔夫表示,"穿越北极是欧洲到远东和太平洋地区的最短海上通道。我认为,根据国际关系正常化进展程度,在我方破冰船护卫下,我们可以向外国船舶开放北方海航线。"此后不久,北方海航线开始向国际航运开放。⑤ 两年后,苏联"季克西"号船将货物从德国运往日本,苏联借此从北方海航线赚取了第一笔外汇。⑥ 1991 年,法国籍"星盘"号船成为通过北方海航线的第一艘非苏联籍船舶。⑦

国际社会对北方海航线的兴趣推动了两份报告的出炉。挪威、日本和俄罗斯在 1993 至 1999 年开展了"国际北方海航线项目",重点关注

---

① discussion, above, pp. 130 and pp. 137.
② Donald R. Rothwell, The Polar Regions and the Development of International Law (Cambridge University Press, 1996), 205.
③ Tullio Scovazzi, "New Developments Concerning Soviet Straight Baselines." (1988) 3 International Journal of Estuarine and Coastal Law 37; Vladimir Golitsyn, "The Arctic-On the Way to Regional Cooperation." (1989) 1 Marine Policy Report 91. For a discussion of the Canadian baselines, also adopted in 1985, see above, pp. 133 - 134 and 137 - 138.
④ Pharand, "The Arctic Waters and the Northwest Passage," 15.
⑤ Quoted in Rothwell, The Polar Regions and the Development of International Law, n. 85 above, p. 206.
⑥ Erik Franckx, "The Legal Regime of Navigation in the Russian Arctic." (2009) 18 Journal of Transnational Law and Policy 327 at 329.
⑦ Erik Franckx, "The Legal Regime of Navigation in the Russian Arctic." (2009) 18 Journal of Transnational Law and Policy 327 at 329.

该水道用于国际航运的可行性。其总结道：

> 就经济、技术和环境而言，国际商业航运大规模增长是可行的。最大和最明显的货物潜力蕴藏在俄罗斯北极陆上和近海巨大石油和天然气储备之中，针对西方市场的海上出口很可能在新世纪初开始。在交通运输方面，"国际北方海航线项目"对北方海航线东西两端（西北欧、东北亚和北美西海岸）主要揽货区的研究发现，存在主要为干散货的过境货物运输稳定潜能。①

第二份报告《北极行动纲领》，由欧盟委员会于 2002 至 2006 年间资助并主持完成，旨在帮助北方海航线在环境和经济方面成为可行选项，以便从俄罗斯北极地区运输石油和天然气。其结论是："北方海航线的石油和天然气运输具备技术可能性和经济可行性。"②

2009 年 9 月，随着俄罗斯海岸厚实坚硬的多年冰层消失，两艘德国集装箱船由韩国蔚山出发，经北方海航线，成功抵达目的港荷兰鹿特丹。③ 2010 年 11 月，俄罗斯最大的矿业公司诺里尔斯克镍业公司报告称，该公司一艘船舶完成从摩尔曼斯克至上海的往返航程。这趟 9836 海里的旅程耗时 41 天，相比之下经苏伊士运河则需要航行 20942 海里并耗时 84 天。④ 2011 年 8 月，长 300 米的超级油轮"弗拉基米尔·蒂克霍诺夫"号装载天然气冷凝物从摩尔曼斯克驶往泰国麦普塔普特港，成为完成北方海航线航行的最大船只。其之所以能够这样做，是因为现在夏末海冰情况已可满足船舶向北航行至新西伯利亚群岛的要求，从而

---

① International Northern Sea Route Program, http://www.fni.no/insrop/.

② Arctic Operational Platform, http://www.transport-research.info/web/projects/project_details.cfm?id=38216.

③ Tony Halpin, "Cargo Ships Navigate Northeast Passage for the First Time," The Times, September 14, 2009, p. 1.

④ "DJ Norilsk Nickel Vessel Completes First Northern Sea Route Trip," Waves Newsletter, November 22, 2010, http://wavesnewsletter.com/? p. 1475.

绕过了这些岛屿和大陆之间的浅水区。① 2012年8月，中国科考破冰船"雪龙"号在俄罗斯核动力破冰船"瓦伊加奇"号护航下，穿越北方海航线。"瓦伊加奇"号的存在所体现出的重要一点是：航运量增加并不表明俄罗斯认为北方海航线可以不受限制地对外开放。

三、加拿大和俄罗斯法律立场评估

由于不存在外国水面船只单方面通过以及仅有一个国家明确反对俄罗斯的立场，维利基茨基、绍卡利斯基、德米特里·拉普捷夫以及桑尼科夫海峡几乎肯定是俄罗斯的内水。道格拉斯·布鲁贝克同意该评价，尽管他假定（但没有经过事实证明）至少存在一些单方面通过的情况并且除美国以外也有别国对俄罗斯立场表达抗议。② 罗思韦尔写道："考虑到外国船只通过这些海峡频率相对较低，与西北航道同类航行相比则更低，似乎很难将东北航道中任何主要海峡归类为'国际海峡'。"③ 就上述评论，罗宾·丘吉尔和沃恩·劳写道：

> 东北航道中除被囊括在1985年划设的直线基线内的部分单独海峡外，鉴于通过其他海峡（通常处于冰封状态）的实际航行次数屈指可数，因而存在关于其他海峡是否可被称为"用于国际航行"并由此产生过境通行权的疑问。④

确定俄罗斯的主张关系到争议的"关键日期"是1964年还是1965年的问题，也即各方不同立场变得清晰，随后采取的支持行为对法律分

---

① Wang Qian, "Breaking the Ice," China Daily, September 30, 2012, http://www.chinadaily.com.cn/sunday/2012-09/30/content_15793745.htm.

② R. Douglas Brubaker, Russian Arctic Straits (Dordrecht: Martinus Nijhoff, 2004), pp. 41 and 189.

③ Rothwell, The Polar Regions and the Development of International Law, n. 85, above, p. 206.

④ Robin Churchill and Vaughan Lowe, The Law of the Sea, 3rd edn. (Manchester University Press, 1999), p. 106.

析无关紧要的日期。①

只有一个因素对俄罗斯法律地位产生不利影响，即由直线基线包围的近海北极岛屿似乎并未沿着"海岸的一般方向"。② 然而，俄罗斯的内水立场比划设支线基线要早数十年，也因此是基于其他国家长期的默认，这种默认包括但不限于不存在单方面通过。

西北航道的情况更为模糊。尽管加拿大1969年为美国"曼哈顿"号提供大量协助，两次均授予许可，对1985年美国"极地海"号航行做出"权利不受损害"的声明，但实际上还是存在两次未经申请水面航行的现实。此外，仅有美国持续反对加拿大法律立场。加拿大因纽特人已使用并占有西北航道海冰达数千年，他们的支持也巩固了加拿大的立场。尽管加拿大数个基线长度不同寻常，在一个由19000个紧密交织岛屿构成的沿岸群岛周围划设直线基线，似乎与"英挪渔业案"中明确阐述的直线基线目的是一致的，也即要符合内水制度的话，该海域应该"与大陆存在足够紧密联系"。这一思想"应被公平地运用于海岸地理结构与挪威一样不同寻常的案例中"。③

最后，西北航道争议在1969年或1985年到达"关键日期"，当时加拿大清楚阐明了其内水立场并采用直线基线。据此，即使今天一艘外国船舶未经加拿大许可航行通过西北航道，虽然会造成政治后果，但不会损害加拿大法律主张。因此，加拿大需要应对的只有两次通行问题。这两次通行虽未申请许可，但加拿大均通过隐含或明确的方式对其授予了许可；在后一案例中，两国就该通行不会对法律争议造成损害达成一致。对"用于国际航行"要求进行仔细分析后，罗斯韦尔正确地总结道："若不对国际海峡问题提供进一步司法指导，最终确定西北航道是否属于国际海峡将变得极端困难"。④

---

① On the critical date principle, references, Chapter 1, n. 9, above.
② discussion, above, p. 138.
③ Fisheries Case (UK v. Norway) (1951) ICJ Reports 116 at 133.
④ Rothwell, The Polar Regions and the Development of International Law, n. 85, above, p. 200.

四、加拿大和俄罗斯合作

俄罗斯和加拿大均坚持本国北极海峡为内水的法律立场,北方海航线和西北航道的相似之处不仅限于此。1982年,苏联和加拿大外交官在《联合国海洋法公约》第二百三十四条谈判中互相协作,该条允许沿岸国在海岸外200海里范围内易结冰区域行使航运管理权,以进一步预防、减少和控制海洋污染。① 美国"曼哈顿"号航行之后,第二百三十四条赋予加拿大1970年《加拿大北极水域污染防治法》以合法性,② 该法也为苏联此后于1990年制定北方海航线规则提供了参照。③

正如上文所述,1985年加拿大和苏联分别沿本国北极海岸线划设直线基线。④ 同年,美国派遣海岸警卫队"极地海"号通过西北航道,苏联驻渥太华大使馆新闻随员叶夫根尼·波兹尼亚科夫公开表示支持加拿大法律立场并称:"无论是对西北航道还是北方海航线,我们的立场都基于国际法规定。一国岛屿周边水域是该国内水。"⑤

然而,没有证据表明苏联或俄罗斯在此之前或之后再度发表支持加拿大立场的声明,也没有证据显示加拿大发表声明对此作出回应。考虑到两国相似的法律境地,这就显得十分奇怪。对这种奇怪现象最合理的解释是政治因素:加拿大和苏联属于冷战不同阵营。美国对加拿大主张的反对一直基于更为广泛的战略考虑,即对全球范围内航行权利最大化的需求。加拿大和美国通过北约、北美防空司令部和五眼情报共享网络构建安全联系,加拿大政府很难在西北航道问题上采取独立立场。而在北方海航线争议中支持苏联立场根本就不是一个备选项。

---

① discussion, below, pp. 164 – 165.

② Arctic Waters Pollution Prevention Act, 1969 – 70 Statutes of Canada, chap. 47, http://laws.justice.gc.ca/eng/acts/A – 12/index.html.

③ For a recent overview of the regulations, see Franckx, "The Legal Regime of Navigation in the Russian Arctic," pp. 330 – 339.

④ discussions, above, pp. 131 and pp. 146 – 147.

⑤ Matthew Fisher, "Soviets Back Canada's Claim to Northwest Passage Waters," Globe and Mail, August 7, 1985.

至于如何解释苏联对西北航道问题近乎完全沉默的态度,可以假定苏联决定不破坏这种微妙的平衡,允许加拿大和美国在该问题上"同意各自保留不同意见"。如果苏联坚决支持加拿大立场,美国或决定不再容忍加拿大的单独立场,然后在一个紧密但非对等的双边关系中,对加拿大施加强大的压力。另一种或其他解释是,苏联并不担心任何国家会借由公开航行通过北方海航线的方式直接挑战其主张。引发核冲突的风险太大,并且唯一能够在海面航行执行任务的美国船舶是轻度武装的海岸警卫队破冰船,其与俄罗斯北方舰队实力过于悬殊。

　　今天,随着冷战结束和海冰融化,环境问题和经济发展主导了政策领域。俄罗斯是八国集团、二十国集团、世界贸易组织、欧洲委员会、巴伦支海欧洲—北极理事会和北极理事会成员国。其最大贸易伙伴是主要由北约成员国组成的欧盟。俄罗斯军事力量也大幅下降,2011年,其军费开支只有美国的十分之一(分别为719亿和7110亿美元)。①

　　2007年11月,加拿大总理斯蒂芬·哈珀和时任俄罗斯总理维克托·祖布科夫就加拿大和俄罗斯的经济合作发表共同声明。② 2010年1月,据维基解密披露,哈珀对北约秘书长安德斯·福格·拉斯穆森表示,因为加拿大与俄罗斯在北极问题上存在"很好的工作关系","北极国家不可能开战",所以军事同盟在北极地区没有用武之地。③ 2010年9月,俄罗斯总统弗拉基米尔·普京在莫斯科一次会议上称:"如果你孤身一人,你无法在北极生存。自然条件迫使人们和国家互相帮助。"④ 正像上文所解释的那样,就在普京发表这番言论的一周之前,

---

① "The 15 Countries with the Highest Military Expenditure in 2009," Stockholm International Peace Research Institute, 2010, http://www.sipri.org/research/armaments/milex/resultoutput/milex_15 (China: $143bn./France: $62.5bn./Germany: $46.7bn./Italy: $34.5bn.).

② Joint Statement on Canada-Russia Economic Cooperation, November 28, 2007, http://www.cbern.ca/cms/One.aspx?portalId=625751andpageId=9815452.

③ US State Department cable # VZCZCXR03302, January 20, 2010, http://aptn.ca/pages/news/2011/05/11/while-harper-talked-tough-with-nato-on-arctic-u-s-believed-pm-all-bark-no-bite/ (original cables are reproduced below the article).

④ Luke Harding, "Vladimir Putin Calls for Arctic Claims to Be Resolved under UN Law," Guardian, September 23, 2010, http://www.guardian.co.uk/world/2010/sep/23/putin-arctic-claims-international-law.

俄罗斯和挪威外交部长签署巴伦支海的海上边界条约。① 此后，俄罗斯、加拿大、美国、丹麦、挪威、瑞典、芬兰和冰岛于 2011 年 5 月签署多边搜索和救助条约，这是在北极理事会框架下谈判达成的首份法律文件。②

所有这些都对北方海航线和西北航道造成了影响。2009 年 2 月，加拿大外交部长法律顾问艾伦·凯塞尔在莫斯科会见俄罗斯的同僚罗曼·科洛德金。俄罗斯对本次会议总结道：

> 双方在加拿大西北航道和俄罗斯北方海航线国际航运问题上具有高度一致的立场，认同为保护脆弱的海洋环境而在这些区域适用限制措施是必要的，一致认为《联合国海洋法公约》承认沿岸国在冰封区域所享有的权利。双方同意就此议题展开更详细磋商，包括两国与美国就历史性水域权利问题存在的争议。③

冷战结束 20 多年来，俄罗斯和加拿大均已融入全球经济，成为北极合作的积极参与方。但现在，随着海冰消融和外国船运公司的加入，其他国家与美国一道公开反对加拿大或俄罗斯在本国北极海峡的法律立场（甚至如上文建议，即使一些作法实际上并不符合相关国家利益）可能只是时间问题。鉴于两个航道情况的高度相似性，对加拿大和俄罗斯一方主张反对的增加，同时也会削弱另一方主张。在此急剧变化和富有挑战的环境中，两国明智的作法是寻求就北方海航线和西北航道法律

---

① 2010 Treaty between the Kingdom of Norway and the Russian Federation concerning Maritime Delimitation and Cooperation in the Barents Sea and the Arctic Ocean, English translation http://www.regjeringen.no/upload/ud/vedlegg/folkerett/ avtale_engelsk.pdf. See discussion, Chapter 2, above.

② Agreement on Aeronautical and Maritime Search and Rescue in the Arctic, May 12, 2011, http://arctic-council.npolar.no/en/meetings/2011-nuuk-ministerial/docs/. See discussion, Chapter 8, below.

③ Russia-Canada consultations on the legal status of the Arctic, February 20, 2009, Moscow, http://byers.typepad.com/arctic/russiacanada-consultations-on-the-legal-status-of-the-arctic.html.

状态形成共同立场。在其他方面，例如两国可以单独或联合与美国进行谈判以达成某种长期妥协，就特定问题展开外交合作也将有助于强化两国所需要的影响力。

五、加拿大和美国合作

加拿大一直以来很难与美国讨论西北航道问题。从大西洋到太平洋的北方航线曾经是自卡伯特到哈德逊和弗兰克林等一系列探险家心目中的"圣杯"，他们的发现有助于奠定加拿大的国家基础。[①] 西北航道也成为加拿大与其更为强大的领国之间最为重要和持久的争议，比如对很多加拿大人而言，该航道是骄傲和焦虑的来源之一。尽管如此，两国在时机成熟时，还是设法就西北航道问题进行了讨论。正如上文所提及，加拿大总理布赖恩·马尔罗尼通过达成相关船舶在进入该水道前需要请求加拿大批准，并且相关航行不会对法律争议造成影响的协议，解决了美国海岸警卫队破冰船所造成的挑战。[②] 1988年《北极合作协议》虽然实际上已解决该难题，但却没有考虑到目前正在发生的海冰急剧融化问题。

海冰融化对"同意各自保留不同意见"的安排构成了根本性挑战。西北航道国际航运增加将需要改善治安、搜救、溢油反应和其他在实践中只有沿岸国才能提供的基本服务。然而，只要加拿大对航运监管的管辖权存在争议，其对上述领域增加投入的积极性就会降低。

未来两个变化结合在一起，可为加拿大和美国展开新的谈判提供动力。2001年9月11日发生的恐怖袭击将美国安全担忧的焦点从国家行为体转移到非国家行为体上。正如上文所述，2005年美国大使保罗·塞卢奇披露，他曾要求美国国务院根据恐怖主义威胁，重新审查美国对西北航道立场。[③] 塞卢奇担忧恐怖分子可能利用北极无冰的条件，运输

[①] Pierre Berton, The Arctic Grail: The Quest for the Northwest Passage and the North Pole, 1818-1909 (Toronto: McClelland and Stewart, 1988).

[②] discussion, above, pp. 139-140.

[③] discussion, above, pp. 140-141.

第五章 北极航道

大规模杀伤性武器进入北美。他甚至公开表示,加拿大的法律立场目前对美国可能是有利的。

2008年,塞卢奇参加由双方非官方专家组成的"北方航运模式谈判"。① 该活动为期两天,目的是就相关问题展开讨论并找出可能的解决办法,向两国政府提出联合建议。双方专家一致认为,美国和加拿大在北极地区合作的悠久历史表明,两国可以参考圣罗伦斯水道等其他国家管辖下水域的航运合作历史案例,制定一项新的双边协议。他们提出了九项建议,包括两国就阿拉斯加和加拿大北部水域通报和封锁工作建立类似规则和执法合作机制,以及建立航道、交通管理和溢油反应计划。他们还建议,最大限度发挥两国目前对进出加拿大和美国港口和在两国登记船舶的强大法律权力。

第三个变化发生在2009年,奥巴马政府上台伊始即在北极政治方面采取高度合作态度,着手"重启"与此前冷战对手俄罗斯的关系。2010年4月,新版《削减和限制进攻性战略武器条约》承诺,两国将减少核武器储备并提交新的核查措施。② 考虑到大部分俄罗斯核导弹潜艇都部署在北极圈以北区域,该协议对北极地区发展而言具有重要意义。除此之外,奥巴马政府还采纳了一系列专门为北极制定的其他倡议。美国与俄罗斯共同主导了多边搜索和救助条约谈判,③ 与加拿大合作开展波弗特海大陆架测绘活动。正如第三章中解释的那样,美国和加拿大两国目前正处于就波弗特海海上边界谈判达成协议的早期阶段。

奥巴马政府明白,加拿大总理哈珀有时就北极问题发表十分强硬的言论,主要对象是加拿大选民而非外国政府。根据维基解密公开的信息,美国大使戴维·雅各布森在2010年1月一份电报中做了这样的解

---

① "Model Negotiation on Northern Waters," Annex II in Michael Byers, Who Owns the Arctic? Understanding Sovereignty Disputes in the North (Vancouver, BC and Berkeley, Calif.: Douglas & McIntyre, 2009); also http://byers.typepad.com/arctic/model-negotiation-on-northern-waters.html.

② Measures for the Further Reduction and Limitation of Strategic Offensive Arms (US-Russian Federation), April 8, 2010, http://www.state.gov/t/avc/newstart/index.htm.

③ Agreement on Aeronautical and Maritime Search and Rescue in the Arctic, n. 113, above. See discussion, Chapter 8, below.

释："保守派将对'北方'的担忧作为政治招牌……并取得成功。"① 在同一份电报中，美国外交官称："总理在北极问题上的公开立场可能并不能反映其更为务实的个人观点和政策优先方向，相关证据是，哈珀于1月7日和8日与雅各布森大使就长期和广泛问题进行了长达数小时谈话，期间总理一次都没有提及北极地区。"

在环境根本改变的情况下，加拿大和美国应该重启对西北航道问题的讨论。正如雅各布森在2010年1月那份电报中所阐述，美国政府愿意：

> 当此之时，加拿大推进其"主权"利益，就必须把重点放在与北极邻国的双边和多边伙伴关系方面。在北极沿岸国家中（也许是所有国家），加拿大和美国通常具有最紧密的同盟政策利益，对国际法持有共同观点，并在多边场合（例如北极理事会）中具有共同目标。就加拿大而言，如果两国可在北极问题上找到共同点，那么加拿大获得成功的概率将远大于其单独对抗其他国家或国家集团的利益。

在为这些讨论做必要准备之时，加拿大将不得不考虑美方可能合理要求加方在进入、治安、搜救等服务和基础设施方面做出承诺，以换取美国承认加拿大的"内水"立场。新的协议可以通过缔结双边条约的形式体现出来，在理想情况下，其后加拿大可以通过与其他国家达成相同或至少相似的双边条约方式使之多边化。这种方法已被证明是成功的，美国和加勒比国家之间就海上毒品禁运达成了很多相同双边条约，美国主导的"防扩散安全倡议"下"方便旗"国之间也达成了相似双边条约。②

---

① US State Department cable # VZCZCXYZ0001, January 21, 2010, http://aptn.ca/pages/news/2011/05/11/while-harper-talked-tough-with-nato-on-arctic-u-s-belived-pm-all-bark-no-bite/ (original cables are reproduced below the article).

② Michael Byers, "Policing the High Seas: The Proliferation Security Initiative." (2004) 98 American Journal of International Law 526 at 530 (on bilateral treaties concerning the interdiction of vessels suspected of carrying weapons of mass destruction) and pp. 538 – 540 (on bilateral treaties concerning the interdiction of vessels suspected of smuggling drugs).

这些国家可包括加拿大的其他北约伙伴国，韩国、日本等美国和加拿大的其他共同盟国，以及利比亚和巴拿马两个主要航运登记国。显然，美国对该方案的支持是必不可少的。

与此类似的是，美国和俄罗斯可以通过有效谈判达成关于北方海航线的双边条约；之后俄罗斯可以与其他国家复制该条约相关内容，以实现多边化。还有个一个更具雄心的想法，加拿大、美国和俄罗斯或许有意愿就北极海峡问题展开三边条约谈判，该条约也许同样能够有效解决阿拉斯加和俄罗斯远东之间的白令海峡问题。

六、白令海峡

凶猛的风暴和严寒的温度，再加上大雾、冰冻和地处偏远等自然条件，使得白令海峡成为对航海者极具挑战之地。但白令海峡正逐渐变为一条重要的航道，因为该海峡是太平洋与西北航道、北方海航线连接的枢纽。美国和俄罗斯在该地区的地理位置十分接近，该水道长期以来一直都是两国战略利益所在。两国大陆海岸最窄处只相隔45海里，海峡中俄罗斯的大代奥米德岛与美国的小代奥米德岛之间的距离更是不足3海里。

美国和俄罗斯两国均承认白令海峡是国际海峡，外国船舶通过无需经过两国批准。这两个沿岸国家已经就搜索和救助、助航规定等展开合作，并将进一步深化此类合作。根据维基解密公布的美国机密外交电报，俄罗斯外交部于2009年4月联系美国驻莫斯科大使馆，"要求就一系列长期停滞的白令海峡相关倡议展开合作，内容包括自然保护、石油和天然气勘探、海上运输和交通。"[①]

在同一份电报中，美国大使馆讨论了俄罗斯不同官员对于北极政策常常互相矛盾的公开声明，并向国务院提出以下建议：

> 外交部和总统梅德韦杰夫的声明表明，温和派将北极视为

---

① State Department reference # VZCZCXRO2637. Sent May 26, 2009, http://wikileaks.ch/cable/2009/05/09MOSCOW1346.html.

合作区域。我们对北极理事会的支持和通过双边途径就北极问题（包括拟议的"美俄北极计划"）进行的接触，均有助于支持温和派并鼓励俄罗斯政府继续合作。加强科学合作，特别是在气候变化方面，能够增进信任和建立信心。在多边或双边合作框架下，我们还可以提供所有梅德韦杰夫在2008年9月17日谈话中要求俄罗斯政府开展，但在缺乏外部专业支持下很难完成的任务，包括共同开发航行辅助和港口设施，持续研究和分享海流和气象数据，促进原住民社会发展，就应急反应和溢油修复展开合作等。①

两年后，在法国多维尔举行的八国集团峰会间隙，奥巴马总统和梅德韦杰夫总统就白令海区域合作发表联合声明。该声明没有提起航运问题，而是侧重于环保合作，即"扩大两国阿拉斯加州和楚科奇自治区承担受特别保护的自然领土/区域管理职责的政府机构之间的互动"。② 然而，根据维基解密公开的电报显示，两国在其他领域的合作亦将很快出现。

如前文所述，1990年美国和苏联谈判划定了白令海峡、白令海和楚科奇海总长1600海里的海上边界。③ 尽管俄罗斯杜马尚未批准该条约，但是美国和俄罗斯已经同意根据1969年《维也纳条约法公约》第25条之规定，视其具有临时约束力。④

即使两国边界条约被解除，白令海峡本身的法律地位也不会改变。

---

① State Department reference # VZCZCXRO2637. Sent May 26, 2009, http://wikileaks.ch/cable/2009/05/09MOSCOW1346.html.

② US-Russia Statement on Cooperation in Bering Strait Region, May 26, 2011, http://iipdigital.usembassy.gov/st/english/texttrans/2011/05/20110526082231su0.7241262.html#axzz1SOGSoeUE.

③ Agreement between the United States of America and the Union of Soviet Socialist Republics on the Maritime Boundary (1990) 29 ILM 941, http://www.state.gov/documents/organization/125431.pdf. See discussion, Chapter 2, above.

④ Article 25 reads, in part: "A treaty or a part of a treaty is applied provisionally pending its entry into force if: the treaty itself so provides; or the negotiating States have in some other manner so agreed." 1969 Vienna Convention on the Law of Treaties, http://untreaty.un.org/ilc/texts/instruments/english/conventions/1_1_1969.pdf.

俄罗斯国内对该条约的反对声主要集中于白令海峡南部一段白令海边界的位置，但对于两国在海峡内的边界位置没有分歧，包括经过大代奥米德岛和小代奥米德岛之间较为窄浅水道的部分。因为存在这些岛屿，并且它们各自距离本国海岸线的距离都小于24海里，所以任何希望通过该海峡的外国船舶必须经由俄罗斯或者美国的领水。同样，这些船舶享有通过的权利，因为两个沿岸国均认为大小代奥米德岛两侧水道为国际海峡。然而，国际海峡的定位也意味着这些水道中不存在航道限制、通报制度或引航员年龄限制。考虑到这个地处偏远且风险较高的水道船舶交通量增加的情况，建议俄罗斯和美国合作寻求国际海事组织同意采取上述管理措施，相关程序将在第六章中详细阐述。

七、乌尼马克海峡

地球是一个球体，从美国西北部和加拿大西部前往中国、日本和韩国最近的航运线路是经由狭窄的乌尼马克海峡通过阿拉斯加的阿留申群岛。[①] 乌尼马克海峡只有9海里宽，但每年有超过5000艘船舶使用该海峡，其中很多是大型集装箱船和散装货船。[②]

在潮汐作用下，乌尼马克海峡周边水域温度较低但养分丰富，浮游生物大量生长，为丰富的食物链提供了坚实的基础。[③] 该区域是阿拉斯加国家海洋野生动物保护区的一部分，是4000万只海鸟和大量海洋哺乳动物的家园，其中包括濒临灭绝的北海狮、北方海狗、海獭以及多种鲸类。该生态系统具有相当大的经济价值。乌尼马克海峡北部的白令海支撑着美国最大的商业渔场，年产值高达20亿美元。[④]

恶劣天气和海况伴随着巨大的潮汐流在乌尼马克海峡十分常见。

---

① the map at www.nap.edu/openbook.php?record_id=12443&page=58.

② For the 2006–2007 numbers and a breakdown of vessel types, see Risk of Vessel Accidents and Spills in the Aleutian Islands: Designing a Comprehensive Risk Assessment-Special Report 293 (Washington, DC: National Academies Press, 2009), pp. 73–77, http://www.nap.edu/catalog.php?record_id=12443.

③ Ibid., pp. 59–63.

④ Ibid., p. 62.

2004年12月,一艘225米长的马来西亚籍货轮"色冷当·阿育"号刚进入该海峡就在暴风中失去动力。① 这艘船被风暴吹得搁浅并解体,造成120万升燃油泄漏。因地处偏远,天气恶劣,阿留申也完全缺乏清理溢油的设备和人员,导致石油几乎都没有得到回收。更为复杂的是,美国长期承认乌尼马克海峡为国际海峡,外国船舶可以在未经许可或监管限制的情况下进入。② 由此,该海峡也没有建立航道、通知或引航要求。

"埃克森·瓦尔迪兹"号在威廉王子湾泄漏超过8000万升石油事件发生20年之后,③ 加拿大对中国的重油出口活动正导致新的威胁向乌尼马克海峡蔓延。两家石油管道公司计划在阿尔伯塔省使用天然气凝析油稀释焦油沥青,以便将其向西输送至不列颠哥伦比亚省,然后再使用油轮运输。④ 2012年,美国海岸警卫队司令罗伯特·帕普在向参议院小组委员会解释美国海洋安全挑战时,将乌尼马克海峡称为"重要的咽喉要道",他表示:"有成千上万的船舶装载着燃料和货物通过那里,存在导致环境灾难、沉船和其他事故的风险。"⑤

美国政府能够采取一些行动,其可以在荷兰港附近驻扎大型救援拖船和数艘溢油清理船,要求国际海事组织将乌尼马克海峡认定为"特别敏感海域",以便美国能够要求船舶通过该海峡时须提前通知并遵守船

---

① For the 2006 – 2007 numbers and a breakdown of vessel types, see Risk of Vessel Accidents and Spills in the Aleutian Islands: Designing a Comprehensive Risk Assessment-Special Report 293 (Washington, DC: National Academies Press, 2009), pp. 73 – 77, http://www.nap.edu/catalog.php?record_id = 12443., p. 81.

② Annotated Supplement to the Commander's Handbook on the Law of Naval Operations (Naval War College: Newport, Rhode Island, 1997), pp. 2 – 86, Table A2 – 5, http://www.scribd.com/doc/36391405/US – Navy – Commander – s – Handbook – Annotated – Supplement – 1997.

③ Art Davidson, In the Wake of the Exxon Valdez (San Francisco, Calif.: Sierra Club Books, 1990); Lila Guterman, "Exxon Valdez Turns 20" (March 20, 2009) 323 (5921) Science 1558.

④ Jane Stevenson, "Enbridge Pushes Oil Tanker Safety Strategy," March 18, 2010, TheTyee.ca, http://thetyee.ca/News/2010/03/18/TankerSafety/; Mitchell Anderson, "Kinder Morgan's Grand Plan to Pipe Oil Sands Crude," June 2, 2011, TheTyee.ca, http://thetyee.ca/News/2011/06/02/KinderMorganGrandPlan/.

⑤ US Coast Guard Commandant Robert Papp, Testimony before Senate Appropriations Subcommittee on Homeland Security, May 9, 2012, http://www.c – spanvideo.org/program/299429 – 1.

舶交通分道航行规则。① 美国还可以设法说服航运公司主动安排油轮改道阿留申群岛南部水域，但此举将增加运输的距离和成本。上述措施可能都无法改变每年有数百艘油轮通过乌尼马克海峡的现实情况。更有意义的做法是美国重新考虑其在国际海峡问题上的立场，改变一直强调航行自由最大化的态度，并与加拿大、俄罗斯等国合作，强化多边标准和沿岸国权利。②

八、内尔斯海峡

内尔斯海峡狭窄的水道将格陵兰和加拿大埃尔斯米尔岛分隔开，并连接着巴芬湾和林肯海。它也是北极唯一有争议领土——汉斯岛的所在地。③

内尔斯海峡长 300 多海里，部分区域仅有 12 海里宽。大部分区域完全处于丹麦或加拿大一方领海内，这些海域（及其之外大陆架）的划界已由两国 1973 年签订的条约所确定。④ 内尔斯海峡相对较深，凯恩海湾西部最浅处也在船舶龙骨下 200 米。但该海峡冬季和春季结着坚硬的海冰；夏季和秋季则被北冰洋冲来的海冰、格陵兰彼得曼和洪堡冰川崩落的冰山所占据，因而并不适宜水面船舶活动。尽管如此，近年来至少有一艘，甚至可能更多的破冰船从内尔斯海峡两端破冰而入。⑤

加拿大和丹麦均认为内尔斯海峡既不是国际海峡，也不是内水，因

---

① discussion, below, pp. 163 – 165.
② discussion, below, pp. 163 – 167.
③ For more on Hans Island, Chapter 1, above.
④ For more on the 1973 Canada-Denmark boundary treaty, Chapter 2, above.
⑤ The Greenpeace icebreaker Arctic Sunrise reportedly made the voyage in 2009. See Patrick Barkham, "The Sermilik Fjord in Greenland: A Chilling View of a Warming World," Guardian, September 1, 2009, http://www.guardian.co.uk/environment/2009/sep/01/sermilik-fjord-greenland-global-warming.

为该海峡经过两国领海,所以两国均认可存在"无害通过"权。① 这一观点可从1983年两国签订的一份条约中找到佐证,该条约主要涉及加拿大和格陵兰之间的海洋环境保护问题,② 未提及任何国际海峡问题。条约还对沿岸国在领海之内和之外的权利作出区分,明确认为各国在领海内享有实施"船舶交通管理或船舶报告服务"的充分权利。③

几乎可以确定,美国采取把内尔斯海峡视为国际海峡的立场,因为美国海军的律师们认为,"用于国际航行"的标准可以是指目前尚不存在国际航行,但存在被用于国际航行的可能性。④ 此外,潜艇可以在国际海峡中潜航,但在一般领水内则不行,而美国潜艇经常并且有时是公开使用内尔斯海峡。潜艇操作人员出于安全因素通常会倾向于保持水下航行状态,但由于内尔斯海峡存在海冰和冰山,潜艇在此别无选择,只有保持潜航一种方式。

内尔斯海峡转变为一条重要航运线路的可能性较小。相较于经西北航道连接白令海峡和北美东部、经格陵兰东岸弗拉姆海峡连接白令海峡和欧洲的两条线路,通过内尔斯海峡并不会节省时间或缩短距离。然而随着海冰融化,邮轮或许会经常在此出没,渔船和石油勘探船也有可能

---

① The legal regime of innocent passage is set out in Articles 17 - 26 of UNCLOS, Chapter 4, n. 12, above. Essentially, foreign ships have a right of passage, provided that they do not threaten the security of the coastal state and that they abide by its laws concerning the safety of navigation, the preservation of the environment, the prevention of infringement of its customs, fiscal, immigration, or sanitary laws, etc.

② 1983 Agreement for Cooperation Relating to the Marine Environment (1984) 23 (2) ILM 269, http://treaties.un.org/doc/Publication/UNTS/Volume%201348/volume - 1348 - I - 22693 - English. pdf.

③ Ibid., Article 7 reads, in part: "1. The Parties shall cooperate and assist each other in their respective vessel traffic management or ship reporting services in relation to ships navigating in the area covered by this Agreement. 2. (i) The Parties shall cooperate in identifying, monitoring and reviewing as necessary appropriate routing areas for vessels in the area covered by this Agreement outside territorial waters with a view to avoiding harmful effects to the marine environment and to the economic and social conditions in the area covered by this Agreement."

④ discussion, above, p. 137. James C. Kraska of the US Naval War College has expressed the unusual view that Nares Strait is one of the routes of the Northwest Passage. Kraska, "The New Arctic Geography and US Strategy," in James C. Kraska (ed.), Arctic Security in an Age of Climate Change (New York: Cambridge University Press, 2011), 244 at 260.

会经此前往北冰洋中部。若是如此，则该水道的地位或将开始引发关注，而出于环境保护、航行安全和国家安全的目的，加拿大和格陵兰会对该海峡加以监管。

九、"海峡国"的多边机制

此外，加拿大和俄罗斯可以放弃两国在西北航道和北方海航线问题上的内水立场，转而赞成利用国际法为沿岸国提供的条件，保护两国在国际海峡的利益。例如，《联合国海洋法公约》第三十九条要求船舶在"过境通行"时应"毫不延迟"，"避免对海峡沿岸国的主权、领土完整或政治独立施加任何武力威胁或使用武力"，同时"避免以通常方式进行不间断地和迅速地航行所附带发生的活动以外的任何活动"。该条款还要求这些船舶"遵守普遍接受的有关海上安全的国际规则、程序和实践"，以及"普遍接受的有关预防、减少和控制船舶污染的国际规则、程序和实践"。[①]

《联合国海洋法公约》第四十条禁止在未获得沿岸国或数国事先授权的情况下，在国际海峡中从事"任何研究或调查活动"。第四十一条规定，沿岸国在与国际海事组织等"主管国际组织"协商后，可在国际海峡中"必要时为航行指定海道和规定分道通航制"。第四十二条规定，国际海峡沿岸国可对"航行安全和海上交通"进行管理，以及"使有关在海峡内排放油类、油污废物和其他有毒物质的适用的国际规章有效，以防止、减少和控制污染"。根据第四十二条，沿岸国也可禁止捕鱼，以及"上下任何商品、货币或人员"，并规定这些法律和规定"不应在形式上或事实上在外国船舶间有所歧视，或在其适用上有否定、妨碍或损害本节规定的过境通行权的实际后果。"[②]

然而，为支持这些监管权力，沿岸国在国际海峡中可采取的执法措施极为有限。正如玛丽·乔治所指出，"海峡国家很难在不违反第四十二条第二款'妨碍或损害过境通行权'的情况下，将第四十二条第一

① Chapter 4, n.12, above.
② Ibid.

款下规定的法律和规定付诸实施。"① 斯图亚特·凯同样总结道:"沿岸国适用于过境船舶的权利非常有限。"②

如上所述,沿岸国确已根据《联合国海洋法公约》第二百三十四条之规定,强化冰封水域污染控制权。

沿岸国有权采取和实施非歧视性的法律和法规,以预防、减少和控制船舶在专属经济区内冰封水域造成的海洋污染,这些水域中特别严峻的气候条件和常年冰封的状况将对航行造成阻碍或异常危险,海洋环境污染也会对生态平衡造成重大危害或者不可逆的干扰。这些法律和规章应当适当考虑航行要求,根据现有最佳科学证据保护海洋环境。③

《联合国海洋法公约》第二百三十四条的谈判正是受到加拿大通过1970年《北极水域污染预防法》的推动。④ 然而,目前还不清楚该条款是否会允许加拿大或俄罗斯至少在发生污染事故之时,在国际海峡拦截不符合规定的船只。休·卡米诺斯对第二百三十三条(该条款对在非冰封水域进行污染预防设置了更为有限的管辖权)在国际海峡适用性的分析体现了该问题的严重性:

> 毗邻海峡的国家依据第二百三十三条之规定采取任何强制措施,必须证明过境船舶违反第四十二条第一款(a)和(b)项所指的法律和规章与对海峡的海洋环境造成重大损害之间存在直接联系。如果对海洋环境已经造成实际损害,并且与船只

---

① Mary George, "The Regulation of Maritime Traffic in Straits Used for International Navigation," in Alex G. Oude Elferink and Donald R. Rothwell (eds.), Oceans Management in the 21st Century: Institutional Frameworks and Responses (Leiden: Martinus Nijhoff, 2004), p. 24.

② Stuart Kaye, "Regulation of Navigation in the Torres Strait: Law of the Sea Issues," in Donald R. Rothwell and Sam Bateman (eds.), Navigation Rights and Freedoms and the New Law of the Sea (Dordrecht: Kluwer, 2000), 119 at 123.

③ Article 38, UNCLOS, Chapter 4, n. 12, above.

④ Arctic Waters Pollution Prevention Act, n. 104, above, sec. 2. For a detailed account of the legal and diplomatic history, Justin DeMowbray Nankivell, "Arctic Legal Tides: The Politics of International Law in the Northwest Passage," Ph. D. thesis, University of British Columbia, 2010, http://circle.ubc.ca/bitstream/handle/2429/26642/ubc_2010_fall_nankivell_justin.pdf?sequence=1.

的违法行为有关，那么"海峡沿岸国可采取适当强制措施"。①

也有人质疑，第二百三十四条是否将继续适用于先前冰封，但逐渐变为无冰的水域。第二百三十四条并未表明，因常年冰封而从属于污染预防管辖权的相关水域，在海冰长期消失之时，是否还可以维持这种法律地位。根据二百三十四条所赋予的权利根植于当地洋面的性质，而不是基于状态不定的特定海洋区域。

如上文所述，沿岸国可以要求国际海事组织将一个国际海峡的部分或全部指定为"特别敏感海域"，例如 2005 年澳大利亚在托雷斯海峡的成功案例。② 然而，目前尚不清楚他们是否因此获得了任何新的权利。当澳大利亚随后要求在托雷斯海峡采取强制引航计划时，美国和新加坡提出抗议，认为不得在国际海峡中采取相关措施。③

然而，尽管存在抗议，与先前采取自愿原则的方案低于 50% 的遵守率相比，强制引航措施已获得 100% 的遵守。④ 这表明该制度值得寻求获得国际海事组织的承认。加拿大和俄罗斯也无需放弃其内水立场，以寻求国际海事组织认定"特别敏感海域"，进而由其批准采取强制船舶登记计划、分航通行以及引航措施。相关认定不会对监管措施的法律效力起到决定性作用，却至少可为他们提供更多合法性。只要明确承认不会对法律争议造成任何损害，即可申请该认定并且授予的可能性较大。

2010 年，加拿大在未与国际海事组织接触的情况下，将先前属于

---

① Hugo Caminos, "The Legal Re′gime of Straits in the 1982 United Nations Convention on the Law of the Sea." (1987) 205 Recueil des cours 128 at 172.

② "Designation of the Torres Strait as an Extension of the Great Barrier Reef Particularly Sensitive Sea Area," IMO Doc. MEPC 53/24/Add. 2, Annex 21, July 22, 2005, http://www.amsa.gov.au/marine_environment_protection/torres_strait/133 – 53. pdf.

③ Robert C. Beckman, "PSSAs and Transit Passage-Australia's Pilotage System in the Torres Strait Challenges the IMO and UNCLOS." (2007) 38 Ocean Development and International Law 325 at 326.

④ Sam Bateman and Michael White, "Compulsory Pilotage in the Torres Strait: Overcoming Unacceptable Risks to a Sensitive Marine Environment." (2009) 40 Ocean Development and International Law 184 at 191.

自愿性质的北极航运登记制度改为强制性。① 随后国际海事组织内部就此表示担忧,主要集中于加拿大事前未经协商即推行这种强制性制度。② 然而,正如麦克道曼指出的那样:"第二百三十四条的措辞和谈判历史表明该条强烈支持以下观点,即符合第二百三十四条措辞的相关措施不需要经过国际海事组织的事前审查和事后复核,沿岸国可依据第二百三十四条单方面采取比现有国际公认规则更为严格的标准和措施。"③

如果国际海事组织的2009年《极地水域操作船舶指南》如原先设想那样被赋予强制性,其也将有助于促进所有北极海峡的环境保护和争端解决。④ 事实上,北极理事会在2009年和2011年两次呼吁国际海事组织将该指导方针转变为具有法律约束力的"极地规则"。⑤ 此举将有助于消除加拿大和俄罗斯在西北航道和北方海航线相对清晰和严格的规则与第二百三十四条等更为模糊的国际法标准之间的一些差异。这反过来也可使得美国和其他国家更易于接受加拿大和俄罗斯的法律立场。

---

① The new regulations (http://laws-lois.justice.gc.ca/eng/regulations/SOR-2010-127/page-1.html) came into force in 2010. See Ted L. McDorman, "National Measures for the Safety of Navigation in Arctic Waters: NORDREG, Article 234 and Canada," in Myron H. Nordquist, et al., The Law of the Sea Convention: US Accession and Globalization (Leiden: Martinus Nijhoff, 2012), 409.

② Singapore, for example, stated that "it is not apparent how the mandatory ship reporting and VTS system established under NORDREG ties in with the fundamental purpose of Article 234 of UNCLOS...which is to allow for the prevention, reduction and control of marine pollution. The need for such a mandatory system should be supported by best available evidence." Singapore, "Statement to MSC," in Annex 28 of IMO, "Report of the Maritime Safety Committee in its Eighty-Eighth Session," IMO Doc. MSC/88/26, December 15, 2010, pp. 11-36.

③ McDorman, "National Measures for the Safety of Navigation in Arctic Waters," n. 156, above.

④ Guidelines for Ships Operating in Polar Waters, December 2, 2009, http://www.imo.org/blast/blastDataHelper.asp?data_id=29985&filename=A1024 (26).pdf.

⑤ Tromso Declaration (2009) and Nuuk Declaration (2011), both, http://www.arctic-council.org/index.php/en/about/documents/category/5-declarations; and discussion, Chapter 6, below.

十、潜艇航行

冷战期间，苏联潜艇曾在未经批准的情况下进入西北航道。[①] 但是他们从未威胁到加拿大在北极的法律立场，因为潜艇的全部意图是保持隐秘，而只有公开行动才能损害或创设国际法权利。[②] 同样，任何可能通过苏联北部海峡的北约潜艇也不会对苏联主张产生任何法律后果。

美国对西北航道的使用并没有如此神秘，尤其是在内尔斯海峡。我们知道，1960年"海龙"号成为第一艘自东向西航行通过西北航道的美国潜艇。[③] 我们也知道1962年"鳐鱼"号从大西洋经内尔斯海峡前往北冰洋。[④] 1970年"撞木鲛"号、[⑤] 1979年"射水鱼"号均航行通过相同航线。[⑥] 或许还发生过其他数次航行：2005年11月，"夏洛特"号在北极水面出现，随后潜入大洋，前往哈利法克斯、新斯科舍进行港口访问。[⑦] 尽

[①] Bob Weber, "Soviet Subs Cruised Canadian Arctic Maps Suggest," Canadian Press, December 6, 2011, http://www.thestar.com/news/canada/article/1097530-soviet-subs-cruised-canadian-arctic-maps-suggest.

[②] Anthony D'Amato, The Concept of Custom in International Law (Ithaca, NY: Cornell University Press, 1971), 469, where the author writes, with respect to the widespread use of torture by states, that the "objective evidence shows hiding, cover-up, minimization, and non-justification-all the things that betoken a violation of the law."

[③] Alfred S. McLaren, Unknown Waters: A First-Hand Account of the Historic Under-Ice Survey of the Siberian Continental Shelf by USS Queenfish (Tuscaloosa, Ala.: University of Alabama Press, 2008), 19. See also Donat Pharand and Leonard Legault, The Northwest Passage: Arctic Straits (Dordrecht: Martinus Nijhoff, 1984), 148.

[④] McLaren, Unknown Waters, p. 20. Pharand and Legault report on the return trip through the Northwest Passage but not the outbound trip through Nares Strait. See Pharand and Legault, The Northwest Passage, 148.

[⑤] Alfred S. McLaren, "The Evolution and Potential of the Arctic Submarine." (1985) 2 POAC Conference Proceedings (Danish Hydraulic Institute) 848 at 854, http://www.poac.com/Papers/POAC85_V2_all.pdf.

[⑥] "Research Guide to Submarine Arctic Operations," chap. 12, "US Submarine Arctic Operations-Historical Timeline," http://www.navsource.org/archives/08/pdf/08046001.pdf.

[⑦] "US Sub May Have Toured Canadian Arctic Zone," National Post, December 19, 2005, http://www.canada.com/nationalpost/story.html?id=fb21432a-1d28-415e-b323-ceb22d477732andk=69493.

管美国海军不会向记者提供该艇详细路径,但是最短的航线经过内尔斯海峡。

2009年2月,《洛杉矶时报》报道了当年名为"冰雪演习2009"的机密任务,美国海军称通过该演习在北冰洋"测试潜艇可操作性和作战能力"。美国海军"海伦娜"号和"安那波利斯"号向北航行,在位于阿拉斯加普拉德霍湾以北160海里的一处建于海冰之上的研究站的周边和水下测试通讯设备。根据报道,"海伦娜"号从位于圣迭戈的母港出发。虽然不清楚"安那波利斯"号何时出发前往北极,但该潜艇的基地位于康涅狄格州格罗顿,两条最短的航线分别经过西北航道和内尔斯海峡。2011年3月,基地同样位于格罗顿的"新罕布什尔"号前往普拉德霍湾以北相同区域参与"冰雪演习2011"。①

尚不清楚在这些案例中美国是否寻求并获得了加拿大的批准。在公开场合,加拿大选择忽略潜艇过境问题,完全忽略该问题对加拿大有利,因为秘密行动不能创设或改变国际法。然而,作为美国在北约和北美防空司令部的军事盟友,加拿大可能至少已获悉一部分潜艇活动情况,只是保持沉默而已。这种知悉和被动默许相结合,可能会对加拿大法律立场产生致命影响,若相关证据被公开将构成单方面将西北航道用于国际航行的事实。

美国潜艇航行或许是在加拿大同意下发生。1995年,时任国防部长戴维·科隆内特在众议院被问及潜艇通过西北航道的问题。他回答称:"我相信我们与美国存在新的外交安排,美方将向我方通报其核潜艇的冰下活动,这使我们至少可以说,美方这么做经过我们的默许。"②当一名反对派议员试图核实该陈述时,科隆内特纠正自己发言称:

> 不存在任何关于别国潜艇通过加拿大北极水域的正式协议。然而,加拿大作为拥有潜艇的国家,确实从盟国处获得潜

---

① "Navy Announces ICEX 2011 Subs," Navy News, March 18, 2011, http://www.military.com/news/article/navy-news/navy-announces-icex-2011-subs.html.

② Terry Fenge, Letter to the Editor ("Submarines and Arctic Sovereignty"), Globe and Mail, February 10, 1996.

艇活动信息。交换相关信息是出于操作和安全原因,主要为减小潜航状态的潜艇之间发生相互干扰和水下碰撞的可能性。①

10年后,另一位国防部长称此安排为一项"协议"。比尔·格雷厄姆向《环球邮报》保证说,美国在其任何潜艇过境加拿大水域之前"将会告诉我们"。②

如果关于潜艇航行的双边协议存在的话,其很有可能是根据1988年的《北极合作协议》,该协议规定美国海岸警卫队破冰船航行"不影响"双方法律立场。③ 但是,若不存在相关协议并且未向加拿大提出批准请求,而仅是告知相关航行,一旦相关情况被公之于众,这种知悉和默许相结合将损害加拿大法律立场。但从法律角度讲,只要加拿大和美国继续将相关活动视为机密,那么潜艇航行问题就不会被摆上台面。

十一、小结

美国认为,北方海航线和西北航道都是"国际海峡",外国船舶可在未经批准或受到监管限制的情况下通行。俄罗斯和加拿大持相反观点:沿两国北方海岸线的海峡构成"内水",外国船舶进入必须获得批准,国内法对其具有完全效力。

北极海冰迅速融化将促使美国重新考虑其在两条水道的法律立场。每年可能会有成百上千的外国船舶在加拿大北极区域航行,这将对美国国家安全构成威胁,该问题只有通过加拿大这种具有执行力的沿岸国行使权力才能得到妥善解决。北冰洋的另一边,俄罗斯已经慑止外国对其在北方海航线法律立场的任何直接挑战,并将继续维持这种作法,这意味着美国无法在北方海航线占据上风。

---

① Terry Fenge, Letter to the Editor ("Submarines and Arctic Sovereignty"), Globe and Mail, February 10, 1996.

② Jane Taber, "Harper Breaks Ice on Arctic Sovereignty," Globe and Mail, December 23, 2005.

③ discussion, above, pp. 139 – 140.

第六章 环境保护

在加拿大北极高地的比奇岛度过了一个夏日,我目睹了令人敬畏的"喂食狂潮"。水中充满着生命,成千上百万的数厘米长的海蝴蝶(一种以浮游生物为食的自由流动的软体动物)被一大群幼年北极鳕鱼驱赶至海面。海鸥、燕鸥、飞蛾和其他海鸟的嘈杂集合止在盛宴,还有一群明显欢乐的竖琴海豹。一只白鲸鲸鱼掠过,它们的背部在它们喂食时轻轻地打破了表面。一只年轻的北极熊耐心地看着岸边的动作;秋天海冰回来时,它的禁食将结束。

北极大部分生物都存在于海洋中,这就是为什么石油泄漏的可能性会引发如此担忧,尤其是因为石油在冰水中降解和扩散的速度非常缓慢。北极地区的气候变化比地球上其他任何地方都表现得更为明显,这已经给该地区高度特殊化的生态系统带来了巨大压力。尽管气候变化和石油泄漏已成为当今北极地区环境保护的焦点,但是环境合作的一个例子还是要比这些担忧早了一个多世纪。

一、物种保护

(一)北海狗

根据1867年《转让阿拉斯加条约》,[①] 美国获得普利比洛夫群岛主权,该群岛由位于阿留申群岛以北180海里的四个火山岛组成。这些岛屿是北海狗的主要繁殖地,而人类对它们皮毛的需求量很大。外国猎

---

① Treaty concerning the Cession of the Russian Possessions in North America, Chapter 2, n. 21, above.

人，主要是加拿大人，会在 3 海里领海范围之外等待并在这些海狗进入公海时将其猎杀。这种"远洋猎捕海豹"的作法（即在公海猎杀海狗）正使北海狗的数量大幅减少。

美国在 1868—1873 年间通过了几项法律，禁止在普利比洛夫群岛及其邻近水域猎杀海狗。[①] 1886 年，美国海岸警卫队开始严格执行这一禁令，并在距离海岸 60 海里处执法，远超领海界限。三艘"英国"海狗捕猎船只被逮捕（给英国加引号是因为当时联合王国仍在包括船舶登记在内的所有国际事务中代表加拿大）。英国和美国同意将此事提交仲裁，1893 年仲裁庭做出有利于英国的裁决，同时建议两国禁止本国国民参与普利比洛夫群岛周边 60 海里以内的远洋海狗猎捕活动。[②]

该仲裁决定导致第一个旨在保护野生动物的国际条约——1911 年美国、英国（代表加拿大）、日本和俄罗斯达成《北太平洋海狗公约》。[③] 1957 年通过了一项后续条约，但于 1984 年失效，当时美国参议院没有向延长该条约适用期限的议定书提供"建议和同意"。[④] 幸运的是，目前北海狗皮的市场已经消失，现存数量也并未受到捕猎威胁。

（二）北极熊

标志性的北极熊可重达 700 千克，后腿直立可超过 3 米，通常被认为是世界上最大的陆地肉食动物。[⑤] 然而，北极熊的学名"Ursus maritimus"表明其已经进化为专门在冰冻海面上狩猎的事实。北极熊生活在

[①] generally, James Thomas Gay, American Fur Seal Diplomacy: The Alaskan Fur Seal Controversy (New York: Peter Lang, 1987); Natalia S. Mirovitskaya, Margaret Clark, and Ronald G. Purver, "North Pacific Fur Seals: Regime Formation as a Means of Resolving Conflict," in Oran Young and Gail Osherenko, Polar Politics: Creating International Environmental Regimes (Ithaca, NY: Cornell University Press, 1993), 22.

[②] Bering Sea Fur Seals Arbitration (1893) 1 Moore International Arbitrations 755, http://archive.org/details/fursealarbitrati03ber.

[③] 1911 Convention Respecting Measures for the Preservation and Protection of Fur Seals in the North Pacific Ocean, 214 Canada Treaty Series 80, http://archive.org/details/fursealsconventi00unit.

[④] 1957 Interim Convention on Conservation of North Pacific Fur Seals, 314 UNTS 105, http://sedac.ciesin.org/entri/texts/acrc/1957FS.txt.html.

[⑤] generally, Ian Stirling, Polar Bears: The Natural History of a Threatened Species (Markham, Ont.: Fitzhenry and Whiteside, 2011).

加拿大北部、格陵兰、挪威、俄罗斯和阿拉斯加生物丰富的浅水区冰面上。数量约为2—2.5万头的泛北极种群被分为19个亚种，其中一些在自然中是存在交叉的，这使得对它们的管理和保护成为一个国际关注的问题。[1]

在20世纪中期，使用破冰船和飞机对北极熊进行猎捕的活动引起人们对该物种能否长期生存的担忧。1973年，加拿大、丹麦、挪威、苏联和美国共同签署《养护北极熊协定》。[2] 这个所谓的"北极熊条约"要求五国"采取适当行动保护北极熊所处的生态系统"并"符合根据现有最佳科学数据所采取的合理保护措施"管理种群数量。[3] 它还禁止使用"大型机动船只"和飞机来捕猎北极熊。[4]

2000年，俄罗斯和美国签署双边协议作为对该条约的补充。[5]《阿拉斯加和楚科塔北极熊种群保护和管理协议》引入一项关于禁止携带"有幼崽的雌性，小于一岁的幼崽，以及洞穴中的熊，包括准备进入洞穴或刚离开洞穴"的新禁令。[6] 它还建立了由两国各派遣一位代表组成的美国和俄罗斯北极熊委员会，"以包括当地居民传统知识在内的可靠科学数据为依据"，决定楚科奇海、东西伯利亚海和白令海"北极熊种群的年度可持续捕获水平"。[7] 随之，两国都有权获得年度配额的一半。

两个土著团体之间也达成了一项类似的协议，加拿大的因努维阿勒伊特人和美国的因纽皮特人（Inupiat）[8] 1988年签署了《因努维阿勒伊特和因纽皮特北极熊管理协议》，并于2000年更新。该协议建立了由因

---

[1] "Population Status Reviews" on the website of the Polar Bear Specialist Group of the IUCN Species Survival Commission, http://pbsg.npolar.no/en/status/.

[2] 1973 International Agreement on the Conservation of Polar Bears, http://pbsg.npolar.no/en/agreements/agreement1973.html.

[3] Ibid., Art. 2.

[4] Ibid., Art. 4.

[5] 2000 Agreement between the Government of the United States of America and the Government of the Russian Federation on the Conservation and Management of the Alaska - Chukotka Polar Bear Population, http://pbsg.npolar.no/en/agreements/US - Russia.html.

[6] Ibid., Art. 6 (b).

[7] Ibid., Art. 8.

[8] 2000 Inuvialuit - Inupiat Polar Bear Management Agreement in the Southern Beaufort Sea, http://pbsg.npolar.no/en/agreements/USA - Canada.html.

努维阿勒伊特人和因纽皮特人组成的联合委员会,也是根据科学数据,决定波弗特海南部北极熊年度可持续捕获量,并划分给这两个土著团体。值得注意的是,美国、加拿大、阿拉斯加、育空或西北地区的国家、州/领地政府都不是这个次国家协议的签字方,尽管它们均默认该协议。

加拿大、努纳武特和格陵兰政府于 2009 年达成第三项协议[1],并据此成立了一个主要由因纽特人组成的联合委员会,就凯恩盆地、巴芬湾北极熊总可捕获水平以及努纳武特和格陵兰之间配额分配提出建议。虽然丹麦仍然负责格陵兰的外交事务,但其并不是该协议缔约方,大概因为该协议涉及自然资源,所以属于格陵兰管辖范围。

尽管这些保护协议意义重大,不过从长远来看,它们能否获得成功仍存疑。气候变化延长了每年的无冰期,迫使北极熊延长了在岸上的停留时间。虽然北极熊已经进化到可以长期储存脂肪,但夏季无冰时间延长还是让它们感受到了压力,影响它们的繁殖成功率并导致在南部区域生活的北极熊死亡率上升。[2] 海冰消失也影响生态系统的其他部分,包括北极鳕鱼以及北极熊捕食的海豹。美国地质调查局在 2007 年预测,全球北极熊数量到 2050 年将减少 2/3。[3]

世界上有 2/3 的北极熊生活在加拿大,科学家和因纽特人在该物种是否丰富的问题上关系紧张。[4] 科学家声称北极熊的数量正在减少,需要进一步保护;而因纽特人则称北极熊的数量在增加;科学家们回应

---

[1] 2009 Memorandum of Understanding between the Government of Canada, the Government of Nunavut, and the Government of Greenland for the Conservation and Management of Polar Bear Populations, http://pbsg.npolar.no/export/sites/pbsg/en/docs/GN-MOU-PB.pdf.

[2] Ian Stirling and Andrew E. Derocher, "Effects of Climate Warming on Polar Bears: A Review of the Evidence." (2012) 18 (9) Global Change Biology 2694; Ed Struzik, "Climate Change Threatens to Disrupt the Denning Habits of Polar Bears," Edmonton Journal, June 23, 2012, http://www.edmontonjournal.com/news/Climate+change+threatens+disrupt+denning+habits+polar/6831844/story.html.

[3] Steven C. Amstrup, et al., "Forecasting the Range-Wide Status of Polar Bears at Selected Times in the 21st Century," US Geological Survey Administrative Report, 2007, http://www.usgs.gov/newsroom/special/polar_bears/docs/USGS_PolarBear_Amstrup_Forecast_lowres.pdf.

[4] Randy Boswell, "Inuit to Fight US Effort to Ban International Trade in Polar Bear Parts," Postmedia News, June 14, 2012, http://www.canada.com/business/Inuit+fight+effort+international+trade+polar+bear+parts/6782983/story.html#ixzz1yiwmbhmq.

说，饥饿的熊造访社区的可能性更大，因此更容易被人看到。[①]

2008 年，美国政府根据《濒危物种法》将北极熊列为濒危物种，禁止进口北极熊兽皮。[②] 这项禁令对加拿大因纽特人社区产生了立竿见影的效果，那里的猎人此前通过向美国狩猎运动爱好者出售配额和提供指导而获取利润。现在，由于无法证明是在美国国内猎杀，越来越少的美国猎人前往北方。但是每年仍有数百张北极熊皮被剥下，主要被出口到欧洲。[③]

2010 年，美国政府提议将北极熊从《濒危野生动植物种国际贸易公约》附录二移至附录一，此举将禁止全球范围内北极熊的商业交易。[④] 受因纽特人对北极熊种群数量观点的影响，加拿大政府能够争取到足够多的其他国家来阻止美国的提议。[⑤] 但是，关于北极熊的外交斗争还没有结束：2012 年 6 月，一个由环保组织和美国议员组成的联盟开始推动美国采取新措施确保《濒危野生动植物种国际贸易公约》对北极熊设置禁令。[⑥]

（三）鲸鱼

北极露脊鲸是体型最大的纯北极或亚北极动物，可以长到 20 多米长，130 吨重。尽管它们体型庞大，但却以北极一些最小的动物为食（被称为"桡足动物"的微小甲壳类生物），鲸鱼利用其筛状的鲸须板将这些生物从水体中分离出来。在北极的一些地区，因纽特人和他们之前的图勒人依靠这些温和的巨兽作为肉、鲸脂，以及建造冬天覆盖茅草房屋所需鲸须的来源。在 19 世纪末和 20 世纪初，欧洲和美国的捕鲸者屠杀了成千上万头北极露脊鲸，导致这一物种濒临灭绝。据估计，到

[①] e. g. , Ian Stirling and Claire Parkinson, "Possible Effects of Climate Warming on Selected Populations of Polar Bears (Ursus maritimus) in the Canadian Arctic." (2006) 59 Arctic 261.

[②] Felicity Barringer, "Polar Bear Is Made a Protected Species," New York Times, May 15, 2008, http://www.nytimes.com/2008/05/15/us/15polar.html.

[③] "CITES Turns Down Protections for Polar Bear, Bluefin Tuna," Environmental News Service, March 18, 2010, http://www.ens-newswire.com/ens/mar2010/2010-03-18-02.html.

[④] 1973 Convention on International Trade in Endangered Species of Wild Fauna and Flora, http://www.cites.org/.

[⑤] "CITES Turns Down Protections for Polar Bear, Bluefin Tuna," n. 21, above.

[⑥] Boswell, "Inuit to Fight US Effort," n. 18, above.

20世纪20年代，只有3000头左右个体存活。[1]

1946年，《国际捕鲸管制公约》获得通过。该公约目的是"为适当保护鲸鱼种群制定规则，从而使捕鲸业得到有序发展成为可能。"[2] 根据该公约还成立了国际捕鲸委员会，该委员会于1982年通过了一项无限期商业捕鲸禁令。

该公约和委员会所取得的成功不可否认。今天，在北极圈周围可发现超过1万多头北极露脊鲸。但是一些国家，特别是日本、冰岛和挪威，反对这项禁令，强调公约目标是"使捕鲸业有序发展成为可能"。[3] 他们质疑，是否存在科学证据支持对所有鲸鱼种类实施禁令，因此允许本国公民开展有限捕猎。为此，日本以该公约第八条有关科学研究的内容为根据，冰岛和挪威则利用第五条规定国家可以将其自身排除在委员会所做决定之外的机制。[4]

也有其他国家完全在国际捕鲸委员会制度之外运作，其中最重要的是加拿大，它在1972年禁止商业捕鲸，但于1982年退出该委员会。之后其在1984年与因努维阿勒伊特人、1993年与因纽特人达成的土地所有权协定中，确保了原住民的捕鲸权利。[5] 国际捕鲸委员会[6]和美国总统比尔·克林顿谴责了加拿大的行为，后者写道：

> 加拿大的行为危害了国际社会使鲸鱼种群开始从历史上捕鲸活动的破坏性影响中恢复的努力……根据1982年《联合国海洋法公约》所反映的国际法，各国有义务通过保护和管理鲸

---

[1] NOAA Fisheries Service, Office of Protected Resources, "Bowhead Whale (Balaena mysticetus)," http：//www. nmfs. noaa. gov/pr/species/mammals/cetaceans/bowheadwhale. htm.

[2] 1946 International Convention for the Regulation of Whaling, 161 UNTS 72, http：//www. iwcoffice. org/cache/downloads/1r2jdhu5xtuswws0ocw04wgcw/convention. pdf.

[3] Ibid.

[4] Ibid.

[5] 1984 Inuvialuit Final Agreement (as amended), sec. 14 (6), http：//www. daair. gov. nt. ca/_live/documents/documentManagerUpload/InuvialuitFinalAgreement1984. pdf; 1993 Nunavut Land Claims Agreement, sec. 5. 6. 1, http：//nlca. tunngavik. com/.

[6] e. g. , IWC Resolution 2000-2002 (Resolution on Whaling of Highly Endangered Bowhead Whales in the Eastern Canadian Arctic), http：//iwcoffice. org/meetings/resolutions/resolution2000. htm#2.

鱼的适当国际组织开展合作。加拿大已经实施的捕鲸活动削弱了国际捕鲸委员会保护项目的有效性。[1]

克林顿政府认定加拿大的行为符合《培利修正案》，该法是《渔民保护法》的一项条款。根据该法案，任何国家违反国际捕鲸委员会捕鲸制度，美国总统均有权对其捕鱼活动采取贸易制裁措施。[2] 然而，克林顿最终没有实施任何制裁，只是不予考虑加拿大请求美国豁免对其海豹产品的贸易禁令。[3]

近年来，国际捕鲸委员会已经接受了阿拉斯加的因纽皮特人和格陵兰的因纽特人数量有限的"维持生计"捕鲸活动，并为此授予其北极露脊鲸配额。这就引发了加拿大是否应该重新加入国际捕鲸委员会机制的问题。[4] 与此同时，气候变化给北极露脊鲸、白鲸、独角鲸等其他北极物种的未来增添了新的不确定性。随着冰层融化，虎鲸向北迁移的数量显著增加，捕食那些先前本可躲在浮冰之间狭窄通道中的鲸鱼和海豹。[5]

二、渔业

北冰洋的捕鱼活动一直规模有限，这主要是由于物种缺乏商业吸引力，以及几乎终年结冰。但是随着海洋变暖和冰层融化，红大马哈鱼、大西洋鳕鱼、鳕鱼和其他具有商业吸引力的物种可能很快将向北迁徙。此外，一旦北冰洋本地物种具备开发条件，很快就会具备商业吸引力，

---

[1] President William J. Clinton, "Message to the Congress on Canadian Whaling Activities," February 10, 1997, http://www.gpo.gov/fdsys/pkg/WCPD-1997-02-17/pdf/WCPD-1997-02-17-Pg175.pdf.

[2] Ibid.

[3] Ibid.

[4] For an excellent discussion of the issue, see Anthony Speca, "In the Belly of the Whaling Commission." Northern Public Affairs, June 18, 2012, http://www.northernpublicaffairs.ca/index/in-the-belly-of-the-whaling-commission/.

[5] Steven H. Ferguson, J. W. Higdon, and E. G. Chmelnitsky, "The Rise of the Killer Whales as a Major Arctic Predator," in Ferguson, et al., A Little Less Arctic: Top Predators in the World's Largest Northern Inland Sea, Hudson Bay (Dordrecht: Springer, 2010), 117.

例如：北极鳕鱼成为鱼粉减量渔业的对象。

在距离海岸 200 海里范围内，沿岸国拥有排他性的渔业管辖权。然而，生活在专属经济区以外公海中或在公海和专属经济区之间转移的渔业种群，很容易受到非北极国家远洋捕鱼船队的过度捕捞。科学上对鱼类种群如何应对变化的水温和冰况尚不清楚，为此需要制定一项关于距海岸 200 海里外北冰洋中部渔业保护和管理的国际协议。理想情况下，这种协议应在商业捕鱼开始之前即展开谈判并付诸实施，并且该区域捕鱼的这种不确定性和固有的脆弱性将使非北极国家获益。

此类协议拥有有力和令人信服的先例，有关巴伦支海（如第二章中讨论的）公海区域捕鱼和白令海的现有条约，以及 1995 年《联合国跨界鱼类种群和高度洄游鱼类种群协议》、西北大西洋渔业组织和东北大西洋渔业委员会。

（一）北冰洋"甜甜圈洞"

白令海海域面积约为 67 万平方海里。在此区域内，"甜甜圈洞"（donut hole）是一块面积达 3.6 万平方海里的椭圆形公海飞地，被俄罗斯和美国的专属经济区向海界限所包围并界定。

20 世纪 80 年代，来自中国、日本、波兰、韩国和其他国家的捕鱼船开始在甜甜圈洞中捕捞狭鳕鱼，这种鱼会在国际水域和俄罗斯、美国的专属经济区之间迁徙。捕鱼活动迅速发展为过度捕捞，1992 年鳕鱼种群数量锐减。俄罗斯和美国政府的应对措施是谈判达成 1994 年《白令海狭鳕资源养护与管理公约》。[①] 值得注意的是，中国、日本、波兰和韩国也签署了该条约。

该条约建立"甜甜圈洞"内狭鳕鱼捕捞临时禁止制度并成立一个科学和技术委员会，负责持续评估该物种的生物量。缔约方年度会议利用这些评估确定下一年允许捕获水平。如果生物量小于 167 万公吨，允许捕获量即为零并且不允许在"甜甜圈洞"中直接捕捞狭鳕鱼。公约

---

① 1994 Convention on the Conservation and Management of Pollock Resources in the Central Bering Sea, 34 ILM 67, http：//www.afsc.noaa.gov/REFM/CBS/Docs/Convention% 20on% 20Conservation% 20of% 20Pollock% 20in% 20Central% 20Bering% 20Sea.pdf.

要求缔约方采取包括强制观察程序在内的执法措施，允许其他缔约方官员登船检查该国船只。公约还要求将违反其规定的行为列为犯罪行为，但是这些行为只能由违反规定船舶的船旗国进行审判和处罚。然而令人印象深刻的是，公约对狭鳕鱼种群而言来得太晚了，狭鳕鱼数量到目前为止仍未达到允许捕捞的最低水平。

（二）北冰洋渔业组织

北冰洋中部商业捕鱼的潜力和利益不断增长，2012年皮尤环境组织发表了一份公开信，并征得来自67个国家2000多位科学家联署。① 科学家们建议，在缺乏足够科学信息管理的情况下，北冰洋中部面临着被破坏的风险，这种破坏包括但不限于过度捕捞。他们呼吁设立一个国际渔业协定，通过"基于健全的科学和预防原则，从零捕捞水平开始，以反映对该地区渔业生态的了解程度"的方式，保护北冰洋中部区域。② 科学家们还指出，与白令海中鳕鱼资源的情况不同，在达到高水平捕鱼之前和"预防性管理不再是一种选项之前"，仍有机会获得该地区相关数据并建立管理制度。③

一些国家对此表示关注。2008年，来自阿拉斯加州的联邦参议员特德·史蒂文斯和丽莎·穆尔科斯基共同发起一项参议院决议，要求美国行政部门"谈判达成一项协议或数项协议，以管理北冰洋中迁徙、跨境和跨界鱼类种群，并建立一个新的国际渔业管理组织或数个区域组织。"该决议进一步指明，该协议或数项协议"应符合《联合国鱼类种群协定》的要求"，与此同时，美国应"支持停止在北冰洋公海扩大商业捕鱼活动的国际努力"。④ 这项决议获得一致通过并经乔治·W. 布什

---

① Pew Environment Group, "More than 2,000 Scientists Worldwide Urge Protection of Central Arctic Ocean Fisheries," http://www.oceansnorth.org/arctic-fisheries-letter.

② Ibid.

③ "An Open Letter from International Scientists." (2012), http://www.oceansnorth.org/arctic-fisheries-letter.

④ SJ Res. 17 [110th], "A joint resolution directing the United States to initiate international discussions and take necessary steps with other Nations to negotiate an agreement for managing migratory and transboundary fish stocks in the Arctic Ocean," http://www.govtrack.us/congress/billtext.xpd?bill=sj110-17.

总统签署后成为法律。

2009年,奥巴马政府遵循国会指示,禁止在阿拉斯加北部联邦水域进行商业捕鱼活动。[1] 商务部长骆家辉在宣布禁令时表示:

> 气候变化导致北极海冰消退,人们对北极水域商业捕鱼的兴趣不断增加。我们正在规划可持续的捕鱼活动,不会伤害这个脆弱生态系统的整体健康。该计划将对过去不存在任何商业捕鱼活动的区域中的相关活动采取预防性措施。[2]

美国北极水域捕鱼的禁令在加拿大引起一些争议,因为其声称将包括波弗特海6250平方海里的争议区域。[3] 加拿大政府还表达了这种暂停是"解决可持续性风险的唯一手段。探索性捕鱼规定、区域封锁等其他手段是基于风险的,与可持续性使用不相符"的观点。[4] 然而,若加

---

[1] Allison Winter, "US Bans Commercial Fishing in Warming Arctic," New York Times, August 21, 2010, www.nytimes.com/gwire/2009/08/21/21greenwire-us-bans-commercial-fishing-in-warming-arctic-33236.html.

[2] Ibid.; Randy Boswell, PostMedia News, "Advocates Push for Temporary Ban on Arctic Fishing," May 1, 2011, http://www.nunatsiaqonline.ca/stories/article/185776_advocates_push_for_temporary_ban_on_arctic_fishing/.

[3] Randy Boswell, "Canada Protests US Arctic Fishing Ban," CanWest News Service, September 4, 2009, http://www.canada.com/nanaimodailynews/news/nation/story.html?id=b8757b5b-0b10-4769-9696-cdf9c315a754.

[4] Randy Boswell, "Canada, US May Be at Odds over Conservation; Beaufort Sea Policy," National Post, August 26, 2009. In April 2011, the Canadian government and the Inuvialuit Regional Corporation signed a memorandum of understanding acknowledging that current scientific information is insufficient to start a commercial fishery in the Beaufort Sea and pledging jointly to develop a precautionary fisheries plan. "Beaufort Sea Commercial Fishing Banned," CBC News, April 15, 2011, http://www.cbc.ca/news/canada/north/story/2011/04/15/beaufort-sea-commercial-fishing-ban.html. In April 2012, the Canadian government accepted that "any possible future commercial fishery in the high seas of the central Arctic Ocean must be governed by effective management and conservation measures that are based on sound scientific advice, in consultation with Northerners and are agreed upon internationally." It also stated: "To that end, Canada continues to engage in discussions with the other four Arctic Ocean coastal states, including the United States, to address all relevant issues." Joint Statement by Keith Ashfield, Minister of Fisheries and Oceans and Leona Aglukkaq, Minister of Health and Minister of the Canadian Northern Economic Development Agency, April 25, 2012, http://www.dfo-mpo.gc.ca/media/statement-declarations/2012/20120425-eng.htm.

拿大不采取完全禁止的措施，一旦商业捕鱼出现在波弗特海的加拿大一侧，就会引发加拿大和美国之间艰难的谈判。因为在边界一侧允许捕鱼，而另一侧则禁止的情况，就好比打开一个共享泳池一侧的排水阀。

美国和俄罗斯在楚科奇海的边界也存在同样的风险，特别是在白令海峡北部和《白令海渔业协定》所涉之外的区域。幸运的是，这种渔业种群共享安排是专属经济区相邻或相对国家之间相对标准的做法。正如美国国会决议所预见到的，更为有益的前景是成立北冰洋中部区域渔业组织，该组织在1995年建立并于六年后生效的《联合国跨界鱼类种群和高度洄游鱼类种群协议》框架下运行。①

就像19世纪的海狗一样，跨界种群还包括沿海国专属经济区和公海之间迁徙的鱼类。同样，这在传统上对渔业管理提出了一个问题，因为沿海国采取的任何保护措施都可能由于其专属经济区外不受管制的捕鱼而无效。1995年《联合国跨界鱼类种群和高度洄游鱼类种群协议》使得沿海国能够建立一个区域渔业组织，通过设立配额等手段，在离海岸200海里外区域管理跨界和高度洄游鱼类。但是，任何此类组织必须在非歧视性基础上向域外国家开放。任何希望在该区域内捕鱼的国家都必须加入该组织，但是在加入后就应进行充分参与，包括参与制定配额等。例如，西北大西洋渔业组织的成员国中包括日本和韩国，尽管该组织公约仅适用于美国东北部、加拿大东部和格陵兰西南部的专属经济区附近水域。②

在西北大西洋渔业组织公约区域东部，东北大西洋渔业委员会拥有大面积的管理区域，分为包括挪威海和巴伦支海中部区域在内的三个部分，这些区域正好位于北极之内。③ 东北大西洋渔业委员会依据1980年《东北大西洋未来渔业多边合作公约》成立，成员包括冰岛、挪威、

---

① 1995 UN Agreement on Straddling Fish Stocks and Highly Migratory Fish Stocks, http://www.un.org/Depts/los/convention_agreements/convention_overview_fish_stocks.htm.

② For a useful map, http://www.nafo.int/about/frames/about.html.

③ For a useful map, http://www.neafc.org/page/27.

俄罗斯、欧盟，以及代表格陵兰和法罗群岛的丹麦。[1] 该委员会负责在尊重海洋自由的前提下，管理非成员捕鱼活动的难题。如果非成员国船舶在东北大西洋渔业组织区域内以"破坏委员会规定之有效性"的方式进行捕鱼，则可禁止这些船舶在该委员会成员国卸渔或者获得燃料和补给。[2] 它们还会被列入推定从事"非法、不报告和不管制捕鱼"的船只名单，这一名单将转交给其他区域渔业组织，这些组织的成员国也可拒绝这些船只进入港口。

因此，建立一个北冰洋渔业组织很可能需要一些非北极国家的参与，只要这些国家愿意就必须允许它们加入。届时，这些国家将可以进入200海里之外区域捕鱼，前提是就相关配合措施达成基于科学的共识。然而，在等待弄清哪些非北极国家表现出在北冰洋捕鱼的兴趣之时，没有必要拖延谈判。沿海国已经有意向并依据《联合国跨界鱼类种群和高度洄游鱼类种群协议》第八条，自行建立区域渔业组织，只要该组织向"相关渔业资源享有真正利益"的其他国家保持开放。[3]

此外，在引发利益冲突和公众舆论介入之前，有时更容易找到缔结条约的政治意愿。美国方面明显具备支持成立一个北冰洋渔业组织的政治意愿，尽管该国一贯对国际组织保持谨慎，但却在该问题上采取主动态度。其他北极国家应该明智地考虑一下，不应错失这一良机。白令海峡以北的公海在夏末就已经完全无冰了，而且其与韩国、日本和中国的距离要比区域中很多国家远洋渔船前往目前作业的区域更短。

在北极理事会中进行北冰洋渔业组织的谈判和管理是不明智的，因为非该理事会成员国也需要直接参与决策。值得注意的是，2001年《北极搜救协议》也不是在北极理事会内部进行谈判或通过的。相反，

---

[1] 1980 Convention on Future Multilateral Co-operation in the North East Atlantic Fisheries, Official Journal of the European Communities, http://www.jus.uio.no/english/services/library/treaties/08/8-02/northeast-atlantic-fisheries.xml. The NEAFC adopted amendments to the Convention in 2004 and 2006 that the parties have accepted on a provisional basis, pending ratification. http://www.neafc.org/system/files/londondeclaration_and_new_convention.pdf.

[2] "NEAFC Scheme of Control and Enforcement," especially chap. 7 (Measures to Promote Compliance by Non-Contracting Party Fishing Vessels), http://www.neafc.org/scheme/chapter7.

[3] UN Agreement on Straddling Fish Stocks and Highly Migratory Fish Stocks, n. 45, above.

成员国成立了一个独立于北极理事会运作的特别工作组,这些国家签署了该条约,而不是由理事会通过了条约。简言之,该条约是在北极理事会框架下达成的,但不是由理事会本身通过。

对北冰洋渔业组织采用相同方法可以解决涉及北极理事会的另一个问题,即丹麦、瑞典和芬兰是欧盟成员国,不能决定本国渔业政策,所以欧盟委员会将不得不代表这三个国家进行谈判。[①] 但欧盟委员会没有理由不能以正式成员身份加入北极理事会框架下成立的特别工作组。

将欧盟纳入北极理事会下的渔业谈判可以带来其他好处。第一,为了使北冰洋渔业组织获得成功,欧盟将必须在未来某个时间点加入该组织。因为西班牙、葡萄牙和英国等欧盟成员国的远洋捕鱼船队规模较大,地理位置接近。为了确保欧盟充分和及时的参与,从一开始就将其纳入在内是有利的。第二,欧盟已经表示强烈支持对北冰洋渔业开展以科学为基础的合作管理。2009年,欧盟部长理事会同意"推动对北极公海新渔业活动采取预防性措施的必要性,并采取措施保护国家管辖以外区域的海洋生物多样性"。[②] 其表示,"愿意考虑通过扩大相关区域渔业管理组织授权范围的方式,在未受国际保护体系覆盖的部分海域建立监管框架的提议,或者由相关方商定的任何其他提议。"它还表示支持"对那些水域中新的渔业活动实施临时禁令"。第三,将欧盟作为北极理事会框架下渔业谈判一方,或许与欧盟申请北极理事会正式观察员地位之间存在有益联系。[③] 吸纳强大的非本区域参与者扮演协商和支持角色,对一个区域组织而言利大于弊,这也正是加拿大和美国在欧洲理事会获得观察员地位的原因。接纳欧盟作为正式观察员并将其纳入渔业谈判,可以很快形成一个获得广泛和热情支持的北冰洋渔业组织。显然,同样的道理也适用于中国,鉴于其也申请获得北极理事会正式观察员地位,以及其作为远洋捕鱼国的利益和影响。

[①] The European Commission would not have to negotiate on behalf of Greenland, for, while Denmark is a member of the EU, Greenland is not-a decision, implemented in 1985, that was rooted in a desire to manage its own fishery. "Greenland Out of EEC," Chapter 1, n. 47, above.

[②] Council of the European Union, "Council Conclusions on Arctic Issues," December 8, 2009, http://oceansnorth.org/resources/council – european – union – conclusions arctic – issues.

[③] discussion, below, pp. 236 – 237.

三、航运

2010年7月,俄罗斯冰区加强大型游轮"柳波芙·奥尔洛娃"号前往加拿大北极地区时,加拿大运输部检查人员认定该船管道系统存在问题并将之暂时扣留在纽芬兰。① 在船主承诺夏季航行旺季结束解决该问题之后,才被授予许可。那年8月,我在"柳波芙·奥尔洛娃"号上生活了两个星期,被其破旧和锈迹斑斑的状况所震撼,尤其是那些在北极风暴中基本无法使用的开敞式救生艇。按照租用该船并向船主提供25万美元贷款的因纽特人公司的要求,该船于2010年9月返回纽芬兰时被扣押。当发现船主还拖欠船员5个月工资之时,该公司放弃了这艘船。②

(一)船只安全

不安全的船舶能够进入北极水域的情况并非源于沿岸国缺乏管辖权。即使西北航道和北方海航线的咽喉要道被认为是"国际海峡",加拿大和俄罗斯在这些水道仍有一定的监管权力。③ 在美国"曼哈顿"号穿越西北航道之后,加拿大政府于1970年通过了《北极水域污染防治法》。④ 该法对加拿大北极海岸周边100海里范围内所有航运实施了严格的安全和环境要求。这部法律在当时是违反国际法的,国际法不承认沿海国享有超过12海里的权利,也即领海所允许的外部限制。但是该

---

① Chris Windeyer, "Transport Canada Raps Cruise North for Safety Issues," Nunatsiaq News, July 20, 2012, http://www.nunatsiaqonline.ca/stories/article/200710_Transport_Canada_raps_Cruise_North_for_safety_issues/.

② "Deteriorating Russian Cruise Ship's Future Unclear," CBC News, April 11, 2012, http://www.cbc.ca/news/canada/newfoundland-labrador/story/2012/04/11/nl orlova-update-411.html.

③ On the disputes over the legal status of the Northwest Passage and the Northern Sea Route, Chapter 5, above.

④ Arctic Waters Pollution Prevention Act, Chapter 5, n. 46, above. In June 2009, Canada took full advantage of Article 234 by extending the reach of the AWPPA to 200 nautical miles. An Act to Amend the Arctic Waters Pollution Prevention Act, SC 2009, c. 11, http://laws-lois.justice.gc.ca/eng/AnnualStatutes/2009_11/page-1.html.

法推动了 1982 年《联合国海洋法公约》第二百三十四条的谈判和通过，允许沿海国在几乎常年冰封导致异常航行危险时，针对 200 海里范围内海洋污染问题制定法律。沿海国有权制定和执行非歧视性的法律和规章，以防止、减少和控制船只在专属经济区范围内冰封区域对海洋的污染，这种区域内的特别严寒气候和一年中大部分时候冰封的情形对航行造成障碍或特别危险，而且海洋环境污染可能对生态平衡造成重大的损害或无可挽救的干扰。这种法律和规章应适当顾及航行，并以对海洋环境保护现有最可靠的科学证据为基础。①

第二百三十四条的通过也有助于国际习惯法平行规则的发展。1985 年，这一结果使得加拿大可以取消其对接受国际法院强制管辖权的保留，当其于 1970 年通过《北极水域污染防治法》时，曾提出保留意见。② 1990 年，俄罗斯通过了北方海航线航运规定，这与加拿大法律中的规定非常相似。③

《北极海运评估报告》是由北极理事会下属的北极海洋环境保护工作组撰写并经北极理事会 2009 年部长会议批准。④

该报告认为，"船舶对北极海洋环境的最大威胁是意外或非法排放石油。北极船舶的其他潜在影响还包括，船只撞击海洋哺乳动物，引入外来物种，扰乱海洋哺乳动物迁徙模式以及海洋运输活动产生的噪音。"⑤ 报告还发现，"在极地条件下，对冰区领航员，以及海员在北极安全和生存都缺乏统一的国际标准"。⑥ 该评估报告建议北极国家"认识到北极独特环境和航行条件……在国际海事组织中提供合作支持相关努力，以强化、协调和定期更新北极地区船舶作业的国际标准"，包括通过强制适用国际海事组织 2009 年制定的《在北极冰覆盖水域内船舶

---

① UNCLOS, Introduction, n. 15, above.

② The reservation was withdrawn nine years before UNCLOS came into force, and a full eighteen years before Canada ratified the treaty. (1985 – 1986) 40 International Court of Justice Yearbook 64.

③ Erik Franckx, "The Legal Regime of Navigation in the Russian Arctic." (2009) 18 Journal of Transnational Law and Policy 327 at 330 – 339.

④ 2009 Arctic Marine Shipping Assessment, http://www.arctic.noaa.gov/detect/documents/AMSA_2009_Report_2nd_print.pdf.

⑤ Ibid., p. 5.

⑥ Ibid., p. 4.

航行指南》的升级版。[1]

该指南强调了为北极水域作业船舶加装冰区加强外壳的重要性,携带潜在污染物进入北极水域的油轮应当拥有双层船壳,所有船只的导航和通讯设备应该适合偏远和具有挑战性的北极条件。北极理事会部长们同意该评估报告的建议,并曾在两个场合下呼吁国际海事组织将该指南转变为具有法律约束力的"极地规则"。[2] 国际海事组织船舶设计与设备分委会目前正就该文件进行磋商,将对北极船舶的认证、设计、建造、装备和操作制定详细规则,尤其突出环境保护。[3]

美国在磋商中扮演了突出角色,显然取得了良好的进展。然而,该规则对各国产生约束力的方式成为一个棘手问题。国际海事组织海洋环境保护委员会草拟了一个需要各国批准的新条约,尽管这将延缓该规则生效,并且基本可以预言美国不会批准。美国正在推动将"极地规则"视为1974年《国际海上人命安全公约》[4] 的一系列修正案,该公约长期以来一直使用"默认接受程序"更新其义务,有时是以相当实质性的方式。[5] 前一种方法提供了更大程度的合法性,后一种方法则提供了更大的效力,"极地规则"最终将选择哪种方式仍有待观察。

(二)压载水

轻载货船在其压载舱中装载大量水,以便在外海航行时保持稳定。压载水通常在最后一个停靠港装载上船,并在下一个停靠港或在航程中较浅或平静的水域排放。成千上万的物种通过压载水被传播到世界各

---

[1] Ibid., p. 6. International Maritime Organization, "Guidelines for Ships Operating in Polar Waters," A26/Res. 1024, adopted December 2, 2009, http://www.imo.org/blast/blastDataHelper.asp?data_id=29985&filename=A1024(26).pdf.

[2] Tromso Declaration (2009) and Nuuk Declaration (2011), both http://www.arctic-council.org/index.php/en/about/documents/category/5-declarations.

[3] e.g., Turid Stemre, "Background and Status of the IMO Initiative to Develop a Mandatory Polar Code," IMO Workshop, Cambridge, September 27-30, 2011, http://www.imo.org/MediaCentre/HotTopics/polar/Documents/Polarkoden%20-Cambridgeclean%20session%201-1.pdf.

[4] 1974 International Convention for the Safety of Life at Sea, consolidated 2004 version http://library.arcticportal.org/1696/1/SOLAS_consolidated_edition2004.pdf.

[5] Lei Shi, "Successful Use of the Tacit Acceptance Procedure to Effectuate Progress in International Maritime Law." (1998-1999) 11 University of San Francisco Maritime Law Journal 299.

地，其中一些成为新生态系统中的入侵物种，往往会损害本土物种。有一些已经造成了相当大的经济损失，例如压舱水将斑马纹贻贝带入美国和加拿大五大湖的案例。① 2004 年，国际海事组织通过了《国际船舶压载水和沉积物控制与管理公约》，简称《压载水管理公约》。② 《压载水管理公约》要求新建船舶必须安装压载水处理系统，而且现有船舶也必须通过改造加装这一系统。改造要求将随时间推移逐步实施，最后期限取决于船龄和压载舱大小。作为一项中期措施，《压载水管理公约》要求船舶将其压载水排放至距离海岸至少 50 海里，水深大于 200 米的水域。③ 然而，只有在代表全球航运吨位 35% 的 30 个国家批准之后，《压舱水管理公约》才会生效。截至 2012 年 11 月，已有 36 个国家批准该条约，包括加拿大、挪威、瑞典、俄罗斯以及最为重要的利比亚，但总吨位仍仅有 29%。④ 与此同时，美国海岸警卫队和环境保护署已经通过了他们自己的规则，主要目的在于保护五大湖地区，相关规则将于 2021 年在美国水域生效。⑤ 不幸的是，在北极排放压舱水总体上仍不受管制，并由此带来了真正的风险。由于北极港口主要用于出口原材料，船舶到达时通常装载少量货物并满载压载舱。⑥ 船舶进入西北航道和北方海航线水深较浅和保护水域时，会排放压舱水以减少船只吃水。作为一种临时保护措施，可以在入侵物种较难生存的深水区设立排放压舱水

---

① Among other things, zebra mussels clog the intake pipes of water treatment and power plants. generally, Great Lakes Information Network, "Zebra Mussels in the Great Lakes Region." http://www.great-lakes.net/envt/flora-fauna/invasive/zebra.html.

② 2004 International Convention for the Control and Management of Ships' Ballast Water and Sediments. http://www.cep.unep.org/meetings-events/11th-igm/bw-convention-final-text.

③ Ibid., Annex, Regulation B-4.

④ International Maritime Organization, "Status of Conventions," http://www.imo.org/About/Conventions/StatusOfConventions/Pages/Default.aspx.

⑤ Felicity Barringer, "New Rules Seek to Prevent Invasive Stowaways," New York Times, April 7, 2012, http://www.nytimes.com/2012/04/08/science/earth/invasive-species-target-of-new-ballast-water-rule.html.

⑥ Arthur J. Niimi, "Environmental and Economic Factors Can Increase the Risk of Exotic Species Introductions to the Arctic Region through Increased Ballast Water Discharge." (2004) 33 Environmental Management 712.

的指定位置。① 然而，深水区排放本身也有危险：2006 年，一艘 200 米长的汽车运输船"美洲豹王牌"号，在阿拉斯加沿岸转移压载水时船体突然向一侧倾斜。② 尽管该船被成功打捞上来，但是船上 4812 辆新车受损并最终报废。在这种情况下，代表全球另外 6% 航运吨位的国家批准《压载水管理公约》并使该公约生效就变得非常重要，其中占航运总吨位 22% 的巴拿马一个国家就可发挥很大作用。

四、核事故

尽管海洋广袤无垠，但核潜艇还是存在发生碰撞的可能，这或许是因为它们大部分时间都在相互躲藏。1992 年，美国海军"巴吞鲁日"号核潜艇在摩尔曼斯克附近撞上一艘俄罗斯潜艇。1993 年，美国海军"茴鱼"号核潜艇在巴伦支海与一艘俄罗斯潜艇发生碰撞。2009 年，一艘英国潜艇和法国潜艇在大西洋中部相撞。③ 还有核潜艇发生过搁浅、起火或其他严重事故，其中最著名的就是"库尔斯克"号核潜艇，这艘俄罗斯巡航导弹潜艇 2000 年在巴伦支海沉没。世界范围内至少已有 8 艘核潜艇发生事故，其中两艘美国、六艘苏联或俄罗斯的。④ 考虑到北冰洋对俄罗斯和美国潜艇舰队的重要性，在那里发生事故的风险特别高。显然需要制定一项用于沟通和协调潜艇航行的国际安全规则，可以基于 1972 年《美苏关于防止公海及其上空意外事故的协定》，但是该协议主要解决水面舰艇的问题。⑤ 这样的协议应当包括北约国家和俄罗

---

① Paul Brodie, "Ballast Water Rules Are Long Overdue." Chronicle Herald, October 17, 2010, D3, http://byers.typepad.com/arctic/2010/10/ballast - water - rules - are - long - overdue.html.

② Rachel D'Oro, "Insufficient Stability Is Blamed for Turning Ship." Associated Press, July 27, 2006, http://juneauempire.com/stories/072706/sta_20060727006.shtml.

③ "Nuclear Subs Collide in Atlantic," BBC News, February 16, 2009, news.bbc.co.uk/2/hi/7892294.stm.

④ Christopher Tingle, "Submarine Accidents: A 60 - Year Statistical Assessment." (2009) Professional Safety: Journal of the American Society of Safety Engineers 31.

⑤ 1972 Agreement between the Government of the United States of America and the Government of the Union of Soviet Socialist Republics on the Prevention of Incidents On and Over the High Seas, http://www.fas.org/nuke/control/sea/text/sea1.htm.

斯，可能还包括印度和中国，在理想情况下应具有全球性视角，但最好可以从北冰洋开始。核事故也可能发生在北极地区，因为其他船只上也装备有反应堆，尤其是俄罗斯运营的一些破冰船。[①] 此外，世界上第一座漂浮核电站，"罗蒙诺索夫院士"号，于2012年被部署到俄罗斯远东的堪察加地区。[②] 1986年切尔诺贝利核事故之后，在国际原子能机构框架下很快通过两项公约：第一个是1986年的《及早通报核事故国际公约》，该公约建立了可能导致重大跨界辐射泄漏事故的通报制度；[③]第二个是1986年的《核事故或辐射紧急情况援助公约》，该公约为各国在没有发生跨界辐射风险的核事故中提供了快速沟通和协作的框架。[④] 但是，上述条约本身只能促进而不能要求强制遵守。日本是上述两公约的缔约国，但在2011年因海啸引发的核危机之后，日本对外界援助缺乏透明度和开放性的情况令人不安。[⑤]

五、深海采矿

国际海底管理局是根据1982年《联合国海洋法公约》设立的，[⑥]总部位于牙买加的金斯敦，负责组织和控制所谓"区域"中所有海床上的矿物资源，基本上所有这些海底都处于国家管辖范围之外。国际

[①] Bellona Foundation, "Nuclear Icebreakers," http://www.bellona.org/english_import_area/international/russia/civilian_nuclear_vessels/icebreakers/30107.

[②] "Akademik Lomonosov: The World's First Floating Nuclear Plant," Marine Insight News Network, October 12, 2011, http://www.marineinsight.com/marine/marine-news/featured/akademik-lomonosov-the-worlds-first-floating-nuclear-plant/.

[③] 1986 Convention on Early Notification of a Nuclear Accident, http://www.iaea.org/Publications/Documents/Infcircs/Others/infcirc335.shtml.

[④] 1986 Convention on Assistance in the Case of a Nuclear Accident or Radiological Emergency, http://www.iaea.org/Publications/Documents/Infcircs/Others/infcirc336.shtml.

[⑤] e.g., Chico Harlan, "Report Blasts Japan's Preparation for, Response to Fukushima Disaster," Washington Post, July 5, 2012, http://www.washingtonpost.com/world/new-report-blasts-japans-preparation-for-response-to-fukushima-disaster/2012/07/05/gJQAN1OEPW_story.html. On the status of the 1986 Conventions, http://www.iaea.org/Publications/Documents/Conventions/cenna_status.pdf and http://www.iaea.org/Publications/Documents/Conventions/cacnare_status.pdf.

[⑥] the ISA website http://www.isa.org.jm/.

海底管理局与公营和私营公司订立合同,授权它们勘探和开发指定区域。根据《联合国海洋法公约》规定,国际海底管理局也应拥有自己的采矿实体,被称为"企业",但其尚未就成立该实体采取任何行动。

就连还未加入《联合国海洋法公约》的美国也承认国际海底管理局的合法性。20世纪90年代早期,美国利用其冷战后的主导地位对《联合国海洋法公约》的深海采矿条款进行了修改,允许包括美国公司在内的私营企业获得进入这一新资源前沿的权利。①

国际海底管理局起初专注于锰结核的开采潜力,它是一种苹果大小的块状锰、镍、铜和钴,在一些地方覆盖深海平原的大片区域。该机构于2000年通过了对此类结核勘探的规章。② 2001年起,该机构与保加利亚、中国、古巴、捷克、法国、德国、印度、日本、韩国、波兰、俄罗斯和斯洛伐克公司签署了一系列为期15年的合同。③ 目前这些勘探区主要位于太平洋和印度洋,但开采活动还没有展开。众所周知,北冰洋存在锰结核区域。事实上,这种结核于1868年首次在西伯利亚沿岸的喀拉海被发现,④ 它们将来某一天可能会引发商业兴趣。

经过六年谈判,国际海底管理局于2012年通过了第二套关于多金属硫化物的规章。⑤ 这些含硫矿物是在被称为"热液喷口"的水下间歇喷泉周围被发现的具有经济价值的浓聚物,通常含有包括铜、镍、钴和稀土元素等在内战略性矿物。中国迫切需要这类战略性矿产来支撑其快速发展的高科技经济产业,所以已经迅速采取行动对其加以利用。在新

---

① Christopher Joyner, "The United States and the New Law of the Sea." (1996) 27 Ocean Development and International Law 41. The new provisions on deep seabed mining, along with the opportunity to secure widely recognized rights over extended continental shelves, constitute significant incentives for US accession.

② Regulations on Prospecting and Exploration for Polymetallic Nodules in the Area, adopted 13 July 2000, http://www.isa.org.jm/en/documents/mcode.

③ For information on the contractors, http://www.isa.org.jm/en/scientific/exploration/contractors.

④ International Seabed Authority, "Polymetallic Nodules," http://www.isa.org.jm/files/documents/EN/Brochures/ENG7.pdf.

⑤ Regulations on Prospecting and Exploration for Polymetallic Sulphides, May 7, 2010, http://www.isa.org.jm/files/documents/EN/Regs/PolymetallicSulphides.pdf.

规章通过后的几天内,国有的中国大洋矿产资源研究开发协会就向国际海底管理局递交了一份申请,要求在印度洋一处海脊开采矿石。① 但中国进军深海采矿不会对其他国家构成严重威胁,因为它们也可以提交自己的申请。

深海采矿制度并不完美。《联合国海洋法公约》要求各国在深海采矿过程中确保对环境的"有效保护",但没有就有效保护的具体内容提供指导。近期通过的关于多金属硫化物的规章规定,国际海底管理局"制订并定期审查环境规则、规章和程序,以确保有效保护海洋环境,使其免受有害影响,"并且这些规则应当反映"预防性措施"。② 这种措施可能包括禁止在热液喷口周围进行采矿,因为扰动海底可能会导致有毒硫化物扩散,并可能扰乱存在于富含矿物质的高温水体中的特殊生态系统。

2003年,加拿大将"奋进热液喷口"确定为"海洋保护区",成为首个将预防措施运用于深海采矿的国家。③ 该喷口位于温哥华岛西南逾2000米深水中,喷口属于加拿大200海里专属经济区内。禁止在那里开采可能最终带来意想不到的商业利益,因为热液喷口周围的生态系统是以独特的耐高温生物为基础。在完全黑暗的深海中,它们通过化学合成的方式将化学能转化为有机物质,就像植物通过光合作用转化太阳能一样。来自于"奋进热液喷口"附近的一些特殊生物酶,已经被用于工业和医学应用领域研究。

在其他例子中,可能会在矿物开采和生态系统保护之间寻求平衡。加拿大的鹦鹉螺矿业公司目前正在巴布亚新几内亚领海内的俾斯麦海进行硫化物开采项目的工程阶段。④ 作为巴布亚新几内亚政府所要求的环境影响评估一部分,该公司承诺减少悬浮物卷流,降低对海底生态系统

---

① "Comra Applies for Approval of Plan of Work for Exploration for Polymetallic Sulphides," International Seabed Authority Press Release, May 25, 2010, http://www.isa.org.jm/en/node/518.

② Regulations on Prospecting and Exploration for Polymetallic Sulphides, n. 90, above.

③ Fisheries and Oceans Canada, "Endeavour Hydrothermal Vents," http://www.dfo-mpo.gc.ca/oceans/marineareas-zonesmarines/mpa-zpm/pacific-pacifique/endeavour-eng.htm.

④ Nautilus Minerals, "Solwara 1 Project-High Grade Copper and Gold," http://www.nautilusminerals.com/s/Projects-Solwara.asp.

的长期损害,包括在热液喷口周边设置保留区域,以使得一些特有生物能够让矿区重新恢复原状。由于国际海底管理局建立了详细的规章和审查采矿申请,该公司应确保在200海里之外的实践至少应当遵循该模式的某些版本。

对热液喷口的保护和开发在某个时候可能会成为北极地区的一个议题。人们沿着格陵兰和挪威之间的哈克尔海岭发现了超过12个这样的热液喷口,里面存在大量的硫化物矿产。沿着别的北冰洋海脊还可能分布着其他的喷口,存在于沿岸国管辖范围内外。

北冰洋大陆架也蕴藏着大量的甲烷水合物,即天然气受高压和低温作用转变为压缩并冻结的冰状。对这些甲烷水合物进行商业采集的技术还不存在,当这种技术成为现实时,其成本也将高得令人望而却步。沿海国管辖范围之外的深海海底也可能存在甲烷水合物,这最终可能会引起非北极国家的关注。但就像锰结核和多金属硫化物一样,这些资源将受到国际海底管理局的组织和控制,从而避免出现不受监管的财富争夺。此外,在遥远的,通常是黑暗、寒冷和多风暴的北冰洋深处进行采矿活动所带来的风险和成本将是巨大的。在北冰洋进行深海采矿还需要数十年甚至几个世纪。

六、经空气传播的污染物

(一)持久性有机污染物

持久性有机污染物是有毒化学物质,包括主要工业国家生产和使用的二氯二苯三氯乙烷(DDT)和多氯联苯(PCBs)。一直以来,这些有毒物质通过低纬度挥发和高纬度冷凝等全球蒸馏过程而大量存在,有时也被称为"蚱蜢效应"。在北极地区沉淀之后,毒素会向食物链上层移转,在海豹、北极熊等捕食者的脂肪组织中积累并最终被人类摄入。就此问题展开的多边谈判最终达成了2001年《关于持久性有机污染物的斯德哥尔摩公约》,该公约要求各国采取具体措施,减少或消除持久性有机污染物,并安全处置现有库存。① 截至目前,已有178个国家批准了该公约,包括加拿大、中国、欧盟、印度和日本。② 2009年,修订后的公约增加了9种新化学品,其中一些仍被广泛用作杀虫剂和阻燃剂将逐步被淘汰。两年后,农作物杀虫剂硫丹也被列入名单。③

在《斯德哥尔摩公约》谈判中,该问题的北极方面内容发挥了决定性作用。④ 希拉·瓦特·克劳狄尔代表因纽特人北极圈理事会参与会谈,她后来因气候变化方面的工作,与美国前副总统阿尔·戈尔共同获得诺贝尔和平奖提名。瓦特·克劳狄尔强调,因纽特人是全球范围内持久性有机污染物最脆弱的受害者,以至于妇女必须再三考虑是否用母乳喂养她们的婴儿。在一个特别关键的阶段,她向联合国环境规划署执行主任克劳斯·托普弗展示了一尊因纽特妇女和婴儿的皂石雕刻。⑤ 该雕刻在会谈期间一直被放在谈判桌的最前端。

(二)北极雾霾

"北极雾霾"一词最初见于小默里·米切尔于1956年发表的一篇论文,主要用于描述来源不明的可见大气层。⑥ 米切尔参与了美国空军在1948—1967年间记录北极气象情况的"雷鸟飞行"项目。⑦ 但直到

---

① 2001 Stockholm Convention on Persistent Organic Pollutants, http://chm.pops.int/Convention/tabid/54/Default.aspx.

② Status of Ratifications, http://chm.pops.int/Countries/StatusofRatifications/tabid/252/Default.aspx.

③ "The New POPs under the Stockholm Convention," http://chm.pops.int/Convention/ThePOPs/TheNewPOPs/tabid/2511/Default.aspx.

④ David Downie and Terry Fenge, Northern Lights Against POPs: Combating Toxic Threats in the Arctic (Montreal and Kingston: McGill-Queen's University Press, 2003); Bruce E. Johansen, "The Inuit's Struggle with Dioxins and Other Organic Pollutants." (2002) 26 American Indian Law Quarterly 479.

⑤ Marla Cone, Silent Snow: The Slow Poisoning of the Arctic (New York: Grove Press, 2005), 200.

⑥ J. M. Mitchell, Jr., "Visual Range in the Polar Regions with Particular Reference to the Alaskan Arctic." (1956) Journal of Atmospheric and Terrestrial Physics 195.

⑦ Ken Wilkening, "Science and International Environmental Nonregimes: The Case of Arctic Haze." (2011) 28 Review of Policy Research 131, http://www.highbeam.com/doc/1G1-253536411.html.

20世纪70年代末，其他研究人员才确定北极雾霾是由人类活动造成的，① 20世纪80年代中期，米切尔的论文被用于更好地理解这一现象。其中一项发现涉及"晚冬发生的频率更高"，这是因为在"寒冷、黑暗和相当稳定的系统"中颗粒和气体移动率更低，而这种系统在北极冬季较为盛行。② 研究人员还发现，只有一小部分的北极雾霾源自于北极当地。③ 大多数情况下，这属于"远距离传来空气污染"，④ 主要是硫酸盐混合数量不等的"有机微粒、氮化合物、尘埃和黑碳，以及重金属和其他污染物等微量元素"。⑤ 硫酸盐的来源较多，包括发电厂、石油和天然气生产、冶炼厂、纸浆和造纸厂，而氮化合物主要来自于汽车尾气的氧化。⑥

北极雾霾对环境和气候存在直接和间接的影响。它在北极吸收光线的冰雪表面之上制造一个"光线吸收层"，改变了北极"辐射平衡"。⑦ 雾霾中的悬浮微粒甚至可能影响云层的特性，尤其是它们的"辐射率"，即云层发出辐射的速率。北极雾霾增加了保留在地球表面的太阳辐射数值，导致冰雪融化速度加快，尤其是在春季。

1979年，联合国欧洲经济委员会通过了《远程越境空气污染公约》。⑧ 该公约为科学合作和政策协调提供了框架，包含规定了具体减排措施的八个议定书。其中之一是1999年《减少酸化、富营养化和地

---

① Arctic Monitoring and Assessment Programme, "AMAP Assessment 2006: Acidifying Pollutants, Arctic Haze, and Acidification in the Arctic," 1, http://amap.no/documents/index.cfm?dirsub = %2FAMAP%20Assessment%202006%20 - %20Acidifying%20Pollutants%2C%20Arctic%20Haze%20and%20Acidification%20in%20the%20Arcticandsort = default.

② Glen E. Shaw, "The Arctic Haze Phenomenon." (August 16, 1995) 76 Bulletin of the American Meteorological Society 2403, http://journals.ametsoc.org/doi/pdf/10.1175/1520 - 0477 (1995) 076%3C2403%3ATAHP%3E2.0.CO%3B2; and Arctic Monitoring and Assessment Programme, "AMAP Assessment 2006," ibid., p. ix.

③ Arctic Monitoring and Assessment Programme, "AMAP Assessment 2006."

④ Ibid.

⑤ Show, n. 103, above, p. 2405.

⑥ Arctic Monitoring and Assessment Programme, "AMAP Assessment 2006," n. 102, above, p. 1.

⑦ Ibid., p. 38.

⑧ United Nations Economic Commission for Europe, 1979 Convention on Long - Range Transboundary Air Pollution, http://www.unece.org/env/lrtap/lrtap_h1.html.

面臭氧的哥德堡议定书》，① 其已经得到北极理事会北极监测与评估工作组的确认，对减少北极雾霾具有特别重要的意义。② 《哥德堡议定书》规定了硫酸盐、一氧化碳、挥发性有机化合物和氨的排放上限，还为发电厂和车辆等特定排放源制定了严格的排放标准，并要求通过现有最佳方法减少排放。③ 美国、芬兰、瑞典、挪威和丹麦已经批准了《哥德堡议定书》；俄罗斯、加拿大和冰岛还没有批准。④

北极监测与评估工作组还建议，在美国、加拿大和俄罗斯北极地区建立更多空气和降水化学监测站。⑤ 这些站点将有助于科学家更好地了解一段时期内北极雾霾运行和变化的机理。⑥ 不幸的是，加拿大在2012年采取了相反的做法，关闭了该国位于北纬80度，努纳武特尤里卡的极地环境空气研究实验室。⑦

（三）黑碳

黑碳是碳氢燃料在燃烧过程中，由于氧气不足导致燃料没有完全转化为二氧化碳和水，而产生的颗粒物质。⑧ 它有时被称为"煤烟"，一

---

① Protocol to Abate Acidification, Eutrophication, and Ground – Level Ozone, http：//www.unece.org/fileadmin/DAM/env/lrtap/full%20text/1999%20Multi. E. Amended. 2005. pdf.

② Arctic Monitoring and Assessment Programme, "AMAP Assessment 2006," n. 102, above, p. ix.

③ Protocol to Abate Acidification, Eutrophication, and Ground – Level Ozone, n. 110, above.

④ United Nations Economic Commission for Europe, "Status of Ratification of the 1999 Gothenburg Protocol to Abate Acidification, Eutrophication and Ground – Level Ozone as of 24 May 2012," http：//www.unece.org/env/lrtap/status/99multi_st. html.

⑤ United Nations Economic Commission for Europe, "Status of Ratification of the 1999 Gothenburg Protocol to Abate Acidification, Eutrophication and Ground – Level Ozone as of 24 May 2012," http：//www.unece.org/env/lrtap/status/99multi_st. html. , p. 97.

⑥ Ibid. , p. 98.

⑦ "High Arctic Research Station Forced to Close：PEARL Played a Key Role in Ozone Measurements, International Collaborations." CBC News, February 28, 2012, http：//www.cbc.ca/news/politics/story/2012/02/28/science – pearl – arctic – research. html.

⑧ P. K. Quinn, et al. , The Impact of Black Carbon on the Arctic Climate (Oslo：Arctic Monitoring and Assessment Programme, 2011), 4, http：//www.amap.no/documents/.

个包含多种碳基微粒的词语。① 在发达国家,黑碳的主要来源是柴油发动机的废气。在发展中国家,黑碳通常源于木材、植物油和动物粪便等生物质燃料的燃烧。②

当黑碳沉积在冰雪之上时,会显著降低"反照率"或反射率,导致冰雪更快速融化。③ 随着融化过程进行,颗粒会更加集中于冰雪表面,从而进一步加速融化。即使碳颗粒停留在空气中,它们仍然可以通过吸收太阳能和加热周围空气来提高融化速度。④

直至目前,黑碳和其他"短期气候污染物"对气候变化的影响在很大程度上一直被忽视。虽然黑碳微粒在大气中仅停留数周(而二氧化碳分子会持续数年),但是最近的研究表明,它可能是"过去一个世纪中所观测到的四分之一全球变暖现象"的罪魁祸首。⑤ 毫无疑问,黑碳是北极海冰、冰川和永久冻土融化的重要因素。⑥

黑碳在大气中较短的寿命意味着,减少此类排放是减缓全球变暖的捷径。斯坦福大学大气和能源项目主任马克·雅各布森认为,这"也许是拯救北极海冰的唯一方法。"⑦ 2009 年,北极理事会成立工作组确定黑碳主要来源并建议"立即采取行动"。⑧ 尽管减少这个星球上任何地

---

① James Hansen and Larissa Nazarenko, "Soot Climate Forcing Via Snow and Ice Albedos." (2004) 101 (2) Proceedings of the National Academy of Sciences 423, http://www.pnas.org/content/101/2/423.full.pdf+html.

② Cath O'Driscoll, "Soot Warming Significant." (2011) 17 Chemistry and Industry 10.

③ Arctic Council Task Force on Short - Lived Climate Forcers, "Technical Report: An Assessment of Emissions and Mitigation Options for Black Carbon for the Arctic Council," May 2, 2011, p. 2, http://arctic - council.npolar.no/accms/export/sites/default/en/meetings/2011 - nuuk - ministerial/docs/3_1_ACTF_Report_02May2011 v2.pdf.

④ National Aeronautics and Space Administration, "Black Soot and Snow: A Warmer Combination," December 22, 2003, http://www.nasa.gov/centers/goddard/news/topstory/2003/1223blacksoot.html.

⑤ National Aeronautics and Space Administration, "Black Soot and Snow: A Warmer Combination," December 22, 2003, http://www.nasa.gov/centers/goddard/news/topstory/2003/1223blacksoot.html.

⑥ Ibid..

⑦ O'Driscoll, n. 119, above, p. 10.

⑧ Alister Doyle, "Arctic Nations Plan Soot Crackdown," Boston Globe, April 30, 2009, http://www.boston.com/news/world/europe/articles/2009/04/30/arctic_nations_plan_soot_crackdown/.

方的黑碳排放都将对北极产生积极影响,但是该工作组报告称,减少北极内部及附近碳源将可产生更大的影响。① 研究发现,北极地区黑碳的最大来源是柴油车辆、农业,以及合法的森林燃烧、野火和住宅供暖。报告指出,海上运输"是一个潜在重要来源,特别是在北极,因为随着时间推移海运量预计会增加,而且距离冰雪较近"。②

美国副国务卿吉姆·斯坦伯格在2011年北极理事会部长会议筹备期间表示,不会就黑碳进行具体条约谈判;但是,将会"共同聚焦"采取"强有力的国内行动"。③ 大多数北极国家尚未就解决黑碳问题采取具体措施,尽管这些国家已经存在限制短期气候污染物排放的项目并间接限制黑碳。④ 2011年,美国环境保护署曾就有关缓解俄罗斯北极地区柴油导致黑碳的研究征求建议,然后再将该研究成果适用于其他北极国家。⑤

此外,美国正在牵头减少北极以外区域黑碳排放的努力。2012年2月,美国、加拿大、孟加拉国、加纳、墨西哥、瑞典和联合国环境规划署宣布成立气候和清洁空气联盟以减少短期气候污染物。⑥ 该联盟是一

---

① Arctic Council Task Force on Short-Lived Climate Forcers, "Technical Report," n. 120, above, p. 2.

② Arctic Council Task Force on Short-Lived Climate Forcers, "Progress Report and Recommendations for Ministers," May 2, 2011, p. 3, http://arctic-council.npolar.no/accms/export/sites/default/en/meetings/2011-nuuk-ministerial/docs/3-0a_TF_SPM_recommendations_2May11_final.pdf.

③ Joby Warrick and Juliet Eilperin, "Arctic Council to Address Role of Soot in Global Warming." Washington Post, May 11, 2011, http://www.washingtonpost.com/national/arctic-council-to-address-role-of-soot-in-global-warming/2011/05/11/AFourXsG_story.html.

④ For an overview of each Arctic country's pollution measures that may affect black carbon emissions, Arctic Council Task Force on Short-Lived Climate Forcers, "Technical Report," n. 120, above, sec. 5, pp. 34-51.

⑤ Environmental Protection Agency, Request for Proposals: "Arctic Black Carbon: Reduction of Black Carbon from Diesel Sources," 2011, pp. 1-2, http://www.epa.gov/international/grants/Arctic-Black-Carbon-ModifiedRFP.pdf.

⑥ United Nations Environment Programme, "New Climate and Clean Air Coalition Expands to 13 Members: New Initiatives Assessed for Fast and Scaled-Up Action on Black Carbon, Methane, and HFCs," April 24, 2012, http://www.unep.org/newscentre/default.aspx?DocumentID=2678andArticleID=9116. The coalition website is located http://www.unep.org/ccac/Home/tabid/101612/Default.aspx.

项自愿性倡议，旨在推动减少黑碳等短期气候污染物的相关措施，并确定了包括"重型柴油车辆和发动机"和"石油和天然气生产"在内需要"立即采取行动"的领域。① 2012 年 5 月，法国、德国、意大利、日本、俄罗斯和英国等八国集团其他成员国同意加入该联盟。②

七、石油泄漏

石油泄漏的巨大风险，世人时时记起。2010 年 4 月，在距离路易斯安那州海岸 35 海里处，英国石油公司租用的"深水地平线"钻井平台发生爆炸并沉没。在封堵破裂井口的 3 个月时间内，至少有 8 亿升原油喷涌而出，对墨西哥湾的环境以及美国至少 4 个州的捕鱼和旅游产业造成不可估量的代际损害。③

发生在北极的石油泄漏将带来更大的风险。正如上文所述，石油在寒冷温度下分散和降解非常缓慢。④ "埃克森·瓦尔迪兹"号曾在阿拉斯加南部海岸的威廉王子湾泄漏超过 8000 万升原油，二十多年后，此次事故造成的溢油仍在当地生态系统中挥之不去。⑤ 偏远、海冰、季节性极夜、恶劣天气以及缺乏沿岸基础设施和人口中心，使得成功实施清理工作的预期更为遥不可及。北极海洋生态系统中物种的高度特殊化使

---

① Climate and Clean Air Coalition to Reduce Short - Lived Climate Pollutants, "Focal Areas," http://www.unep.org/ccac/FocalAreas/tabid/102153/Default.aspx.

② UNEP News Centre, "All G8 Countries Back Action on Black Carbon, Methane and Other Short Lived Climate Pollutants," May 22, 2012, http://www.unep.org/newscentre/default.aspx? DocumentID = 2683andArticleID = 9134.

③ e. g., National Oceanic and Atmospheric Administration, "Natural Resource Damage Assessment, Status Update for the Deepwater Horizon Oil Spill." (April 2012), http://www.gulfspillrestoration.noaa.gov/wp - content/uploads/FINAL _ NRDA _ StatusUpdate _ April2012.pdf.

④ Pew Environment Group, "Oil Spill Prevention and Response in the US Arctic Ocean: Unexamined Risks, Unacceptable Consequences." (November 2010), http://www.pewtrusts.org/uploadedFiles/wwwpewtrustsorg/Reports/Protecting_ocean_life/PEW - 1010_ARTIC_Report.pdf.

⑤ Lila Guterman, "Exxon Valdez Turns 20" (March 20, 2009) 323 (5921) Science 1558. See also Art Davidson, In the Wake of the Exxon Valdez (San Francisco, Calif.: Sierra Club Books, 1990).

其极易受到破坏,并且该生态系统已经因水温升高和海冰消失而承受着巨大的压力。最后但同样重要的是,北极很多土著居民仍然依赖鱼类和海洋哺乳动物作为食物来源。

(一)美国

北极石油和天然气开发的速度因国家而异。连续几届美国政府都支持在阿拉斯加北部大陆架进行近海勘探,以减少对外国能源依赖。20 世纪 80 年代,壳牌石油公司钻探了 16 口探井;2005 年,该公司出价 4400 万美元购买波弗特海勘探租约,2008 年又另花费 22 亿美元买下楚科奇海租约。① 2010 年,壳牌石油公司和英国石油公司都在波弗特海美国一侧钻探近海油井。随后,为应对"深水地平线"井喷事故,奥巴马政府暂停了近海石油租赁销售。2011 年,美国海岸警卫队司令罗伯特·帕普向国会发出警告称,美国没有准备好应对北极地区的重大溢油事件。②

石油公司则回应称,他们在阿拉斯加近海石油项目是在水深小于 70 米的人工岛礁或锚泊于海底的平台上进行的。两家公司声称,这使得北极钻井与墨西哥湾浮动平台的深水钻探完全不同。③ 奥巴马政府接受了这一观点。2012 年,壳牌石油公司在阿拉斯加以北的美国海域部署了 2 艘钻井船和另外 20 艘船只。④ 尽管由于设备问题和海

---

① John M. Broder and Clifford Krauss, "New and Frozen Frontier Awaits Offshore Oil Drilling," New York Times, May 23, 2012, http://www.nytimes.com/2012/05/24/science/earth/shell-arctic-ocean-drilling-stands-to-open-new-oil-frontier.html.

② "Testimony of Commandant Admiral Robert Papp Jr., US Coast Guard, before the Senate Committee on Commerce, Science, and Transportation, Subcommittee on Oceans, Atmosphere, Fisheries, and Coast Guard," August 12, 2011, http://www.dhs.gov/ynews/testimony/20110812-papp-keeping-coast-guard-ready-alaska.shtm.

③ Broder and Krauss, n. 137, above. In 2010, the World Wildlife Fund responded: "[T]he risk of a blowout is not related to depth, per se. Last year's blowout in the Timor Sea, which took 74 days to cap, occurred in 261 feet of water. The IXTOC I, the worst accidental spill in history until the Deepwater Horizon disaster, took place in only 160 feet of water. Both of these catastrophes occurred in depths and pressures comparable to those found in the Beaufort and Chukchi seas." World Wildlife Fund, "Drilling for Oil in the Arctic: Too Soon, Too Risky," December 1, 2010, p. 18, http://www.worldwildlife.org/what/wherewework/arctic/WWFBinaryitem18711.pdf.

④ Broder and Krauss, n. 137, above.

冰漂移,① 壳牌石油公司最终未能在当年夏季完成钻井作业,但美国政府仍要求其额外部署2艘钻井船,以具备在相同季节条件下,为主井钻探减压井的能力。当井喷发生时,钻探一个相邻的拦截井可以减少原油泄漏的压力,从而可以更容易地将主井封闭。

(二)加拿大

20世纪七八十年代,波弗特海的加拿大部分共钻探了93口井,在加拿大高北极岛屿周边近海区域另钻了40口井。② 当时,加拿大在为北极近海钻井提供监管制度方面处于世界领先地位,包括1976年引入的石油公司需具备钻探同季减压井的要求。

20世纪90年代,加拿大政府取消北极石油和天然气勘探补贴,也没有进行近海钻探。然而,随着石油价格上涨,石油公司重回波弗特海,从加拿大政府购买大面积的勘探租约。③ 其中一些租约处于深水区域,而在此类区域中无论是钻探第一口井还是减压井,都必须经过多年演习。④ 因此,其中一些租赁方开始游说负责加拿大北极区域近海钻探管制的联邦机构——加拿大国家能源委员会,要求放松同季减压井的要求。⑤ 在"深水地平线"钻井平台井喷事故后,这些公司主动要求暂停相关钻探活动,以便从该事件中汲取教训并修改监管规定。⑥

2011年,国家能源委员会发布一份关于北极近海石油钻探的报告,

---

① Kim Murphy, "Drill Rigs Wind Up Operations in Arctic Alaska Seas," Los Angeles Times, October 31, 2012, http://www.latimes.com/news/nation/nationnow/la-na-nn-arctic-drill-alaska-20121031,0,6809964.story.

② National Energy Board, "Review of Offshore Drilling in the Canadian Arctic," December 2011, p.3, http://www.neb-one.gc.ca/clf-nsi/rthnb/pplctnsbfrthnb/rctcffshrdrllngrvw/fnlrprt2011/fnlrprt2011-eng.pdf.

③ discussion, Chapter 3, above.

④ Oceans North Canada, "Becoming Arctic-Ready: Policy Recommendations for Reforming Canada's Approach to Licensing and Regulating Offshore Arctic Oil and Gas." (September 2011), Fig.1, p.1, http://oceansnorth.org/becoming-arctic-ready.

⑤ National Energy Board, n.142, above, p.5.

⑥ Shawn McCarthy, "Oil Giants Contest Arctic Relief Well Requirement," Globe and Mail, April 5, 2011, http://www.theglobeandmail.com/report-on-business/industry-news/energy-and-resources/oil-giants-contest-arctic-relief-well-requirement/article582755/.

报告虽然保留了同季减压井的要求，却为该政策开了一个重要口子：

> 同季减压井政策的预期结果是消除同一季节中出现的失控井，以尽量减少对环境的有害影响。我们将继续要求任何申请近海钻探授权的公司向我们提供它们将如何满足该政策的具体细节。想绕过该政策的申请人，必须展示将如何达到或超过我们这项政策的预期结果。我们将采取个案审查的方法，决定哪些措施符合达到或超过同季减压井政策的预期结果。我们承认，世界范围内技术不断进步，包括消除失控井所需的技术。我们对技术改变和发展持开放态度。①

与此同时，国家石油委员会对加拿大北极区域近海钻探提出一套新的文件要求。② 所有申请监管批准的公司必须确定任何"对重大溢油事故特别敏感"的动物，解释其钻探计划处理"海洋保护区和海洋动物季节性迁徙"的方法，以及"北极环境因素，包括极端温度、黑暗、冰间湖（例如冬季开放水域的部分区域）、冰盖、海冰移动、海况、洋流、海岸线特征和海底特征对该项目的潜在影响"。③ 这些公司还需要描述"包括预计流速、总体流量、原油性质和潜在井喷最大持续时间等最坏情形"以及"通过同井干预和钻探减压井等方式恢复油井控制的措施"。④

2012年，加拿大政府又开放波弗特海2638平方海里区域的勘探招标。⑤ 新区域被分为6块，其中4个位于波弗特海南部，2个位于班克

---

① National Energy Board, n. 142, above, p. 40.

② National Energy Board, "Filing Requirements for Offshore Drilling in the Canadian Arctic," December 2011, http：//www. neb－one. gc. ca/clf－nsi/rthnb/pplctnsbfrthnb/rctcffshrdrllngrvw/rctcrvwflngrqrmnt/rctcrvwflngrqmnt－eng. pdf.

③ Ibid., p. 9.

④ Ibid., p. 21.

⑤ Nathan Valderklippe, "Reviving Arctic Oil Rush, Ottawa to Auction Rights in Massive Area," Globe and Mail, May 16, 2012, http：//www. theglobeandmail. com/news/politics/reviving－arctic－oil－rush－ottawa－to－auction－rights－in－massive－area/ article2435284/.

斯岛附近的波弗特海东部。① 加拿大《环球邮报》在报道拍卖时写道："返回波弗特海的兴趣或许表明，石油公司能够适应国家能源委员会去年公布的新规则，该规则允许相关公司偏离在事故中应急井的建设必须在冬季来临之前完成的要求，如果他们能够表明其他方法可以提供同等的安全措施。"② 《环球邮报》错了，至少是在对波弗特海兴趣的程度上。只有总部位于英国的一家小公司富兰克林石油参与了投标，该公司仅仅承诺投资750万美元用于勘探，就获得了所有的新租约。③ 但是事实仍然是，加拿大在同季减压井要求上已经略有让步。

（三）挪威

挪威石油公司对在北海和挪威海近海区域开展钻探活动拥有相当丰富的经验，而挪威海是北海、巴伦支海、格陵兰和挪威西海岸之间的北大西洋的一部分。面对因北海石油产量不断下降，而导致政府特许权使用费减少的现实状况，大多数挪威人已经接受开放挪威北极近海钻探的必要性。然而，在"深水地平线"井喷事故之后，这种共识变得支离破碎，开发罗弗敦群岛周边资源的计划受到了特别严格的审查。该岛链绵延200公里，位于北极圈以北的挪威大陆近海，以从海中蹿出呈锯齿状的山脉、冷水暗礁和一个大型鳕鱼渔场而闻名。④ 2011年各方就保护罗弗敦群岛，但允许在更北的地方进行近海钻探达成妥协。⑤ 不久之后，在卑尔根以南附近区域发现了一块至少蕴藏5亿桶高质量石油的巨

---

① the map on p. 3 of the "Call for Bids," April 28, 2012, http：//www.aadncaandc.gc.ca/DAM/DAM－INTER－HQ/STAGING/texte－text/nog_rm_ri_bsm_bsm12_ bid_1334948912303_eng.pdf.

② Ibid.

③ "Low－Ball Arctic Oil Lease Earns Opposition Scorn," Canadian Press, September 21, 2012, http：//www.cbc.ca/news/canada/north/story/2012/09/20/beaufort－franklin ndp.html.

④ In 2002, Norway included the Lofoten Islands in its "tentative list," the first stage in the acquisition of "World Heritage Site" status at UNESCO. http：//whc.unesco.org/en/tentativelists/1751/.

⑤ Bjoern H. Amland, Associated Press, "Norway Blocks Oil Drilling in Fish－Spawning Area," March 11, 2011, http：//seattletimes.nwsource.com/html/businesstechnology/2014465947_apeunorwayoildrilling.html.

大油田，这可能会减缓石油公司向更北水域推进的速度。① 但是挪威政府在 2012 年宣布，正在对巴伦支海 72 个新勘探区块和挪威海另外 14 个区块进行公开招标。②

幸运的是，挪威拥有世界上安全标准最高的近海钻井技术，包括长期要求相关企业具备在出现井喷后 12 天内启动减压井能力。③ 世界各地都需要挪威在北极的专业知识和技术，包括格陵兰和俄罗斯。

（四）格陵兰

格陵兰政府将石油和天然气开发视为从丹麦获得财政和政治独立的关键因素，并一直热衷于颁发近海勘探许可证。跨国石油公司纷纷抢购许可证，因为格陵兰西部和东北部沿海地区蕴藏着丰富的油气资源。

戴维斯海峡位于格陵兰和加拿大的巴芬岛之间。由于这里存在数千座从格陵兰岛西部冰川上崩落并被洋流带至北大西洋的冰山，所以其有时被称为"冰川胡同"。戴维斯海峡距离任何重要港口或人口中心都有 800 海里以上距离，此地存在强烈风暴并且每年都有几个月处于完全黑暗之中。该海峡也是几种濒临灭绝鲸鱼的家园，同时也是商业捕虾和大菱鲆渔业重要区域。

格陵兰仿照挪威，对近海钻探采取高标准要求。苏格兰的凯恩能源公司于 2010 - 2011 年在戴维斯海峡钻探多口油井之时，2 艘钻井船被要求一直停留在该区域，如果一艘出现井喷，另一艘还可以钻探减压井。④ 数艘"海冰管理船"也随时准备拖走有威胁的冰山。⑤ 在这些标准监管下以及媒体和环保组织密切关注下，凯恩能源公司还是承担了后来被认为是不可接受的风险。具体来说，该公司使用了超过 160 吨的钻

---

① Bjoern H. Amland, Associated Press, "Statoil Announces Huge North Sea Oil Discovery," August 16, 2011, http：//abcnews. go. com/Business/wireStory? id =14313838#. T - pFPI7O5UQ.

② "Norway Offers Exploration Licenses in Arctic Waters," Reuters, June 26, 2012, http：//www. reuters. com/article/2012/06/26/norway - licences idUSL6E8HQ3FW20120626.

③ "Norsok Standard D - 010 Rev. 3 (Well Integrity in Drilling and Well Operations)," August 2004, sec. 4. 8. 2, http：//www. standard. no/PageFiles/1315/D - 010r3. pdf.

④ "Media Backgrounder: Cairn's Prevention and Response Capabilities Offshore Greenland," http：//www. cairnenergy. com/files/pdf/greenland/PreventionandResponseCapabilities. pdf.

⑤ Ibid.

井液抑制剂,这是一种被欧盟监管规定列入"红色名单"的钻探润滑剂,其在环境中分解非常缓慢。尽管丹麦国家环境研究所在2011年批准凯恩能源公司使用此类钻井液抑制剂,但其随后表示该公司的使用量"不可接受"并且"违反了国际性决议"。①

因为污染不会顾及国家之间的边界,在格陵兰一侧的戴维斯海峡出现的任何石油或钻探润滑剂泄漏都可能会很快影响加拿大水域。2010年,加拿大环境部长潘迪斯对国会众议院表示,政府官员已同格陵兰政府就计划中的钻探活动进行讨论,"加拿大民众可以放心,环境将得到保护。"② 与此同时,外交部发言人却对加拿大通讯社表示,加拿大和格陵兰的官员仍不清楚1983年与丹麦就海上环境污染防治和减少达成的协议是否仍然有效,因为格陵兰现在已对其自然资源享有管辖权。③ 外交部后来表示,格陵兰是丹麦对该协议义务的继承方。④ 包括1991年各方就1983年协议达成的修正案在内的义务,主要涉及溢油防备和反应、装备和人员共享,以及明确油气资源等。⑤

凯恩能源公司因未能在格陵兰周边发现石油或天然气,而遭受了10亿美元的损失。⑥ 然而,格陵兰政府却继续颁发该岛西海岸的勘探许

---

① Ray Weaver, "Oil Company Criticized for Release of Hazardous Chemical," Copenhagen Post, May 23, 2012, http://www.cphpost.dk/business/oil-company-criticised-release-hazardous-chemical.

② "Drilling Plans Near Greenland Spark Concern," Canadian Press, April 30, 2010, http://www.ctvnews.ca/drilling-plans-near-greenland-spark-concern-1.507833.

③ Ibid. 1983 Agreement for Cooperation relating to the Marine Environment (Canada and Denmark) (1984) 23 (2) ILM 269, http://treaties.un.org/doc/Publication/UNTS/Volume%201348/volume-1348-I-22693-English.pdf.

④ the website of the Canadian Department of Foreign Affairs and International Trade, "Denmark (Faroe Islands/Greenland)," Chapter 1, n. 50, above.

⑤ 1991 Exchange of Notes Constituting an Agreement to Amend Annex B of the 1983 Agreement for Cooperation Relating to the Marine Environment (Canada and Denmark), http://treaties.un.org/doc/Publication/UNTS/Volume%201853/volume-1853-I-22693-English.pdf.

⑥ "Davis Strait Oil Well Comes Up Dry Again," CBC News, September 13, 2011, http://www.cbc.ca/news/canada/north/story/2011/09/13/north-cairn-davis-strait-oil-wells-dry.html; Terry Macalister, "City Investors Are Getting Cold Feet about Arctic Oil Prospecting," Guardian, June 21, 2012, http://www.guardian.co.uk/environment/2012/jun/21/investment-arctic-oil-drilling.

可证,其中包括部分靠近加拿大兰开斯特海峡的海域,该海峡生物资源非常丰富,以至于有时被称为"北极的塞伦盖蒂"。①

(五)俄罗斯

俄罗斯是世界上最大的石油生产国之一,目前大部分石油产量来自于西伯利亚陆上区域。俄罗斯近海主要生产天然气,巴伦支海面积巨大的什托克曼油田引发广泛关注。天然气对于环境的危害要小于石油,因为任何泄漏出来的气体要么蒸发,要么爆炸,可能造成的后果虽然严重但影响相对有限。埃克森美孚目前计划与俄罗斯国有企业俄罗斯石油公司合作,在喀拉海投资30亿美元开展石油勘探活动。俄罗斯副总理伊戈尔·谢琴预计,喀拉海石油项目将在未来十年吸引2000—3000亿美元直接投资,②尽管如查尔斯·埃默森和格拉达·拉恩所指出的那样,"这个数字非常值得怀疑。"③

俄罗斯的环境保护记录令人非常不满。2011年,俄罗斯紧急情况部官员奥列格·库兹涅佐夫透露,在俄罗斯水域存在近2.5万个含有固体放射性废料的装置,其中大多位于北部海岸,包括新地群岛附近沉没的老旧核潜艇反应堆。④此外,堆放在近岸附近的核废料正在向北冰洋泄漏。⑤至于石油泄漏问题,俄罗斯泄漏和溢油每年至少造成石油产量

---

① Government of Greenland, Bureau of Mines and Petroleum, "Current Licenses," http://www.bmp.gl/petroleum/current-licences. On Lancaster Sound, see Gloria Galloway, "Ottawa Moves to Protect Serengeti of the Arctic," Globe and Mail, December 6, 2010, http://www.theglobeandmail.com/news/politics/ottawa-moves-to-protect-serengeti-of-the-arctic/article4081939/.

② Isabel Gorst, Charles Clover, and Ed Crooks, "Exxon and Rosneft Sign Arctic Deal," Financial Times, August 30, 2011. Sechin is quoted as saying: "One ice-proof platform costs $15bn minimum. For the Kara Sea, we require at least 10 platforms."

③ Charles Emmerson and Glada Lahn, Arctic Opening: Opportunity and Risk in the High North (London: Lloyd's, 2012), p. 25 (Box 3), http://www.chathamhouse.org/publications/papers/view/182839.

④ "Russia Reports 25,000 Undersea Radioactive Waste Sites," RIA Novosti, December 26, 2011, http://en.rian.ru/Environment/20111226/170500108.html.

⑤ Jorn Madslien, "Nuclear Waste Poses Arctic Threat," BBC News, October 19, 2006, http://news.bbc.co.uk/2/hi/6058302.stm.

1%的损失。① 其中10%左右,约50万吨,流进了汇入北冰洋的河流。②根据石油密度,50万吨大约是5.5亿万升,超过"深水地平线"事故中泄漏数量的一半。

鉴于这一悲惨的记录,有理由对俄罗斯是否具备安全开展近海石油勘探、生产和运输能力产生严重质疑。2011年,一座浮动石油平台在被拖进俄罗斯远东鄂霍次克海时发生倾覆并沉没,造成53人死亡,此地就位于日本以北不远处。③ 该钻井平台属于俄罗斯天然气工业股份公司,该公司在数月前刚刚宣布将派遣另一个浮动平台参加俄罗斯北极地区伯朝拉海的勘探钻井活动。这第二个平台是为在边远地区作业而设计,在油轮抵达的间隙最多可以储存1.3亿升石油。④

俄罗斯与邻国签订了溢油合作条约。1989年,苏联和美国缔结一项《有关紧急情况下在白令海和楚科奇海合作防止污染的协议》。⑤ 根据该协议,两国"承诺在防治污染事故中互相提供协助……无论该事故发生在何处",制定"联合应急预案"并"定期根据该预案条款举行联合污染反应演习和会议"。1994年,俄罗斯和挪威就巴伦支海溢油反应签署协议。该协议也要求两国制定联合应急预案,并在发生溢油事件时

---

① Nataliya Vasilyeva, "Russia Oil Spills Wreak Devastation," Associated Press, December 17, 2011, http: //www. boston. com/business/articles/2011/12/17/ap_enterprise_russia_oil_spills_wreak_devastation/.

② Ibid.

③ Nataliya Vasilyeva, "Kolskaya Oil Rig Sinking Sparks Doubt Over Arctic Plan," Associated Press, December 23, 2001, http: //www. huffingtonpost. com/2011/12/23/kolskaya - oil - rig - sinking - arctic_n_1167103. html.

④ Nataliya Vasilyeva, "Kolskaya Oil Rig Sinking Sparks Doubt Over Arctic Plan," Associated Press, December 23, 2001, http: //www. huffingtonpost. com/2011/12/23/kolskaya - oil - rig - sinking - arctic_n_1167103. html.

⑤ 1989 Agreement between the Government of the United States of America and the Government of the Union of Soviet Socialist Republics concerning Cooperation in Combating Pollution in the Bering and Chukchi Seas in Emergency Situations, 2190 UNTS 180, http: //www. akrrt. org/mou/Kp - US_USSR_89. pdf.

相互通报。①

(六) 溢油事故责任

至今已有几个条约规定了油轮的污染责任，1969 年《国际油污损害民事责任公约》和 1971 年《设立国际油污损害赔偿基金国际公约》算是开个头。② 在国际海事组织的框架下进行谈判和管理的这些条约，要求船主在承担严格责任（也即无过错责任）和建立强制责任保险制度的基础上开展相关活动。作为回报，船主可从基于船舶吨位的责任上限中获益，超过上限的损害将由石油运输税款支持的基金进行赔偿，但存在最高限额。1992 年，两项议定书扩大了这些条约的范围，将《国际油污损害民事责任公约》的赔偿限额增至 1.39 亿美元，《设立国际油污损害赔偿基金国际公约》的赔偿限额提升至 3.15 亿美元。③ 2000 年，该限额又提高了 50%，2003 年新的议定书创设任择性的"补充基金"，选择批准该议定书的国家将赔偿限额提高至 12 亿美元。④

美国没有批准这些条约，选择完全根据国内法处理责任问题。当外籍的油轮在靠近美国海岸处发生溢油事件时，尤其是在经过白令海峡和乌尼马克海峡等国际海峡中的美国领水时，可能会导致严重法律问题。⑤ 所有其他北极国家都已经批准最新版的《国际油污损害民事责任

---

① "Overenskomst mellom Norge og Russland anga？ ende samarbeid om bekjempelse av olje-forurensning i Barentshavet, 28 April 1994," in Overenskomster med fremmede makter (Oslo: Norwegian Ministry of Foreign Affairs, 1996), pp. 94 – 98, cited in Olav Schram Stokke, "Sub – regional Cooperation and Protection of the Arctic Marine Environment: The Barents Sea," in Davor Vidas (ed.), Protecting the Polar Marine Environment: Law and Policy for Pollution Prevention (Cambridge University Press, 2000), 124 at 138.

② International Oil Pollution Compensation Funds, Liability and Compensation for Oil Pollution Damage: Texts of the 1992 Civil Liability Convention, the 1992 Fund Convention and the Supplementary Fund Protocol (2011 edn.), http://www.iopcfunds.org/uploads/tx_iopcpublications/Text_of_Conventions_e.pdf.

③ International Oil Pollution Compensation Funds, Liability and Compensation for Oil Pollution Damage: Texts of the 1992 Civil Liability Convention, the 1992 Fund Convention and the Supplementary Fund Protocol (2011 edn.), http://www.iopcfunds.org/uploads/tx_iopcpublications/Text_of_Conventions_e.pdf.

④ Ibid.

⑤ discussion, Chapter 5, above.

公约》和《设立国际油污损害赔偿基金国际公约》，世界上两大航运登记国利比亚和巴拿马也批准了这些公约。① 此外，加拿大、丹麦、挪威、瑞典和芬兰"北极五国"也加入了该基金。②

随着货船吨位和航程增加，油轮不再是唯一能够造成大量石油泄漏的船只。如上所述，2004年一艘马来西亚货船通过乌尼马克海峡时，船体破裂并泄漏120万升燃油（重油）；因地处偏远、天气恶劣，以及阿留申群岛几乎没有溢油清理设备，这些油几乎都没有被回收。③ 另一项条约，2001年《国际燃油污染损害民事责任公约》要求船主为该风险投保。然而，该公约第六条保留了船主和保险公司"根据任何适当的国家或国际制度，例如修改后的1976年《海事赔偿责任限制公约》"限制其责任的权利。④ 上述1976年公约规定了远远低于北极地区大规模燃油泄漏可能造成的潜在结果的责任限制。⑤

目前尚未订立任何处理海上石油平台、管道或水下井口生产系统所造成污染的责任和赔偿问题。在各国政府努力应对北极地区近海钻井监管的独特挑战之际，一个特别重要的问题涉及到国内法律规定的责任上限。英国石油公司估计其"深水地平线"井喷所造成的全部损失约为410亿美元，其中包括对环境和经济损失的赔偿。⑥ 这些成本超过了美国法律规定的责任限制。美国1990年《石油污染法》规定，自然资源

---

① For list of the States Parties to the 1992 CLC, 1992 Fund Convention, and 2003 Supplementary Fund, http://www.iopcfunds.org/about-us/legal-framework/1992-fund-convention-and-supplementary-fund-protocol/.
② Ibid.
③ discussion, Chapter 5, above.
④ For the text of the "Bunker Convention," http://www.gard.no/ikbViewer/Content/3210767/Bunkers%20Convention%20and%20ratifications%20March%202012.pdf.
⑤ 1976 Convention on Limitation of Liability for Maritime Claims, as amended by the 1996 Protocol, http://www.emsa.europa.eu/main/enforcement-eu-legislation/topics-a-instruments/download/974/595/23.html.
⑥ Jonathan L. Ramseur, "Liability and Compensation Issues Raised by the 2010 Gulf Oil Spill," Congressional Research Service, March 11, 2011, http://assets.opencrs.com/rpts/R41679_20110311.pdf.

和经济损害的赔偿限额为7500万美元。① 然而，这一限制并不适用于过错或重大过失的情形，但是英国石油公司没有就此提出异议，而是从一开始就放弃主张这一限额。2010年5月，来自阿拉斯州的参议员丽莎·穆尔科斯基否决了一项将《石油污染法》中上限提高至100亿美元的法案。②

根据1970年《北极水域污染防治法》规定，在加拿大北极地区近海石油泄漏的责任限额仅有4000万美元。③ 然而，1984年《因努维阿勒伊特最终协议》规定："若实际野生动物收获损失或未来收获损失是由开发造成，开发人员承担绝对责任，负有对因努维阿勒伊特人进行赔偿并承担缓和和补救措施成本的责任，无需证明存在过错或过失。"这一规定使问题变得复杂。④《因努维阿勒伊特最终协议》适用于因努维阿勒伊特人安置区，包括波弗特海加拿大部分的绝大部分区域。⑤《环球邮报》记者内森·范德克里普写道："因努维阿勒伊特协议下的责任范围存在问题。它适用于与"收获损失"和"未来收获损失"相关的成本，还不清楚是否会涵盖所有石油泄漏成本。"⑥ 虽然责任的全部范围尚不清楚，一场重大石油泄漏事件显然会对因努维阿勒伊特人赖以生存的海洋生态系统造成损害，其规模将远超4000万美元。

可以提出很好的理由取消北极石油勘探、开发和运输的责任上限。

---

① PL 101-380, primarily codified at 33 USC § 2701, et seq. For a useful summary of the issues, Ramseur, "Liability and Compensation Issues," ibid.

② Jake Sherman, "Murkowski Blocks Oil Liability Bill," Politico, May 13, 2010, http://www.politico.com/news/stories/0510/37207.html.

③ Arctic Waters Pollution Prevention Regulations, CRC, c. 354, s. 8 ("For the purposes of section 6 of the Act, the maximum amount of liability of an operator in respect of each deposit of waste is as follows: ... (f) in the case of an operation engaged in exploring for, developing or exploiting oil and gas, $40 million").

④ Inuvialuit Final Agreement (as amended), Art. 13 (15), http://www.daair.gov.nt.ca/_live/documents/documentManagerUpload/InuvialuitFinalAgreement1984.pdf.

⑤ discussion, above, pp. 80-82.

⑥ Nathan Vanderklippe, "Oil Drillers Willing to Accept Liability for Accidents in Arctic," Globe and Mail, September 13, 2011, http://www.theglobeandmail.com/report-on-business/industry-news/energy-and-resources/oil-drillers-willing-to-accept-liability-for-accidents-in-arctic/article4199962/.

现有限额是对石油工业提供公共补贴的一种形式,因为超过限额的潜在费用无需计入保险费,因而也无需对一个潜在项目的经济可行性进行任何评估。责任上限有碍成本的充分内部化,因而可能促进在整体上不具有经济意义的活动。格陵兰在该问题上表现出一定领导力,要求石油公司在勘探钻井前提供20亿美元担保。较小的公司被要求提前提供资金,该"债券"被指定用于支付任何泄漏造成的清理费用。①

（七）溢油防备和反应协议

北极理事会8个成员国均已批准1990年《国际油污防备、反应和合作公约》,这是在国际海事组织框架内谈判达成的一项条约。② 该公约缔约国需要制定处理污染事件的措施,包括储备溢油设备、制定清理预案并举行演习。发生溢油事件时,各方需进行合作,这可能包括另一方要求提供设备的情况。公约还要求推动在区域基础上为石油污染防备和反应制定双边和多边协议。1997年,北极理事会通过一整套"北极近海石油天然气指南",并在2002年和2009年进行了更新。③ 尽管这些指导方针既有一般原则,也有更详细的建议,但是却存在两方面不足。首先,它们不具有约束力,可能会出现各种合规问题。其次,它们回避了一些较为困难和重要的问题,比如是否应该要求石油公司具备钻探同季减压井的能力。④

2011年,北极理事会成立特别工作组,就海洋石油污染防备和反应的条约进行谈判。⑤ 这个由挪威、俄罗斯和美国共同主持的特别工作组,将于2013年提交一份完整条约,该条约将借鉴2011年《北极搜

---

① Tim Webb, "Greenland Wants ＄2bn Bond from Oil Firms Keen to Drill in its Arctic Waters," Guardian, November 12, 2010, http://www.guardian.co.uk/business/2010/nov/12/greenland-oil-drilling-bond.

② 1990 International Convention on Oil Pollution Preparedness, Response and Co operation, http://www.ifrc.org/docs/idrl/I245EN.pdf.

③ For the 2009 version, http://arctic-council.org/filearchive/Arctic%20Offhsore%20Oil%20and%20Gas%20Guidelines%202009.pdf.

④ discussion, above, pp.201 - 205.

⑤ Task Force on Arctic Marine Oil Pollution Preparedness and Response, http://www.arctic-council.org/index.php/en/about-us/task-forces/280-oil-spill-task-force.

救协定》，因此是侧重于提升事故发生时的沟通和协调。[1] 就实质性义务而言，新条约不太可能超越1990年《国际油污防备、反应和合作公约》，解决诸如同季减压井能力、设备和人员安装部署最低限度要求，亦或是提高或取消责任上限等难题。就该条约将填补空白的程度而言，它可能在促进区域协商、协调和合作方面取得进展，因为就北极地区多边海上石油污染反应而言，目前尚无具有法律约束力的文书。

尽管改善沟通和协调可能会有所帮助，但管理北极石油相关风险仍将是一项艰巨的任务。2010年世界野生生物基金会报告中提出一个关键性问题："鉴于巨大的环境挑战、能力缺乏和当前冰覆水域反应手段的严重限制，目前无法对北极地区发生的重大溢油事故进行有效反应。"[2] 该报告更是提出所谓的"反应缺口"，即"由于北极地处偏远和极端气候，在大部分时间都无法采取任何反应措施。"[3] 在此情况下，真正需要的是一份聚焦北极区域范围内溢油预防的条约，这可能迫使企业内化在该地区开展近海钻井的所有成本。石油公司将开发并实施北极地区所需的强化安全措施，但前提是它们必须承担钻井造成损害的所有风险和损失。

八、基于生态系统的管理

基于生态体系的管理包括把污染和过度捕捞等所有环境压力来源进行一揽子处理。这种方法已经在其他区域环境中得到运用，例如地中海、波罗的海和相当大一部分位于北极区域之内的东北大西洋。[4] 基于生态体系的管理也已被运用在北极的巴伦支海。北欧国家、俄罗斯和欧

---

[1] discussion, below, pp. 277 – 279.
[2] World Wildlife Fund, "Drilling for Oil in the Arctic," n. 139, above.
[3] Ibid.
[4] e. g. , Peter M. Haas, Saving the Mediterranean: The Politics of International Environmental Cooperation (New York: Columbia University Press, 1990); Martin Lindegren, et al. , "Preventing the Collapse of the Baltic Cod Stock through an Ecosystem – Based Management Approach. " (2009) 106 Proceedings of the National Academy of Science of the United States of America 14722; Chris Frid, et al. , "Ecosystem – Based Fisheries Management: Progress in the NE Atlantic. " (2005) 29 Marine Policy 461.

盟委员会于1993年通过了《巴伦支海欧洲—北极地区合作宣言》，因其签署地为挪威北部的希尔克内斯小镇，故被称为《希尔克内斯宣言》。① 该宣言聚焦就可持续发展问题展开区域合作，并为此成立了被称为巴伦支海欧洲—北极理事会的政府间论坛。② 与此同时，一些省级政府和土著人民成立了一个平行论坛，也即巴伦支区域理事会。③ 北冰洋沿岸国正在努力在北冰洋中部采取相同做法，尽管迄今为止，它们通过北极理事会中一系列补充性安排（《北极海洋运输评估》、即将达成的《溢油防备和反应协议》），国际海事组织（《北极航运规则》、即将达成的《极地规则》）以及联合国（《气候变化框架公约》）等途径实现这一目标，而不是通过单一文件或机构来完成。罗布·休伯特和布鲁克斯·耶格尔于2008年为世界野生生物基金会撰写的一份报告中提出了一项专门针对北极的倡议。他们呼吁根据《联合国海洋法公约》成立区域渔业组织或达成区域海洋协定，并将《保护东北大西洋海洋环境公约》确定为一种可能的模式。④ 本章此前已经讨论了成立一个区域渔业组织的想法。至于达成一项区域海洋协议的问题，根据联合国环境规划署的"区域海洋项目"，这当然是可行的。⑤ 但是，尽管区域海洋已经成为世界其他地区多边环境合作的焦点，但仍有人会质疑，是否仅仅存在一个区域性海洋就能够创设法律义务。⑥

休伯特和耶格尔进一步认为，根据《联合国海洋法公约》第一百二十二条，北冰洋属于"封闭"或"半闭海"，这一地位将为沿岸国提供更大的监管权力。但是恩诺·哈德斯指出，"第一百二十二条要求通

---

① "Declaration on Cooperation in the Barents Euro – Arctic Region," Kirkenes, Norway, January 11, 1993, http：//www.unep.org/dewa/giwa/areas/kirkenes.htm.

② the website of the Barents Euro – Arctic Council http：//www.beac.st/in_English/Barents_Euro – Arctic_Council.iw3.

③ the website of the Barents Regional Council http：//www.beac.st/in_English/Barents_Euro – Arctic_Council/Barents_Regional_Council.iw3.

④ Rob Huebert and Brooks Yeager, "A New Sea: The Need for a Regional Agreement on Management and Conservation of the Arctic Marine Environment."(World Wildlife Fund, 2008), http：//awsassets.panda.org/downloads/ a_new_sea_jan08_final_11jan08.pdf.

⑤ United Nations Environmental Programme, "Regional Seas Program," http：//www.unep.org/regionalseas/default.asp.

⑥ Ibid.

过一个'狭窄的出口'连接到另一个海或洋……格陵兰海、挪威海和白令海的开放海域显然与北冰洋作为半闭海的地位不符,无论是从地理还是法律角度来看。"① 话虽如此,北冰洋沿岸国家显然希望将北冰洋中部作为一个整体来加强环境保护,包括但不限于溢油预防、准备和应对,渔业管理以及航行安全。

九、小结

我在比奇岛精彩展馆中目睹了北极海洋生态系统,同样,北极环境保护的所有必要元素紧密相连。国际环境法在北极地区有着悠久的历史,发端于19世纪保护北方的海狗,冷战期间为保护鲸鱼和北极熊得以延续。今天,主要的环境挑战来自于海冰融化和石油价格上涨,掺杂着悲剧性和讽刺意味,这两个因素正迅速吸引航运业和资源开发向北延伸。北极国家刚刚开始就航运安全、溢油防备和反应采取新的立法举措,并且有望成立新的区域性渔业组织。需要尽快就溢油预防、提高溢油责任上限、减少北极阴霾和黑炭等气候强迫物质的排放等方面的区域标准展开更多合作。该地区的冰与水之间存在着历史和脆弱的平衡,在应对气候变化时表现出独特的脆弱性并将对全球气候产生至关重要的影响。从这个意义上讲,北极地区环境问题的国际合作正是开始之时,也是结束之日。

---

① J. Enno Harders, "In Quest of an Arctic Legal Regime: Marine Regionalism-A Concept of International Law Evaluated." (1987) 11 Marine Policy 285 at 295 – 296. See, similarly, Erik Molenaar, "Current and Prospective Roles of the Arctic Council System within the Context of the Law of the Sea." (2012) 27 International Journal of Marine and Coastal Law 553 at 563. Harders goes on to argue that the Arctic Ocean's status as a "regional sea" creates legal obligations for the coastal states to manage cooperatively the environment under both UNCLOS and general principles of international environmental law.

第七章 土著人民

千百年来，人类一直沿着北冰洋海岸线生活。在国家和领土所有权概念产生之前，以及欧洲探险家和定居者到来之前，就已经有人类在那里繁衍生息。欧洲人将土著人的家园视为不属于任何人的无主之地，结果造成如今数个北极土著民族跨越国家边界生活的状况。因纽特人生活在加拿大、丹麦、俄罗斯和美国四个国家。萨米人（the Saami，也写作 Sami 或 Sa'mi）同样生活在四个国家，即挪威、瑞典、芬兰和俄罗斯。阿萨巴斯卡人（Athabaskans）和哥威迅人（Gwich'in）生活在加拿大和美国，而阿留申人（Aleut）生活在位于阿拉斯加和俄罗斯（一小部分）的阿留申群岛。① 在北极，土著民族和国际法之间的关系与世界其他地方的此类关系较为相似。大多数土著民族不寻求独立国家意义上的自决，而是争取获得"内部自决"，也即在现有国家边界内争取人权和自治权。②

北极土著民族与欧洲人的接触发生在不同时期。萨米人与非萨米人已经共处了数千年，并融入了挪威、瑞典和芬兰的经济、教育系统以及政府架构。③ 他们也受益于最早见于 1751 年的国内法和国际法对其权利提供的保护，当时瑞典、丹麦和挪威依据《斯特伦斯塔德条约》划分边界，这对萨米人及其驯鹿的迁徙构成潜在障碍。该问题通过在《斯

---

① For a useful map, Winfried K. Dallmann, "Indigenous Peoples of the Arctic Countries," Norwegian Polar Institute, http://www.arctic-council.org/images/maps/indig_peoples.pdf.

② generally, S. James Anaya, Indigenous Peoples in International Law, 2nd edn. (Oxford University Press, 2004); Joshua Castellino and Niamh Walsh (eds.), International Law and Indigenous Peoples (Dordrecht: Martinus Nijhoff, 2004).

③ Galdu, the Resource Centre for the Rights of Indigenous Peoples, has published numerous reports on Saami political representation, resource management, and cultural and educational self-determination. http://www.galdu.org.

特伦斯塔德条约》后增加被称为《拉普附录》附件的方式加以解决，其中部分条款规定：

> 萨米人需要两国的土地。因此，他们可以根据传统，被允许在秋天和春天将其驯鹿跨过边界进入另一国。在此之后，他们应该像所在国治下的臣民一样，一如既往地被允许使用土地、其自身和动物所享有的配给，除下文所述位置之外，他们应得到友好、保护和帮助。①

《拉普附录》有时被称为《萨米人大宪章》，现在仍然具有效力。

格陵兰的因纽特人早在12世纪就开始接触维京定居者。相比之下，加拿大和阿拉斯加的因纽特人一直延续其传统的生活方式，直到20世纪之前都没有明显中断，而且即使到了20世纪，他们主要接触的还是偶尔造访的毛皮商人、捕鲸者、传教士和警察，而不是定居者。更为晚近，冷战时期建立雷达站以及20世纪六七十年代首次寻找石油资源的活动，导致大批军事人员和石油工人涌入该地。由于尝试开展驯鹿放牧集体化运作以及约瑟夫·斯大林为开发北极将数百万工人和囚犯转移到此地，俄罗斯境内的土著民族面临着更为特殊的挑战。这种压力仍在继续，俄罗斯北极石油和天然气工业目前已占该国国内生产总值的20%左右。②

大约有7万萨米人生活在挪威、瑞典、芬兰和俄罗斯，15.5万因纽特人生活在阿拉斯加、加拿大、格陵兰和俄罗斯，5.5万阿萨巴斯卡人和哥威迅人生活在阿拉斯加和加拿大，1.5万阿留申人生活在阿拉斯加和俄罗斯，以及25万其他土著群体生活在俄罗斯北部地区。在教育、住房、医疗保健和工资就业等方面，北欧国家的萨米人最为富有，其次是格陵兰的因纽特人。其他地方土著民族的状况只能用贫穷一词来概

---

① Lennard Sillanpaä, Impact of International Law on Indigenous Rights in Northern Europe (Ottawa: Indian and Northern Affairs Canada, 1992), p. 6.

② Timothy Bancroft - Hinchey, "Climate Change, the Arctic and Russia's National Security," Pravda, March 25, 2010, http://english.pravda.ru/russia/politics/25 - 03 - 2010/112732 - climate_russia - 0/.

括。举个例子,加拿大因纽特青年的自杀率是全国平均水平的 30 倍。[1]落后的经济条件是主要原因,这也导致传统文化的流失和缺乏有意义的政治参与机会。[2]

一、政治参与和自决

包括《联合国宪章》在内的许多条约都提到了自决权,其被广泛认为属于国际习惯法的一部分。[3] 1966 年《公民权利和政治权利国际公约》和《经济、社会及文化权利国际公约》第一条的内容都是:"所有人民都有自决权。他们凭这种权利自由决定他们的政治地位,并自由谋求他们的经济、社会和文化的发展。"[4]

尽管土著人民的自决权一般认为不包含独立建国的权利,但是各国需要向其领土之内的土著人民提供有意义的政治参与和地方决策机会,通常被称为"自治"。[5] 萨米人是首个获得重要政治参与机会的北极土著人,正如莎娜·普劳特解释道:

萨米人委员会成立于 1956 年,当时正值第二次世界大战后自由主义、人权和社会正义浪潮席卷北欧。这一浪潮助长了北欧国家在平等和人权领域担当领袖的宏愿。萨米人委员会的支持者因而能够确保在设立萨米人议会方面获得政府支持,该议会在北欧各国的行政和经济力量不断增长。它的主要目标是扭转语言和文化的同化政策,该政策当时已经成为这些国家的国内政策并且阻止萨米人享有作为一个民族而拥有的集

---

[1] Helen Branswell, "Death, Suicide Rates among Inuit Kids Soar over Rest of Canada," Globe and Mail, July 18, 2012, http://www.theglobeandmail.com/news/national/death-suicide-rates-among-inuit-kids-soar-over-rest-of-canada/article4426600/.

[2] For an equally dark picture of the situation in Alaska, and some explanations, William Yardley, "In Native Alaskan Villages, a Culture of Sorrow," New York Times, May 14, 2007, http://www.nytimes.com/2007/05/14/us/14alaska.html.

[3] Article 1 (2) of the UN Charter refers to "the principle of equal rights and self determination of peoples." http://www.un.org/en/documents/charter/chapter1.shtml.

[4] International Covenant on Civil and Political Rights, http://www2.ohchr.org/english/law/ccpr.htm. International Covenant on Economic, Social and Cultural Rights, http://www.ohchr.org/english/law/cescr.htm.

[5] e.g., Anaya, Indigenous Peoples in International Law, n. 2, above, pp. 153-184.

体权利。①

1989 年在挪威、1993 年在瑞典、1996 年在芬兰先后设立民选的萨米人议会。虽然这些机构的立法能力有限,但是他们通过确保萨米人的观点和利益被融入国家层面决策进程,发挥了重要的协商作用。② 他们还管理着萨米语和教育项目的资金。

自 2001 年以来,三个议会每年都召开一次萨米议会会议。2005 年,萨米议会理事会向挪威、瑞典和芬兰政府提交了《北欧萨米公约》草案。③ 五年后,三国政府同意将该公约草案作为谈判基础,并于 2011 年启动正式谈判。公约草案确认萨米人是土著民族,"特别需要跨越国边界发展其社会",并且这三个国家"承担为萨米文化和社会提供适当条件的国家和国际责任"。这些条件包括相当程度的自治,正如公约草案第三条明确指出:

> 作为一个民族,萨米人依据国际法和该公约的条款和规定,享有自决权。萨米人享有决定其经济、社会和文化发展的权利,并有权为其自身利益处分其自然资源。④

正如第一章中解释的,格陵兰因纽特人在 2008 年公投中获得了广泛的自治权力,国家将司法实务、治安和自然资源的责任交由格陵兰政府。由于政府施行民主政治,而因纽特人占人口的 88%,这个世界上最大的岛屿将成为第一个由因纽特人统治的国家。

美国国会通过了 1971 年《阿拉斯加原住民土地权利处理法案》,该法案为石油工业提供了更大的保障性,也为美国阿拉斯加州的土著人

---

① Shayna Plaut, "'Cooperation Is the Story'-Best Practices of Transnational Indigenous Activism in the North." (2012) 16 International Journal of Human Rights 193 at 197.

② Else Grete Broderstad, "Political Autonomy and Integration of Authority: The Understanding of Saami Self-Determination." (2001) 8 International Journal on Minority and Group Rights 151.

③ For the text of the initial draft, http://www.regjeringen.no/Upload/AID/temadokumenter/sami/sami_samekonv_engelsk.pdf.

④ Ibid.

提供了一定程度的自治。① 该法案提供近 10 亿美元现金,并设立 12 家区域盈利性机构,共计拥有 18 万平方千米土地的地上权和采矿权。将投资和石油工业活动相结合,为一些组织提供了客观的持续收入,特别是北极大陆坡区域公司所代表的 1.1 万因纽皮特人,数额更是可观。②该企业现在是归阿拉斯加州所有的最大公司,在全球拥有大约 1 万名员工。③ 此外,由于北坡自治市的成立,因纽皮特人控制的自治政府能够对石油和天然气设施征收财产税,从而成为该地区唯一服务提供商(目前也是最大的雇主),几乎与英国一样大。④ 然而,相较于其他十分之九的美国最大的州,《阿拉斯加原住民土地权利处理法案》对土著人权利提供了相对较少的保护,包括维持生计的狩猎和捕鱼权。

通过一系列土地权利协议,从因努维阿勒伊特人在育空和西北地区的安置区到拉布拉多的努纳齐亚福特的一系列土地权利协议,加拿大因纽特人已经获得一定程度的自治。最重要的是,高北极岛屿和哈德逊湾西岸的因纽特人,已经在加拿大联邦架构中获得了他们自己的政治实体。土著人占 85% 的努纳武特领地,他们拥有一个多数主义的治理体系,为因纽特人提供了事实上的自治。尽管努纳武特政府在社会服务、教育、医疗保健和司法行政方面拥有相当大的自主权,加拿大政府仍然牢牢控制着资源性收入。这使得该领地几乎完全依赖于财政转移,但这种财政转移与人口增长并不同步,部分原因在于努纳武特的出生率是全国平均水平的两倍。⑤ 控制资源性收入已经成为努纳武特政府的关键问题,当地政府相信财政自治和采掘业进一步发展将使其能够改善教育、医疗保健和生活条件。毫不奇怪,资源性收入是加拿大和努纳武特政府

---

① 1971 Alaska Native Claims Settlement Act, 43 USC Chapter 33, http://www.law.cornell.edu/uscode/text/43/chapter-33.
② the ASRC website http://www.asrc.com.
③ Ibid.
④ North Slope Borough Corporation, at www.co.north-slope.ak.us/.
⑤ "Nunavut Still Canada's Youngest, Fastest Growing Jurisdiction: Statistics Canada," Nunatsiaq News, July 20, 2011, http://www.nunatsiaqonline.ca/stories/article/206678_nunavut_is_canadas_youngest_fastest_growing_place_stats_can_report/.

之间权力转移谈判的症结所在。①

因纽特人自决权在加拿大北部其他地区采取了不同的形式。2005年,拉布拉多的因纽特人、联邦政府以及纽芬兰和拉布拉多两省政府签订了《拉布拉多因纽特人土地所有权协定》。②尽管努纳齐亚福特仍然是纽芬兰和拉布拉多省一部分,但是将由新成立的政府负责健康、教育和文化事务。努那维克的因纽特人也在寻求类似的权力,他们居住在魁北克并于1975年与联邦和省政府达成了土地所有权协定。③

俄罗斯北部的土著人民几乎没有机会获得有意义的政治参与,部分原因是他们在传统居住区的人口中处于少数,另一部分原因是苏联和现在俄罗斯的集权和专制性质政治。话虽如此,俄罗斯萨米人的确与萨米人委员会、萨米议会会议进行了磋商。此外,他们和其他土著人在北极理事会中的代表是俄罗斯北方、西伯利亚和远东土著人民协会,这个组织由34个区域和民族组织共同创建于1990年,最初称为苏联北方民族协会。④

然而,俄罗斯北方、西伯利亚和远东土著人民协会在其网站上抱怨称:

> 在很多地区,当局的强烈反对态度表现为完全无视土著人民并侵犯他们的合法权利和利益。政府代表正努力继续维系着家长式的政策,以控制土著人民;他们往往不知道或不承认人权和原住民权利的国际标准,也不了解该运动的目标。⑤

2012年11月,俄罗斯司法部命令俄罗斯北方、西伯利亚和远东土

---

① Anthony Speca, "Nunavut, Greenland and the Politics of Resource Revenues."(May 2012)Policy Options 62, http://www.irpp.org/po/archive/may12/speca.pdf.

② 2005 Labrador and Inuit Land Claims Agreement, http://www.exec.gov.nl.ca/exec/igas/land_claims/agreement.html.

③ Makivik Corporation, "Nunavik Government," http://www.makivik.org/buildingnunavik/nunavik-government/.

④ RAIPON, http://www.raipon.info/en/.

⑤ Section on "Social" at RAIPON website: http://www.raipon.info/en/history/social.html.

著人民协会暂停运作六个月,表面上是因该组织不遵守俄罗斯法律。此举促使北极理事会成员国的"高级北极官员"以及其他土著"永久参与方"发表一份关切声明,这份声明得到了俄罗斯北极大使安东·瓦西里耶夫的支持,非常引人注目。① 这表明,司法部的行动未得到俄罗斯政府其他部门的支持。不管这场争论如何发展,俄罗斯土著人的处境在未来几年中可能只会变得更糟,因为资源开发公司大幅扩大在俄罗斯北极地区的活动,进一步排挤土著人民和他们的传统生活方式。②

在实施层面,自决权仍然是北极土著民族正在推进的工作。尽管北极人民的土著权利尚不完善,但是这并没有阻止几个北极国家援引这些相同民族的历史性存在来支持以国家为中心的主权主张。

二、土著人权利和主张

较为普遍的观点认为,"持续和平地展示主权"可以为领土所有权提供基础。③ 尤其是国际法院在"西撒哈拉案"中同时还承认,土著人所享有的权利属于国家对领土所有权。④ 因此,加拿大和丹麦有时会援引北极土著人对土地和冰层的"使用和占有",作为两国主权主张的来源之一。

1930 年,关于西北航道北部的斯弗德鲁普群岛所有权问题的一次照会交换中,挪威驻伦敦代办承认加拿大主权并紧随其后要求允许挪威公民在该群岛从事商业活动。⑤ 正如在第一章所解释的,英国驻奥斯陆

---

① Jane George, "Arctic Council Officials Call for Reinstatement of Russian Indigenous Org," Nunatsiaq News, November 15, 2012, http://www.nunatsiaqonline.ca/stories/article/65674arctic_council_calls_for_russian_indigenous_orgs_return/.

② e.g., Lucy Ash, "Yamal reindeer herders hemmed in by gas fields and pipelines," BBC News, May 10, 2012, http://www.bbc.co.uk/news/magazine-17956108.

③ Island of Palmas Case (Netherlands v. USA) (1928) 2 Reports of International Arbitral Awards 829 at 869 (Max Huber, arbitrator), http://untreaty.un.org/cod/riaa/cases/vol_II/829-871.pdf.

④ Western Sahara, Advisory Opinion (1975) ICJ Reports 12 at 38-39, pp. 79-80. See discussion, above, pp. 132-133.

⑤ discussion, Chapter 1, above.

代办以加拿大政府已经指明"只有西北地区原住民可以在北极区域进行狩猎和诱捕,以避免因白人猎人和商人对野生动物资源开发导致土著居民的贫困和饥饿"为由,拒绝了这一要求。①

加拿大政府在1935年和1955年将17个因纽特家庭从魁北克北部迁至雷索卢特湾和格里斯峡湾,在加拿大最北部建立了两个永久社区。因纽特人基本上是被作为"旗杆",也即加拿大在当地主权的标志。正如希拉·格兰特所解释的,重新安置活动受到第二次世界大战和冷战期间美国军事存在大幅增加,以及格陵兰因纽特人造访埃尔斯米尔岛报道的驱使,加拿大人希望展现其对高北极岛屿的使用和占有。② 因纽特人从未到达如此之北地区,就将这些小村庄称为"Qausuittuq"(意即太阳永不落山之地)和"Auyuittuq"(意即冰雪永不融化之地)。

1984年,加拿大政府和北极西北部因努维阿勒伊特人达成《因努维阿勒伊特最终协议》,该协议将波弗特海西经141度经线作为因努维阿勒伊特定居区的西部边界。③ 正如第三章中解释的,该经线在陆地上是作为阿拉斯加和育空之间的边界,也是加拿大在与美国海上边界争端中所倾向的边界线。在最终协议中使用这一有争议的界限可能是为了帮助加拿大的主张获得国际社会的支持。若是这样,这将是一种错误的努力。边界争议的"关键日期"在签署该协议前十多年即已到达,从而否定了旨在强化一方立场的后续行动的法律相关性。④ 此外,因努维阿勒伊特人在国际法下对争议近海区域享有的任何权利都将需要与阿拉斯加的因纽皮特人共享。由于因努维阿勒伊特人和因纽皮特人基本上属于同一民族,因此很难将前者的土著权利转化为一条确定的边界线。尽管

---

① Letter from the British charge'd'affaires in Oslo to the Norwegian Minister for Foreign Affairs, November 5, 1930, in Exchange of Notes Regarding the Recognition by the Norwegian Government of the Sovereignty of His Majesty over the Sverdrup Islands, Canada Treaty Series 1930, No. 17, http://byers.typepad.com/arctic/1930.html.

② Shelagh D. Grant, "A Case of Compounded Error: The Inuit Resettlement Project, 1953, and the Government Response, 1990." (1991) 19 (1) Northern Perspectives (Canadian Arctic Resources Committee) 3.

③ 1984 Inuvialuit Final Agreement (as amended), http://www.daair.gov.nt.ca/_live/documents/documentManagerUpload/InuvialuitFinalAgreement1984.pdf.

④ On the critical date principle, Chapter 1, n. 9, above.

该最终协议缺乏国际法层面的相关性,但是因努维阿勒伊特人确实通过该协议为加拿大政府参与国与国边界谈判提供了重要的国内工具,因为根据加拿大法律,因努维阿勒伊特人的权利受到宪法性保护。①

1985年,加拿大外交部长乔·克拉克在提出加拿大对西北航道的法律立场时,引用了因纽特人的历史性存在:"自古以来,加拿大因纽特人就已使用并占有这块冰层,就像他们已使用和占有这块土地一样。"② 1993年,《努纳武特领土声明协议》确认加拿大高北极地区因纽特人将"他们在加拿大以及加拿大主权或管辖权之下相邻近海区域内,对土地、水域等所有的原住民主张、权利、所有权和利益"转让给联邦政府。③《努纳武特领土声明协议》另一条款明确了因纽特人强化加拿大在国际法中地位的意愿:"加拿大对高北极岛屿水域的主权得到因纽特人使用和占有的支持"。④ 不幸的是,这一互利安排自此受到压力。2006年,因纽特土地索赔组织努纳武特通格维克公司起诉加拿大政府,指控其未履行《努纳武特领土声明协议》中作出的承诺。⑤

最后,2005年丹麦前格陵兰部长汤姆·贺耶姆将因纽特人对北极的使用作为丹麦对汉斯岛主张的重要组成部分:

> 几个世纪以来,格陵兰因纽特人一直将汉斯岛作为了解冰层状况和狩猎前景的有利理想位置,特别是猎捕北极熊和海豹。加拿大因纽特人从未使用过该岛……事实上,汉斯岛是因

---

① discussion, Chapter 3, above.

② Joe Clark, Secretary of State for External Affairs, Statement on Sovereignty, Chapter 5, n. 15, above, p. 270.

③ 1993 Nunavut Land Claims Agreement, Chapter 5, n. 16, above, sec. 2. 7. 1 (a).

④ Ibid. , sec. 15. 1. 1 (c).

⑤ Terry Fenge, "Inuit and the Nunavut Land Claims Agreement: Supporting Canada's Arctic Sovereignty. " (December 2007 – January 2008) Policy Options 84, http: //www. irpp. org/po/archive/dec07/fenge. pdf. In June 2012, the Nunavut Court of Justice granted a summary judgment on the first aspect of the case, namely the failure of the Canadian government to create a Nunavut General Monitoring Plan, and awarded \$ 14. 8 million in damages to the land claims organization. Nunavut Tunngavik Inc. , "Historic Ruling from the Nunavut Court of Justice Upholding Inuit Rights," June 28, 2012, http: //www. tunngavik. com/blog/2012/06/28/historic – ruling – from – the – nunavut – court – of – justice – upholding – inuit – rights/.

纽特人的狩猎地图里不可分割的一部分。他们甚至为这里起了一个当地的名字"Tartupaluk",意即"肾脏"。①

正如第一章中解释的,提及格陵兰因纽特人的活动并不具有决定性,因为同样的因纽特人经常前往埃尔斯米尔岛,该岛现在被普遍认为属于加拿大领土。在某些情况下,援引土著人的历史使用和占有可能会具有重要性,例如在西北航道问题上。② 在其他情况下,其可能只意味着对政府施加道德和政治义务,希望政府能够支持土著人民的利益。无论如何,北极土著人并不满足于等待政府的援助。相反,他们在努力影响国家外交和国际立法方面展开了密切和战略性的合作。

三、土著跨国主义与国际立法

北极土著人民的跨国属性为其影响和参与国际立法创造了独特的机会,具体方法包括与边界另一侧相同土著团体合作,与其他地区土著人民接触,以及在下面的例子中简单地绕过各国政府进行合作。

如上所述,加拿大北极西部地区的因努维阿勒伊特人和阿拉斯加的因纽皮特人基本上是同一个民族,却被难以察觉、很少执行的国际陆上边界和有争议的国际海上边界所分开。因此,他们愿意就共同关心的问题进行合作不会令人感到奇怪,包括保护和管理北极熊等与他们文化不可分割的物种。正如第六章所解释,1988年达成《因努维阿勒伊特与因纽皮特北极熊管理协议》。③ 该协议设立了由因努维阿勒伊特和因纽皮特代表组成的联合委员会,以确定和划分每年波弗特海南部北极熊的可持续捕获量。无论美国、加拿大、阿拉斯加、育空或西北地区的联邦、州或领地的政府都不是这个次国家协议的签字方,尽管它们都通过默认同意的方式许可了这一协议。

---

① Tom Høyem, "Mr. Graham, You Should Have Told Us You Were Coming," Globe and Mail, July 29, 2005.

② discussion, Chapter 5, above.

③ Inuvialuit-Inupiat Polar Bear Management Agreement in the Southern Beaufort Sea, as updated in 2000, http://pbsg.npolar.no/en/agreements/USA-Canada.html.

第七章 土著人民

北极土著人民已经出于对由各国政府参与的国际立法施加影响的目的展开合作。正如蒂莫·科维罗瓦和莉娜·海纳马基所解释的:

> 土著人民通常将国际法视为推进其政治目标的一个非常重要工具。这很可能是因为在很多国家,他们影响政治发展的机会相当有限。所以对他们而言,设法影响国际法发展似乎是一项值得采取的战略,因为国际法拥有对所有国家(习惯法)或国际条约缔约国施加法律义务的权威。由于今天的许多问题只能在全球或区域层面加以解决,土著人民自然也有兴趣参与国际条约的制定进程。①

同一土著民族分布在两个或更多国家里,要寻求立法影响,首先涉及统一发声,并具有整合这些拥有不同国籍人员的组织职能。例如,因纽特人北极圈理事会是一个非政府组织,它将阿拉斯加、加拿大、格陵兰和俄罗斯的因纽特人聚集成单一的政治力量。因纽特人北极圈会议成立于1977年,是一个权力分散和高度民主的机构,在四个国家设有分支,与加拿大"因纽特联合组织"等因纽特人团体保持密切合作。② 这四个国家的分支共同组成了一个超国家机构,并选举主席和罢工委员会,进而在北极理事会和联合国土著问题常设论坛中代表因纽特人,该论坛是联合国经济及社会理事会的咨询机构。③

在1979年格陵兰实现自治和六年后退出欧洲经济共同体的进程中,因纽特人北极圈会议都发挥了一定作用。④ 在国际环境问题上,跨国因纽特人组织影响最为显著。正如第六章中解释的,因纽特人北极圈会议在《关于持久性有机污染物的斯德哥尔摩公约》的谈判和表决中发挥

---

① Timo Koivurova and Leena Heinämäki, "The Participation of Indigenous Peoples in International Norm‑making in the Arctic." (2006) 42 Polar Record 101.

② generally, Gary N. Wilson, "Inuit Diplomacy in the Circumpolar North." (2007) 13 Canadian Foreign Policy Journal 65.

③ UN Permanent Forum on Indigenous Peoples. http://social.un.org/index/Indigenous Peoples.aspx.

④ Wilson, n. 43, above, p. 67.

了作用。该公约要求各国停止生产相关毒素，这些毒素被大气带到北极地区，并在海豹、熊以及最终还有人类等捕食者的脂肪组织中累积。

因纽特人在提醒其他人关注气候变化的规模和紧迫性方面也取得了进展。气候变化直接和深刻影响因纽特人，因为冰雪条件变得难以预测，作为他们食物来源的动物数量也正在下降。2005年，希拉·瓦特·克劳狄尔以及其他62名来自加拿大和阿拉斯加的因纽特人向位于华盛顿特区的美洲人权委员会提交请愿书。① 他们认为美国没有减少二氧化碳和其他温室气体的大量排放，侵犯了因纽特人的文化和环境权利。2006年，该委员会拒绝就该请愿书举行听证并写道，"所提供的信息不能使我们确定，所谓的事实是否会最终构成对《美洲宣言》所保护之权利的侵犯。"② 然而，委员会随后举行了一次一般性听证会，有史以来首次对气候变化和人权之间的关系展开调查。③ 这一进展以及围绕请愿书的全部努力，都有助于提高美国媒体和公众对气候变化的认知水平。正如第六章中所提及的，瓦特·克劳狄尔2007年获得了诺贝尔和平奖提名，以表彰她在国际环境问题上的工作。④

因纽特人还与小岛屿发展中国家进行了接触，这一群体主要包括地势低洼的太平洋岛国，这些国家之间相互合作，以提高人们对气候变化的认识并推动采取国际行动。正如瓦特·克劳狄尔所解释："当我们融化时，小岛屿发展中国家会沉没。"⑤ 该联盟被称为发出"许多强有力的声音"，自2005年起，它一直致力于影响《联合国气候变化框架公约》缔约方会议上的跨国谈判。⑥

---

① Inuit Circumpolar Council Canada, "Inuit Petition Inter - American Commission on Human Rights to Oppose Climate Change Caused by the United States of America," December 7, 2005, http：//www. inuitcircumpolar. com/index. php? Lang = En&ID = 316.

② Jane George, "ICC Climate Change Petition Rejected," Nunatsiaq News, December 15, 2006, http：//www. nunatsiaqonline. ca/archives/61215/news/nunavut/61215_02. html.

③ Jessica Gordon, "Inter - American Commission on Human Rights to Hold Hearing After Rejecting Inuit Climate Change Petition." (2007) 7 Sustainable Development Law and Policy 55.

④ "Gore Nominated for Nobel Peace Prize," Environmental News Service, February 1, 2007, http：//www. ens - newswire. com/ens/feb2007/2007 - 02 - 01 - 09. html.

⑤ Quoted http：//www. manystrongvoices. org/media. aspx.

⑥ Many Strong Voices http：//www. manystrongvoices. org/.

萨米人理事会创建于 1956 年，代表挪威、瑞典、芬兰和俄罗斯的萨米人。[1] 萨米人理事会的主要目标是扭转语言同化的历史，促进文化权利和跨界自由迁徙，这对于分布在四个国家，以驯鹿放牧为生的半游牧民族而言尤为重要。[2] 萨米人理事会最初是萨米人在国家和地区（北欧）层级的代言人，但该工作已经被萨米人议会所接管。萨米人理事会现在专注于在国际层面代表萨米人并联系其他土著人民和组织。成立伊始，萨米人委员会的工作就得到挪威、瑞典和芬兰等国政府的支持，这些国家在国内和国际人权运动中一直位居前列。

正如普劳特解释道，因纽特人和萨米人"已经花费几代人的时间来建立和维持合作与协作关系。"[3] 他们"除参加彼此的执行会议外，还在联合国土著人问题常设论坛中轮流代表北极……"[4] 1996 年，因纽特人和萨米人在成立北极理事会中发挥了影响力，包括为他们自己和其他北极土著人民争取"永久参与方"的有意义地位。[5] 正如戴维·斯克里夫纳解释的，取得这一结果并不容易：

> 加拿大和因纽特人北极圈会议很快注意到，美国早前制定的程序规则草案虽然正确地强调了北极理事会的政府间性质，但是却有意削弱了永久参与方相对于观察国的优势，在某种程度上将前者等同于后者。除俄罗斯外，其他北极国家支持加拿大重申永久参与方的"特殊性"，以及他们有权要求成员国政府达成集体决定之前充分征求他们的意见。[6]

永久参与方的地位对北极理事会中六个组织所代表的土著人民而言

---

[1] Saami Council http：//www.saamicouncil.net/? deptid =1116.
[2] Plaut, n.11, above, p.197.
[3] Ibid., p.194.
[4] Ibid.
[5] generally, Frances Abele and Thierry Rodon, "Inuit Diplomacy in the Global Era: The Strengths of Multilateral Internationalism." (2007) 13 (3) Canadian Foreign Policy 46.
[6] David Scrivener, "Arctic Environmental Cooperation in Transition." (1999) 35 (192) Polar Record 51 at 56.

具有非常重要的意义，包括阿留申人国际协会、北极阿萨巴斯卡人理事会、哥威迅人国际协会、因纽特人北极圈理事会、萨米人理事会以及俄罗斯北方土著人民协会等。①

因纽特人北极圈理事会和萨米人理事会也共同推动北极理事会在决策中采取协商一致的方式，认为这将减少他们的劣势，因为作为永久参与方而非成员国，他们没有投票权。② 正如萨米人理事会的奥拉夫·马赛厄斯·埃拉向普劳特所解释的那样，对全体同意的要求意味着个别成员国有时可以代表土著人民来阻止达成一致意见：

> "永久参与方地位比观察员地位要好很多，后者是我们在联合国中拥有的地位。北极理事会的所有决定都必须以一致同意的方式达成。尽管我们没有投票权，但是我们可以阻止投标。"埃拉停下来笑道，"我们可以请求冰岛提供帮助或做点什么，说'不！'之类的。看，我们萨米人和美国几乎拥有同样的权力，我们只是缺钱。"③

正如关于成立北极理事会的《渥太华宣言》中第二条所规定的："设立永久参与方这一分类是为了北极土著代表在北极理事会中能够积极参与和充分协商"。④ 虽然不是《渥太华宣言》所要求的，但是采用一致同意的决策方式是完全符合其目标的。

---

① http://www.arcticpeoples.org/index.php?option=com_k2&view=item&layout=item&id=237&Itemid=6. The permanent participants are supported administratively by an Indigenous Peoples' Secretariat, though this body suffers from not having a permanent funding mechanism.

② Evan T. Bloom, "Establishment of the Arctic Council." (1999) 93 American Journal of International Law 712 at 716.

③ Olav Mathias Eira, personal communication quoted in Plaut, n. 11, above, p. 203. Ironically, as Plaut explains, "The Saami Council and the ICC found a strange friend and advocate for the consensus model in America's historical reluctance to join formal, contentious driven, political bodies." Plaut, n. 11, above, citing Bloom, n. 59, above.

④ Declaration on the Establishment of the Arctic Council, Ottawa, September 19, 1996 (1996) 35 ILM 1387, http://www.arctic-council.org/index.php/en/about/documents/category/5-declarations.

四、《极地因纽特人在北极主权的宣言》

获得北极理事会永久参与方地位对于北方土著民族而言并不是完全的胜利。1996 年成立北极理事会的《渥太华宣言》中仅有两个注脚,其中之一规定,"本宣言中使用的'人民'(peoples)一词不应被解释为对国际法下赋予该词的权利构成任何影响"。[①] 2007 年通过的《联合国土著人民权利宣言》全文中"people"一词均为复数形式,这在一定程度上解决了关于使用"people"还是"peoples"的争议以及"peoples"中暗含自决权的问题。[②] 但是,令北方土著人民懊恼的是,他们作为北极理事会永久参与方的地位并没有保证他们在每次关于该地区议题的谈判中都能坐上台面。2008 年 5 月,6 个永久参与方,连同冰岛、瑞典和芬兰都没有受邀参加由丹麦在格陵兰的伊卢利萨特举办的北冰洋沿岸五国会议。

因纽特人北极圈理事会发布了一份《极地因纽特人在北极主权的宣言》,以此方式作出回应,其中特别提到被排除于伊卢利萨特会议:

> 尽管北极沿岸五国(挪威、丹麦、加拿大、美国和俄罗斯)认为需要使用国际机制和国际法解决主权争端(参见 2008 年《伊卢利萨特宣言》),这些国家在讨论北极主权问题时,却没有提及促进和保护土著人民权利的现有国际文件。在采用与北极理事会相似的方式讨论北极主权问题之时,他们也

[①] Declaration on the Establishment of the Arctic Council, Ottawa, September 19, 1996 (1996) 35 ILM 1387, http://www.arctic-council.org/index.php/en/about/documents/category/5-declarations.

[②] 2007 UN Declaration on the Rights of Indigenous Peoples, http://www.un.org/esa/socdev/unpfii/documents/DRIPS_en.pdf. For a contrary view, Karen Engle, "On Fragile Architecture: The UN Declaration on the Rights of Indigenous Peoples in the Context of Human Rights." (2011) 22 European Journal of International Law 141.

未将因纽特人纳入其中。①

《极地因纽特人在北极主权的宣言》本质上是将因纽特人纳入未来任何关于北极的决策之中主张的进一步延伸。这是一个"关于"（on）主权而不是主权"的"（of）宣言，并非是在追求独立国家地位的意义上主张主权。该文件开篇即表明，因纽特人作为一个民族"享有所有人民的权利"，包括《联合国宪章》和两个人权国际公约等国际文件中所承认的权利。在这方面，它提出了一种稳健的"内部"自决形式：

> 作为一个民族，我们所有权利中至关重要的是自决权。我们有权自由决定我们的政治地位，自由追求我们经济、社会、文化和语言的发展，自由处分我们的自然财富和资源。各国有义务尊重和促进我们自决权的实现。②

该文件接着列出了因纽特人作为土著民族的一系列权利：

> 我们作为土著民族的权利包括《联合国土著人民权利宣言》所承认的以下权利，所有这些权利均与北极主权和主权权利相关：享有自决权，以自由决定我们的政治地位，自由谋求自身的经济、社会和文化发展（第三条）；内部自主权或自治权（第四条）；有权要求与各国或其继承国订立的条约、协定和其他建设性安排得到承认、遵守和执行（第三十七条）；维护和加强我们特有的政治、法律、经济、社会和文化机构，同时保有充分参与国家政治、经济、社会和文化生活的权利（第五条）；参与事关自身权利的事务决策的权利，有权保持和发展自己的土著人决策机构（第十八条）；拥有、使用、开发和

---

① "A Circumpolar Inuit Declaration on Sovereignty in the Arctic," April 2009, sec. 2. 6, https：//www.itk.ca/publication/circumpolar - declaration - sovereignty - arctic (emphasis in original).

② Ibid., sec. 1. 4.

控制我们的土地、领土和资源的权利,未获得我们自由知情同意不在我们的土地、领土或资源进行任何项目(第二十五至三十二条);享有和平与安全的权利(第七条);养护和保护我们环境的权利(第二十九条)。①

与《联合国土著人民权利宣言》一样,《极地因纽特人在北极主权的宣言》亦寻求巩固和发展国际法。出于该原因,它并没有提及《联合国土著人民权利宣言》等联合国大会的决议,并不是具有法律约束力的文件。此外,《联合国土著人民权利宣言》中某些条款的国际习惯法地位仍存在争议,特别是关于各国政府必须与土著人民协商,"以便在采取和实施可能影响土著人民的立法或行政措施之前,获得他们自由、事先和知情的同意"。② 也即,新的国际法规定在获得有约束力的"硬法"地位的过程中,经常采用"软法"形式,这种情况很可能发生在此处。③

《极地因纽特人在北极主权的宣言》接着直接讨论了其标题中所确定的主题,即"主权"一词经常被用于指代一个社会或国家在国内和

---

① "A Circumpolar Inuit Declaration on Sovereignty in the Arctic," April 2009, sec. 2.6, https://www.itk.ca/publication/circumpolar-declaration-sovereignty-arctic (emphasis in original). (emphasis in original).

② S. James Anaya, "Indigenous Peoples' Participatory Rights in Relation to Decisions about Natural Resource Extraction: The More Fundamental Issue of What Rights Indigenous Peoples Have in Lands and Resources." (2005) 22 Arizona Journal of International and Comparative Law 7. Canada has expressed the view that "the Declaration is a non-legally binding document that does not reflect customary international law" ("Canada's Statement of Support on the United Nations Declaration on the Rights of Indigenous Peoples," November 12, 2010, http://www.ainc-inac.gc.ca/ap/ia/dcl/stmt-eng.asp). The United States has similarly stated that "While the Declaration is not legally binding, it carries considerable moral and political force" ("Announcement of US Support for the United Nations Declaration on the Rights of Indigenous Peoples," December 16, 2010, http://www.state.gov/r/pa/prs/ps/2010/12/153027.htm).

③ Mauro Barelli, "The Role of Soft Law in the International Legal System: The Case of the United Nations Declaration on the Rights of Indigenous Peoples." (2009) 58 International and Comparative Law Quarterly 957. On soft law generally, Christine Chinkin, "The Challenge of Soft Law: Development and Change in International Law." (1989) 38 International and Comparative Law Quarterly 850.

国外所享有的绝对和独立的权威。主权是一个有争议的概念,然而它没有固定的含义。随着欧盟等不同治理模式的演变,旧的主权观念正在瓦解。主权与主权之间存在重叠,并且经常在联邦内部进行分割,以创造性的方式承认人民的权利。对生活在俄罗斯、加拿大、美国和丹麦(格陵兰)等国的因纽特人而言,主权和主权权利的问题必须在通过长期斗争,获得作为一个有权对生命、领土、文化和语言行使自决权的北极土著民族之承认和尊重的背景下,加以验证和评估。①

主权的可分割性确实使得各国政府更容易满足土著人民的自决权。但是,与《极地因纽特人在北极主权的宣言》中所表达的观点相反,可以认为当需要在国家、国际组织或次国家政府之间分享主权时,需要获得最初拥有所有主权的一国政府之同意。在某种程度上,在加拿大、美国或格陵兰政府,主权都是通过领土协定的方式转移给土著人政府,这同样是在获得同意的情况下发生的。因此,将该论点推导至逻辑结论就是,国家实践中不存在支持一个土著民族未经本国政府同意而获得该国主权权利的权利。

即使《极地因纽特人在北极主权的宣言》中提出的论点在法律上无法令人信服,但是由此仍能得出一个清晰和道德上强有力的结论:"北极地区的主权和主权权利与因纽特人自决和其他权利两者之间存在不可分割的联系,这就要求各国接受因纽特人在北极地区国际关系实践中作为伙伴的存在和角色"。② 不仅如此,这一结论是出于完全政治目的而进行的战略部署,甚至需要将美国国务卿作为其游说工作的目标之一。

2010年3月,加拿大政府决定继续举办伊卢利萨特会议的后续会议,这次会议是在魁北克的切尔西举行。正如丹麦两年前所做的那样,加拿大选择只邀请其他四个北冰洋沿岸国家,不邀请土著人永久参与方,也不邀请冰岛、瑞典或芬兰。③ 美国国务卿希拉里·克林顿公开谴

---

① "A Circumpolar Inuit Declaration on Sovereignty in the Arctic," n. 64, above, sec. 2. 1.
② Ibid., sec. 3. 3.
③ Rob Gillies, "Clinton Rebukes Canada on Arctic Meeting," Associated Press, March 29, 2010, http://www.guardian.co.uk/world/feedarticle/9009648.

责东道主的这一决定,并表示,"就北极问题举行的重大国际讨论,应包含那些在该地区拥有合法利益的群体。我希望在北极地区永远展示我们合作的能力,而不是制造新的分裂。"此前她曾表示,被排除在外的土著团体代表曾联系过她。① 希拉里不满的另一个表现是,她没有出席加拿大政府会后为外长们安排的新闻发布会。② 此后再没有举行"北极五国"会议,从这个意义上讲,《极地因纽特人在北极主权的宣言》被证明是相当成功的。

五、主权是否"源于国内"?

2007 年,斯蒂芬·哈珀表示:"在捍卫我们在北极主权的问题上,加拿大必须做出选择:或要么利用它,要么失去它。"③ 在同一次讲话中,加拿大总理承诺将向该国海军提供多达 8 艘冰区加强舰艇和北极燃料补给站。因纽特领导人回答称,他们已经"利用"北极几千年了,并在此基础上提出健康的社区对加拿大北极主权的重要性不亚于军事装备和人员。此外,正如"因纽特联合组织"的玛丽·西蒙所解释的,只有通过与因纽特人合作才能实现健康的社区,进而获得主权。

> 北极主权意味着政府必须认识到因纽特人随时准备成为改善北极社区健康、教育和基础设施协作战略的积极合作伙伴。北极政策必须建立在尊敬加拿大因纽特人并与之长期合作的基础之上。④

因纽特人北极圈理事会也提出了同样的论点,在《极地因纽特人在

---

① Rob Gillies, "Clinton Rebukes Canada on Arctic Meeting," Associated Press, March 29, 2010, http://www.guardian.co.uk/world/feedarticle/9009648.

② Ibid.

③ "Harper on Arctic: 'Use it or Lose it'," Victoria Times Colonist, July 10, 2007, http://www.canada.com/topics/news/story.html?id=7ca93d97-3b26-4dd1-8d92-8568f9b7cc2a.

④ Mary Simon, "Inuit and the Canadian Arctic: Sovereignty Begins at Home." (2009) 43 Journal of Canadian Studies 250 at 259.

北极主权的宣言》中，该组织表示："北极主权和主权权利的基础、表现和享有均需要北极地区的健康和可持续的社区。从这个意义上讲，'主权源于国内'"。①

但是，正如本书之前章节中所解释的，整个北极圈唯一有争议的领土是无人居住的汉斯岛。唯一尚未解决的北极海上边界争端是波弗特海，在此因努维阿勒伊特人的历史性存在对国际法争论没有多大关系。至于北冰洋中部地区扩展大陆架相关问题，它们也与因纽特人"使用和占有"无关，部分原因是因纽特人从未到过如此北方之地。剩下的就是西北航道问题，在这里因纽特人"使用和占有"确实具有相关性，但仅限于1969年或1985年两个争议的"关键日期"之前。

虽然当代土著人民的存在并不会强化国家的法律立场，但与土著组织的合作关系可以加强国家的道德和政治权威，并且国家推进环境保护等有利于北极土著人民的政策时，该国影响力也会因此提升。2007年，加拿大三个领地的政府针对21世纪的土著人民提出一个更为微妙和引人注目的观点，将其称为"主权管家"并值得获得各国政府的感激和支持。

> 北方地区不由有地图上的线或点，而是由我们的人民确定的。加拿大对北方岛屿、内水和冰层覆盖水域的主权根植于历史、国际法和原住民对其的占有和使用。在人类层面而言，北方人是加拿大北极主权的体现。
>
> 但是为了使得北方人继续作为加拿大主权的管家，北方地区需要可持续的社区。必须支持北方人将其社区建设成为满足健康生活所需，提供就业、教育和培训，家庭可享有足够、合适和可负担住房，拥有与加拿大其他地区相媲美的健康和社区服务之所。我们可以为我们自己和孩子们打造明天。②

---

① "A Circumpolar Inuit Declaration on Sovereignty," n. 64, above, sec. 3. 1. 2.
② The Yukon, Northwest Territories, and Nunavut, "A Northern Vision: A Stronger North and a Better Canada," 2007, p. 7, http://www.anorthernvision.ca/documents/newvision_english.pdf.

六、海豹产品出口

近年来，因纽特人与非北极国家关系最为艰难，其中尤数与欧盟的关系。为了回应公众对捕猎海豹相关残酷行为的广泛关注，欧盟委员会（欧盟的执行机构）于2009年禁止进口海豹产品。① 捕猎海豹是因纽特人文化中不可分割的一部分，也是他们重要的食物来源，海豹皮的销售为他们提供了亟需的收入。然而，加拿大大西洋沿岸的非因纽特人同样进行了更大规模的海豹捕猎活动，非因纽特人的捕猎占到加拿大海豹产品出口的95%以上。公平地讲，欧盟委员会确实对"因纽特人和其他土著社区传统狩猎活动得到的并且有助其生存的海豹产品"进行了豁免。② 但是，有些出乎意料的是，禁令的影响是同时破坏了非因纽特人和因纽特人两者的海豹产品在欧盟内的市场。

欧盟委员会引入进口禁令的时机欠妥，北极理事会成员国当时正在考虑欧盟提出获得其正式观察员地位的申请。加拿大政府在因纽特人组织和努纳武特政府鼓动下，利用协商一致决策固有的否决权阻挠对该申请的审议。③ 其后，北极理事会于2011年通过了确定观察员地位申请的"一般适当性"标准，其中包括"观察员……尊重北极土著人和其他北极居民的价值、利益、文化和传统的程度"。④ 采取该标准可让加拿大今后阻止欧盟申请时更容易找到正当理由，尽管最终排除或承认的决定将基于政治考量而非（故意）模糊的标准。

2010年，加拿大全国性的因纽特人组织"因纽特联合组织"针对

---

① The import ban is set out in Regulation (EC) No. 1007/2009, http://eur-lex.europa.eu/LexUriServ/LexUriServ.do?uri=OJ:L:2009:286:0036:0039:EN:PDF. On the politics and policy development leading to the ban, Njord Wegge, "Politics between Science, Law and Sentiments: Explaining the European Union's Ban on Trade in Seal Products." (2012) 6 Environmental Politics 1.

② Ibid.

③ "Canada against EU Entry to Arctic Council because of Seal Trade Ban," CBC News, April 29, 2009, http://www.cbc.ca/news/world/story/2009/04/29/cda-eu-arctic-seal.html.

④ "Observers" http://www.arctic-council.org/index.php/en/about-us/partners-links.

欧盟委员会进口禁令向欧洲普通法院提出诉讼。① 该组织认为，禁止因纽特人向欧盟出口海豹产品造成"严重和无法弥补的损害"，从而影响到他们社区的社会结构。其特别指出，这项禁令违反了因纽特人根据《欧洲人权公约》第八条所享有的尊重私人和家庭生活之权利。2011 年 9 月，法院裁定不予受理此案，但没有提供理由。② 2011 年 11 月，因纽特人组织就该裁定向欧洲法院提出上诉。③ 在另一个同样由"因纽特联合组织"提出的案件中，该组织质疑所谓"因纽特豁免"的有效性，因其认为无效的豁免将使得整个禁令失去效力。在撰写本书时，欧洲法院尚未对第二起案件做出判决。

2009 年，加拿大和挪威（非欧盟成员国）均要求与欧盟委员会就海豹产品禁令进行"磋商"，这是世界贸易组织争端解决程序的第一步。④ 2011 年，世界贸易组织成立争端解决小组对两起申诉进行听审。⑤ 2012 年，加拿大和挪威采取下一步行动，要求任命专家。⑥ 加拿大和挪威主张，进口禁令违反了《关税和贸易总协定》和《技术性贸易壁垒协议》中"国民待遇"和"最惠国"条款中的非歧视性原则。他们还主张，这项禁令违反了《技术性贸易壁垒协议》第二条规定，因为禁令不是"实现合法目标所必需的限度"并且构成了"对国际贸

---

① Inuit Tapiriit Kanatami and Others v. Parliament and Council, Case T – 8/10, [2010] OJ C 100/ 41, http：//eur – lex. europa. eu/LexUriServ/LexUriServ. do? uri = OJ：C：2010：100：0041：0041：EN：PDF.

② Order of the General Court of 6 September 2011 – Inuit Tapiritt Kanatami and Others v. Parliament and Council (Case T – 18/10), http：//eur – lex. europa. eu/LexUriServ/LexUriServ. do? uri = OJ%3AC%3A2011%3A319%3A0020%3A0021%3Aen%3APDF.

③ (February 25, 2012) Official Journal of the European Union C58/3, http：//eurlex. europa. eu/LexUriServ/LexUriServ. do? uri = OJ：C：2012：058：0003：0003：EN：PDF.

④ Simon Lester, "The WTO Seal Products Dispute: A Preview of the Key Legal Issues." 14 (2) ASIL Insight, January 13, 2010, http：//www. asil. org/insights100113. cfm.

⑤ WTO Dispute Settlement Board, decision of April 21, 2011, http：//www. wto. org/english/news_e/news11_e/dsb_21apr11_e. htm. For the current status of the case, European Communities-Measures Prohibiting the Importation and Marketing of Seal Products, Dispute DS400, http：//www. wto. org/english/tratop_e/dispu_e/cases_e/ds400_e. htm.

⑥ "Canada Calls for WTO Action on Seal Ban Dispute," Nunatsiaq News, September 24, 2012, http：//www. nunatsiaqonline. ca/stories/article/65674canada_calls_for_wto_action_on_seal_ban_dispute/.

易造成不必要的障碍"。① 欧盟委员会主张,这一禁令是基于"公共道德"的理由,因为许多欧洲人对猎杀海豹感到厌恶。世界贸易组织在此之前的一个案例中接受了相似论点,② 但在另一个案例中对其予以否定。③

无论世界贸易组织专家组和随后世界贸易组织上诉机构如何裁决,鉴于双方政府所受到的国内政治压力,围绕海豹产品的争议不太可能消失。此外,唯一可能有效的贸易补救措施是,在不考虑原产地的情况下,向所有海豹产品开放欧洲共同市场,但该方法与相对少数的因纽特人所遭受的经济损失不成比例。世界贸易组织能否成为土著人人权等问题的最终仲裁者仍存质疑,因而该问题只能在国际贸易法下得到一定程度的解决。④

七、土著人民和人权

无论根据何种标准,1953 年和 1955 年将 17 个家庭重新安置于雷索卢特湾和格里斯峡湾的做法侵犯了被迁徙者的人权。对于起初来自魁北克北部的因纽特人而言,向北 1600 千米的迁徙之路就像一次登月之旅。他们的传统知识和狩猎技巧都无法适应新环境,没有足够的冰雪建

---

① For two papers that explain the legal arguments in depth and predict entirely different results, Xinjie Luan and Julien Chaisse, "Preliminary Comments on the WTO Seals Products Dispute: Traditional Hunting, Public Morals and Technical Barriers to Trade." (2011) 22 Colorado Journal of International Environmental Law and Policy 79, http://www.colorado.edu/law/sites/default/files/Vol.22.1.pdf and Robert Howse and Joanna Langille, "Permitting Pluralism: The Seal Products Dispute and Why the WTO Should Accept Trade Restrictions Justified by Noninstrumental Moral Values." (2012) 37 Yale Journal of International Law 367, http://www.yjil.org/docs/pub/37-2-howse-langille permitting-pluralism.pdf.

② United States-Measures Affecting the Cross-Border Supply of Gambling and Betting Services, Dispute DS285, https://www.wto.org/english/tratop_e/dispu_e/cases_e/ds285_e.htm.

③ China-Measures Affecting Trading Rights and Distribution Services for Certain Publications and Audiovisual Entertainment Products, Dispute DS363, https://www.wto.org/english/tratop_e/dispu_e/cases_e/ds363_e.htm.

④ Kamrul Hossain, "The EU Ban on the Import of Seal Products and the WTO Regulations: Neglected Human Rights of the Arctic Indigenous Peoples?" (2013) 49 Polar Record 154.

造冰屋,从11月至来年2月的极夜对他们而言是既陌生又难以忍受。

半个多世纪以来,加拿大国内一直存在关于重新安置是被迫亦或自愿的激烈争论,至少对于因纽特人得到了更好的狩猎和生活条件的承诺存在相当程度的误传。① 然而,随后的辩论将赔偿规定推迟了四十多年。直至1996年,加拿大政府才同意一项1000万美元的一揽子计划,但政府仍忽略了加拿大众议院原住民事务和北方发展委员会、加拿大人权委员会和皇家原住民族委员会等三个不同机构的建议,拒绝就此道歉。尽管赔偿协议承认因纽特人遭受"痛苦、苦楚和苦难",其还称,"当时政府官员出于高尚意图行事,认为这符合因纽特人的最大利益"。②

类似的因纽特人迁徙事件还发生在格陵兰,同样是在1953年,当时有116人的整个社区被从图勒重新安置到夸那,以便美国空军可以在原位置扩建基地。③ "被驱逐53"("Hingitaq 53",其中"Hingitaq"意即"被驱逐","53"意指重新安置发生于1953年)随后起诉丹麦政府。1999年,丹麦上诉法院认为,"被驱逐53"的权利确受侵犯,决定给予他们每人1.7万克朗(约3000美元)个人赔偿和共50万克朗(约9万美元)集体赔偿。④ 然而,法院否决了他们返回的权利。2003年,丹麦最高法院维持了这一判决,随后又以司法管辖权为由驳回该组织向欧洲人权法院上诉的请求。⑤

特别是在加拿大和俄罗斯,北方土著人目前的社会和经济条件明显

---

① For the different sides of the debate, Frank Tester and Peter Kulchyski, Tammarniit (Mistakes): Inuit Relocation in the Eastern Arctic, 1939 – 63 (Vancouver: University of British Columbia Press, 1994); Gerard Kenney, Arctic Smoke and Mirrors (Prescott, Ontario: Voyageur Publishing, 1994).

② Jim Bell, "What Are the Exiles Signing?" Nunatsiaq News, March 15, 1996, http://www.nunatsiaqonline.ca/archives/back-issues/week/60315.html#1.

③ Jean Malaurie, The Last Kings of Thule: With the Polar Eskimos, as They Face their Destiny (trans. Adrienne Foulke) (London: Jonathan Cape, 1982); Stephen Fottrell, "Inuit Survival Battle against US Base," BBC News, May 27, 2004, http://news.bbc.co.uk/1/hi/world/europe/3753677.stm.

④ Fottrell, "Inuit Survival Battle," ibid.

⑤ HINGITAQ 53 v. Denmark, Application No. 18584/04, decision from the European Court of Human Rights on admissibility, https://www.elaw.org/node/3834.

违反了《经济、社会、文化权利国际公约》中相关权利规定,包括第十一条"足够的食物、衣着和住房",第十二条"能达到的最高的体质和心理健康的标准"以及第十三条教育方面规定。① 虽然加拿大和俄罗斯均批准了该公约,但都没有批准公约的任择议定书,② 也没有同意其他执行机制。

在北欧国家,萨米人的经济和社会权利受到相对较好的保护。他们现在的主要问题是对土地、水和自然资源(尤其是石油和天然气开发、伐木和气候变化)全面实现民族自决权利,保护他们的语言并提供适当的文化教育。③

八、土著人和捕鲸

土著人最关心的问题是能否按照传统方式生活。但是,正如第六章中所解释的那样,北极土著人捕鲸已经引发了相当大的争议。1982年国际捕鲸委员会发布了一项全球范围内的捕鲸禁令后,加拿大退出该委员会,并于1984年和1983年达成的土地权利协议中保证因努维阿勒伊特人和因纽特人拥有捕鲸权。④ 尽管国际捕鲸委员会已经接受了阿拉斯加的因纽皮特人和格陵兰的因纽特人为"维持生计"可以猎捕数量有限鲸鱼,但加拿大政府以及加拿大因纽特人仍旧游离于该制度管辖

---

① 1966 International Covenant on Economic, Social and Cultural Rights, http://www.ohchr.org/english/law/cescr.htm.

② 2008 Optional Protocol to the International Covenant on Economic, Social and Cultural Rights, UN General Assembly Resolution A/RES/63/117, http://www.ohchr.org/english/law/docs/a.RES.63.117_en.pdf.

③ James Anaya, UN Special Rapporteur on the Rights of Indigenous Peoples, "The Situation of the Sami People in the Sa′pmi Region of Norway, Sweden and Finland," June 6, 2011, UN Doc. A/HRC/18/35/Add.2, http://unsr.jamesanaya.org/country-reports/the-situation-of-the-sami-people-in-the-sapmi-region-of-norway-sweden-and-finland-2011.

④ Inuvialuit Final Agreement, n. 32, above, sec. 14 (6); 1993 Nunavut Land Claims Agreement, sec. 5.6.1, http://nlca.tunngavik.com/.

之外。①

值得赞扬的是，因纽特人正在推动北极露脊鲸主要栖息地的保护工作。坐落于巴芬岛东海岸的克莱德里弗社区已经说服加拿大政府指定伊莎贝拉湾及其周边领水为"国家野生动物保护区"。② 成百上千的北极露脊鲸在伊莎贝拉湾度过夏天，以湾内丰富的桡足类浮游生物为食。根据加拿大法律，除非获得特别许可，国家野生动物保护区内禁止进行商业活动。

由此往北700千米处，兰开斯特海峡是西北航道东部主要入口，它也是北极露脊鲸、世界上大多数独角鲸、北美1/3的白鲸、海象、北极熊、环斑海豹、髯海豹、鞍背海豹和数百万只海鸟的家园。二十多年来，加拿大和联合国教科文组织一直考虑将兰开斯特海峡列为世界遗产。③ 这一行动将有助于推动引入航道制度，以减少船舶噪音对海洋哺乳动物的影响。在某种程度上这一做法也可以支持加拿大立场，即西北航道属于完全处于其管理和控制下的"内水"。但历届加拿大政府都未能推动联合国教科文组织完成该程序，或许是因为担忧此举可能引发美国对加拿大西北航道立场的挑战。④

---

① For an excellent discussion of the issue, Anthony Speca, "In the Belly of the Whaling Commission," Northern Public Affairs, June 18, 2012, http://www.northernpublicaffairs.ca/index/in-the-belly-of-the-whaling-commission/.

② "Canada Preserves Arctic Wilderness for Whales, Bears, Birds," Environmental News, September 4, 2008, http://www.ens-newswire.com/ens/sep2008/2008-09-04-01.html.

③ As a party to the 1972 Convention Concerning the Protection of the World Cultural and Natural Heritage, Canada is required to identify the natural sites of outstanding universal value on its territory (Art. 3), http://whc.unesco.org/archive/convention-en.pdf). However, nominations to the World Heritage List are not considered unless the nominated property has previously been included on the state party's "tentative list" of the properties it intends to consider for nomination in subsequent years. Parties are encouraged to re-examine and re-submit their tentative list at least once every decade. Under Canada's original tentative list of world heritage sites (1980), Lancaster Sound was included as part of Sirmilik National Park. However, the proposal was subsequently abandoned and Lancaster Sound does not currently appear on Canada's updated tentative list (2004). UNESCO World Heritage Centre, Tentative Lists: Canada, http://whc.unesco.org/en/tentativelists/state=ca. There are at present no marine World Heritage Sites in the Arctic. UNESCO World Heritage Lists at, http://whc.unesco.org.

④ discussion, Chapter 5, above.

第七章 土著人民

  一个争议较少的国内举措是将兰开斯特海峡列为"国家海洋保护区"（相当于国家公园），该想法也已提出了数十年，由于因纽特人担忧可能对其捕猎权造成限制而一再拖延。[1] 2009 年，加拿大政府宣布将花费 500 万美元研究此类保护区是否将成为对"兰开斯特海峡可持续管理的切实可行办法"。[2] 然而，答案并不明确，因为缺乏世界遗产名录带来的国际承认，外国船舶可能不会过多关注加拿大国内法规限制。加拿大设立国家海洋保护区还可以与重新获得联合国教科文组织认定的努力有效结合起来，从而以互相支持的方式将国内与国际认定联系起来。

  在宣布兰开斯特海峡有关事项的同时，加拿大政府、努纳武特政府和当地因纽特人协会签署了一份关于因纽特人参与可行性研究的谅解备忘录，但至此各方就没有再进行显著的合作。[3] 2010 年，加拿大政府租用德国科考破冰船"极星"号对该地区进行地震测试。因纽特人担忧地震波对海洋哺乳动物造成影响，并且认为加拿大政府在该地区地震研究安排与其禁止石油和天然气开发的禁令相矛盾，因此请求并获得了努纳武特最高法院的禁制令。[4] 这艘已经横跨大西洋并正在前往兰开斯特海峡途中的德国破冰船，不得不掉头返航。

---

[1] According to Parks Canada, a proposal for a national marine conservation area was prepared in 1987, but the feasibility assessment was suspended at the request of the local Inuit. Parks Canada, "Canada's National Marine Conservation Areas System Plan: Lancaster Sound," http://www.pc.gc.ca/progs/amnc－nmca/systemplan/itm1－/arc6_E.asp.

[2] Gloria Galloway, "Ottawa Moves to Protect Serengeti of the Arctic," Globe and Mail, December 6, 2010, http://www.theglobeandmail.com/news/politics/ottawa－moves－to－protect－serengeti－of－the－arctic/article4081939/; and "Health of the Oceans Initiatives-A Listing by Lead Department or Agency," http://www.dfo－mpo.gc.ca/oceans/management－gestion/healthyoceans－santedesoceans/initiatives－eng.htm.

[3] "Ottawa Proposes Boundaries for Lancaster Sound Marine Conservation Area: Promised Steering Committee Yet to Be Created," Nunatsiaq News, December 6, 2010, http://www.nunatsiaqonline.ca/stories/article/987678_ottawa_proposes_boundaries_for_lancaster/.

[4] Josh Wingrove, "Lancaster Sound: A Seismic Victory for the Inuit," Globe and Mail, August 13, 2010, http://www.theglobeandmail.com/news/politics/lancaster－sound－a－seismic－victory－for－the－inuit/article1377067/.

九、土著人与核武器

1968 年,一架美国 B-52 轰炸机在位于格陵兰岛图勒的美国基地附近坠毁,导致一枚未爆核弹丢失在冰层之下。① 与此同时,美国和苏联核潜艇在格陵兰和加拿大高北极岛屿周边水域出没变得更为常见。② 这些事态发展引发因纽特人关注,他们也注意到美国、英国和法国在南太平洋进行的大气层核试验,受此直接影响,当地土著人做出了一致反应。太平洋土著岛民在推动各国谈判并最终达成 1985 年《南太平洋无核区条约》中发挥了重要作用。这一文件通常被称为《拉罗汤加岛条约》,澳大利亚、库克群岛、斐济、基里巴斯、瑙鲁、新西兰、纽埃、巴布亚新几内亚、所罗门群岛、汤加、图瓦卢、瓦努阿图以及西萨摩亚均已批准该条约。③ 与此同时,因纽特人北极圈理事会在 1983 年通过一项决议,呼吁"不在北极或亚北极地区进行核试验或部署核装置"。④ 虽然该决议没有发展为一项国家间协议,但是正如第八章中所讨论的,冷战结束和近期北极圈合作增加使得类似努力在当代变得更有希望。

十、小结

北极土著人民的历史性存在被用来支持一国对领土所有权的主张,在西北航道问题上,也被用来支持群岛中海峡和水道的"内水"地位。

---

① Gordon Corera, "Mystery of Lost US Nuclear Bomb," BBC News, November 10, 2008, http://news.bbc.co.uk/1/hi/7720049.stm.

② For more on submarines, Chapter 5, above, as well as the first paragraph of Chapter 8, below.

③ For more information on the Treaty of Rarotonga, http://www.nti.org/treaties-and-regimes/south-pacific-nuclear-free-zone-spnfz-treaty-rarotonga/. For the text of the treaty, http://cns.miis.edu/inventory/pdfs/aptspnfz.pdf.

④ ICC, "Resolution on a Nuclear Free Zone," http://web.archive.org/web/20110826020556/, http://www.arcticnwfz.ca/documents/I%20N%20U%20I%20T%20CIRCUMPOLAR%20RES%20ON%20nwfz%201983.pdf. A similar statement had been made six years earlier, though not in the form of a resolution. Russel Barsh, "Demilitarizing the Arctic as an Exercise of Indigenous Self-Determination." (1986) 55 Nordic Journal of International Law 208.

北极土著人民也参与了国际立法进程,通过跨边界民族内部以及各民族之间在战略上的并且有时是非常成功的努力,影响国家做出决策。这一成功关系到土著人民在北极理事会中作为"永久参与方"的法律地位,将他们置于与成员国同等地位。另一项成功是关系到北极理事会采用协商一致的决策方式,这就有效消除了永久参与方没有投票权的劣势。第三个成功是,结束北冰洋沿岸国家在北极理事会之外,也即在排除永久参与方的情况下,召开所谓"北极五国"会议的惯例。尽管北极土著人民的影响是更为普遍和世界范围内国际立法程序向非国家行为体开放的体现,但在国家间合作相对较新的区域,这种发展似乎来得更快和更容易。

第八章 安全

> 北极不仅是指北冰洋,也是包含欧洲、亚洲和美洲三大洲的北部边缘地区。这里是欧亚、北美和亚太地区交汇处,边界相互接近,各国分属于相互对立的军事集团或不结盟国家,利益彼此交叉。
>
> 米哈伊尔·戈尔巴乔夫[1]

1958年,美国海军"鹦鹉螺"号核潜艇在北极点水下航行。一年之后,"鳐鱼"号核潜艇在北极点水面航行。作为导弹平台,核动力潜艇可提供比陆基或远程轰炸机更好的隐秘性、航程和移动性。由于具备在水下潜伏数月的能力,这些潜艇全年都可以在北极海冰之下执行任务。1980年,苏联北方舰队拥有56艘配备核导弹的潜艇。[2] 这些潜艇中有些不会离开北冰洋;另一些则会通过"格陵兰-冰岛-英国缺口"进入大西洋。有的潜艇会穿越加拿大和格陵兰之间冰雪覆盖的西北航道或内利斯海峡。2011年,我登上俄罗斯科学院"伊奥芙院士"号科考船,有机会对苏联的旧海图和加拿大的最新海图进行比较研究。前者的探测深度明显优于后者,特别是在格陵兰岛图勒的美国空军基地和加拿大雷索

---

[1] Mikhail Gorbachev, "Presentation of the Order of Lenin and the Gold Star to the City of Murmansk," October 1, 1987, http://www.barentsinfo.org/? DeptID = 3473.

[2] John Kristen Skogan, "The Evolution of the Four Soviet Fleets 1968 – 1987," in John Kristen Skogan and Arne Olav Brundtland, Soviet Seapower in Northern Waters: Facts, Motivation, Impact and Responses (London: Pinter, 1990), 18.

卢特湾空军基地附近。①

苏联人还将北极作为核试验场所，1961年人类史上测试过的最大武器，50兆吨级的"沙皇炸弹"在新地群岛上空被引爆。在巴伦支海东侧的这个群岛及其上空总共进行了超过200次核试验，遗留的放射性尘埃将持续数个世纪。②

在冷战初期，远程轰炸机成为运载核武器的主要手段。美国B-52轰炸机挂载着致命武器，在加拿大高北极地区上空不停盘旋，等待着进入苏联空域的指示。北冰洋的另一边，图-95"熊"式轰炸机也在进行着同样恐怖的仪式。1968年，一架B-52轰炸机在图勒附近冰面坠毁，机上携带有4枚氢弹。虽然用以触发核弹头的高爆炸药发生爆炸，但核弹头本身未出现问题，因为机组人员没有给它安装引爆装置。美国、丹麦和当地因纽特人冒着极大风险开展大规模回收作业。③ 三个核弹头被找回，但第四个仍被埋在某处冰层之下，含有半衰期为24000年的钚元素。④

北约与苏联在北极甚至拥有长达200千米的北极陆地边界——沿着挪威北部高度军事化的科拉半岛，巴伦支海近海漫长而有争议的边界。⑤ 还有第二个同样具有争议的海上边界位于在阿拉斯加和苏联远东之间，两国大陆海岸线在白令海峡中仅相隔45海里，在该水道中央苏联大代奥米德岛和美国小代奥米德岛更是仅相距3海里。⑥

---

① Bob Weber, "Russian Maps Suggest Soviet Subs Cruised Canadian Arctic," Canadian Press, December 6, 2011, http://www.theglobeandmail.com/news/national/russian-maps-suggest-soviet-subs-cruised-canadian-arctic/article2261379/. The soundings were also in slightly different locations, with different measurements, which confirm the Soviet charts were not compiled from Canadian charts.

② International Atomic Energy Agency, Nuclear Explosions in the USSR: The North Test Site Reference Material (Vienna: Division of Nuclear Safety and Security, 2004), pp. 5 and 29, http://www-ns.iaea.org/downloads/rw/waste-safety/north-test-site-final.pdf.

③ Stephen Mulvey, "Denmark Challenged over B52 Crash," BBC News, May 11, 2007, http://news.bbc.co.uk/2/hi/europe/6647421.stm.

④ Gordon Corera, "Mystery of Lost US Nuclear Bomb," BBC News, November 10, 2008, http://news.bbc.co.uk/2/hi/europe/7720049.stm.

⑤ For more on the Barents Sea boundary, see Chapter 2, above.

⑥ Ibid..

在冷战期间，国际法在北极安全方面作用虽小，但重要性突出。1949 年《北大西洋公约》的第五条规定了冰岛、挪威、丹麦、加拿大和美国等北约国家间的集体防御义务，因此该公约也覆盖格陵兰、加拿大高北极岛屿和阿拉斯加。[1] 1958 年，加拿大和美国达成《北美防空司令部协议》，将北美大陆防空力量集中于一个两国指挥架构之下。该协议已经续签十次，联合司令部的授权也随之两度扩大，首先是纳入航空航天防御，后又加入海上监视的内容。[2]

1941 年，丹麦和美国签署《格陵兰防务协定》，由美国接管该岛防卫义务直至第二次世界大战结束。[3] 1951 年的一项新协议允许美国扩建在图勒的空军基地并行使专属管辖权。[4] 2004 年，尽管当地因纽特人表示担忧，但是双方还是进一步达成协议，允许升级在图勒的雷达系统，编入美国弹道导弹防御系统的组成部分。[5]

美国和苏联之间的许多军控协议同样与北极相关，包括 1963 年《部分禁止核试验条约》,[6] 1971 年《禁止在海床洋底及其底土安置核

---

[1] 1949 North Atlantic Treaty, http://www.nato.int/cps/en/natolive/official_texts_17120.htm. Article 5 reads, in part: "The Parties agree that an armed attack against one or more of them in Europe or North America shall be considered an attack against them all and consequently they agree that, if such an armed attack occurs, each of them, in exercise of the right of individual or collective self-defense recognised by Article 51 of the Charter of the United Nations, will assist the Party or Parties so attacked by taking forthwith, individually and in concert with the other Parties, such action as it deems necessary, including the use of armed force, to restore and maintain the security of the North Atlantic area."

[2] The most recent, 2006, version of the NORAD Agreement, http://www.state.gov/documents/organization/69727.pdf.

[3] 1941 Agreement Relating to the Defense of Greenland (1941) 35 (3) American Journal of International Law Supplement 129.

[4] 1951 Agreement on the Defense of Greenland, http://avalon.law.yale.edu/20th_century/den001.asp.

[5] "US Expands Greenland Relations in Support of Missile Defense," Environment News Service, August 9, 2004, http://www.ens-newswire.com/ens/aug2004/2004-08-09-02.asp.

[6] 1963 Treaty Banning Nuclear Weapon Tests in the Atmosphere, in Outer Space and Under Water, 480 (1) UNTS 6964, http://treaties.un.org/doc/Publication/UNTS/Volume%20480/volume-480-I-6964-English.pdf.

武器和其他大规模毁灭性武器条约》,① 1972 年《战略武器限制条约》② 以及 1972 年《限制反弹道导弹系统条约》,③ 2001 年美国小布什政府正式退出该条约,之后美国开始在阿拉斯加的格里利堡部署弹道导弹防御拦截器。④

一、缓和中的北极局势

冷战结束二十年后,北极地区爆发冲突的风险大大降低。如上所述,俄罗斯现在是二十国集团、世界贸易组织、欧洲理事会、巴伦支海欧洲—北极理事会和北极理事会的成员。其最大贸易伙伴主要由北约成员国组成的欧盟。俄罗斯军事实力也大幅下降,2011 年军费为 720 亿美元,仅为美国 7110 亿美元军事开支的十分之一。⑤

北极国家的领导人一致认为,该地区几乎没有爆发冲突的风险。正如上文提及,2010 年 1 月,加拿大总理史蒂芬·哈珀对北约秘书长表示,加拿大与俄罗斯就北极问题拥有良好的工作关系,北约的存在反而会适得其反,加剧局势紧张,而且北极国家没有爆发战争的可能性。⑥ 9 个月后,俄罗斯总理(现为总统)弗拉基米尔·普京发表关于试图在

---

① 1971 Treaty on the Prohibition of the Emplacement of Nuclear Weapons and Other Weapons of Mass Destruction on the Sea – Bed and the Ocean Floor and in the Subsoil Thereof, 955 UNTS 115, http://disarmament.un.org/treaties/t/sea_bed/text.

② 1972 Interim Agreement between the United States of America and the Union of Soviet Socialist Republics on Certain Measures with respect to the Limitation of Strategic Offensive Arms (SALT I), http://cns.miis.edu/inventory/pdfs/aptsaltI.pdf.

③ 1972 Treaty between the United States of America and the Union of Soviet Socialist Republics on the Limitation of Anti – Ballistic Missile Systems (ABM Treaty), http://www.nti.org/media/pdfs/aptabm.pdf?_=1316631917and_=1316631917.

④ "Statement by the Press Secretary: Announcement of Withdrawal from the ABM Treaty," December 13, 2001, http://georgewbush – whitehouse.archives.gov/news/releases/2001/12/20011213 – 2.html.

⑤ "The 15 Countries with the Highest Military Expenditure in 2009," Stockholm International Peace Research Institute, 2010, http://www.sipri.org/research/armaments/milex/resultoutput/milex_15 (China: $43bn./US: $711bn./France: $52.5bn./Germany: $46.7bn./Italy: $4.5bn.).

⑥ US State Department cable # VZCZCXR03302, Chapter 5, n.110, above.

北极独立生存和大自然使得人们和国家互相帮助的演讲。①

加拿大和美国军方的高层官员已证实这些观点。2009 年，加拿大参谋长纳廷齐克将军表示，"如果有人打算入侵加拿大北极地区，我首要任务就是营救他们。"② 2010 年，美国海军作战部长加里·拉夫黑德海军上将发表一份关于"海军北极战略目标"的备忘录称，"北极地区发生冲突的可能性很低。"③

尽管如此，所有北极国家都已采取措施改善在该地区的军事能力。加拿大政府已承诺为该国海军建造多达 8 艘冰区加强巡逻舰，尽管（截至 2013 年 1 月）尚未签署合同。④ 他还承诺在巴芬岛北部设立海军深水港，但相关计划已经大幅缩水。⑤ 加拿大骑兵巡逻队是一支由北方社区兼职志愿者组成的预备队，其规模已由 4100 人小幅增加到 4700 人。⑥

丹麦拥有四艘可以在 80 厘米厚的一年冰中航行的护卫舰，并分别于 2008 和 2009 年增加了两艘稍小的冰区加强巡逻舰。只要北部海冰条件允许，这些舰艇及其直升机就可以在格陵兰周边部署。⑦

挪威作为一个有着 500 万人口的国家，拥有装备精良的军事力量。

---

① Luke Harding, "Vladimir Putin Calls for Arctic Claims to Be Resolved under UN Law," Guardian, September 23, 2010, http：//www.guardian.co.uk/world/2010/sep/23/putin-arctic-claims-international-law.

② Pierre-Henry Deshayes, "Arctic Threats and Challenges from Climate Change," Agence France-Presse, December 6, 2009, http：//www.google.com/hostednews/afp/article/ALeqM5iESW9KN4XHyuP2QpnDqDf5wGxJVg.

③ US Chief of Naval Operations, "Navy Strategic Objectives for the Arctic," May 21, 2010, p.3, http：//greenfleet.dodlive.mil/files/2010/09/US-Navy-Arctic-Strategic-Objectives-21-May-2010.pdf.

④ Lee Berthiaume, "Armed Arctic Vessels Face Delay in Latest Procurement Setback," Postmedia News, May 8, 2012, http：//www.nunatsiaqonline.ca/stories/article/65674armed_arctic_vessels_face_delay_in_latest_procurement_setback/.

⑤ Bob Weber, "Ottawa Scraps Big Plans for Arctic Naval Facility," Canadian Press, March 23, 2012, http：//thechronicleherald.ca/canada/76576-ottawa-scraps-big-plans-arctic-naval-facility.

⑥ David Pugliese, "Canadian Rangers Increase in Size. Ranks are at around 4,700," Ottawa Citizen, July 25, 2011, http：//blogs.ottawacitizen.com/2011/07/25/canadian-rangers-increase-in-size-ranks-are-at-around-4700/.

⑦ quotation from Danish Rear-Admiral Henrik Kudsk, n.135, below, pp.272-273.

该国拥有5艘配备宙斯盾系统的护卫舰,6艘柴电潜艇和1艘104米长的冰区加强巡逻舰"斯瓦尔巴"号。挪威同时还装备和使用F-16战斗机,但仍在考虑是否将这些飞机替换为F-35战斗机。① 2010年,挪威军队将该国联合作战司令部迁至位于北极圈内的冷战时期地下综合设置中,此举在国际上引发一些非议。② 事实上,新地点位于这个狭长国家的中间位置附近。

2011年,俄罗斯国防部长阿纳托里·谢尔久科夫宣布将成立两个陆军旅,以保护俄罗斯北极资源,但拒绝透露该计划具体细节。③ 2012年,据"今日俄罗斯电视台"新闻报道,该国另一项计划是沿着北方海航线等北极地区建立二十个边境哨所,每个哨所驻扎15—20名守卫。④ 这两项计划似乎均未针对其他国家;相反,它们似乎是为应对走私、非法移民和恐怖主义等伴随北部地区商业活动增加而出现的非国家行为体的威胁。⑤

俄罗斯其他的军事计划遭受到一些人的质疑,从气候和能源解决方案中心2012年发布的一份报告摘录中可见一斑:

> 《2007—2015年俄罗斯国家军备计划》强调重建其北方海军力量。根据该计划,俄罗斯将新建核动力潜艇,包括攻击型和弹道导弹型。俄罗斯地理实际情况表明这些舰艇将驻扎在北方水域。俄罗斯海军司令表示,俄罗斯还计划建造5至6个航母战斗群并将主要驻扎在北方基地……俄罗斯还恢复了在北极的一处重要军事存在。2007年8月,他们重启远程轰炸机巡

---

① Andrea Shalal-Esa, "Lockheed Welcomes Norway Backing of F-35 Fighter," Reuters, March 23, 2012, http://uk.reuters.com/article/2012/03/23/us-lockheed-fighter-norway-idUKBRE82M1CQ20120323.

② "Inside Norway's Underground Military HQ," BBC News, September 22, 2010, http://www.bbc.co.uk/news/world-europe-11386699.

③ Thomas Grove, "Russia Creates Two Brigades of Arctic Troops," Reuters, July 1, 2011, http://uk.reuters.com/article/2011/07/01/russia-arctic-troops-idUKLDE76017D20110701.

④ "Russia to Set Up Arctic Frontier Posts," RT News, April 16, 2012, http://rt.com/politics/arctic-border-posts-russia-132/.

⑤ On non-state threats, discussion below.

逻,并于同年恢复了海军水面部队在北方的巡逻。俄罗斯一直小心翼翼地保持在国际空域活动,但在某些情况下也接近过加拿大、挪威和美国的边界。[1]

评估俄罗斯政府在北极问题上的声明和行动往往具有挑战性,尤其是因为该国主要海军港口必然位于巴伦支海西南部沿岸。苏联解体后,俄罗斯失去位于波罗的海国家的海军设施,白俄罗斯和立陶宛的独立更使得加里宁格勒成为飞地,这就使得摩尔曼斯克和其他北极不冻港的重要性增加。这些因素使得要把专为北极进行部署与投资和旨在保持俄罗斯在其他地区能力的部署和投资加以区分变得较为困难。[2]

俄罗斯和美国在北冰洋持续部署核潜艇并派遣军用飞机在其上空飞行。有时,一些行为会过度刺激邻国。2009年一次演习之后,两架"熊"式轰炸机在距加拿大波弗特海岸90海里处上空被拦截。加拿大国防部长彼得·麦凯召开新闻发布会,指出这起事件发生在美国总统巴拉克·奥巴马访问渥太华之前仅一天,并表示:"我不会站在这里并指责俄罗斯人有意在总统访问期间进行此类活动,但这实在是太巧合了"。[3] 此后,当斯蒂芬·哈珀总理被问及该事件时,他表示俄罗斯飞机事实上已经进入加拿大空域,该空域和领海一样扩展至距海岸12海里的近海。"这是我们真正关心的问题",他说,"我曾多次表达我国政府对俄罗斯在全球范围内日益咄咄逼人的行动和对我国空域的侵犯感到深切担忧。"哈珀承诺称,他会对"俄罗斯任何对加拿大北极主权的侵犯做出回应。"[4]

---

[1] Rob Huebert, et al., "Climate Change and International Security: The Arctic as a Bellwether." 2012, Center for Climate and Energy Solutions, p. 18, http://www.c2es.org/publications/climate-change-international-arctic-security/.

[2] Rob Huebert, "The Newly Emerging Arctic Security Environment," Canadian Defence and Foreign Affairs Institute, March 2010, p. 16, http://www.cdfai.org/PDF/The% 20Newly% 20Emerging% 20Arctic% 20Security% 20Environment.pdf.

[3] Steven Chase, "Ottawa Rebukes Russia for Military Flights in Arctic," Globe and Mail, February 28, 2009, http://www.theglobeandmail.com/news/politics/ottawa-rebukes-russia-for-military-flights-in-arctic/article1149408/.

[4] Ibid.

美国和俄罗斯对加拿大评论的回应为了解北极实际的安全形势提供了更多信息。掌管北美防空司令部的美国四星上将向记者们保证,俄罗斯人的"操作专业",没有进入加拿大或美国空域,而一名俄罗斯外交官解释称,已根据华盛顿和莫斯科长期协议,事先向北美防空司令部通报了这些飞行活动。①

正如查尔斯·埃默森所提醒的那样,"当代俄罗斯的力量投射能力已不及苏联时期",并且"普京和梅德韦杰夫政权的国内合法性更依赖于经济繁荣,而不是军事力量。"② 西蒙·韦泽曼在斯德哥尔摩国际和平研究所2012年发布的一篇文章中准确描述了该情况。

虽然一些媒体、政客和研究人员已经将北极沿岸国家能力的变化描述为重大军事力量建设和对安全的潜在威胁,但总体情况是装备、兵力水平和力量结构的现代化、增长或变化均有限。其中一些变化,例如加拿大强化骑兵巡逻队,挪威主要陆上部队进驻该国北部或者俄罗斯新建北极部队等,对主权不明的北极地区力量投射几乎或根本没有影响;相反,他们是为了巡逻和保护公认的国家领土,非法活动正愈来愈容易在这些领土滋生。③

此外,各国已采取许多措施降低北极军事化,包括2006年美国退出冰岛基夫拉维克空军基地,俄罗斯接受西方国家帮助退役和清除俄罗斯北极沿岸苏联时期遗留的核潜艇和弹头。之后,2011年《新削减战略武器条约》对美国和俄罗斯生效。④ 作为奥巴马"重启"俄美两国关系努力的一部分,该条约要求将战略核导弹发射装置的数量削减50%。

所有这些均引发了一个问题,即对北极而言,北约是否仍继续具有

---

① Ibid., testimony of Dmitry Trofimov before Canadian House of Commons Standing Committee on National Defence, March 23, 2009, http://www.parl.gc.ca/HousePublications/Publication.aspx? DocId = 3760417&Language = E&Mode = 1.

② Charles Emmerson, The Future History of the Arctic (New York: Public Affairs, 2010), p. 121.

③ Siemon T. Wezeman, "Military Capabilities in the Arctic." SIPRI Background Paper, Stockholm, March 2012, pp. 13 – 14, http://books.sipri.org/product_info? c_product_id = 442.

④ New START Treaty, Chapter 2, n. 71, above.

相关性。① 在可预见的将来，问题的答案可能是"不"，至少就北约在《北大西洋公约》下的传统集体防御授权而言是如此。然而，北约已经逐步寻求扩大其授权，最重要的是通过2010年北约部长们采纳一项新的"战略概念"。② 在这份文件中，北约自身任务不仅包括集体防御，还包括危机管理以及贸易路线、能源供应和油气管道方面的"合作安全"。尽管该战略概念没有提及北极，但北约扩大授权很可能将其引向北方，而且当它与北极理事会等其他组织之间开展协调与合作之时，向北扩张就成为需要。

迄今为止，因为1996年《渥太华宣言》中的一段脚注："北极理事会不应处理有关军事安全的问题"，③ 北极理事会一直回避安全问题。该脚注是在美国的坚持下写入的，其大概担心这个新设立的政府间论坛对美国和俄罗斯在该地区微妙的核平衡产生潜在影响。④ 今天，北极理事会已经取得适度成功的记录，在此相当不同的情况中，建议成员国可以重新审议这一决议。他们这样做也没有任何阻碍，正如埃里克·穆伦纳尔温和地指出：

《渥太华宣言》使用"应当"（should）这一自愿性词语，该词一般适用于不具有法律约束力的文书，这表明北极理事会可以处理这些问题，只要协商达成一致意见。事实上，由于《渥太华宣言》没有法律约束力，如果成员国有意超越北极理事会现已非常广泛的职权范围，该宣言不会对成员国构成多大

---

① e. g., Helga Haftendorn, "NATO and the Arctic: Is the Atlantic Alliance a Cold War Relic in a Peaceful Region Now Faced with Non – Military Challenges?" (2011) 20 European Security 337; Sven G. Holtsmark, "Towards Cooperation or Confrontation? Security in the High North." Research Paper No. 45, NATO Defense College, February 2009, http://www.ndc.nato.int/research/series.php? icode = 1.

② "Strategic Concept for the Defence and Security of the Members of the North Atlantic Treaty Organization," http://www.nato.int/lisbon2010/strategic – concept – 2010 – eng. pdf.

③ Declaration on the Establishment of the Arctic Council, Chapter 7, n. 61, above.

④ Rob Huebert, "New Directions in Circumpolar Cooperation: Canada, the Arctic Environmental Protection Strategy and the Arctic Council." (1998) 5 Canadian Foreign Policy 37 at 54.

障碍。①

二、中国

北极远离中国海岸，中国在北极不构成军事威胁。作为世界上最大的贸易国家，中国是二十国集团（G20）和世界贸易组织成员，拥有与北极国家保持友好关系的长期利益。尽管中国军费开始迅速增长，但是2011年其国防支出仍仅相当于美国的1/5，或者大致相当于法国、德国和意大利的总和。②

中国长期致力于北极科研活动，特别是在气候变化方面。据琳达·雅各布森称，1984年以来，中国已经组织了26次北极考察并建立了三个北极科考站，③ 其中一个坐落于挪威斯瓦尔巴群岛。中国还拥有一艘长163米的科考破冰船"雪龙"号，并正在建造第二艘稍小一些的科考破冰船。

中国政府充分认识到北极地区近海石油和天然气开发的巨大潜力，但也知道大部分石油和天然气位于大陆架沉积岩中。根据海洋法，沿岸国对距海岸200海里内的自然资源享有排他性权利。④ 中国人还意识到，如果沿岸国能够从科学上证明北冰洋洋底的地形和地质属于该国陆块的"自然延伸"，这些国家可能会对更远的海床资源拥有管辖权。⑤ 中国不挑战这些权利主张。中国已经批准《联合国海洋法公约》，并使用该公约中的相关条款主张对东海外大陆架的主权权利，这与北极国家

---

① Erik Molenaar, "Current and Prospective Roles of the Arctic Council System within the Context of the Law of the Sea." (2012) 27 International Journal of Marine and Coastal Law 553 at 570.
② "The 15 Countries with the Highest Military Expenditure in 2011," n. 19, above.
③ "China's Perspective on Arctic Matters." (2009) 55 (15) Shijie Zhishi, translated in Linda Jakobson, "China Prepares for an Ice–Free Arctic." SIPRI Insights on Peace and Security, No. 2010/2, March 2010, p. 3, http: //books. sipri. org/files/insight/SIPRIInsight1002. pdf.
④ discussion, Chapter 4, above.
⑤ Ibid.

在本地区的作法相似。① 与此同时，中国明确表示，希望北极国家尊重国际法有关外大陆架外部界限的规定，所有国家均享有获取该区域以外国际"区域"资源的权利。②

中国没有必要挑战北极国家的主张。近海石油和天然气勘探、开采和运输费用高昂，尤其是在极其偏远和不适宜人类定居的区域。为获得这些财富，北极国家将需要强大的市场和大量的资本，中国在这两方面具有优势。至于北冰洋渔业，中国已经与数个区域渔业组织开展了良好的合作，作为回报，中国获得了以科学研究为目的的捕鱼配额。③

然而，中国以合法方式参与北极活动的努力正因北极理事会推迟批准其正式观察员国地位申请一事而动摇。不幸的是，中国是与欧盟一同提出的请求，因为欧盟对海豹产品进口禁令问题，两者申请就被同时搁置。④ 2011 年，北极理事会通过了对正式观察员国的新标准，其中包括承认"北极国家依据《联合国海洋法公约》管理北冰洋之权利"的条件。⑤ 中国不太可能接受这一条件，因为这句话目前的措辞暗示北极国家有权管理整个北冰洋。事实上，中国和其他非北极国家完全有权利在距离海岸 12 海里以外自由航行，在 200 海里之外捕鱼以及开发大陆架之外的海底资源。

北极理事会成员国犯了一个错误，没有认识到其虽然拥有广泛权利，但这种权利不是无限的。就目前情况而言，他们很难想出更好的策略，以缓解中国人对这些国家在北极地区意图的担忧。2012 年，中国官员在接受琳达·雅各布森和彭景超采访时，"私下表示对一些标准的不满，例如规定申请方必须展现'致力于永久参与方工作的政治意愿和

---

① Alexander M. Peterson, "Sino-Japanese Cooperation in the East China Sea: A Lasting Arrangement?" (2009) 42 Cornell International Law Journal 441. China's disputes in the South China Sea revolve around quite different issues of title to land territory, in the form of islands and shoals, and the entitlements of such features to maritime zones.
② discussion, Chapter 4, above.
③ discussion, Chapter 6, above.
④ discussion, Chapter 7, above.
⑤ "Observers," http://www.arctic-council.org/index.php/en/about-us/partners-links.

经济能力'和'承认北极国家'在北极地区的主权、主权权利和管辖权"。① 雅各布森和彭景超还报道称,中国学者批评该标准提高"政治门槛,以阻止非北极国家干预"北极事务;"北极国家向世界宣布:北极属于北极国家",并且"如果很多国家被排除于北极理事会之外,该理事会的影响力将被削弱,其将很难继续成为商讨北极事务的首要机构"。②

中国尊重国际法,在北极地区拥有合法利益。中国申请永久观察员地位的请求,应予立即批准。(译者注:中国于2013年5月成为北极理事会观察员。)

三、北极无核武器区

1982年,当北约和苏联还处于冷战状态时,因纽特人北极圈理事会通过一项决议,反对在北极地区储存或试验核武器。③ 由于北冰洋是核潜艇的主要战场,因纽特人的倡议必然以失败告终。但现在,在形势发生根本性转变的情况下,或许是时候回到在北极建立无核武器区这一想法之上了。

几十年来,已有两个条约禁止在北极特定区域使用核武器。1920年《斯瓦尔巴条约》通过禁止设立任何"海军基地"或"防御工事"并声明该岛"永远不可被用于战争目的"的方式,有效地实现这个挪威群岛的非军事化。④ 目前已有40个国家批准了《斯瓦尔巴条约》,包括全部北极国家。⑤ 1971年,适用于世界所有海洋的《禁止在海床洋底

---

① Linda Jakobson and Jingchao Peng, "China's Arctic Ambitions." SIPRI Policy Paper 34, November 2012, http://books.sipri.org/product_info?c_product_id = 449.

② Ibid., citing and translating Y. Qian, "How Far Is China from the Arctic." (2011) 29 Liaowang Dongfang Zhoukan, http://www.lwdf.cn/wwwroot/dfzk/Focuseast/252093.shtml; and Peiqing Guo, "Making Preparations against an Arctic Monroe Doctrine." (2011) 42 Liaowang 71 – 72.

③ discussion, Chapter 7, above.

④ Treaty concerning the Archipelago of Spitsbergen, Chapter 1, n. 24, above, Art. 9.

⑤ "Traktat anga'ende Spitsbergen (Svalbardtraktaten)," http://www.lovdata.no/cgi-bin/udoffles?doc = tra – 1920 – 02 – 09 – 001.txt.

及其底土安置核武器和其他大规模毁灭性武器条约》禁止在距离海岸12海里之外的海床部署核武器。[1] 已有94个国家批准了该条约,包括所有北极国家和除法国外的所有已宣布拥有核武器的国家。[2] 同样可以认为,根据国际习惯法的最新发展,沿岸国有权禁止运输危险核货物的船舶通过其专属经济区。[3] 然而,在北极设立无核武器区的大多数支持者正计划通过一项类似于1959年《南极条约》的全面区域性安排,而该条约要求整个南极维持非军事化。[4]

1968年《不扩散核武器条约》提高了设立无核武器区的可能性,该条约第七条规定:"本条约的任何规定均不影响任何国家集团为了保证其各自领土上完全没有核武器而缔结区域性条约的权利。"[5] 联合国大会于1975年将无核武器区定义为:

任何国家集团在自由行使其主权的前提下,根据条约或公约而建立的,并经联合国大会承认为无核武器区的任何地区,据此:

(a) 确定了该地区所应遵守的完全没有核武器存在的法规,包括划定该地区界限的程序;

(b) 建立了核查和控制的国际体系,以保证该法规所产生的义务得到遵守。[6]

---

[1] 1971 Treaty on the Prohibition of the Emplacement of Nuclear Weapons and Other Weapons of Mass Destruction on the Sea‐Bed and the Ocean Floor and in the Subsoil Thereof, 955 UNTS 115, http://disarmament.un.org/treaties/t/sea_bed/text. generally, Jozef Goldblat, "The Seabed Treaty and Arms Control," in Richard Fieldhouse (ed.), Security at Sea: Naval Forces and Arms Control (Oxford University Press and Stockholm International Peace Research Institute, 1990), 187.

[2] "Status of the Treaty," http://disarmament.un.org/treaties/t/sea_bed.

[3] Jon M. Van Dyke, "The Disappearing Right to Navigational Freedom in the Exclusive Economic Zone." (2005) 29 Marine Policy 107 at 110 – 112.

[4] 1959 Antarctic Treaty, 402 UNTS 71, http://www.ats.aq/documents/ats/treaty_original.pdf. Article 1 (1) reads: "Antarctica shall be used for peaceful purposes only. There shall be prohibited, inter alia, any measure of a military nature, such as the establishment of military bases and fortifications, the carrying out of military manoeuvres, as well as the testing of any type of weapons."

[5] 1968 Treaty on the Non‐Proliferation of Nuclear Weapons, 729 UNTS 161, http://www.iaea.org/Publications/Documents/Infcircs/Others/infcirc140.pdf.

[6] UNGA Res. 3472 B (1975), http://www.opanal.org/Docs/UN/UNAG30res3472i.pdf.

第八章 安全

目前世界范围内存在五个无核武器区：拉丁美洲①、南太平洋②、东南亚③、非洲④以及中亚⑤。

在1975年的同一份决议中，联合国大会试图给宣布拥有核武器的中国、法国、俄罗斯、英国以及美国创设一项义务，要求这些国家通过协议或承诺的方式声明"尊重完全没有核武器存在的全部法规"以及"不对无核武器区的国家使用或威胁使用核武器"。⑥ 然而，联合国大会没有权力施加法律义务，这些所谓的"消极安全保证"也并非总是唾手可得。美国只向拉丁美洲无核武器区提供保证，⑦ 俄罗斯则向拉丁美洲⑧和南太平洋两个区域提供保证。⑨

目前最成功的无核武器区都建立在那些尚未部署核武器的地区。这一事实条件可能解释了就斯瓦尔巴、南极和海床等区域达成条约的成功之处。北极则呈现出完全不同的现实情况，数十年来这里一直是数千枚核弹头及其导弹、轰炸机和核潜艇等运载系统的基地。考虑到北冰洋作为俄罗斯和北约核导弹潜艇部署区域的持续重要性，在全球核裁军实现之前，北极实现全面无核武器区似乎是不可能的。

尽管如此，2009年由美国起草并获得一致通过的联合国安理会第1887号决议，明确支持将设立无核武器区作为防止核扩散的有效途径之一。该决议的序言部分如下：

---

① 1967 Treaty for the Prohibition of Nuclear Weapons in Latin America and the Caribbean (Treaty of Tlatelolco), http：//disarmament.un.org/treaties/t/tlatelolco/text.

② 1985 South Pacific Nuclear Free Zone Treaty (Treaty of Rarotonga), http：//disarmament.un.org/treaties/t/rarotonga/text.

③ 1995 Treaty on the Southeast Asia Nuclear Weapon - Free Zone (Treaty of Bangkok), http：//disarmament.un.org/treaties/t/bangkok/text.

④ 1996 African Nuclear Weapon Free Zone Treaty (Treaty of Pelindaba), http：//disarmament.un.org/treaties/t/pelindaba/text.

⑤ 2006 Treaty on a Nuclear - Weapon - Free Zone in Central Asia (Treaty of Semipalatinsk), http：//disarmament.un.org/treaties/t/canwfz/text.

⑥ UNGA Res. 3472 B (1975), n. 65, above.

⑦ The negative security assurance is set out in Additional Protocol II to the Treaty of Tlatelolco, http：//disarmament.un.org/treaties/t/tlateloco_p2/text. On US ratification, see http：//disarmament.un.org/treaties/t/tlateloco_p2.

⑧ Ibid.

⑨ "Status of the Protocol," http：//disarmament.un.org/treaties/t/rarotonga_p2.

欢迎并支持在缔结无核武器区条约方面已采取的步骤，重申坚信在有关地区各国间自由达成的安排基础上，按照1999年联合国裁军审议委员会的指导方针建立国际公认的无核武器区，将增进全球和区域的和平与安全，加强核不扩散机制，并有助于实现核裁军目标。①

另一个表明对无核武器区态度转变的信号是：2011年奥巴马政府宣布将向美国参议院提交两份关于消极安全保证的议定书，即《南太平洋无核武器区条约》和《非洲无核武器区条约》的议定书，以征询参议院意见并批准该文件。②

北极在通往区域无核武器区的道路上可以采取一些循序渐进的有效措施。选项之一是北极六个无核国家中的一个或多个仿效蒙古国1992年所采取的行动，宣布本国是无核武器区。③ 五个拥核国家发表联合声明，依据蒙古无核武器区地位向其提供安全保证后，联合国大会于2001年正式承认了该地位。④

没有什么可以阻止诸如努纳武特和格陵兰这样的次国家主体像世界上数百个城市那样，做出类似声明，尽管他们的行动对所在国政府没有约束力。⑤ 努纳武特和格陵兰仅仅承认不存在核武器的声明也不会损害加拿大和丹麦政府在国防和外交事务上的权力。

更有雄心的是，北极六个无核武器国家中的两个或多个可以通过谈

---

① S/RES/1887 (2009), adopted September 24, 2009, http://www.europarl.europa.eu/meetdocs/2009_2014/documents/sede/dv/sede301109unscr1887_/sede301109unscr1887_en.pdf.

② Alfred Nurja, "Obama Submits NWFZ Protocols to Senate," Arms Control Today, June 2011, http://www.armscontrol.org/act/2011_06/NWFZ.

③ "Nuclear-Weapon-Free Status of Mongolia," http://cns.miis.edu/inventory/pdfs/mongol.pdf.

④ UNGA Res. 55/33/S, November 20, 2000, http://www.un.org/depts/dhl/resguide/r55.htm.

⑤ Nigel Young, "Peace Movements in History: Perspectives from Social Movements," in S. Mendlovitz and R. B. Walker (eds.), Towards a Just World Peace (London: Butterworths, 1987), 137 at 154-157.

判的方式,在这些国家之间设立无核武器区,除非之后涉及消极安全保证方面问题,否则无需寻求俄罗斯或美国参与其中。的确,北欧无核武器区的可能性已经被讨论了半个多世纪。① 可以说,任何类似条约均将违背加拿大、丹麦、冰岛或挪威在北约框架下,允许战时在其领土部署核武器的承诺。② 但是这些国家可以通过退出北约核计划小组的方式避免法律冲突,该小组成员国身份即不是盟国所必须,也已不具有冷战时期的重要性。

最有希望和最直接的机会三十多年前就出现了,当时富兰克林·格利菲斯提出达成一项多边协议,以实现北冰洋中部水面和海冰的非军事化。③ 通过聚焦维持一个尚未军事化区域的非军事化状态,该建议遵循了《海床洋底及其底土安置核武器和其他大规模毁灭性武器条约》的模式。当时,北冰洋中部水面几乎没有军事化的风险,因此该条约的主要好处将是促进美国和苏联之间的合作。现在,随着北极海冰消失,海军水面舰艇部署至北冰洋(超出历史上巴伦支海和挪威海的无冰区域)的风险逐年上升,格利菲斯的建议因而值得认真考虑。

格利菲斯提议的一个附带但具有战略意义的好处是,通过阻止将用于水面反舰作战的舰艇部署至北冰洋,可保护并维持核潜艇提供的威慑力。当然,这是海冰在历史上曾发挥的作用。显然,搜索和救助、潜艇在紧急情况下上浮等和平军事行动的例外情况必须被纳入该条约。

就北冰洋中部海面和海冰非军事化的条约进行谈判、实施和核实,

---

① Ingemar Lindahl, The Soviet Union and the Nordic Nuclear – Weapons – Free – Zone Proposal (London: Macmillan, 1988); Clive Archer, "Plans for a Nordic Nuclear – Weapon Free Zone." (2004) 34 Kosmopolis 201 (supplement), http://helda.helsinki.fi/bitstream/handle/10224/3635/archer201 – 207.pdf.

② Douglas Roche and Ernie Regehr, "Canada, NATO and Nuclear Weapons." Project Ploughshares Working Paper 01 – 3 (2001), http://www.ploughshares.ca/content/canada – nato – and – nuclear – weapons.

③ Franklyn Griffiths, "A Northern Foreign Policy." (1979) 7 Wellesley Papers (Toronto: Canadian Institute of International Affairs), 61. In 2010, Griffiths raised the idea again, at a NATO – related workshop, where he reports: "It was right away shot down as unrealistic and as undesirable in proposing to alter the high – seas regime in international law." Griffiths, "Arctic Security: The Indirect Approach," in James Kraska (ed.), Arctic Security in an Age of Climate Change (New York: Cambridge University Press, 2011), 3 at 5 n. 2.

相对容易。因此，如果成员国选择超越"渥太华宣言"框架下不合时宜的建议，那么它可能是与北极理事会进行的"军事安全"有关的第一个主题。①

四、非国家行为体

今天，北极地区最为严重的安全威胁出现在其南部边缘、西北航道、北方海航线，以及巴伦支海、白令海、波弗特海和挪威海沿岸。这些威胁包括毒品走私、非法移民，甚至是恐怖分子等非国家行为体，他们可能会利用无冰水域将违禁品、人口或大规模杀伤性武器运送至北美或欧洲，亦或实现太平洋和大西洋之间运输。但是，遥远的距离、恶劣的天气和人口稀少（外界很难忽视）结合在一起也使得该地区的威胁水平远低于南方地区。此外，开通北极航运线后一些货船可以经此避开印度洋和马六甲海峡中海盗出没的水域，或许至少起到减少世界其他地区非国家行为体安全威胁的效果，海盗每年给国际航运业造成的损失高达80亿美元。②

（一）毒品走私

非法毒品在大多数北极社区随处可得，这就增加了将向北运送毒品的相同路线反过来作为毒品进入欧洲或北美之通道的可能性。2007年，加拿大当局在努纳武特的剑桥湾拦截一艘悬挂挪威旗，名为"狂怒二世"号的私人快艇，船上数人拥有犯罪背景，包括毒品走私。③尽管此次航行可能只是一次挑战加拿大对西北航道主张的不成熟尝试，但其也可能是一次侦查任务。四年之后，在一次北极航行期间，我在富兰克林湾上岸，此地位于"狂怒二世"号被拦截处以西600千米。富兰克林

---

① discussion, above, p. 253.
② Geopolicity, "The Economics of Piracy." May 2011, http://www.geopolicity.com/upload/content/pub_1305229189_regular.pdf.
③ Testimony of Philip Whitehorne, Canada Border Services Agency, to the Senate Committee on Fisheries and Oceans, November 5, 2009, http://www.parl.gc.ca/Content/SEN/Committee/402/fish/13evb-e.htm?Language=EandParl=40andSes=2andcomm_id=7.

湾是一个长期废置的冷战时期雷达站所在地,但旧的沙砾跑道中间竟有三个崭新的飞机起降时留下的轮胎印迹。在西北航道沿线的废弃军事、勘探和科研站点中存在着数百个类似的跑道,这些都是过往游船、货船或私人快艇很容易到达的地方。

北极毒品走私几乎没有引起国际法问题,因为各国对其领土、领海内以及靠近国际海峡的犯罪活动拥有无可争议的管辖权。[1] 此外,沿岸国可以对距离海岸12海里至24海里之间的"毗连区"内对毒品走私行使管辖权已被普遍接受。[2] 也有主张认为可以根据"保护管辖"或"普遍管辖"原则行使管辖权。[3] 然而,当涉及到经过适当注册的船只时,船旗国管辖的优先地位使得上述论断难以为继。[4] 更为常见的情况是,通过"登临检查"协议解决毒品走私问题,该协议允许一国拦截另一国船只,或者企图逃往另一国领海的船只。"登临检查"一词指的是来自第二国的执法部门官员在此类行动中被部署于拦截船只上。加拿大和美国之间存在类似协议,主要为两国东西海岸和五大湖区域所设计,这一做法也可被应用到波弗特海执法合作当中。[5] 将来,加拿大和丹麦可就加拿大和格陵兰之间的水域达成类似协议,挪威和俄罗斯就巴伦支海,俄罗斯和美国就楚科奇海、白令海峡和白令海也一样。尽管与俄罗斯达成登临检查协议似乎不太可能,但俄罗斯和美国自1994年以

---

[1] Article 42 (1) of the UNCLOS reads, in part: "Subject to the provisions of this section, States bordering straits may adopt laws and regulations relating to transit passage through straits, in respect of all or any of the following: ... (d) the loading or unloading of any commodity, currency or person in contravention of the customs, fiscal, immigration or sanitary laws and regulations of States bordering straits," Introduction, n. 15, above.

[2] Article 33 (1) of UNCLOS reads, in part: "In a zone contiguous to its territorial sea, described as the contiguous zone, the coastal State may exercise the control necessary to ... prevent infringement of its customs, fiscal, immigration or sanitary laws and regulations within its territory or territorial sea," ibid.

[3] e.g., Christina Sorensen, "Drug Trafficking on the High Seas: A Move Toward Universal Jurisdiction under International Law." (1990) 4 Emory International Law Review 207.

[4] For a brief but useful discussion, see Robin Churchill and Vaughan Lowe, The Law of the Sea, 3rd edn. (Manchester University Press, 1999), 217 – 218.

[5] "Framework Agreement on Integrated Cross – Border Maritime Law Enforcement Operations between the Government of Canada and the Government of the United States of America," May 2009, http://www.publicsafety.gc.ca/prg/le/_fl/int – cross – brdr – maritime – eng.pdf.

来一直在使用类似登临检查的作法，在白令海进行渔业管理合作。①

（二）非法移民

非法移民问题在北极地区日益引起关注，包括在俄罗斯与芬兰和挪威的陆地边界沿线。正如查尔斯·埃默森所解释的：

> 在冷战时期，挪威政府一贯的政策是，任何跨越该边界的人都不会被遣返回苏联。平均每年只有一至两人可以成功。如今，这一数字要大得多，并且其动机趋向于经济性而非政治性。挪威在20世纪90年代初对俄罗斯大规模移民的担忧已被对有组织犯罪分子试图将非法移民偷渡至该国的可能性所取代，挪威属于欧洲申根区域的一部分……另一方俄罗斯人则担忧"恐怖分子"的渗透。②

一些非法移民的尝试也发生在北极的其他地方。2006年9月，一名罗马尼亚男子驾驶一艘6米长的摩托艇从格陵兰驶往加拿大埃尔斯米尔岛的格里斯峡湾。③ 其后一个月，两名土耳其水手在马尼托巴省的丘吉尔港跳船，并购买前往温尼伯的火车票。④ 与更为南方的区域不同，尽管此类事件不会引发国际法问题，但是它们确实表明，北极地区的边境监控需要得到加强。

最重大的挑战来自于航运量增加，包括但不限于游轮，其已经将数百名外国游客带入这个没有任何边境管控措施，却提供飞往南方航班的北方小型社区。政府当局才刚刚认识到这一挑战。在加拿大，根据《海

---

① Convention on the Conservation and Management of Pollock Resources, Chapter 6, n. 36, above. discussion, Chapter 6, above.

② Emmerson, The Future History of the Arctic, n. 38, above, p. 104.

③ "Romanian Who Boated to High Arctic Fesses Up," CBC News, November 15, 2006, http://www.cbc.ca/news/canada/north/story/2006/11/14/grise-romanian.html.

④ Michel Comte, "Turkish Sailors Jump Ship in Canada Arctic, Prompt Security Review," Agence France-Presse, October 30, 2006, http://dl1.yukoncollege.yk.ca/agraham/discuss/msgReader＄3341? mode=topicandy=2006andm=11andd=2.

上运输安全法》所实施的规章,海员需要进入加拿大领水时,必须提前 96 个小时通知并且提供"所携带货物的一般说明"。① 强制性北极航行登记系统要求他们向官员通知船上人数并且每天提供更新的船只位置。② 最后,任何希望踏上加拿大土地的人必须通知加拿大边境服务局和加拿大公民及移民部,因此北极游轮运营者将经常在加拿大第一个停靠港安排检查人员在场。

加拿大在实施强制性北极航行登记系统之前未与其他国家协商,除此之外,这些措施都没有产生争议。③ 但这些措施不太可能阻止专业的犯罪分子或恐怖分子潜入北美。或许需要采取进一步措施,例如要求提供计划使用西北航道的全体船员和乘客清单,或在这些船只航行期间进行实际的检查。这些措施将引发关于该水道法律地位和第五章中讨论的沿岸国权力扩张等所有复杂的问题。

最后,北极非法移民很可能将增加,这不仅是因为海冰融化使得进入北极更为便利,还因为同样的气候变化过程将迫使数亿人离开他们在发展中国家的家园。加拿大、美国和欧洲国家已经面临逃离贫困、迫害和战乱的移民潮,但是在海冰融化为进入北极提供新入口的同时,难民数量预计将成倍地增加。

(三)大规模杀伤性武器运输

2007 年,保罗·塞卢奇称:"我认为在恐怖主义时代,认定西北航道属于加拿大部分地符合我们的安全利益。这将使得加拿大海军能够拦截西北航道中的船只,以确保他们不会试图携带大规模杀伤性武器进入北美地区。"④ 这位前美国驻加拿大大使是对的——一个沿岸国在"国

---

① Marine Transportation Security Regulations, SOR/2004 – 144, Section 221 (1), http://laws – lois. justice. gc. ca/eng/regulations/SOR – 2004 – 144/index. html.
② Northern Canada Vessel Traffic Services Zone Regulations, SOR/2010 – 127, http://laws – lois. justice. gc. ca/eng/regulations/SOR – 2010 – 127/page – 1. html. McDorman, "National Measures for the Safety of Navigation in Arctic Waters," Chapter 5, n. 156, above.
③ discussion, above, p. 166.
④ Jim Brown, Canadian Press, "Ex – US Envoy Backs Canada's Arctic Claim," Chapter 5, n. 60, above.

际水域"中的管辖权多于其在一个"国际海峡"中的管辖权。但是正如第五章中提到的,沿岸国对此几乎无能为力,特别是在事关国家安全的问题上。① 例如,《联合国海洋法公约》第三十九条第1款规定:

> 船舶和飞机在行使过境通行权时应:(a)毫不迟延地通过或飞越海峡;(b)不对海峡沿岸国的主权、领土完整或政治独立进行任何武力威胁或使用武力,或以任何其他违反《联合国宪章》所体现的国际法原则的方式进行武力威胁或使用武力;(c)除因不可抗力或遇难而有必要外,不从事其继续不停和迅速过境的通常方式所附带发生的活动以外的任何活动。②

此外,《联合国海洋法公约》第四十二条第1款称:

> 海峡沿岸国可对下列各项或任何一项制定关于通过海峡的过境通行的法律和规定:……(d)违反海峡沿岸国海关、财政、移民或卫生的法律和规章,上下任何商品、货币或人员。③

根据《联合国宪章》和国际习惯法,沿岸国有自卫的权利,这一权利超过外籍船只作为船旗国领土延伸所具有的不可侵犯性。④ 这一权利可以在同盟国集体自卫中使用,正如《北大西洋公约》第五条所述。⑤ 而且,在此限制下自卫的权利可以被先发制人地行使,自2001年9月11日之后该限制一直饱受争议并且至少出现了一些变化。⑥

---

① discussion, above, pp. 163 – 167.
② Introduction, n. 15, above.
③ Ibid.
④ Article 51 reads, in part: "Nothing in the present Charter shall impair the inherent right of individual or collective self – defense if an armed attack occurs against a Member of the United Nations, until the Security Council has taken measures necessary to maintain international peace and security." 1945 UN Charter, http: //www. un. org/en/documents/charter/index. shtml.
⑤ discussion, above, p. 247.
⑥ Tom Ruys, "Armed Attack" and Article 51 of the UN Charter: Evolutions in Customary Law and Practice (Cambridge University Press, 2010).

在任何情况下都不应自卫权,该权利仅是负责任的国家诉诸最后手段正当性来源。正是基于这一认识,美国主导的"防扩散安全倡议"已被用来促进国际间就打击大规模杀伤性武器的空中和海上运输展开合作,方法是利用沿海国、港口国和船旗国现有管辖权,而不是根据国际法寻求新的权利。① 例如,一艘悬挂利比亚或巴拿马国旗的船舶穿越白令海峡时,可能被美国海军或海岸警卫队拦截,由于已经在"防扩散安全倡议"下达成了双边条约,所以那些国家作为船旗国的权力已经自愿地委托予美国。加拿大或俄罗斯与两个世界上最大的船运登记国利比亚和巴拿马之间达成类似条约,对此可以乐观其成,值得点赞。

最后,尽管关于西北航道地位的争论还在继续,但加拿大和美国就安全管理和其他共同关心问题仍存在合作的机会。正如上文所述,2006年5月,《北美防空司令部协议》扩展至包含共享海上通道和"国内航道"监视。② 时任加拿大国防部长戈登·奥康纳后来证实,该协议包括西北航道。③

(四) 针对航班的恐怖袭击

美国、俄罗斯和加拿大的军事人员在 2010—2012 年间连续三个夏天举行联合演习,以测试他们对阿拉斯加和俄罗斯远东之间空域商业航班劫持事件的反应能力。④ 据报道,北美防空司令部发布的一则新闻稿称,代号为"警惕之鹰"的演习"继续促进俄罗斯联邦空军和北美防

---

① Byers, "Policing the High Seas," Chapter 5, n. 122, above.

② The most recent, 2006, version of the NORAD Agreement, http://www.state.gov/documents/organization/69727.pdf.

③ Parliament of Canada, House of Commons, Debates, 1st Session, 39th Parliament, 8 May 2006, 15:00. For other ways in which the US and Canada could cooperate, "Model Negotiation on Northern Waters," Chapter 5, n. 118, above.

④ "Norad Tests Hijacked Jetliner Response," CBC News, August 10, 2010, http://www.cbc.ca/news/canada/story/2010/08/10/norad-russia-terrorist-hijacking.html; David Pugliese, "Russia, Canada and the US to Launch Vigilant Eagle Exercise Aimed at Preventing Air Terrorism," Ottawa Citizen, August 10, 2012, http://blogs.ottawacitizen.com/2012/08/10/russia-canada-and-the-u-s-to-launch-vigilant-eagle-exercise-aimed-at-preventing-air-terrorism/.

空司令部之间就防范可能的空中恐怖威胁展开合作"。①

针对飞行器的恐怖袭击已经成为联合国安理会多项决议和条约的主题。1970年,安理会第286号决议呼吁各国"采取一切可能的法律步骤'以防止'劫持或任何其他干扰国际民用航空飞行的行为"。② 1971年,《关于制止危害民用航空安全的非法行为的公约》,即《蒙特利尔公约》规定,"缔约国应根据国际法和国内法,努力采取一切切实可行的措施预防针对飞行器的暴力行为。"③ 2005年,联合国安理会第1624号决议呼吁各国"加强国际边界的警戒,包括打击伪造旅行证件,并尽可能加强恐怖主义筛查和乘客安全程序。"④

尽管这些文件没有一个是专门针对北极的,他们是否能在北极得到充分实施值得怀疑。例如,在加拿大在北纬60度以北的航班不会受到安全检查。这就包括加满燃料的波音737飞机,其航程足以抵达美国主要城市。当被用于执行加拿大南部渥太华和埃德蒙顿等城市起飞或抵达的包机时,这类飞机也不需进行安检。如果机场已经配备了必要的人员和设备,且安检是切实可行的,那么不进行安检就会有安全隐患。

(五)针对石油和天然气设施的抗议活动

2011年,22名绿色和平组织活动人士在格陵兰附近登上石油钻井平台并致使钻井活动中断12小时后被逮捕。⑤ 3个月后,加拿大皇家骑警提供一份威胁评估报告,认定绿色和平组织属于"日益激进的环保主义派别",该组织"反对加拿大北极地区开发,也反对加拿大近海石油

---

① Pugliese, "Russia, Canada and the US," ibid.
② UN Security Council Resolution 286 (1970), http://www.un.org/documents/sc/res/1970/scres70.htm.
③ 1971 Montreal Convention for the Suppression of Unlawful Acts against the Safety of Civil Aviation, Art. 10, http://treaties.un.org/untc//Pages//doc/Publication/UNTS/Volume% 20974/volume-974-I-14118-English.pdf.
④ UN Security Council Resolution 1624 (2005), http://www.un.org/Docs/sc/unsc_resolutions05.htm.
⑤ "Greenpeace Head Naidoo Held in Cairn Oil Rig Protest," BBC News, June 17, 2011, http://www.bbc.co.uk/news/uk-scotland-13814009.

工业。"① 威胁评估还称,绿色和平组织在格陵兰周边活动,"凸显出需要准备好应对近海石油和天然气平台治安与安全的潜在威胁"。2012年,绿色和平组织活动人士将自己吊挂在俄罗斯伯朝拉海一座近海石油平台一侧长达15分钟,但此次未造成钻探中断。② 同样在2012年,美国海岸警卫队向阿拉斯加北部地区部署更多资源,部分原因是环保主义者可能发动反对石油钻井平台的直接行动。③ 与此同时,美国政府通过一项法规,在壳牌石油公司"诺贝尔发现者"号平台周围设立500米禁区。④

激进组织的抗议对石油公司和政府而言无疑是代价高昂的,包括公众舆论方面。然而,和平的温和抵抗行为和暴力行为之间存在重要区别,即后者如果出于政治动机则可能构成恐怖主义。再次,由于距离遥远、天气条件严峻和当地人口稀少等原因,恐怖主义在北极地区不太可能立足。⑤

五、搜索和救助

2012年8月,全球最大的私人游艇利用海冰快速消退之机,穿越了西北航道。⑥ 这艘200米长的巴哈马藉船舶实际上是一个豪华高级公

---

① Jim Bronskill, "Radical Environmentalism Growing, Warns New Report," Canadian Press, July 30, 2012, http://www2.canada.com/nanaimodailynews/news/story.html?id=37448c64-168c-4192-82f0-a9a01d1c2310.

② Andrew E. Kramer, "Greenpeace Activists Climb Russian Oil Rig," New York Times, August 24, 2012, http://www.nytimes.com/2012/08/25/world/europe/greenpeace-activists-climb-russian-oil-rig-in-arctic-ocean.html.

③ Kirk Johnson, "For Coast Guard Patrol North of Alaska, Much to Learn in a Remote New Place," New York Times, July 21, 2012, http://www.nytimes.com/2012/07/22/us/coast-guard-strengthens-presence-north-of-alaska.html.

④ FR Doc. No. 2012-15950, Federal Register, vol. 77, no. 126, June 29, 2012, pp. 38718-38723, http://cryptome.org/2012/06/uscg062912.htm.

⑤ Mary Pemberton, "Officials: Alaska Pipeline Not That Vulnerable," Associated Press, December 2, 2006, http://www.usatoday.com/news/nation/2006-02-12-pipelinethreats_x.htm.

⑥ Jane George, "The World Gets Green Light to Transit Northwest Passage," Nunatsiaq News, August 31, 2012, http://www.nunatsiaqonline.ca/stories/article/65674the_world_gets_the_green_light_to_transit_the_northwest_passage/.

寓，165个单位中有些价值超千万。① 许多大型游轮已经在格陵兰和斯瓦尔巴附近水域航行，包括可容纳3780位乘客的歌诗达邮轮"太平洋"号，其姊妹舰歌诗达邮轮"协和"号2012年1月在意大利附近触礁。②

体型更小且经过冰区加强的"考察性"邮轮航行已经暴露了在北极航行的危险因素，包括被称为"残碎冰山"的小块冰山，这种冰山非常坚硬，潜浮于水面之下，很难被发现。2007年，利比亚藉船舶"探险者"号在南极航行时撞上残碎冰山后沉没。幸运的是，当时海上风平浪静，所有乘客都获救。③

第二种危险是搁浅，特别是在相对较浅的西北航道和北方海航线。1996年，巴哈马藉"汉莎蒂克"号在努纳武特的约阿港附近一个沙洲搁浅。幸运的是当时天气很好，一艘俄罗斯船舶在一周内便救起所有乘客。④ 2010年，巴哈马藉"快船冒险家"号（后来更名为"大海冒险家"号）在努纳武特的库格鲁克图克附近撞上水下礁石。⑤ 这次的天气仍旧很好，而且加拿大海岸警卫队破冰船"阿蒙森"号距离事发地只有两天航程。

缺乏关于加拿大北极地区的优秀航海图导致触底风险增加。2010年，约翰·弗金汉姆对"努纳特希亚克新闻"表示，海图不足是"北

---

① e. g., "A Place on the World -For \$17.5 Million," Wall Street Journal, March 6, 2009, http：//online. wsj. com/article/SB123629449070245501. html.

② "Terror at Sea: The Sinking of the Concordia," Channel 4 television documentary, broadcast January 31, 2012, http：//www. channel4. com/programmes/terror - atsea - the - sinking - of - the - concordia/4od.

③ Bureau of Maritime Affairs, Liberia, "Report of Investigation in the Matter of Sinking of Passenger Vessel EXPLORER (O. N. 8495)," http：//www. photobits. com/dl/Explorer % 20 - % 20Final% 20Report. PDF.

④ Transportation Safety Board, "Marine Investigation Report M96H0016, Grounding-Passenger Vessel 'HANSEATIC'," http：//www. tsb. gc. ca/eng/rapports - reports/marine/1996/m96h0016/m96h0016. asp.

⑤ Transportation Safety Board, "Marine Investigation Report M10H0006, Grounding-Passenger Vessel Clipper Adventurer," http：//www. tsb. gc. ca/eng/rapports - reports/marine/2010/m10h0006/m10h0006. asp.

极地区最大的问题"。① 弗金汉姆在加拿大海冰服务局工作了 30 年,他解释说,只有十分之一的加拿大北极水域按照现代标准绘制了海图,按照目前进度,完成这项工作还要花费数个世纪。

第三个危险是不可预测和经常极端的北极天气。即使在夏天,七级以上的强风和七米高的巨浪也稀松平常。虽然对船员素质良好的船舶而言,这样的风浪通常不是问题,但是它们可以将一艘搁浅的船撕开,使得乘客们别无选择,只能弃船。寒冷天气加上暴风雪还会导致"结冰",当浪花冻结在船舶的上层建筑时,会导致船舶头重脚轻,容易倾覆。②

应对航空事故同样需要搜索和救助能力。1991 年,一架加拿大 C-130 "大力神"飞机在距离埃尔斯米尔岛阿勒特加拿大军事哨所 20 千米处坠毁,18 名乘客和机组人员中有 5 人丧生。13 名幸存者在暴风雪中等待一天多,救援人员才赶到并将其解救。③ 1996 年,一架图-154M 客机在斯瓦尔巴群岛的一座山上坠毁,造成机上 141 人全部遇难。④ 2011 年,一架波音 737 尝试在加拿大高北极地区的雷索卢特湾降落时撞毁在山坡上,12 人死亡,3 名幸存者因惊人的巧合而得到救援,当时数百名加拿大士兵正在 3 千米外开展飞机失事场景下的搜索和救助演习。⑤

每年有成千上万个商业航班使用北极上空的"跨极"或"高纬度"

---

① Jane George, "Expert Sounds Alarm about Dangerous Arctic Waters," Nunatsiaq News, August 30, 2010, http://www.nunatsiaqonline.ca/stories/article/300810_Expert_sounds_alarm_about_dangerous_Arctic_waters/.

② Lasse Makkonen, Atmospheric Icing on Sea Structures (Hanover, NH: US Army Cold Regions Research and Engineering Laboratory, Monograph 84 - 2, 1984), http://www.boemre.gov/tarprojects/056/056AC.PDF.

③ Clyde H. Farnsworth, "After a Plane Crash, 30 Deadly Hours in the Arctic," New York Times, November 5, 1991, http://www.nytimes.com/1991/11/05/world/after-a-plane-crash-30-deadly-hours-in-the-arctic.html?src=pm.

④ Aircraft Accident Investigation Board, Norway, "Report on the Accident to Vnukovo Airline's Tupolev TU-154M RA 85621," Report 07/99, http://www.aibn.no/ra-85621-pdf.

⑤ Transportation Safety Board, "First Air Accident, Resolute Bay, Nunavut, 20 August 2011," http://www.tsb.gc.ca/eng/medias-media/majeures-major/aviation/A11H0002/MI-A11H0002.asp.

航线，尽管现代喷气式客机非常可靠，但是诸如2009年法国航空447号航班坠入南大西洋的事故仍旧时有发生。在北极漫长的冬季，寒冷的气温要求救援人员必须在数小时内发现坠机生还者，尽管所涉及的距离通常非常遥远。退役上校皮埃尔·勒布朗告诉我说，他负责指挥加拿大北方战区（此后更名为"北方联合特遣部队"）多年，发生商业航班事故的可能总是让他夜不能寐。当我问勒布朗的继任者诺姆·库图上校，如果一架大型喷气式飞机在冬天坠毁在埃尔斯米尔岛会发生什么情况时，他强调："我们无法到达那里。"

加拿大在北极的搜索和救助能力特别有限。加拿大军队已经装备了一些远程搜救直升机，但是它们的基地距西北航道约3000千米远，并且需要在中途进行数次加油。C-130 "大力神"飞机也被用于搜索和救助，但是它们也部署于加拿大南部，与直升机不同，该飞机无法将人员吊上飞机。加拿大海岸警卫队破冰船正在老化，加拿大海军则完全缺乏有破冰能力的船只，更换新型"北极/近海巡逻舰"的计划也一再推迟。①

相比之下，俄罗斯在北极拥有突出的搜索和救助能力，主要源于冷战时期该地区的军事化。俄罗斯现在正采取措施维持这一能力。2011年11月，莫斯科拨款9.1亿卢布（约2800万美元）用于沿北方海航线建设10个搜索和救助中心。②

在阿拉斯加，搜索和救助活动主要由美国海岸警卫队执行，他们在阿拉斯加州南部海岸两个地点拥有6架C-130 "大力神"飞机和12架远程直升机。海岸警卫队可以得到美国陆军的支持，他们有在温赖特堡部署的"支奴干"直升机③，阿拉斯加州国民警卫队直升机和"大力

---

① Lee Berthiaume, "Armed Arctic Vessels Face Delay in Latest Procurement Setback," Postmedia News, May 8, 2012, http://www.nunatsiaqonline.ca/stories/article/65674armed_arctic_vessels_face_delay_in_latest_procurement_setback/.

② Trude Pettersen, "Russia to Have Ten Arctic Rescue Centers by 2015," Barents Observer, November 18, 2011, http://barentsobserver.com/en/topics/russia-have-ten-arctic-rescue-centers-2015 (note: the article mistranslates "МЛН" as "billion" rather than "million").

③ Staff Sgt. Patricia McMurphy, "Fort Wainwright Receives New Chinook CH-47F Helicopters," US Army Alaska Public Affairs, July 23, 2012, http://www.usarak.army.mil/main/Stories_Archives/July-23-27-2012/120723_FS3.asp.

神"飞机。① 为应对沿北冰洋海岸线活动不断增加的情况，现在美国海岸警卫队在夏季的几个月里都会在巴罗部署两架直升机。②

丹麦军队为格陵兰周边提供搜索和救助服务，丹麦拥有可观的海军力量，正如海军少将亨里克·库德斯科克所说：

> 对于北极地区特定用途，我们共有7艘舰艇。其中有4艘护卫舰大小（3500吨）的舰艇，具备起降直升机和冰区航行能力。我们通常保持一艘永久驻扎格陵兰周边，另一艘永久驻扎法罗群岛周边。除了这四艘舰艇，我们还有两艘中等大小舰艇（略小于2000吨），一艘巡逻艇"图卢加克"号，该艇名字"图卢加克"在当地因纽特语中是"乌鸦"的意思。该艇有13名船员，具备冰区航行能力。受我们海军能力所限，这些军舰分散在各地。夏天，我们将其中两艘部署至遥远北方的一个固定站点，（在你们加拿大）西北航道的东部，雷索卢特湾东部，但是是在我们这一侧。在图勒地区北部，只要海冰条件允许，我们就会永久性部署一艘军舰。所以，只要海冰融化，就有一艘军舰部署在那儿。在格陵兰海岸东北部我国一侧也是这样的情况。③

挪威方面，其5艘护卫舰都可以起降直升机。④ 该国还在北极地区保持两架陆基搜索和救助直升机，一架在斯瓦尔巴，一架位于巴伦支海南部该国本土的班纳克。⑤ 挪威政府正在进行16架新型搜索和救助直

---

① Alaska National Guard website, http://www.akguard.com/.
② Johnson, "For Coast Guard Patrol North of Alaska," n. 116, above.
③ Jane Kokan, "Greenland: Canada's Arctic Neighbour." (January/February 2012) 9 (1) FrontLine Defence 23 at 24, http://www.frontline-canada.com/downloads/12-1_RAdmKudsk.pdf.
④ "Nansen Class Anti-Submarine Warfare Frigates, Norway," http://www.navaltechnology.com/projects/nansen/.
⑤ Anne Holm Gundersen, "Search and Rescue Cooperation in the Arctic-Experiences and Future Challenges," presentation to the 2012 Arctic Dialogue, Bodø, Norway, http://www.uin.no/Documents/Om% 20UiN/Fakulteter/HHB/Arctic% 20Dialogue/Presentations% 202012/Norwegian% 20research% 20and% 20rescue_Anne_Holm_Gundersen.pdf.

升机的采购程序,预计将于 2016 年开始交付。①

然而,北极是一片非常广袤的地区,一旦发生事故,据离最近的搜索和救助设施也有数千公里。幸运的是,为拯救处于危险之中的生命而进行快速和有效地反应,长期以来都是各国最容易达成共识的事项之一。"泰坦尼克"号的沉没加速了《国际海上人命安全公约》的谈判,并最终于 1914 年通过。正如第六章中提及的,1974 年通过的第五版《国际海上人命安全公约》规定了"默认接受程序",即除非在特定日期之前收到一定数量缔约方的反对,对该公约提出的修正案将生效。②《国际海上人命安全公约》从一开始就要求各方"确保在其海岸周边为海岸监视和营救海上遇险人员做出必要安排"。③

1944 年《国际民用航空公约》的《附件 12》也涉及搜索和救助。该附件于 1951 年通过并且此后不断进行更新。④ 第 2.1.2 条规定,缔约国被要求向事故的幸存者提供援助时不应考虑这些人员的国籍。第 2.1.1 条要求,缔约国"在其领土范围内安排建立并立即提供搜寻与援救服务"。第 2.1.1.1 条规定,在公海或"主权尚未确定的区域"的情况下,缔约方在"主权尚未确定的区域"中提供搜寻与救援服务的责任区,应根据区域航行协议进行划分。《附件 12》还要求相邻缔约国协调其搜寻和援救组织,并根据第 3.1.3 条规定,各缔约国"必须准许另一国搜寻与援救单位为搜寻航空器事故现场并援救事故幸存者之目的,立即进入其领土"。

1979 年《国际海上搜寻和救助公约》第 2.1.1 段要求缔约各方通

---

① "NO – Sola: Search and Rescue Helicopters, 2011/S 207 – 337613, Contract Notice," http://ted.europa.eu/udl? uri = TED: NOTICE: 337613 – 2011: TEXT: EN: HTML. Iceland is taking part in the Norwegian procurement and intends to purchase one helicopter with the option of acquiring two more.

② Lei Shi, "Successful Use of the Tacit Acceptance Procedure to Effectuate Progress in International Maritime Law." (1998 – 1999) 11 University of San Francisco Maritime Law Journal 299.

③ 1974 International Convention for the Safety of Life at Sea, chap. 5, Regulation 15, 1184 UNTS 278, http://www.austlii.edu.au/au/other/dfat/treaties/1983/22.html. The many amendments are listed at http://www.tc.gc.ca/eng/marinesafety/rsqa – imo – solas – 546.htm.

④ 1944 Convention on International Civil Aviation, Annex 12, 7th edn., 2001, http://www.scribd.com/doc/18191224/Anexo – 12 – Search – and – Rescue.

过单独或合作的方式"参与发展搜索和救助服务,以确保为海上遇险人员提供协助",并且第2.1.3段要求在政治上存在重叠的区域设立"充足"和"连续"的"搜救区域"。① 第2.1.7段同样明确:"搜救区域的划分不涉及并且不得损害国家之间边界的划分。"

1979年《国际海上搜寻和救助公约》通过要求和建议的方式强调合作的重要性。第3.1.1段要求各缔约方须协调其搜救组织并建议就具体搜救工作进行配合。第3.1.2段建议各缔约国"在其适用的国家法律、规章制度的约束下,如果其他缔约方的救助单位只是出于搜寻发生海难的地点和救助该海难中遇险人员的目的,应批准其立即进入或越过其领海或领土。"与此相关的是,第3.1.3段要求,缔约方的当局为了搜寻行动的目的,希望进入另一缔约方领土者,"须向该另一缔约方发出请求,详细说明所计划的任务及其必要性。"第3.1.4段要求,被申请一方"须立即告知已收到此项请求"并且"如对执行其计划任务有条件,须尽快说明"。简而言之,除非涉及进入领土等相关问题,缔约方必须提供合作,因为各方保留以任何理由拒绝对方进入其领土的主权权利。

1982年《联合国海洋法公约》对这些早期条约进行了强化,规定"每个沿海国应促进有关海上和上空安全的足敷应用和有效的搜寻和救助服务的建立、经营和维持,并应在情况需要时为此目的通过相互的区域性安排与邻国开展合作。"②

包括苏联和美国在内的许多国家就是这么做的。1988年,这两个冷战时期的对手签署了一项关于海上搜索和救助的双边条约,尽管如人们所预期的那样,这项协议影响不大。③ 它借助两国边界确定了各自的搜索和救助区域,第3.1条要求双方"酌情合作和协调两国行动"。然而,该协议第3.2条还规定:"在任何一方的领海、内水和陆地之内实

---

① 1979 International Convention on Maritime Search and Rescue, 1405 UNTS 119, as amended in 1998 and 2004, http://cil. nus. edu. sg/rp/il/pdf/1979%20International%20Convention%20on%20Maritime%20Search%20and%20Rescue – pdf.

② UNCLOS, Art. 98(2) Introduction, n. 15, above.

③ 1988 Agreement between the Government of the United States of America and the Government of the Union of Soviet Socialist Republics on Maritime Search and Rescue, 2191 UNTS 115, http://treaties. un. org/doc/Publication/UNTS/Volume%202191/v2191. pdf.

施搜索和救助行动应由该方救援单位进行"。

  美国和加拿大早在 1949 年就达成一项照会交换,允许任何参与合作搜索和救助的飞机绕过正常入境程序。① 1999 年,美国、加拿大和英国就空中和海上的搜索和救助达成三方谅解备忘录,使得人员和装备可以在未经通知的情况下,从一国进入或飞跃另一国领土,只要他们参与紧急救援并"在可能情况下尽快"提供入境通知。②

  2003 年,俄罗斯和北约签署一项潜艇救援协议。③ 该协议是为应对三年前俄罗斯攻击型核潜艇"库尔斯克"号失事之类的事件而制定,协议明确规定北约和俄罗斯将致力于制定共同的搜索和救助程序、协调装备开发、交换相关信息,甚至开展联合演习。俄罗斯参与了北约 2005 年和 2008 年举行的搜索和救助演习,④ 并于 2009 年主办自己的国际演习,参与方有芬兰、挪威和瑞典。⑤ 2005 年,一艘英国潜艇被用于解救 7 名俄罗斯水手,他们搭乘的小型潜艇被困在勘察加半岛附近太平洋海面之下 190 米的渔网中。⑥

  2008 年,由挪威、瑞典、芬兰和俄罗斯组成的"巴伦支海欧洲—北极区域"成员国签署《应急预防、准备和响应领域的政府间协议》。⑦

---

① 1949 Exchange of Notes between Canada and the United States of America Constituting an Agreement Relating to Air Search and Rescue Operations along the Common Boundary of the Two Countries, Canada Treaty Series 1949/2, http://www.lexum.com/ca_us/en/cts.1949.02.en.html.

② US Department of Homeland Security and Public Safety Canada, "Compendium of US-Canada Emergency Management Assistance Mechanisms," June 2012, p.9, http://www.dhs.gov/xlibrary/assets/policy/btb-compendium-of-United-States-Canada-emergency-management-assistance-mechanisms.pdf.

③ "NATO and Russia Sign Submarine Rescue Agreement," NATO Update, February 8, 2003, http://www.nato.int/docu/update/2003/02-february/e0208a.htm.

④ "NRC Practical Cooperation Factsheet," http://www.nato-russia-council.info/HTM/EN/news_41.shtm.

⑤ "Barents Rescue - 2009," August 26, 2009, http://barentsobserver.com/en/murmanskobl/barents-rescue-2009.

⑥ "Russians Saved in Deep-Sea Rescue," BBC News, August 7, 2005, http://news.bbc.co.uk/1/hi/world/europe/4128614.stm.

⑦ "Agreement between the Governments in the Barents Euro-Arctic Region on Cooperation within the Field of Emergency Prevention, Preparedness and Response," December 11, 2008, http://www.barentsinfo.fi/beac/docs/Agreement_Emergency_Prevention_Preparedness_and_Response_English.pdf.

该条约规定了当一国向另一国要求获得此项协助时,一些促进搜索和救助设备及人员跨界部署的条款。

作为这一国际立法的结果,当北极理事会于2009年4月批准"设立工作小组,以在2011年下一届部长会议之前,商讨和完成有关北极搜索和救助合作相关国际文件"之时,相关基础工作都已经准备就绪。[1] 该工作小组由美国和俄罗斯共同主持。

2011年5月,北极理事会部长级会议签署《北极海空搜救合作协定》。[2] 其被称为一个重要进展,但正如该协定序言中指出的,所有北极国家均已是1944年《芝加哥公约》和1979年《国际海上搜寻和救助公约》缔约方。第七条第1款接着指出,这两项公约"应作为根据协定实施搜寻与救助行动的基础",而且《北极海空搜救合作协定》各项规定也与两项公约具有密切联系。

《北极海空搜救合作协定》为8个北极国家划设了空中和海上搜救区(第一条和附件第一段),表明在其地理责任区域之内,"各方应推动建立、运行和维持适当和有效的搜救能力"(第三条第3款)。[3] 该协定规定,当一方要求另一方提供搜救协助之时,后一方"应立即决定并通知请求方是否有能力提供所请求的协助,并立即表明可提供协助的范围和条件。"(第七条第3款e项)但是,当一方为搜救目的请求进入另一方领土之时,包括补充燃料,被请求方并非必须给予许可;相反,

---

[1] Tromso Declaration, April 29, 2009, Section on "Arctic Marine Environment," http://arctic-council.org/filearchive/Tromsoe%20Declaration-1.pdf.

[2] Agreement on Cooperation on Aeronautical and Maritime Search and Rescue in the Arctic, May 12, 2011, http://www.arctic-council.org/index.php/en/about/documents/category/20-main-documents-from-nuuk.

[3] Like the 1979 SAR Convention, Art. 3 (2) of the Arctic SAR Convention states: "The delimitation of search and rescue regions is not related to and shall not prejudice the delimitation of any boundary between States or their sovereignty, sovereign rights or jurisdiction." It does so for a reason, namely, that the lines do not necessarily track agreed boundaries. For instance, in the Beaufort Sea the 141W meridian is used to divide the Canadian and American SSRs all the way to the North Pole, notwithstanding the on-going dispute between the two countries as to the location of the maritime boundary, while the remote and nearly unpopulated Norwegian island of Jan Mayen is placed entirely within the Icelandic SRR. For a visual depiction of the SRRs, (2011) Arctic Search and Rescue Delimitation Map, http://library.arcticportal.org/1500/.

其"应当尽快通知是否允许进入其领土,以及若有条件,则该任务应在何种条件下进行。"(第八条第 1 款和第 2 款)

此外,1944 年《芝加哥公约》和 1979 年《国际海上搜寻和救助公约》中相关条款已经为北极国家设立了需要遵守的特定法律义务,《北极搜救协定》对此没有做出新的规定。该协定也没有创设任何"新的行动或资源要求",例如设备配备或人员预期反应时间等。[1] 该协定增加的新内容是鼓励但并不要求缔约国采取的其他合作步骤,包括分享信息服务和程序、技术、设备和设施,联合研究和开发倡议,专家互访以及联合搜救演习。所有这些都很重要,尤其因为参与这些互动的很多人都是军方人员。所以,根据《北极搜救协定》开展的交流与合作可以建立信任并缓解各个北极国家军队之间的紧张关系,包括北约和俄罗斯之间。

2011 年 10 月,《北极搜救协定》通过后仅 5 个月,就举行了第一次联合演习。由加拿大军方主办的这次会议,在育空的怀特霍斯一家酒店举行,来自所有北极理事会成员国的代表均出席,会议重点是搜寻与救助等操作层面。[2] 随后,2012 年 4 月,8 个北极国家军方高层领导人在拉布拉多的古斯贝会面,讨论搜救、救灾和态势感知等方面合作,[3] 将军们同意每年举行会面。[4]

同样重要的是,《北极搜救协定》是北极理事会框架下谈判达成的第一份具有法律约束力的文件。从纯实用主义和短期角度而言,北极理事会各国部长只要简单地宣布保持对 1944 年《芝加哥公约》和 1979 年《国际海上搜寻和救助公约》的承诺即已足够。但是各成员国显然寻求采取更多行动,即为北极的外交合作势头再加一把力,特别是将北

---

[1] Canada Command, "Search and Rescue (SAR) Overview, Arctic Caucus Meeting, 17 – 19 August 2011," http://www.pnwer.org/Portals/18/Arctic% 20Caucus% 20SAR% 20Overview% 20Presentation.pdf.

[2] "Whitehorse Table – Top Exercise Brings Arctic SAR Experts Together," Nunatsiaq News, October 10, 2011, http://www.nunatsiaqonline.ca/stories/article/65674whitehorse_table – top_exercise_brings_arctic_sar_experts_together/.

[3] Reuters, "Arctic Generals Agree on Closer Ties," April 13, 2012, http://www.thestar.com/news/canada/politics/article/1161369 – arctic – generals – agree – on – closer – ties.

[4] Ibid.

极理事会发展成为可以进行国际立法的区域组织。在这方面更为重要的是,各成员国在通过《北极搜救协定》的同时,同意为北极理事会设立常设秘书处。① 从这些行动中可以看出,北极国家作为该地区主要决策者的地位正在加强。

六、小结

虽然北冰洋位于冷战的前沿,但是该地区现正逐渐转变为国家间合作的新区域,包括安全问题合作。俄罗斯现在是世界贸易组织成员,其最大的贸易伙伴是主要由北约成员国组成的欧盟。随着海冰融化,所有北极国家都已采取措施强化在北极的军事实力,但仍坚定地将重点放在应对诸如毒品走私和非法移民等非国家行为体威胁上。新的形势促使北极理事会八个成员国就"北极搜索与救援协议"进行谈判,其他不少倡议现在也似乎具备了实现的可能,包括一项保持北冰洋中部海面和海冰非军事化的条约。同样,加拿大和美国对非国家行为体安全威胁的担忧,有可能为两国就西北航道地位进行的谈判提供动力。

---

① Nuuk Declaration, 7th Ministerial Meeting of the Arctic Council, May 12, 2011, http://arctic-council.org/filearchive/nuuk_declaration_2011_signed_copy-1.pdf.

结 论

在莫斯科俄罗斯外交部那栋斯大林时代的摩天大楼内，一幅由加拿大自然资源部绘制的地图悬挂在俄罗斯北极大使安东·瓦西里耶夫的办公室最醒目的位置。墙上装饰物的选择反映了当代北极的几个关键方面。

首先，尽管俄罗斯和加拿大的全球影响力正在减弱，但这两个世界上面积最大的国家在北极地区仍保持主导地位。尽管美国作为北极大国有些勉强，但仍然是全球超级大国，故而也坐拥这种影响力。其次，对自然资源需求的不断增长和气候变化，推动北极成为国际外交的主流。瓦西里耶夫是俄罗斯最有能力的外交官之一，能说一口流利的英语。或许同样重要的是，他还会说普通话，在中国拥有相当丰富的经验。中国是一个正在崛起的超级大国，也是俄罗斯巨大北极财富最有希望的市场。北极已经进入国际主流外交，主要迹象包括美国国务卿出席北极理事会会议，世界最大和第三大经济体欧盟和中国申请成为正式观察员国等。

北极快速的重新定位让许多记者措手不及，他们还没有准备好，装备也跟不上，来不及对当前形势作出解释和分析。这样一来，有关北极的报道过分强调那些遥不可及的国家间冲突可能一触即发，而对于现实存在的合作潮流重视得远远不够。这种不平衡的作法进一步误导了新闻报道的受众，包括一般公众和至少部分政治人物。然而，正如本书所展示的，北极区域存在着相当大的合作潜力。其中一些合作表现为国际法的发展，越来越多专门针对北极地区的国际法规开始出现，这些规则正帮助各国避免和化解原本可能十分棘手的争端。

北极区域的大多数合作都建立在对土地、毗邻水域和大陆架资源等权利进行明确划分的基础上。这些权利是全球国际法律体系的核心组成部分，这一体系经过数个世纪的争论和协调才得以建立起来，各国据此明确了如何划定各自管辖范围的界限，并朝着共同目标而开展合作。这一成熟的过程体现在这样一个事实上，即面积狭小的汉斯岛是整个北极圈内唯一有争议的陆地领土。

在世界各地，20世纪沿海国权利对外延伸为冲突埋下了隐患，但这一隐患很快就被消除了，因为各国拒绝通过征服的方式获得海洋权利，而是转由建立海上边界划分规则。这种合法化程序的完善可以通过一个事实加以证明，即北极区域唯一遗留的海上边界争端位于加拿大和阿拉斯加以北的波弗特海。在北冰洋中部，石油、天然气和其他资源存在于距离海岸200海里之外的外大陆架，沿岸国权利重叠的争端理论上在这里仍有可能发生，但是所有五个沿岸国均表示将依据现有法律规则和科学数据确定其管辖范围的延伸。北极各国政府清楚地认识到明确各自疆界的价值，在此范围内各国可以开展自然资源开采许可颁发、环境保护、冰情预报和搜救等必要服务。

从某种程度上讲，这种合作的动力即使在冷战时期也不曾消失。1973年《保护北极熊协议》是多边环境保护的第一步，而北极熊在北极国家文化中的标志性地位使这一努力成为可能。更重要的是，随后召开的联合国海洋法会议为苏联和美国在超级大国对抗最为紧张的时期，提供了一次合作机会。在一个由加拿大人担任主席的起草委员会努力下，双方代表团商讨了1982年《联合国海洋法公约》中对北极地区具有直接影响的条款。这其中就包括涉及冰封水域的污染防治的第二百三十四条，即所谓"北极例外"，以及关于外大陆架的第七十六条。

通过为建构跨境和超越国家管辖范围以外的合作提供某种机制，国际法在大片、偏远、荒凉和人口稀少的区域尤其有效。为此，北极国家已经开始进行一些最初不具有约束力的"软法"性质的立法举措，例如创设北极理事会的《渥太华宣言》以及国际海事组织颁布的《北极航行准则》。如今，北极立法正朝着"硬法"条约方向发展，比如《关于持久性有机污染物的斯德哥尔摩公约》和《北极海空搜救合作协定》。后面这一文件特别有趣，因为其未对现有的非北极特别条约中规定的义务做任何增补。《北极海空搜救合作协定》仅是为北极各国政府，特别是北极区域内的军队，建立了新的会面空间，而不是增加新的法律。在这个空间中可能会形成具有共同认识、利益和认同的共同体。《渥太华宣言》中至今阻止北极理事会处理"军事安全"问题的脚注已经过时，《北极海空搜救合作协定》可以为冷战期间分裂的两方阵营就走私和非法移民等北极安全议题开展合作提供新的渠道。

北极土著民族组成跨越国家边界和民族分别的跨国群体，开始在区域外交和国际立法中发挥越来越重要的作用。传统上，土著民族缺乏"法律人格"，对国际关系影响甚微，然而，北极土著民族被吸纳为北极理事会永久参与方，成功阻止北冰洋沿岸国会议（即"北极五国"）将土著民族排除在外的作法。在21世纪，土著民族在国际法中将享有多种权利，包括有权参与涉及他们所居住地区的决策。

对于从冷战对峙到北极合作的转变，很难用主导20世纪国际法和国际关系原则的实证主义和现实主义理论观点进行解释。建构主义的观点现在似乎提供了更多的解释工具，尽管还不能解释全部问题。在安全语境中，本地区仍然存在大规模核武库，美国继续独断专行，将北方海航线和西北航道的法律性质界定为"国际海峡"，由此可见权力政治的重要因素在北极依旧存在。

可以说，现实主义和非现实主义的解释并行不悖，反映了某种不断演变的地缘政治形势。随着冷战结束，国际贸易和投资大幅强化，外交官、政治家，以及企业家、原住民和民间社会领导人在北极理事会等机制中互动频繁，逐步形成共同利益和认同。随着时间的推移，这或将建立起某种信任，北极地区非军事化趋势不断加强。在这方面，随着非北极国家在本地区利益不断增长，北极国家共同拥有的北方敏感性将会有所帮助，因为外部挑战能够引发群体成员之间更大的共同体意识。

有关北极政治更为详尽的理论分析，还有待另一本书，但是我们可以假设，即使在安全担忧和现实思想占主导的区域，也容易受到"跛足合作"的影响：在一个受制度化和法制化驱动的过程中，发展信任和共同解决问题的优势愈发明显。从这个意义上讲，北极以其安全、环境和土著政治的独特结合，将成为21世纪国际关系专业学者的最佳演练场。

参考文献

Abele, Frances and Thierry Rodon, "Inuit Diplomacy in the Global Era: The Strengths of Multilateral Internationalism." (2007) 13 (3) Canadian Foreign Policy 45.

Adams, Marie, Kathryn J. Frostz and Lois A. Harwood, "Alaska and Inuvialuit Beluga Whale Committee (AIBWC) -An Initiative in At Home Management." (1993) 46 Arctic 134.

Amstrup, Steven C., et al., "Forecasting the Range - Wide Status of Polar Bears at Selected Times in the 21st Century," US Geological Survey Administrative Report, 2007, http: //www. usgs. gov/newsroom/special/polar_bears/docs/USGS_PolarBear_Amstrup_Forecast_lowres. pdf.

Anaya, S. James, Indigenous Peoples in International Law, 2nd edn. (Oxford University Press, 2004). "Indigenous Peoples' Participatory Rights in Relation to Decisions about Natural Resource Extraction: The More Fundamental Issue of What Rights Indigenous Peoples Have in Lands and Resources." (2005) 22 Arizona Journal of International and Comparative Law 7. "The Situation of the Sami People in the Sa'pmi Region of Norway, Sweden and Finland." June 6, 2011, UN Doc. A/HRC/18/35/Add. 2, http: //unsr. jamesanaya. org/country - reports/the - situation - of - the - sami - people - in - thesapmi - region - of - norway - sweden - and - finland - 2011.

Anderson, David H., "The Status under International Law of the Maritime Areas around Svalbard." (2009) 40 (4) Ocean Development and International Law 373.

Antinori, Camille M., "The Bering Sea: A Maritime Delimitation

Dispute Between the United States and the Soviet Union." (1987) 18 Ocean Development and International Law 1.

Archer, Clive, "Plans for a Nordic Nuclear - Weapon - FreeZone." (2004) 34 Kosmopolis 201 (supplement), https: //helda. helsinki. fi/bitstream/handle/10224/3635/archer201 - 207. pdf.

Ballantyne, Joe, Sovereignty and Development in the Arctic: Selected Exploration Programs in the 1980s (Whitehorse: self - published, 2009).

Barelli, Mauro, "The Role of Soft Law in the International Legal System: The Case of the United Nations Declaration on the Rights of Indigenous Peoples." (2009) 58 International and Comparative Law Quarterly 957.

Barsh, Russel, "Demilitarizing the Arctic as an Exercise of Indigenous SelfDetermination." (1986) 55 Nordic Journal of International Law 208.

Bateman, Sam and Clive Schofield, "State Practice Regarding Straight Baselines in East Asia-Legal, Technical and Political Issues in a Changing Environment." Paper prepared for a conference at the International Hydrographic Bureau, Monaco, October 16 - 17, 2008, http: //www. gmat. unsw. edu. au/ablos/ABLOS08Folder/Session7 - Paper1 - Bateman. pdf.

Bateman, Sam and Michael White, "Compulsory Pilotage in the Torres Strait: Overcoming Unacceptable Risks to a Sensitive Marine Environment." (2009) 40 Ocean Development and International Law 184. Baxter, Richard R., The Law of International Waterways (Cambridge, Mass.: Harvard University Press, 1964).

Beckman, Robert C., "PSSAs and Transit Passage-Australia's Pilotage System in the Torres Strait Challenges the IMO and UNCLOS." (2007) 38 Ocean Development and International Law 325.

Berton, Pierre, The Arctic Grail: The Quest for the Northwest Passageand the North Pole, 1818 - 1909 (Toronto: McClelland and Stewart, 1988).

Bloom, Evan T., "Establishment of the Arctic Council." (1999) 93 American Journal of International Law 712.

Borgerson, Scott G. , "Arctic Meltdown: The Economic and Security Implications of Climate Change. " (2008) 87 (2) Foreign Affairs 63.

Bourne, Charles B. and Donald M. McRae, "Maritime Jurisdiction in the Dixon Entrance: The Alaska Boundary Re - examined. " (1976) 14 Canadian Yearbook of International Law 183.

Boyd, Susan B. , "The LegalStatus of the Arctic Sea Ice: A Comparative Study and a Proposal. " (1984) 22 Canadian Yearbook of International Law 98.

Broderstad, Else Grete, "Political Autonomy and Integration of Authority: The Understanding of Saami Self - Determination. " (2001) 8 International Journal on Minority and Group Rights 151.

Brubaker, R. Douglas, Russian Arctic Straits (Dordrecht: Martinus Nijhoff, 2004).

Brunnée, Jutta and Stephen Toope, Legitimacy and Legality in International Law (Cambridge University Press, 2010).

Byers, Michael, Custom, Power and the Power of Rules (Cambridge University Press, 1999). "Policing the High Seas: The Proliferation Security Initiative. " (2004) 98 American Journal of International Law 526. Who Owns the Arctic? Understanding Sovereignty Disputes in the North (Vancouver, BC and Berkeley, Calif. : Douglas & McIntyre, 2009).

Caminos, Hugo, "The Legal Régime of Straits in the 1982 United Nations Convention on the Law of the Sea. " (1987) 205 Recueil des cours 128.

Careaga, Luis, "Un condominium franco - espagnol: L'île des faisans ou de la conférence," thesis, Faculté de droit et des sciences politiques, University of Strasbourg, 1932.

Carnaghan, Matthew and Allison Goody, "Canadian Arctic Sovereignty. " (January 26, 2006), Parliamentary Information and Research Service (PRB05 - 61E), Library of Parliament, http: //www. parl. gc. ca/Content/LOP/researchpublications/prb0561 - e. htm.

Castellino, Joshua and Niamh Walsh (eds.), International Law and Indigenous Peoples (Dordrecht: Martinus Nijhoff, 2004).

Charney, Jonathan I., "Rocks that Cannot Sustain Human Habitation." (1999) 93 American Journal of International Law 863.

Charney, Jonathan I. and Lewis Alexander (eds.), International Maritime Boundaries, Vol. 1 (Dordrecht: American Society of International Law/ Martinus Nijhoff, 1993).

Chen, Zhuoheng, et al., "Petroleum Potential in Western Sverdrup Basin, Canadian Arctic Archipelago." (December 2000) 48 (4) Bulletin of Canadian Petroleum Geology 323.

Chinkin, Christine, "The Challenge of Soft Law: Development and Change in International Law." (1989) 38 International and Comparative Law Quarterly 850.

Churchill, Robin and Vaughan Lowe, The Law of the Sea, 3rd edn. (Manchester University Press, 1999).

Churchill, Robin and Geir Ulfstein, Marine Management inDisputed Areas: The Case of the Barents Sea (London: Routledge, 1992).

Colson, David, "The Delimitation of the Outer Continental Shelf between Neighboring States." (2003) 97 American Journal of International Law 91.

Cone, Marla, Silent Snow: The Slow Poisoning of the Arctic (New York: Grove Press, 2005).

Crawford, James, The Creation of States in International Law, 2nd edn. (Oxford University Press, 2006).

D'Amato, Anthony, The Concept of Custom in International Law (Ithaca, NY: Cornell University Press, 1971).

Davidson, Art, In the Wake of the Exxon Valdez (San Francisco, Calif.: Sierra Club Books, 1990).

Downie, David and Terry Fenge, Northern Lights Against POPs: Combating Toxic Threats in the Arctic (Montreal and Kingston: McGill-Queen's University Press, 2003).

Duffy, Helen, The "War on Terror" and the Framework of International Law (Cambridge University Press, 2005).

Elliot - Meisel, Elizabeth B., Arctic Diplomacy: Canada and the United States in the Northwest Passage (New York: Peter Lang, 1998).

Emmerson, Charles, The Future History of the Arctic (New York: Public Affairs, 2010).

Emmerson, Charles and Glada Lahn, Arctic Opening: Opportunity and Risk in the High North (London: Lloyd's, 2012), http: //www. chathamhouse. org/publications/papers/view/182839.

Engle, Karen, "On Fragile Architecture: The UN Declaration on the Rights of Indigenous Peoples in the Context of Human Rights. " (2011) 22 European Journal of International Law 141.

Feldman, Mark B., and David Colson, "The Maritime Boundaries of the United States. " (1981) 75 American Journal of International Law 729.

Fenge, Terry, "Inuit and the Nunavut Land Claims Agreement: Supporting Canada's Arctic Sovereignty. " (December 2007 - January 2008) 29 (1) Policy Options 84.

Ferguson, Steven H., J. W. Higdon and E. G. Chmelnitsky, " The Rise of the Killer Whales as a Major Arctic Predator," in Steven H. Ferguson, et al., A Little Less Arctic: Top Predators in the World's Largest Northern Inland Sea, Hudson Bay (Dordrecht: Springer, 2010).

Finlay, Brian D., "Russian Roulette: Canada's Role in the Race to Secure Loose Nuclear, Biological, and Chemical Weapons. " (2006) 61 International Journal 411.

Fitzmaurice, Gerald, The Law and Procedure of the International Court of Justice, Vol. 1 (Cambridge University Press, 1995).

Fox, Hazel, Paul McDade, Derek Rankin Reid, Anastasia Strati and Peter Huey, Joint Development of Offshore Oil and Gas: A Model Agreement for States for Joint Development with Explanatory Commentary (London: British Institute of International and Comparative Law, 1989).

Franckx, Erik, Maritime Claims in the Arctic: Canadian and Russian Perspectives (Dordrecht: Martinus Nijhoff, 1993). "The Legal Regime of Navigation in the Russian Arctic." (2009) 18 Journal of Transnational Law and Policy 327.

Frid, Chris, et al., "Ecosystem - Based Fisheries Management: Progress in the NE Atlantic." (2005) 29 Marine Policy 461.

Gautier, Donald L., et al., "Assessment of Undiscovered Oil and Gas in the Arctic." (May 2009) 324 (5931) Science 1175.

Gay, James Thomas, American Fur Seal Diplomacy: The Alaskan Fur Seal Controversy (New York: Peter Lang, 1987).

Gedney, Larry and Merritt Helfferich, "Voyage of the Manhattan," December 19, 1983, Alaska Science Forum Article No. 639, http://web.archive.org/web/20120429124511/

Geopolicity, "The Economics of Piracy." May 2011, http://www.geopolicity.com/upload/content/pub_1305229189_regular.pdf.

George, Mary, "The Regulation of Maritime Traffic in Straits Used for International Navigation," in Alex G. Oude Elferink and Donald R. Rothwell (eds.), Oceans Management in the 21st Century: Institutional Frameworks and Responses (Leiden: Martin Nijhoff, 2004).

Goldblat, Jozef, "The Seabed Treaty and Arms Control," in Richard Fieldhouse (ed.), Security at Sea: Naval Forces and Arms Control (Oxford University Press and Stockholm International Peace Research Institute, 1990).

Goldie, L. F. E., "The Critical Date." (1963) 12 International and Comparative Law Quarterly 1251.

Golitsyn, Vladimir, "The Arctic-On the Way to Regional Cooperation." (1989) 1 Marine Policy Report 91.

Gordon, Jessica, "Inter - American Commission on Human Rights to Hold Hearing After Rejecting Inuit Climate Change Petition." (2007) 7 Sustainable Development Law and Policy 55.

Grant, Shelagh D. , "A Case of Compounded Error: The Inuit Resettlement Project, 1953, and the Government Response, 1990. " (1991) 19 (1) Northern Perspectives (Canadian Arctic Resources Committee) 3.

Gray, David H. , "Canada's Unresolved Maritime Boundaries. " (1997) 5 (3) IBRU Boundary and Security Bulletin 61, http: //www. dur. ac. uk/resources/ibru/publications/full/bsb5 - 3_gray. pdf.

Griffiths, Franklyn, "A Northern Foreign Policy. " (1979) 7 Wellesley Papers (Toronto: Canadian Institute of International Affairs), 61. (ed.), Politics of the Northwest Passage (Kingston and Montreal: McGill-Queen's University Press, 1987). "Arctic Security: The Indirect Approach," in James Kraska (ed.), Arctic Security in an Age of Climate Change (New York: Cambridge University Press, 2011).

Grunawalt, Richard J. , "United States Policy on International Straits. " (1987) 18 Ocean Development and International Law 445.

Guo, Peiqing, "Making Preparations against an Arctic Monroe Doctrine. " (2011) 42 Liaowang 71 - 72.

Haas, Peter M. , Saving the Mediterranean: The Politics of International Environmental Cooperation (New York: Columbia University Press, 1990).

Haftendorn, Helga, "NATO and the Arctic: Is the Atlantic Alliance a Cold War Relic in a Peaceful Region Now Faced with Non - Military Challenges?" (2011) 20 European Security 337.

Hansen, James and Larissa Nazarenko, "Soot Climate Forcing Via Snow and Ice Albedos. " (2004) 101 (2) Proceedings of the National Academy of Sciences 423, http: //www. pnas. org/content/101/2/423. full. pdf + html.

Harders, J. Enno, "In Quest of an Arctic Legal Regime: MarineRegionalism-A Concept of International Law Evaluated. " (1987) 11 Marine Policy 285.

Hass, Peter M., Saving the Mediterranean: The Politics of International Environmental Cooperation (New York: Columbia University Press, 1990).

Head, Ivan L., "CanadianClaims to Territorial Sovereignty in the Arctic Regions." (1963) 9 McGill Law Journal 200.

Henriksen, Tore and Geir Ulfstein, "Maritime Delimitation in the Arctic: The Barents Sea Treaty." (2011) 42 Ocean Development and International Law 1.

Holtsmark, Sven G., "Towards Cooperation or Confrontation? Security in the High North." Research Paper No. 45, NATO Defense College, February 2009, http: //www. ndc. nato. int/research/series. php? icode = 1.

Hossain, Kamrul, "The EU Ban on the Import of Seal Products and the WTO Regulations: Neglected Human Rights of the Arctic Indigenous Peoples?" (2013) 49 Polar Record 154.

Howse, Robert and Joanna Langille, "Permitting Pluralism: The Seal Products Dispute and Why the WTO Should Accept Trade Restrictions Justified by Noninstrumental Moral Values." (2012) 37 Yale Journal of International Law 367, http: //www. yjil. org/docs/pub/37 - 2 - howse - langille - permittingpluralism. pdf.

Huebert, Rob, "Steel, Ice and Decision - Making: The Voyage of the Polar Sea and its Aftermath," Ph. D. thesis, Dalhousie University, 1994. "New Directions in Circumpolar Cooperation: Canada, the Arctic Environmental Protection Strategy and the Arctic Council." (1998) 5 Canadian Foreign Policy 37. "The Newly Emerging Arctic Security Environment," Canadian Defence and Foreign Affairs Institute, March 2010, http: //www. cdfai. org/PDF/The% 20Newly% 20Emerging% 20Arctic% 20Security%20Environment. pdf.

Huebert, Rob and Brooks Yeager, "A New Sea: The Need for a Regional Agreement on Management and Conservation of the Arctic Marine Environment." (World Wildlife Fund, 2008), http: //awsassets. panda. org/

downloads/a_new_sea_jan08_final_11jan08.pdf.

Huebert, Rob, et al. , "Climate Change and International Security: The Arctic as a Bellwether. " 2012, Center for Climate and Energy Solutions, http: //www. c2es. org/publications/climate - change - international - arctic - security/.

Jakobson, Linda, "China Prepares for an Ice - Free Arctic. " SIPRI Insights on Peace and Security, No. 2010/2, March 2010, http: // books. sipri. org/files/insight/SIPRIInsight1002. pdf.

Jakobson, Linda and Jingchao Peng, "China's Arctic Ambitions. " SIPRI Policy Paper 34, November 2012, http: //books. sipri. org/product_info? c_product_id = 449.

Jennings, Robert and Arthur Watts, Oppenheim's International Law, 9th edn. (London: Longman, 1992).

Johansen, Bruce E. , "The Inuit's Struggle with Dioxins and Other Organic Pollutants. " (2002) 26 American Indian Law Quarterly 479.

Joyner, Christopher, "The United States and the New Law of the Sea. " (1996) 27 Ocean Development and International Law 41.

Kaczynski, Vlad M. , "US-Russian Bering Sea Marine Border Dispute: Conflict over Strategic Assets, Fisheries and Energy Resources. " (May 2007) 20 Russian Analytical Digest 2.

Kaye, Stuart, "Regulation of Navigation in the Torres Strait: Law of the Sea Issues," in Donald R. Rothwell and Sam Bateman (eds.), Navigation Rights and Freedoms and the New Law of the Sea (Dordrecht: Kluwer, 2000).

Keating, Bern, The Northwest Passage: From the Mathew to the Manhattan, 1497 - 1969 (Chicago: Rand McNally and Company, 1970).
Kenney, Gerard, Arctic Smoke and Mirrors (Prescott, Ont. : Voyageur Publishing, 1994).

Keyuan, Zou, "The Sino-Vietnamese Agreement on Maritime Boundary Delimitation in the Gulf of Tonkin. " (2005) 36 Ocean Development and

International Law 13.

Kirkey, Christopher, "Smoothing Troubled Waters: The 1988 Canada-United States Arctic Co - operation Agreement." (1994 - 1995) 50 International Journal.

"Delineating Maritime Boundaries: The 1977 - 1978 Canada-US Beaufort Sea Continental Shelf Delimitation Boundary Negotiations." (1995) 25 Canadian Review of American Studies 49.

Klein, Natalie, Dispute Settlement in the UN Convention on the Law of the Sea (Cambridge University Press, 2004).

Kohen, Marcelo, Possession conteste'e et souverainete' territorial (Paris: Presses universitaires de France, 1997).

Koivurova, Timo, "Alternatives for an Arctic Treaty - Evaluation and a New Proposal." (2008) 17 Review of European Community and International Environmental Law 14, http: //onlinelibrary. wiley. com/doi/10. 1111/j. 1467 - 9388. 2008. 00580. x/full.

Koivurova, Timo and Leena Heina̋ma̋ki, "The Participation of Indigenous Peoples in International Norm - Making in the Arctic." (2006) 42 Polar Record 101.

Kokan, Jane, "Greenland: Canada's Arctic Neighbour." (January/February 2012) 9 (1) FrontLine Defence 23, http: //www. frontline - canada. com/downloads/12 - 1_RAdmKudsk. pdf.

Kovalev, Aleksandr Antonovich, Contemporary Issues of the Law of the Sea: Modern Russian Approaches (trans. W. E. Butler) (Utrecht: Eleven International Publishing, 2004).

Kraska, James C., "The Law of the Sea Convention and the Northwest Passage." (2007) 22 International Journal of Marine and Coastal Law 257. (ed.), Arctic Security in an Age of Climate Change (New York: Cambridge University Press, 2011).

Kunoy, Bjørn, "Disputed Areas and the 10 - Year Time Frame: A Legal Lacuna?" (2010) 41 Ocean Development and International Law 112.

"The Terms of Reference of the Commission on the Limits of the Continental Shelf: A Creeping Legal Mandate. " (2012) 25 Leiden Journal of International Law 109.

Lalonde, Suzanne and Fre′de′ric Lasserre, "The Position of the United States on the Northwest Passage: Is the Fear of Creating a Precedent Warranted?" (2012) 43 Ocean Development and International Law 28.

Lathrop, Coalter, "Continental Shelf Delimitation Beyond 200 Nautical Miles: Approaches Taken by Coastal States Before the Commission on the Limits of the Continental Shelf," in David A. Colson and Robert W. Smith (eds.), International Maritime Boundaries (Leiden: American Society of International Law/Martinus Nijhoff, 2011), 4139.

Lawson, Karin L., "Delimiting Continental Shelf Boundaries in the Arctic: The United States-Canada Beaufort Sea Boundary. " (1981) 22 Virginia Journal of International Law 221.

Leitzell, Katherine, "When Will the Arctic Lose its Sea Ice?" National Snow and Ice Data Center, May 3, 2011, http://nsidc.org/icelights/2011/05/03/when-will-the-arctic-lose-its-sea-ice/.

Lester, Simon, "The WTO Seal Products Dispute: A Preview of the Key Legal Issues. " 14 (2) ASIL Insight, January 13, 2010, http://www.asil.org/insights100113.cfm.

Lilje-Jensen, Jorgen and Milan Thamborg, "The Role of Natural Prolongation in Relation to Shelf Delimitation Beyond 200 Nautical Miles. " (1995) 64 Nordic Journal of International Law 619.

Lindahl, Ingemar, The Soviet Union and the Nordic Nuclear-Weapons-Free-Zone Proposal (London: Macmillan, 1988).

Lindegren, Martin, et al., "Preventing the Collapse of the Baltic Cod Stock through an Ecosystem-Based Management Approach. " (2009) 106 Proceedings of the National Academy of Science of the United States of America 14722.

Loukacheva, Natalia, The Arctic Promise: Legal and Political Autonomy of Greenland and Nunavut (University of Toronto Press, 2007).

Luan, Xinjie and Julien Chaisse, "Preliminary Comments on the WTO Seals Products Dispute: Traditional Hunting, Public Morals and Technical Barriers to Trade." (2011) 22 Colorado Journal of International Environmental Law and Policy 79.

McDorman, Ted L., "The Role of the Commission on the Limits of the Continental Shelf: A Technical Body in a Political World." (2002) 17 International Journal of Marine and Coastal Law 301. "The Continental Shelf beyond 200 nm: Law and Politics in the Arctic Ocean." (2009) 18 Journal of Transnational Law and Policy 155.

Salt Water Neighbors: International Ocean Law Relations between the United States and Canada (New York: Oxford University Press, 2009). "National Measures for the Safety of Navigation in Arctic Waters: NORDREG, Article 234 and Canada," in Myron H. Nordquist, et al., The Law of the Sea Convention: US Accession and Globalization (Leiden: Martinus Nijhoff, 2012).

McLaren, Alfred S., "The Evolution and Potential of the Arctic Submarine." (1985) 2 POAC Conference Proceedings (Danish Hydraulic Institute) 848. Unknown Waters: A First - Hand Account of the Historic Under - Ice Survey of the Siberian Continental Shelf by USS Queenfish (Tuscaloosa: University of Alabama Press, 2008).

Macnab, Ron, "The Case for Transparency in the Delimitation of the Outer Continental Shelf in Accordance with UNCLOS Article 76." (2004) 35 Ocean Development and International Law 1. "Submarine Elevations and Ridges: Wild Card in the Poker Game of UNCLOS Article 76" (2008) 39 Ocean Development and International Law 223.

McRae, Donald M., "Canada and the Delimitation of Maritime Boundaries," in Donald M. McRae and G. Munro (eds.), Canadian Oceans Policy: National Strategies and the New Law of the Sea (Vancouver, University of British Columbia Press, 1989). "Arctic Sovereignty: What Is at

Stake?" (2007) 64 (1) Behind the Headlines 1.

Makkonen, Lasse, Atmospheric Icing on Sea Structures (Hanover, NH: US Army Cold Regions Research and Engineering Laboratory, Monograph 84-2, 1984).

Malaurie, Jean, The Last Kings of Thule: With the Polar Eskimos, as They Face their Destiny (trans. Adrienne Foulke) (London: Jonathan Cape, 1982).

Mirovitskaya, Natalia S., Margaret Clark and Ronald G. Purver, "North Pacific Fur Seals: Regime Formation as a Means of Resolving Conflict," in Oran Young and Gail Osherenko (eds.), Polar Politics: Creating International Environmental Regimes (Ithaca, NY: Cornell University Press, 1993).

Mitchell, J. M., Jr., "Visual Range in the Polar Regions with Particular Reference to the Alaskan Arctic." (1956) Journal of Atmospheric and Terrestrial Physics 195.

Molenaar, Erik, "Current and Prospective Roles of the Arctic Council System within the Context of the Law of the Sea." (2012) 27 International Journal of Marine and Coastal Law 553.

Mulrennan, Monica and Colin Scott, "Indigenous Rights in Saltwater Environments." (2000) 31 Development and Change 681.

Nankivell, Justin DeMowbray, "Arctic Legal Tides: The Politics of International Law in the Northwest Passage," Ph. D. thesis, University of British Columbia, 2010, https://circle.ubc.ca/bitstream/handle/2429/26642/ubc_2010_fall_nankivell_justin.pdf?sequence=1.

Neumann, Thilo, "Norway and Russia Agree on Maritime Boundary in the Barents Sea and the Arctic Ocean." (November 9, 2010) 14 (34) ASIL Insight, http://www.asil.org/files/2010/insights/insights_101109.pdf.

Niimi, Arthur J., "Environmental and Economic Factors Can Increase the Risk of Exotic Species Introductions to the Arctic Region through Increased Ballast Water Discharge." (2004) 33 Environmental Management

712. Nurja, Alfred, "Obama Submits NWFZ Protocols to Senate." (June 2011) Arms Control Today, http://www.armscontrol.org/act/2011_06/NWFZ. Ochoa-Ruiz, Natalia, and Esther Salamanca-Aguado, "Exploring the Limits of International Law Relating to the Use of Force in Self-Defence." (2005) 16 European Journal of International Law 499.

O'Connell, Daniel P., The InternationalLaw of the Sea, Vol. 1, ed. Ivan Shearer (Oxford: Clarendon Press, 1982).

O'Driscoll, Cath, "Soot Warming Significant." (2011) 17 Chemistry and Industry 10.

Ong, David M., "The 1979 and 1990 Malaysia-Thailand Joint Development Agreements: A Model for International Legal Co-operation in Common Offshore Petroleum Deposits?" (1999) 14 International Journal of Marine and Coastal Law 207.

Østreng, Willy, Delimitation Arrangements in Arctic Seas (Fridtjof Nansen Institute, Study R007-84, 1985). Oude Elferink, Alex G., "The 1990 USSR-USA Maritime Boundary Agreement." (1991) 6 International Journal of Estuarine and Coastal Law 41. "Arctic Maritime Delimitations: The Preponderance of Similarities with Other Regions," in Oude Elferink and Donald Rothwell (eds.), The Law of the Sea and Polar Maritime Delimitation and Jurisdiction (Dordrecht: Kluwer Law International, 2001). "Maritime Delimitation between Denmark/Greenland and Norway." (2007) 38 Ocean Development and International Law 375.

Oude Elferink, Alex G. and Constance Johnson, "Outer Limits of the Continental Shelf and 'Disputed Areas': State Practice Concerning Article 76 (10) of the LOS Convention." (2004) 21 International Journal of Marine and Coastal Law 466.

Pearson, Lester B., "Canada Looks Down North." (1946) 24 Foreign Affairs 638.

Pedersen, Torbjørn, "The Svalbard Continental Shelf Controversy: Legal Disputes and Political Rivalries." (2006) 37 Ocean Development and International Law 339.

Peterson, Alexander M. , "Sino - Japanese Cooperation in the East China Sea: A Lasting Arrangement?" (2009) 42 Cornell International Law Journal 441.

Petrow, Richard, Across the Top of Russia: The Cruise of the US-CGC Northwind into the Polar Seas North of Siberia (London: Hodder and Stoughton, 1968).

Pew Environmental Group, "Oil Spill Prevention and Response in the US Arctic Ocean: Unexamined Risks, Unacceptable Consequences. " (November 2010), http: //www. pewtrusts. org/uploadedFiles/wwwpewtrustsorg/Reports/Protecting_ocean_life/PEW - 1010 _ARTIC_Report. pdf. "More than 2, 000 Scientists Worldwide Urge Protection of Central Arctic Ocean Fisheries. " (April 2012), http: //www. oceansnorth. org/arcticfisheries - letter.

Pharand, Donat, Canada's Arctic Waters in International Law (Cambridge University Press, 1988). "Delimitation Problems of Canada (Second Part)," in Donat Pharand and Umberto Leanza (eds.), The Continental Shelf and the Exclusive Economic Zone: Delimitation and Legal Regime (Dordrecht: Martinus Nijhoff, 1993), 171. "The Arctic Waters and the Northwest Passage: A Final Revisit. " (2007) 38 Ocean Development and International Law 3.

Pharand, Donat and Leonard Legault, The Northwest Passage: Arctic Straits (Dordrecht: Martinus Nijhoff, 1984).

Plaut, Shayna, " 'Cooperation Is the Story' -Best Practices of Transnational Indigenous Activism in the North. " (2012) 16 International Journal of Human Rights 193. Quinn, P. K. , et al. , The Impact of Black Carbon on the Arctic Climate (Oslo: Arctic Monitoring and Assessment Programme, 2011).

Ramseur, Jonathan L. , "Liability and Compensation Issues Raised by the 2010 Gulf Oil Spill. " Congressional Research Service, March 11,

2011, http: //assets. opencrs. com/rpts/R41679_20110311. pdf.

Reid, Robert S. , "The Canadian Claim to Sovereignty over the Waters of the Arctic. " (1974) 12 Canadian Yearbook of International Law 111.

Riddell - Dixon, Elizabeth, "Canada and Arctic Politics: The Continental Shelf Extension. " (2008) 39 Ocean Development and International Law 343.

Roche, Douglas and Ernie Regehr, "Canada, NATO and Nuclear Weapons. " Project Ploughshares Working Paper 01 - 3 (2001), http: //www. ploughshares. ca/content/canada - nato - and - nuclear - weapons.

Roth, R. R. , "Sovereignty and Jurisdiction over Arctic Waters. " (1990) 28 Alberta Law Review 845.

Rothwell, Donald R. , Maritime Boundaries and Resource Development: Options for the Beaufort Sea (Calgary: Canadian Institute of Resources Law, 1988). The Polar Regions and the Development of International Law (Cambridge University Press, 1996).

Russell, Dawn, "International Ocean Boundary Issues and Management Arrangements," in David Vander Zwaag (ed.), Canadian Ocean Law and Policy (Toronto: Butterworths, 1992).

Ruys, Tom, "Armed Attack" and Article 51 of the UN Charter: Evolutions in Customary Law and Practice (Cambridge University Press, 2010).

Sahlins, Peter, Boundaries: The Making of France and Spain in the Pyrenees (Berkeley: University of California Press, 1989).

Samuels, Joel H. , "Condominium Arrangements in International Practice: Reviving an Abandoned Concept of Boundary Dispute Resolution. " (2007 - 2008) 29 Michigan Journal of International Law 727.

Schofield, Clive, "Australia's Final Frontiers? Developments in the Delimitation of Australia's International Maritime Boundaries. " (2008) 158 Maritime Studies 2. "The Trouble with Islands: The Definition and Role of Islands and Rocks in Maritime Boundary Delimitation," in S. Y. Hong and Jon Van Dyke (eds.), Maritime Boundary Disputes, Settlement Processes, and the Law of the Sea (The Hague: Martinus Nijhoff, 2009).

Scott, Colin and Monica Mulrennan, "Reconfiguring Mare Nullius: Torres Strait Islanders, Indigenous Sea Rights and the Divergence of Domestic and International Norms," in Mario Blaser, et al. (eds.), Indigenous Peoples and Autonomy: Insights for a Global Age (Vancouver: UBC Press, 2010).

Scovazzi, Tullio, "New Developments Concerning Soviet Straight Baselines." (1988) 3 International Journal of Estuarine and Coastal Law 37. The Evolution of the International Law of the Sea: New Issues, New Challenges (The Hague: Martinus Nijhoff, 2001).

Scrivener, David, "Arctic Environmental Cooperation in Transition." (1999) 35 (192) Polar Record 51.

Shah, Niaz A., "Self - Defence, Anticipatory Self - Defence and Pre - emption: International Law's Response to Terrorism." (2007) 12 Journal of Conflict and Security Law 95.

Shaw, Glen E., "The Arctic Haze Phenomenon." (August 16, 1995) 76 Bulletin of the American Meteorological Society 2403.

Shi, Lei, "Successful Use of the Tacit Acceptance Procedure to Effectuate Progress in International Maritime Law." (1998 - 1999) 11 University of San Francisco Maritime Law Journal 299.

Shusterich, K. M., "International Jurisdictional Issues in the Arctic Ocean," in W. E. Westermeyer and K. M. Shusterich (eds.), United States Arctic Interests: The 1980s and 1990s (New York: Springer - Verlag, 1984).

Sillanpää, Lennard, Impact of International Law on Indigenous Rights in Northern Europe (Ottawa: Indian and Northern Affairs Canada, 1992).

Simon, Mary, "Inuit and the Canadian Arctic: Sovereignty Begins at Home." (2009) 43 Journal of Canadian Studies 250.

Skogan, John Kristen, "The Evolution of the Four Soviet Fleets 1968 - 1987," in John Kristen Skogan and Arne Olav Brundtland, Soviet Seapower in Northern Waters: Facts, Motivation, Impact and Responses (London: Pinter, 1990).

Smith, Robert W., "United States-Russia Maritime Boundary," in Gerald Henry Blake (ed.), Maritime Boundaries (London: Routledge, 1994).

Sohn, Louis B., "Baseline Considerations," in Jonathan I. Charney and Lewis M. Alexander (eds.), International Maritime Boundaries, Vol. 1 (Dordrecht: Martinus Nijhoff, 1993).

Sorensen, Christina, "Drug Trafficking on the High Seas: A Move Toward Universal Jurisdiction under International Law." (1990) 4 Emory International Law Review 207.

Speca, Anthony, "Nunavut, Greenland and the Politics of Resource Revenues." (May 2012) Policy Options 62, http://www.irpp.org/po/archive/may12/speca.pdf. "In the Belly of the Whaling Commission." Northern Public Affairs, June 18, 2012, http://www.northernpublicaffairs.ca/index/in-the-belly-of-thewhaling-commission/.

Springer, A. L., "Do Fences Make Good Neighbours? The Gulf of Maine Revisited." (1994) 6 International Environmental Affairs 223.

Stabrun, Kristoffer, "The Grey Zone Agreement of 1978: Fishery Concerns, Security Challenges and Territorial Interests." Fridtjof Nansen Institute Report 13/2009, http://www.fni.no/doc&pdf/FNI-R1309.pdf.

Stevenson, Christopher, "Hans Off! The Struggle for Hans Island and the Potential Ramifications for International Border Dispute Resolution." (2007) 30 Boston College International and Comparative Law Review 263.

Stirling, Ian, Polar Bears: The Natural History of a Threatened Species (Markham, Ont.: Fitzhenry and Whiteside, 2011).

Stirling, Ian and Andrew E. Derocher, "Effects of Climate Warming on Polar Bears: A Review of the Evidence." (2012) 18 (9) Global Change Biology 2694.

Stirling, Ian and Claire Parkinson, "Possible Effects of Climate Warming on Selected Populations of Polar Bears (Ursus maritimus) in the Canadian Arctic." (2006) 59 Arctic 261.

Stokke, Olav Schram, "Sub - regional Cooperation and Protection of the Arctic Marine Environment: The Barents Sea," in Davor Vidas (ed.), Protecting the Polar Marine Environment: Law and Policy for Pollution Prevention (Cambridge University Press, 2000), chap. 6.

Tester, Frank and Peter Kulchyski, Tammarniit (Mistakes): Inuit Relocation in the Eastern Arctic, 1939 - 63 (Vancouver: University of British Columbia Press, 1994).

Thorleifsson, ThorleifTobuas, "Norway ' must really drop their absurd claims such as that to the Otto Sverdrup Islands. ' Bi - Polar International Diplomacy: The Sverdrup Islands Question, 1902 - 1930," MA thesis, Simon Fraser University, 2006, http: //ir. lib. sfu. ca/retrieve/3720/etd2367. pdf.

Tingle, Christopher, "Submarine Accidents: A 60 - Year Statistical Assessment." (2009) Professional Safety: Journal of the American Society of Safety Engineers 31.

Trudeau, Pierre, "Remarks to the Press Following the Introduction ofLegislation on Arctic Pollution, Territorial Sea and Fishing Zones in the Canadian House of Commons on April 8, 1970." (1970) 9 ILM 600.

Ulfstein, Geir, "Spitsbergen/Svalbard," in Rudiger Wolfrum (ed.), Max Planck Encyclopedia of Public International Law (Oxford University Press, 2012).

Ünlü, Nihan, The Legal Regime of the Turkish Straits (The Hague: Martinus Nijhoff, 2002).

Van Dyke, Jon M., "The Disappearing Right to Navigational Freedom in the Exclusive Economic Zone." (2005) 29 Marine Policy 107. "Canada's Authority to Prohibit LNG Vessels from Passing through Head Harbor Passage to US Ports." (2008 - 2009) 14 Ocean and Coastal Law Journal 45.

Verhoef, Jacob and Dick MacDougall, "Delineating Canada's Continental Shelf According to the United Nations Convention on the Law of the Sea." (2008) 3 Journal of Ocean Technology 1.

Vidas, Davor (ed.), Protecting the Polar Marine Environment: Law and Policy for Pollution Prevention (Cambridge University Press, 2000).

Wadhams, Peter, "Arctic Ice Cover, Ice Thickness and Tipping Points." (2012) 41 AMBIO: A Journal of the Human Environment 1.

Wegge, Njord, "The EU and the Arctic: European Foreign Policy in the Making." (2012) 3 Arctic Review on Law and Politics 6. "Politics between Science, Law and Sentiments: Explaining the European Union's Ban on Trade in Seal Products." (2012) 6 Environmental Politics 1.

Weil, Prosper, The Law of Maritime Delimitation-Reflections (Cambridge: Grotius Publications, 1989).

Wells, Robert D., "The Icy Nyet." (1968) 94 (782) US Naval Institute Proceedings 73.

Wendt, Alexander, Social Theory of International Politics (Cambridge University Press, 1999).

Wezeman, Siemon T., "Military Capabilities in the Arctic." SIPRI Background Paper, Stockholm, March 2012, http://books.sipri.org/product_info?c_product_id=442.

Wilkening, Ken, "Science and International Environmental Nonregimes: The Case of Arctic Haze." (2011) 28 Review of Policy Research 131, http://www.highbeam.com/doc/1G1-253536411.html.

Wilson, Gary N., "Inuit Diplomacy in the Circumpolar North." (2007) 13 Canadian Foreign Policy Journal 65.

Woehrling, José, "Les Revendications du Canada sur les eaux de l'archipel de l'Arctique et l'utilisation immémoriale des glaces par les Inuit." (1987) 30 German Yearbook of International Law 120.

World Wildlife Fund, "Drilling for Oil in the Arctic: Too Soon, Too Risky." December 2010, http://www.worldwildlife.org/what/wherewework/arctic/WWFBinaryitem18711.pdf.

Young, Nigel, "Peace Movements in History: Perspectives from Social Movements," in S. Mendlovitz and R. B. Walker (eds.), Towards a Just World Peace (London: Butterworths, 1987).

Young, Oran, "Governing the Arctic: From Cold War Theatre to Mosaic of Cooperation." (2005) 11 Global Governance 9.

Young, Oran and Gail Osherenko, Polar Politics: Creating International Environmental Regimes (Ithaca, NY: Cornell University Press, 1993).

中英译名索引

一、地理名称

雷索卢特湾	Resolute Bay
康沃利斯岛	Cornwallis Island
波罗的海	Baltic Sea
圣劳伦斯湾	Gulf of St. Lawrence
伊卢利萨特	Ilulissat
贝洛特海峡	Bellot Strait
加拿大高北极地区	Canada's High Arctic
齐尼思角	Zenith Point
汉斯岛	Hans Island
埃尔斯米尔岛	Ellesmere Island
格陵兰岛	Greenland
内尔斯海峡	Nares Strait
肯尼迪海峡	Kennedy Channel
塔图帕卢克	Tartupaluk
费伦特岛	Pheasant Island
昂代伊	Hendaye
伊伦	Irun
努纳武特	Nunavut
斯瓦尔巴群岛	Svalbard archipelago
巴伦支堡	Barentsburg
朗伊尔	Longyearbyen
维京群岛	Virgin Islands

巴芬湾	Baffin Bay
林肯海	Lincoln Sea
斯弗德鲁普群岛	Sverdrup Islands
加拿大西北地区	Northwest Territories
巴芬岛	Baffin Island
博蒙特岛	Beaumont Island
蒂斯坦特角	Cape Distant
克鲁辛斯特恩岛	Krusenstern 或 Ignalook
拉特曼诺夫岛	Ratmanoff 或 Noonarbook
圣劳伦斯岛	Island of St. Lawrence
楚科奇角	Cape Choukotsky
科曼多尔群岛	Kormandorski couplet
雅图岛	Island of Attou
铜岛	Copper island
托拜厄斯岛	(Tobias Island
芬马克	Finnmark
科拉半岛	Kola Peninsula
法兰士·约瑟夫地群岛	Franz Josef Land
新地群岛	Novaya Zemlya
哈默菲斯特	Hammerfest
瓦朗尼治峡湾	Varangerfjord
布赖恩特角	Cape Bryant
约翰·莫里岛	John Murray Island
哥伦比亚角	Cape Columbia
罗伯逊海峡	Robeson Channel
莫里斯·耶苏普角	Cape Morris Jesup
马更些河	Mackenzie River
图克托亚图克	Tuktoyaktuk
墨西哥湾	Gulf of Mexico
巴罗角	Point Barrow

班克斯岛	Banks Island
克鲁辛斯特恩岛	Krusenstern
拉特曼诺夫岛	Ratmanoff
三王海岭	Three Kings Ridge
楚科奇海台	Chukchi Plateau
海峡群岛	Channel Islands
英吉利海峡	English Channel
维多利亚岛	Victoria Island
巴瑟斯特角	Cape Bathurst
阿蒙森湾	Amundsen Gulf
巴瑟斯特角	Cape Bathurst
巴罗港	Port Barrow
育空北坡	Yukon North Slope
帕特里克王子岛	Prince Patrick Island
阿尔法/门捷列夫海岭	Alpha/Mendeleev Ridge
伊卢利萨特	Ilulissat
亚速尔群岛	Azores
阿森松岛	Ascension Island
威廉姆斯海岭	Williams Ridge
乔伊海岭	Joey Rise
凯尔盖朗海台	Kerguelen Plateau
埃兰暗滩	Elan Bank
加克利海岭	Gakkel Ridge
弗兰格尔岛	Wrangel Island
比斯开湾	Bay of Biscay
罗蒙诺索夫海岭	Lomonosov Ridge
拉森海峡	Larsen Sound
博斯普鲁斯海峡	Bosporus Strait
达达尼尔海峡	Dardanelles Strait
厄勒海峡	Oresund Strait

兰开斯特海峡	Lancaster Sound
麦克卢尔海峡	McClure Strait
威尔士王子海峡	Prince of Wales Strait
大公主岛	Princess Royal Islands
维利基茨基海峡	Vil'kitskii Strait
绍卡利斯基海峡	Shokal'skii Strait
德米特里·拉普捷夫海峡	Dmitrii Laptev Strait
桑尼科夫海峡	Sannikov Strait
卡尔斯基海	Karsky Sea
北地群岛	Severnnaia Zemlia
布尔什维克岛	Bol'Shevik Island
泰梅尔半岛	Taimyr Peninsula
新西伯利亚群岛	New Siberia Islands
大代奥米德岛	Big Diomede
小代奥米德岛	Little Diomede
阿留申群岛	Aleutian Islands
乌尼马克海峡	Unimak Pass
威廉王子湾	Prince William Sound
凯恩海湾	Kane Basin
弗拉姆海峡	Fram Strait
托雷斯海峡	Torres Strait
哈利法克斯	Halifax
新斯科舍	Nova Scotia
普拉德霍湾	Prudhoe Bay
比奇岛	Beechey Island
普利比洛夫群岛	Pribilof Islands
堪察加	Kamchatka
喀拉海	Kara Sea
温哥华岛	Vancouver Island
俾斯麦海	Bismarck Sea

哈克尔海岭	Gakkel Ridge
尤里卡	Eureka
北海	North Sea
罗弗敦群岛	Lofoten Islands
戴维斯海峡	Davis Strait
伯朝拉海	Pechora Sea
地中海	Mediterranean Sea
努纳齐亚福特	Nunatsiavut
哈德逊湾	Hudson Bay
纽芬兰省	Newfoundland
拉布拉多省	Labrador
努那维克	Nunavik
格里斯峡湾	Grise Fiord
图勒	Thule
夸那	Qaanaaq
克莱德里弗	Clyde River
伊莎贝拉湾	Isabella Bay
富兰克林湾	Franklin Bay
马尼托巴省	Manitoba
丘吉尔港	Churchill
温尼伯	Winnipeg
约阿港	Gjoa Haven
库格鲁克图克	Kugluktuk
阿勒特	Alert
温赖特堡	Fort Wainwright
巴罗	Barrow
法罗群岛	Faroe Islands
班纳克	Banak
勘察加半岛	Kamchatka Peninsula
怀特霍斯	Whitehorse

古斯贝	Goose Bay
扬马延岛	Jan Mayen
卡布迪亚角	Ras Kaboudia
塔佐拉角	Ras Tajoura

二、主要法律文件名

《南极条约》(the 1959 Antarctic Treaty)

《北极外交政策声明》(Arctic Foreign Policy Statement)

《联合国海洋法公约》(the 1982 United Nations Convention on the Law of the Sea, UNCLOS)

《极地规则》(Polar Code)

《国际油污防备、反应和合作公约》(the 1990 Convention on Oil Pollution Preparedness, Response and Cooperation, OPRC)

《希尔克内斯宣言》(Kirkenes Declaration)

《北极气候影响评估报告》(the 2004 Arctic Climate Impact Assessment)

《北极海运评估报告》(the 2009 Arctic Marine Shipping Assessment)

《斯匹茨卑尔根条约》(the Spitsbergen Treaty)

《斯瓦尔巴条约》(the Svalbard Treaty)

《维也纳条约法公约》(the 1969 Vienna Convention on the Law of Treaties)

《有关格陵兰岛防务的协议》(Agreement Relating to the Defense of Greenland)

《威斯敏斯特法令》(the Statute of Westminster)

《加拿大和丹麦边界条约》(The Canada-Denmark Boundary Treaty)

《日内瓦大陆架公约》(the 1958 Geneva Convention on the Continental Shelf)

《渔业事务合作协议》(Agreement on Cooperation in the Fishing Industry)

《欧盟共同渔业政策》(the Common Fisheries Policy of the European Union)

《联合国跨界鱼类种群和高度洄游鱼类种群协议》(the 1995 UN Agreement on Straddling Fish Stocks and Highly Migratory Fish Stocks)

《巴伦支海条约》(the Barents Sea Treaty)

《北极外交政策声明》(Arctic Foreign Policy Statement)

《转让阿拉斯加条约》(the 1867 Treaty of Cessation of Alaska to the United States)

《北极水域污染防治法》(the Arctic Waters Pollution Prevention Act)

《因努维阿勒伊特最终协议》(the Inuvialuit Final Agreement)

《托雷斯海峡条约》(the Torres Strait Treaty of 1978)

《杜鲁门大陆架宣言》(the 1945 Truman Proclamation on the Continental Shelf)

《努纳武特领土声明协议》(Nunavut Land Claims Agreement)

《联合国土著人民权利宣言》(the UN Declaration on the Rights of Indigenous People)

《西撒哈拉问题的咨询意见》(Western Sahara Advisory Opinion)

《北极合作协议》(the 1988 Arctic Cooperation Agreement)

《北极行动纲领》(the Arctic Operational Platform)

新版《削减和限制进攻性战略武器条约》("New START" treaty)

《极地水域操作船舶指南》(2009 "Guidelines on Ships Operating in Polar Waters")

《北太平洋海狗公约》(the 1911 Convention Respecting Measures for the Preservation and Protection of Fur Seals in the North Pacific Ocean)

《养护北极熊协定》(the International Agreement on the Conservation of Polar Bears)

《阿拉斯加和楚科塔北极熊种群保护和管理协议》(The Agreement on the Conservation and Management of the Alaska-Chukotka Polar Bear Population)

《因努维阿勒伊特和因纽皮特北极熊管理协议》(the Inuvialuit-Inupiat Polar Bear Management Agreement)

《濒危物种法》(the Endangered Species Act)

《濒危野生动植物种国际贸易公约》(the Convention on International Trade in Endangered Species, CITES)

《国际捕鲸管制公约》(the International Convention for the Regulation of Whaling)

《培利修正案》(the Pelly Amendment)

《渔民保护法》(the Fishermen's Protection Act)

《中白令海狭鳕资源养护与管理公约》(the 1994 Convention on the Conservation and Management of the Pollock Resources in the Central Bering Sea)

《联合国鱼类种群协定》(the United Nations Fish Stocks Agreement)

《白令海渔业协定》(the Bering Sea Fisheries Agreement)

《东北大西洋未来渔业多边合作公约》(the 1980 Convention on Future Multilateral Cooperation in North East Atlantic Fisheries)

《北极搜救协议》(the 2001 Arctic Search and Rescue Agreement)

《北极海运评估报告》(Arctic Marine Shipping Assessment)

《在北极冰覆盖水域内船舶航行指南》(the IMO's 2009 Guidelines for Ships Operating in Arctic Ice - Covered Waters)

《国际海上人命安全公约》(the 1974 Convention for the Safety of Life at Sea)

《国际船舶压载水和沉积物控制与管理公约》,简称《压载水管理公约》(the Convention for the Control and Management of Ships' Ballast Water and Sediments, BWM Convention)

《美苏关于防止公海及其上空意外事故的协定》(the 1972 Agreement between the United States and Soviet Union on the Prevention of Incidents on and over the High Seas)

《及早通报核事故国际公约》(the 1986 Convention on Early Notification of a Nuclear Accident)

《核事故或辐射紧急情况援助公约》(the 1986 Convention on Assistance in the Case of a Nuclear Accident or Radiological Emergency)

《关于持久性有机污染物的斯德哥尔摩公约》(the 2001 Stockholm Convention on Persistent Organic Pollutants)

《远程越境空气污染公约》(the Convention on Long - Range Transboundary Air Pollution)

《减少酸化、富营养化和地面臭氧的哥德堡议定书》(the 1999 Gothenburg Protocol to Abate Acidification, Eutrophication and Ground Level Ozone)

《有关紧急情况下在白令海和楚科奇海合作防止污染的协议》(an Agreement concerning Cooperation in Combating Pollution in the Bering and Chukchi Seas in Emergency Situations)

《国际燃油污染损害民事责任公约》(the 2001 International Convention on Civil Liability for Bunker Oil Pollution Damage)

《石油污染法》(the 1990 Oil Pollution Act)

《国际油污防备、反应和合作公约》(the 1990 Convention on Oil Pollution Preparedness, Response and Cooperation, OPRC)

《巴伦支海欧洲—北极地区合作宣言》(Declaration on Cooperation in the Barents Euro - Arctic Region)

《保护东北大西洋海洋环境公约》(the Convention for the Protection of the Marine Environment of the North - East Atlantic, OSPAR Convention)

《斯特伦斯塔德条约》(the Strömstad Treaty)

《拉普附录》(Lapp Codicil) /《萨米人大宪章》(Saami Magna Carta)

《阿拉斯加原住民土地权利处理法案》(The 1971 Alaska Native Claims Settlement Act)

《关于持久性有机污染物的斯德哥尔摩公约》(the Stockholm Convention on Persistent Organic Pollutants)

《美洲宣言》(the American Declaration)

《联合国气候变化框架公约》(the UN Framework Convention on Climate Change)

《渥太华宣言》(the 1996 Ottawa Declaration on the Establishment of the Arctic Council)

《极地因纽特人在北极主权的宣言》(Circumpolar Inuit Declaration on Sovereignty in the Arctic)

《欧洲人权公约》(European Convention on Human Rights)

《关税和贸易总协定》(GATT)和《技术性贸易壁垒协议》(Agreement on Technical Barriers to Trade, TBT)

《经济、社会、文化权利国际公约》(the International Covenant on Economic, Social and Cultural Rights)

《南太平洋无核区条约》(the 1985 South Pacific Nuclear Free Zone Treaty)/《拉罗汤加岛条约》(Treaty of Rarotonga)

《北美防空司令部协议》(the North American Aerospace Defense Command Agreement)

《格陵兰防务协定》(Agreement Relating to the Defense of Greenland)

《禁止在海床洋底及其底土安置核武器和其他大规模毁灭性武器条约》(Seabed Treaty)

《战略武器限制条约》(Strategic Arms Limitation Treaty, SALTI)

《限制反弹道导弹系统条约》(AntiBallistic Missile Treaty)

《2007-2015年俄罗斯国家军备计划》(the 2007-2015 Russian State Armament Programme)

《北大西洋公约》(the North Atlantic Treaty)

《不扩散核武器条约》(the 1968 Non-Proliferation Treaty)

《海上运输安全法》(the Marine Transportation Security Act)

《联合国宪章》(the UN Charter)

《防扩散安全倡议》(Proliferation Security Initiative, PSI)

《关于制止危害民用航空安全的非法行为的公约》/《蒙特利尔公约》(the Montreal Convention on the Suppression of Unlawful Acts against the Safety of Civil Aviation）

《国际海上人命安全公约》（the International Convention for the Safety of Life at Sea，SOLAS Convention）

《国际民用航空公约》（the 1944 Convention on International Aviation，Chicago Convention）

《1979 年国际海上搜寻和救助公约》 (International Convention on Maritime SAR，SAR Convention)

《应急预防、准备和响应领域的政府间协议》（Agreement between the Governments in the Barents Euro - Arctic Region on Cooperation within the Field of Emergency Prevention，Preparedness and Response）。

《北极海空搜救合作协定》（Agreement on Cooperation on Aeronautical and Maritime Search and Rescue in the Arctic，Arctic SAR Agreement）

《保护北极熊协议》（The 1973 Polar Bear Treaty）

《关于持久性有机污染物的斯德哥尔摩公约》（the Stockholm Convention on Persistent Organic Pollutants）

《北极海空搜救合作协定》（the Arctic Search and Rescue Agreement）

This is a Simplified-Chinese translation edition of the following title published by Cambridge University Press:

Ⓡ€

International Law and the Arctic

ISBN 978-1-107-04275-9 (hardback)

© Michael Byers 2013

This Simplified-Chinese translation edition for the People's Republic of China (excluding Hong Kong, Macau and Taiwan) is published by arrangement with the Press Syndicate of the University of Cambridge, Cambridge, United Kingdom.

© Current Affairs Press 2020

This Simplified-Chinese translation edition is authorized for sale in the People's Republic of China (excluding Hong Kong, Macau and Taiwan) only. Unauthorised export of this Simplified-Chinese translation edition is a violation of the Copyright Act. No part of this publication may be reproduced or distributed by any means, or stored in a database or retrieval system, without the prior written permission of Cambridge University Press and Current Affairs Press.

Copies of this book sold without a Cambridge University Press sticker on the cover are unauthorized and illegal.

本书封面贴有Cambridge University Press防伪标签，无标签者不得销售。

图书在版编目（CIP）数据

国际法与北极/（加）迈克尔·拜尔斯著，陈子楠译，
—北京：时事出版社，2020.8
书名原文：International Law and the Arctic
ISBN 978-7-5195-0337-6

I.①国… II.①迈… ②陈… III.①北极—国际法—研究 IV.①D99

中国版本图书馆 CIP 数据核字（2019）第 252216 号

图字：01-2020-3458

出 版 发 行：时事出版社
地　　　址：北京市海淀区万寿寺甲 2 号
邮　　　编：100081
发 行 热 线：（010）88547590　88547591
读 者 服 务 部：（010）88547595
传　　　真：（010）88547592
电 子 邮 箱：shishichubanshe@sina.com
网　　　址：www.shishishe.com
印　　　刷：北京朝阳印刷厂有限责任公司

开本：787×1092　1/16　印张：20　字数：298 千字
2020 年 8 月第 1 版　2020 年 8 月第 1 次印刷
定价：120.00 元
（如有印装质量问题，请与本社发行部联系调换）